MW01285829

MASTER OF ROME

Sculpture of Julius Caesar by Nicolas Coustou, Louvre Museum, Paris. Wikimedia Commons.

MASTER OF ROME

A LIFE OF JULIUS CAESAR

DAVID POTTER

OXFORD
UNIVERSITY PRESS

OXFORD
UNIVERSITY PRESS

Oxford University Press is a department of the University of Oxford.
It furthers the University's objective of excellence in research, scholarship,
and education by publishing worldwide. Oxford is a registered trade mark of
Oxford University Press in the UK and in certain other countries.

Published in the United States of America by Oxford University Press
198 Madison Avenue, New York, NY 10016, United States of America.

Preassigned Control Number is on file at the Library of Congress

ISBN 9780190867188

DOI: 10.1093/oso/9780190867188.001.0001

Printed by Sheridan Books, Inc., United States of America

The manufacturer's authorised representative in the EU for
product safety is Oxford University Press España S.A. of El Parque
Empresarial San Fernando de Henares, Avenida de Castilla, 2 –
28830 Madrid (www.oup.es/en or product.safety@oup.com).
OUP España S.A. also acts as importer into Spain of products
made by the manufacturer.

Links to third party websites are provided by Oxford in good faith and
for information only. Oxford disclaims any responsibility for the materials
contained in any third party website referenced in this work.

MIX
Paper | Supporting
responsible forestry
FSC® C008955

To the Big Three

Contents

Acknowledgments

This book took shape in the highly agreeable realm of the Institute for Advanced Study during the tenure of a fellowship in the academic year 2021–2022. During that time, I was able to present preliminary versions of key sections of the book to the Department of Classics at the University of Virginia, a meeting of officers at the Marine War College, and at the Institute. A later version of some of this work provided the basis of my Syme Lecture at Oxford in October 2023. I am very grateful to the audiences on these occasions for their feedback.

In fact, this project goes back even further in time than the period already mentioned, and for many years I have been able to teach Caesar at the University of Michigan and have benefited enormously from my students and from the company of my colleagues in the Department of Classical Studies, as well as in the History Department at UCLA in 2018. I have also benefited from the comments of Paco Sze and Sarah Keith on an earlier draft of the manuscript in the summer of 2024. I am grateful to the staff of the library at the Institute for Advanced Study and of the Scoville Memorial Library in Salisbury, Connecticut, for creating welcoming environments in which to work (I cannot say the same for the library in my home institution).

I am extremely grateful to Stefan Vranka at OUP for taking this book on, for his patience as it took shape, and for his helpful criticism. I am also very grateful to Christopher Welser for his careful copyediting of the final manuscript.

My most substantial debt is to my family, which tolerated the long development of this book, especially my wife, Ellen Bauerle. It is a pleasure to thank Ellen and our two daughters, Claire and Natalie—"the big three."

Chapter 1: Descendant of Venus, Coin 1: Julian family history. This coin, issued by Caesar in 49 BCE, represents the elephant killed by Julius Caesar's ancestor (Crawford *RRC* 443/1 reverse/private collection).

Chapter 2: Rage, Coin 2: Coin issued by Saturninus in 104 BCE depicting the god Saturn and suggesting a connection between the god and Saturninus himself, whose name is inscribed below the chariot (Crawford *RRC* 317/3a reverse, American Numismatic Society, 1941, 131).

Chapter 3: Little Caesar, Coin 3: Aeneas leaving Troy carrying his father and the sacred image of Athena (the palladium); this moment of Julian family history is depicted on a coin issued by Caesar's officials in 48 BCE (Crawford *RRC* 458/1 reverse/private collection).

Chapter 4: Teenage Years, Coin 4: Sulla (Crawford *RRC* 434/1 reverse/ private collection).

Chapter 5: Early Adventures, Coin 5: Nicomedes IV, king of Bithynia (American Numismatic Society, 1977.158.250).

Chapter 6: Becoming Caesar, Coin 6: Aediles in their official (curule) seats, depicted on a coin of 86 BCE (Crawford *RRC* 351/1 reverse/ private collection, American Numismatic Society, 1977.158.249).

Chapter 7: Catiline, Coin 7: Voting at Rome. The voter on this coin, minted in 63 BCE, is using a tablet marked with the letter U, indicating a vote in favor of legislation (Crawford *RRC* 413 reverse private collection).

Chapter 8: The Three-Headed Monster, Coin 8: The Villa Publica, an important structure on the Campus Martius, close to where Roman elections were held (American Numismatic Society, 1941.131.261).

Chapter 9: The Land of Opportunity, Coin 9: Coin issued by the Aedui, reflecting the power of Dumnorix (American Numismatic Society, 1957.78.2).

Chapter 10: Caesar on Being Caesar, Coin 10: Seated Gallic captives beneath a trophy on a coin of 46 BCE commemorating Caesar's conquest (American Numismatic Society, 1944.100.3342).

Chapter 11: Opening Phases, Coin 11: Coin of the Veneti, who played a major role in trade between Britain and the continent, Wikipedia.

Chapter 12: Setting Boundaries, Coin 12: Coin of the Aedui (NumisCorner.com).

Chapter 13: Rebellion and Reconstruction, Coin 13: Coin issued by Vercingetorix with his portrait, 52 BCE (www.ambiani.fr.).

Chapter 14: The Rubicon, Coin 14: Portrait of Pompey on coin of Sextus Pompeius (American Numismatic Society, 1944.100.3642).

Chapter 15: Defeating Pompey, Coin 15: Commemoration of the conquest of Gaul on a coin issued for Caesar in 48 BCE (American Numismatic Society, 1948.19.225).

Chapter 16: Cleopatra, Coin 16: Cleopatra coin (American Numismatic Society, 1977.158.621).

Chapter 17: Dictator, Coin 17: The goddess Victoria on a coin issued for Caesar in 45 BCE (American Numismatic Society, 1944.100.3546).

Chapter 18: The Ides of March, Coin 18: Caesar as dictator for life (American Numismatic Society, 1948.19.225).

Chapter 19: Caesar's Legacies, Coin 19: Octavian, shown wearing a beard, which he grew to alter his youthful appearance (Crawford *RRC* 540/2, private collection).

The Roman Empire in 80 BCE.

ATLANTIC OCEAN

GAUL

105 BCE
Cimbrians and Teutons defeat Roman army at Arausio

101 BCE
Marius defeats Cimbrians

TRANSALPINE GAUL

102 BCE
Marius defeats Teutons

CISALPINE GAUL

Arausio
Vercellae
Aquae Sextiae

Massilia

SPAIN

CORSICA

SARDINIA

ROME

Carthage

NUMIDIA

MAURETANIA

AFRICA

ILLYRIA

MACEDONIA

86 BCE
Sulla defeats Mithridates in battle at Chaeronea and Orchomenus

ACHAEA
Athens

SICILY
Syracuse

Mediterranean Sea

Black Sea

BITHYNIA

89 BCE
Mithridates invades province of Asia

ASIA
Pergamum
Ephesus

CRETE

ARMENIA

66 BCE
Mithridates defeated by Pompey

PARTHIAN EMPIRE

CILICIA

67 BCE
Pompey destroys pirate strongholds

CYPRUS

SYRIA
Antioch

JUDEA
Jerusalem

EGYPT
Alexandria

CYRENAICA

N
E
W
S

0 km   200   400
0 miles   200   400

The Campaigns of Caesar in Gaul.

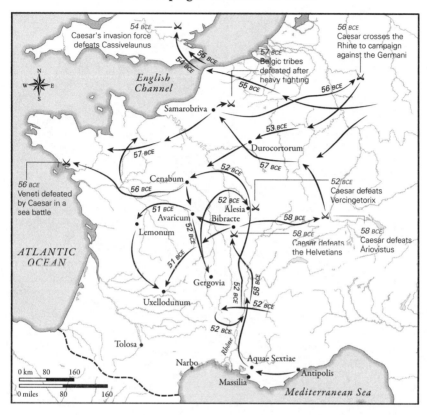

54 BCE
Caesar's invasion force
defeats Cassivelaunus

56 BCE
Caesar crosses the
Rhine to campaign
against the Germani

55 BCE

54 BCE

57 BCE
Belgic tribes
defeated after
heavy fighting

*English
Channel*

N
W — E
S

Samarobriva

55 BCE

56 BCE

53 BCE

57 BCE

Durocortorum

57 BCE

52 BCE

56 BCE
Veneti defeated
by Caesar in a
sea battle

Cenabum

52 BCE

56 BCE

52 BCE
Caesar defeats
Vercingetorix

51 BCE
Avaricum

52 BCE
Alesia
Bibracte

58 BCE

Lemonum

52 BCE

58 BCE
Caesar defeats
the Helvetians

58 BCE
Caesar defeats
Ariovistus

*ATLANTIC
OCEAN*

51 BCE

Gergovia

52 BCE

58 BCE

52 BCE

Uxellodunum

52 BCE

52 BCE

Tolosa

Rhône

Narbo

Aquae Sextiae

0 km   80   160

0 miles   80   160

Massilia

Antipolis

Mediterranean Sea

The Campaigns of the Civil War.

N

Caesar defeats
Pharnaces, who
had invaded Asia
47 BCE

Heraclea

Black Sea

Zela

PONTUS

Nicomedia

Iconium

ASIA

Ephesus

Salamis

CYPRUS

RHODES

Alexandria

EGYPT

Caesar establishes
Cleopatra as queen of Egypt
48–47 BCE

CYRENAICA

Cyrene

Thessalonica

Athens

Sparta

Caesar besieges
Pompey at
Dyrrhachium
Jul. 48 BCE

Caesar defeats Pompey
at Pharsalus; Pompey
escapes to Egypt
Aug. 48 BCE

Domitius's army
surrenders to Caesar
Feb. 49 BCE

Corfinium

ROME

Brundisium

Puteoli

SICILY

Syracuse

Mediterranean Sea

Caesar crosses the
Rubicon river and goes
on to occupy Rome
49 BCE

Lilybaeum

Massilia

CORSICA

SARDINIA

Carthage

Thapsus
46 BCE

AFRICA

Caesar defeats Pompey's Spanish
army
49 BCE

Tarraco

Caesar defeats an army
led by Mettelus Scipio
and Cato the Younger

GAUL

Ilerda

Carthago Nova

NUMIDIA

ATLANTIC
OCEAN

SPAIN

Carteia

Pompey's
sons defeated
at Munda
45 BCE

0 km   200   400

0 miles   200   400

CAESAR'S CAMPAIGNS

49 BCE

48 BCE

47 BCE

46–45 BCE

Central Rome in 55.

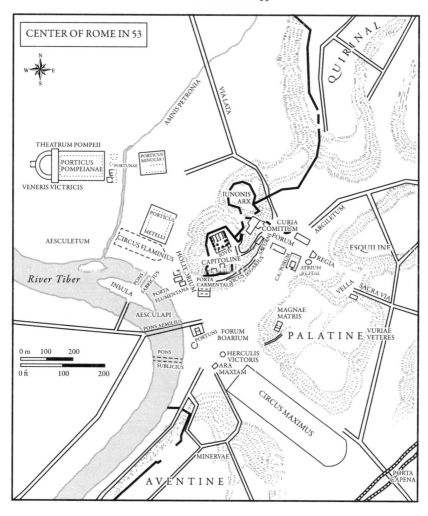

CENTER OF ROME IN 53

N
W E
S

QUIRINAL

AMNIS PETRONIA

VIA LATA

THEATRUM POMPEII

PORTICUS
POMPEIANAE

FORTUNAE

PORTICUS
MINUCIA?

VENERIS VICTRICIS

IUNONIS
ARX

PORTICUS
METELLI

CURIA
COMITIUM

ARGILETUM

AESCULETUM

CIRCUS FLAMINIUS

FORUM

ESQUILINE

HOLITORIUM

CAPITOLINE

IOVIS

CA. TULIANUM

REGIA

ATRIUM
V. ETAE

PORTA
CARMENTALIS

VICUS IUGARIUS SATURNI

River Tiber

INSULA

PONS
FABRICIUS

PORTA
FLUMENTANA

VELIA

SACRA VIA

AESCULAPI

PONS AEMILIUS

MAGNAE
MATRIS

PORTUNI

FORUM
BOARIUM

PALATINE

VURIAE
VETERES

0 m   100   200

PONS
SUBLICIUS

HERCULIS
VICTORIS

ARA
MAXIAM

0 ft   100   200

CIRCUS MAXIMUS

MINERVAE

AVENTINE

PORTA
CAPENA

Introduction

"He doth bestride the narrow world like a colossus." So Cassius to Brutus—one prospective assassin to another—on Caesar, in Shakespeare's *Julius Caesar*. As in Shakespeare, so too elsewhere: Caesar's image is complicated. Often, he appears a flawed genius. A genius, he dominated his generation. Flawed, he was murdered for the way in which he did so.

Caesar changed Rome, destroying the centuries-old Republican form of government based on annually elected magistrates. He also changed the shape of Europe by attaching France to the Mediterranean world. It is not at all clear whether the failing government of Rome in the first century BCE would have accomplished any such thing on its own. The conquest of Gaul required the vision of a man operating outside the bounds of the Roman constitution, and the skill of one of history's greatest military minds.

The fundamental questions which Caesar's career raises are connected with the nature of democratic institutions. Can democratic institutions work effectively and consistently in the interests of the majority of their citizens, delivering the benefits of an orderly society in an equitable fashion? Or are those institutions inherently flawed, enabling self-interested actors to seize control of their operation, and hence doomed to failure when citizens weary of the non-delivery of the benefits they expect? When democratic institutions falter, will the citizens of a democracy turn inevitably to a strongman who promises he will deliver what others have failed to? Is Caesar a model for others or is he a unique political figure whose powerful intelligence and organizational capacity set him apart not only from his contemporaries but from generations of would-be successors?

Being Caesar was not easy. It required patience and a capacity to listen. Even those who didn't like him admitted that Caesar was an exceptionally bright, highly cultivated man with the ability to win others to his side through the power of his arguments. These are not qualities which many aspiring dictators possess. Although Caesar himself was no democrat, he did genuinely care for people who were less fortunate than himself and for the well-being of the individuals who served him. In his writings, he is very clear that his thinking while on campaign included consideration of the welfare of his men, and he inspired genuine loyalty among those who were closest to him.

While Caesar was absolutely convinced that the democratic institutions of the Roman Republic were inefficient and could not provide effective government for the empire Rome had acquired, his understanding of how to fix the situation changed with circumstances. It was the ability to adjust that enabled Caesar to become Cassius's colossus.

This book is a study of leadership, an account of how Caesar ran things as a politician and a general. My essential position is that we can know Caesar better than virtually any other figure prior to Augustine, his contemporary Cicero excepted, through a close reading of his own works. In working with Caesar, I am particularly interested in what he has to say about himself and his principles of administration. He has a great deal to tell us about how he understood his role as a general, about the role of politics in strategic planning, about the management of an organization, and about the enormous attention to detail that is necessary if a leader is to be successful. The organization Caesar built in the decade he was in Gaul was stronger than the state he ostensibly served. He deployed this organization to transform that state. Much of this book is concerned with what Caesar can tells us about how to be a good and effective leader.

Caesar presented himself as a man devoted to bettering the condition of the average person. He defined good government as government that served the interests of the people as a whole. He despised political systems in which the average person was held in thrall to the power and self-interest of aristocrats. In his view of government's purpose he may pass for a "populist" according to both Roman and modern definitions, but a populist need not be, quite often is not, a democrat. Caesar also despised inefficiency, and the Roman democracy in which he grew up was crumbling. The political scene was dominated by wealthy aristocrats who saw the enhancement of their personal wealth and the influence of their families as the purpose of government. The average Roman derived little benefit from the system. If such a person attached him or herself to the interests of the right politician, she or he might see some personal benefit, but there was little freedom of choice. A man (only men could vote) might vote for a program that looked like it could help him or his family, but rarely would it be the case that the program was enacted in the way it had been advertised. We may judge from the conduct of the Roman people that they had little love for their system of government.

Caesar put himself in a position to achieve high office when he adopted an anti-establishment stance. But his vision of what government should do for the average person and of how he could best exercise power did not fit within the institutions of the Roman democracy. His inclination, even before he acquired his army, was dictatorial. It was as a dictator that he finally fulfilled his promises to the Roman people. Because he did that, the Roman people supported the young man who would be heir to Caesar's estate, and that support led to the establishment of a monarchical system of government that would endure for centuries.

In drawing upon Caesar's works as heavily as I do in this book, I offer an interpretation of Caesar that differs from many that have been offered in the past, though I am very aware of the debt I owe to my predecessors, beginning with Theodor Mommsen. Written in the wake of the revolutions of 1848, Mommsen's *History of Rome* presented Caesar as the culmination of Roman Republican history. It was Caesar who realized the vision of left-wing Roman politicians who had hoped to secure the welfare of the Roman people. He was the ultimate representative of the "popular party." No need even to carry Caesar's story through to its conclusion—Mommsen's *History of Rome* ends with Caesar's massive restructuring of Roman political society in 46, more than a year before Caesar's death.

Mommsen's understanding of Caesar was challenged in 1918 by Eduard Meyer in *The Principate of Pompey and the Monarchy of Caesar*, which remains one of the most important and detailed analyses of the sources for Caesar's lifetime. In Meyer's view, the assassins prevented Caesar from realizing the true monarchy to which he aspired, which Meyer thought was unfortunate. Augustus contented himself with restoring the Republic on the model of Pompey's personal domination of the system, his principate.

Meyer's younger contemporary, Matthias Gelzer, took Caesar in a completely different direction in his *Caesar: Politician and Stateman* of 1921. As the title suggests, his Caesar started as a politician (not a good thing) and ended life as a statesman. In 1939, Sir Ronald Syme changed the direction of Roman historical studies with his brilliant *The Roman Revolution*, in which he presented Caesar as the leader of a successful aristocratic faction which laid the foundation for the rise of Augustus and the emergence of the Roman monarchy. Since then, Caesar has tended to be presented as a phenomenon of one model or another of Roman politics. In what follows it will be clear to fellow scholars that my model is significantly influenced both by Syme and by Sir Fergus Millar's *The Crowd in Rome in the Late Republic,* whose stress on the public aspect of Roman politics is critical to understanding Caesar's career. Millar's Rome is the Rome in which Caesar made his way by convincing citizens who participated in public life that he had their interests at heart. Caesar will appear in these pages as a man who emerged from the quarrels which dominated Rome in his youth—quarrels which, despite the vast amount of violence expended in efforts to resolve them, remained unresolved—to offer a new way forward.

This is a book about a man who destroyed a democracy. It is also a book about how a political system can fail and how it can fall victim to a well-organized conspiracy. One of the remarkable facts of Caesar's career is that he didn't conceal his interest in becoming the most powerful man in Rome. He didn't need to. That was an ambition he shared with many other members of a as a vehicle for their own advancement. Well before Caesar's rise to prominence, the Roman democracy had become separated from the principles upon which it had been founded.

I

Descendant of Venus

We'll begin in Rome. It is July. It is hot. Trash piles up. It smells. It is 100 BCE.

You had to be rich to get out of the stench. If you were rich, you would have a house with a generous entranceway, so you would be well away from the street, sitting in an interior garden. You would probably have a bit of incense burning. That improves the atmosphere. Nice smells are associated with the gods, and rich people are closer to the gods than others.

If you were rich, you could also get out of town when things turned nasty. And that is what the aristocratic father of the boy we're interested in, a boy who would be born on July 12, 100 BCE, had done. Perhaps he went to the area of modern San Marino, ancient Bovillae, the family seat. Or, possibly, somewhere around the bay of Naples. This was a preferred refuge for members of Rome's governing class, the people whose family members had held public office and were thus qualified to be members of the Senate, the governing council of the state.[1]

Gaius Julius Caesar, for this is the aristocratic gentleman we are talking about, would likely have been in the house, but not the room, when his wife, Aurelia, gave birth. Childbirth was dangerous and difficult, there was no anesthesia, and it was women's business. All the help Aurelia would get would come from a midwife and the midwife's three assistants, and the divine assistance channeled through the amulets that she, like other Roman women, would have worn to ensure that protection. To give birth she most likely sat on her midwife's crescent-shaped stool.

The story that this child was delivered by caesarian section, which occurs in some ancient biographies, is a myth to explain the family name.[2] The absurdity of the story is betrayed by the fact that the family name was centuries old when the young Gaius Caesar was born.

The year in which Caesar was born would have taken its name from the chief magistrates of the year, the two consuls, Gaius Marius and Lucius Valerius Flaccus. Gaius Marius was the most famous man alive, and he was married to Caesar's aunt Julia. He owed his fame to his ability as a general. Just one year before Caesar's birth, the army he commanded had destroyed the second of two large migratory groups that had once threatened to invade Italy. His army had annihilated the other one in the previous year.

Although Marius would be important to the young Caesar, none of our sources give us details of meetings Caesar had with the great man, and any that he might have had would more likely have been for a hug and a war story than for any serious business. Marius was not a young man, and he would die when Caesar was thirteen.

Marius's story, which we'll be looking at in more detail in our next chapter, was remarkable not just because he was a brilliant soldier but because he rose to the pinnacle of Roman political society without having any ancestors who had held public office at Rome. He was from a wealthy family in the central Italian town of Arpinum, modern Arpino, where he is remembered today with a statue that stares down on the town square.

Descent from a long line of officeholders was typically a critical factor in a political career. The Roman state had once restricted office holding to members of very aristocratic families, known as patricians, and excluded all others, the plebeians, from those opportunities. Those restrictions had been eliminated in the middle of the fourth century BCE, just as Rome took off on the course of conquest that would lead to its dominant position in Italy by the end of the first quarter of the third century. In Marius's time the important families were known as the *nobiles*, "outstanding ones," while people like Marius were *novi*, "new ones."

It made sense for status to stem from the electoral choice of the Roman people. The Roman state was, after all, the *res publica populi Romani*, the "public possession of the Roman people." A public career was known as the *cursus honorum*, or "path of honors." A man (women could not hold office) who chose to follow this path would advance through a series of offices in his thirties and early forties.

Julia's marriage to Marius, which would have looked like a brilliant match in 100, would not have seemed that way when it happened, which was at some point between 115 and 110.[3] That it happened at all points to a curiosity in the history of the Julian clan. Although the Julii claimed to be of great antiquity, the family does not appear to have been well connected with the dominant office-holding aristocracy. The family history prior to the second century existed largely in the world of myth.

Perhaps the most important information about the Julii of the second century comes from an object discovered at San Marino in the nineteenth century. This object is an altar with an inscription recording the devotion of the Julian clan to the god Veiovis, a somewhat obscure divinity who appears to have been a youthful version of the god Jupiter, the chief god of the Roman pantheon.[4] The significance of the text is that it establishes the family base at San Marino. Since, according to local tradition, ancient Bovillae was founded by families that had survived the destruction of Alba Longa many hundreds of years earlier, and since Alba Longa had been founded by Ascanius (a.k.a. Iulus), the son of the Trojan prince Aeneas, the altar suggests that by settling at Bovillae the family was celebrating its historical connection with Alba Longa.

Some aspects of the origin of the Caesars puzzled later Romans. The official story was that the Julian clan descended through Iulus from Aeneas, the son of the goddess Venus. But there was more than one line of Julii, and the connection with Aeneas would not explain the additional family name, or cognomen, Caesar, about which there would be some confusion. Some people said that the name came from the fact that one of the family's early members had been cut (*caesus* in Latin) from his mother's womb, whence our term "Caesarian section." Another story is that a baby Julius was born with a full head of hair (*caesaries*, "flowing hair"). A third was that a Julius had gray eyes—*oculi caesii* in Latin. Yet another story, one that Caesar appears to have thought true, was that an ancestor had killed an elephant, for which the Punic word was *caesai*, in Rome's first war with Carthage, its great rival in North Africa (264–241 BCE). It is quite possibly because this was the story the family told that Caesar placed an image of an elephant on the massive issue of coins he authorized in 49 BCE to pay the army in the civil war he started in that year, completing his ascent to colossal status.[5]

The worship of Veiovis, however, takes us in quite a different direction, and away from Latin derivations for the name, which are all frankly pretty fantastic. The name Caesar is like several other Latin names— Caesius, Caesonius, Caesenmus—which are derived from *aisar*, the Etruscan word for god.[6] An affiliation with Etruria fits with the fact the family belonged to the Fabian tribe. In Caesar's lifetime the Roman people were divided into thirty-five tribes. The number thirty-five had only been reached in the mid-third century, but the Fabian tribe was an early one, centered on the border between Latium and Tuscany.[7] In Caesar's lifetime any connection with Etruria had long been forgotten. The history of the Julian family that has come down in bits and pieces through later biographies descends from a book written, in Caesar's lifetime, by his cousin Lucius. Lucius explained that Aeneas's son Iulus, whose name had been Ascanius, was given his new name because, as a young man, he was an excellent archer (the Greek word for archer being *iobolos*—with the *b*, or beta in Greek. pronounced as a *v*) and killed one of the leaders of the Italian faction that was trying to prevent the settlement of Aeneas's Trojans. Another version of the name held that Ascanius was known as Iullus from the Greek word for a downy beard. The Julian family was one of fifty that claimed direct Trojan ancestry.[8]

The story about the family's connection with Aeneas wasn't an invention on Lucius Caesar's part. The family had been asserting the connection for well over a century and some of them who had held one-year positions as overseers of Rome's mint—a junior position that people would hold before running for senatorial offices—had advertised the connection on coins they minted. One such coin depicted the goddess Roma on the front (obverse) and Venus, the mother of Aeneas on the back (reverse). The claim seems to have annoyed some people when the members of the family were starting to achieve some prominence in Roman politics and it was openly questioned by Marcus Porcius Cato, whose great-grandson would be a trial for our Caesar throughout his life. This elder Cato had been an immensely prominent political figure and was the first person to write a history of Rome in Latin—the few previous histories had all been in Greek. In his history, Cato had written that he was offering an accurate history in place of the bogus stories that were passed down about families at banquets. He also wrote that Ascanius had no descendants.[9]

Cato's comment suggests that the antipathy between his descendent and Caesar was inherited. But it also points to a rather unpleasant fact about the Julian family history. It was fabricated in the later third century. The notion that Aeneas's family had a role in Rome's foundation doesn't seem to have been established until the end of the fourth century, when a Greek historian allowed that Romulus, the founder of Rome, was descended from Aeneas. By Caesar's lifetime most Romans, despite Cato's efforts, probably believed some version of this story that Aeneas was the ancestor of Romulus. But it was a long time before the story became established, and Cato was right to cast doubt on it—and not just because it involved mythical characters who never existed (Cato actually believed that most myths were history). The major problem is that Iulus didn't figure in any early Greek story about the foundation of Rome, and Aeneas seems to have been more popular in Etruria than in Latium in the first few centuries of Rome's existence. His worship as a founding divinity of Latium doesn't seem to have become important until the fifth century BCE. And that doesn't mean Iulus yet had a place in the story, though it is striking that his name shows up in connection with an earlier branch of the Julians, a branch that held office in the fifth century. The members of this clan used the cognomen Iullus. No Iulius Iullus is attested after 379, and no other member of the Julian clan is known to have held office until 267 (he was a Julius Libo). It is not impossible that,

as the creation of family histories became more important in the third
century, a mythical Iulus was born from the cognomen Iullus. The link
between early Aeneas traditions and Etruria points in the same direction
as the derivation of the name Caesar. Before it settled in Bovillae the
Julian clan likely resided in Etruria, and the details of the family history
evolved as the stories about Rome's early history absorbed the Trojan
legend which was already popular in that area.[10]

Despite the Julian clan's claim to great antiquity, the first Julius Caesar
to appear in the public record was one of the praetors—officials one step
below the consuls in the political order—in 208, during the second war
with Carthage, which had begun ten years earlier when the Carthaginian
general Hannibal had invaded Italy, inflicting horrendous losses on badly
led Roman armies. It's likely that the praetor's grandfather was the first
Julius Caesar, the one who killed the elephant. The praetor's grandson
would be the most famous Caesar of the second century, consul in 157. He
led an embassy to Greece in 147 that sparked a disastrous confrontation
between Rome and a league of Greek states in the northern Peloponnese.[11]
After that, no member of the family achieved political distinction during the
next two generations. Then, all of a sudden, in the generation of Caesar's
father, the Julii are immensely prominent.

The Julii in the generation of Caesar's grandfather were still outsiders
to the establishment. Their status is reflected not just in Julia's marriage
to the still relatively unknown Marius but also in the marriage of Caesar's
grandfather to Marcia, whose father would be consul in 118 but who had
no consular ancestors to accompany a pedigree including one of the
seven legendary kings of Rome that seems to have been altogether as
fanciful as that of the Julii. This would change in the next generation.
Caesar's father and uncle would both marry women of unimpeachable
aristocratic credentials.[12]

Gaius Julius Caesar senior was at least thirty years old when his son
was born, a conclusion that can be drawn from the fact that he would
become praetor in 92 and the minimum age for tenure of that office was
thirty-eight. His wife Aurelia was much younger. She lived until 54 BCE

and it is likely that she was in her mid-teens when she gave birth to the young Gaius. Living into her early sixties, she would have been a prodigy. The average Roman who survived childhood lived to be about fifty. Aurelia's longevity was even more remarkable in that women, given the harsh conditions under which they bore their children, had somewhat shorter life expectancies than men, even if they survived their prime years of childbearing (late teens and twenties).[13]

Given the age gap between herself and her husband, Aurelia may not have been her husband's first wife. The typical Roman aristocratic male married in his early twenties to a girl who was a couple of years younger than himself. These marriages had to be approved by the parents of both parties. Under Roman law the senior male in a family, the *paterfamilias*, controlled all the family's property, hence his role in approving a marriage, even if he might leave it up to his son or daughter to select a mate. The Roman father we know best, Marcus Tullius Cicero, did not arrange any of his daughter's marriages, and gave in when she insisted on marrying a man he didn't much like.[14]

The factors influencing a *paterfamilias*'s approval of potential mates for his children were varied. Some were political—would the wedding yield an acceptable alliance that would advance the fathers' careers? Others were economic. Aristocratic women brought substantial dowries to a marriage. The new bride would be expected to support herself with her family's money, and to help her husband pursue his own career. Once her father died the dowry would become her property and she could do with it what she pleased. In theory, she had to have a male guardian, but Roman lawyers treated this requirement as a joke.[15]

At the time he married Aurelia, Gaius Caesar was beginning to ascend the political ladder. Aurelia brought him important connections, for her lineage was a great deal better established in the hierarchy of the office-holding elite than his. Both her father and grandfather had held consulships, and all of her three brothers would ascend to the top of the political order. What made Gaius Caesar an attractive match from a political point of view was presumably his younger sister's marriage to Marius. After 104, with Marius at the peak of his power, the Julii were suddenly far more interesting. The marriage to Aurelia reflects that, and we can be pretty certain that the elder Caesar's first wife had not come from a family as distinguished as the Aurelii.

It is possible, therefore, that the matrimonial connections of the Julii in this generation were a result of the family connection to Marius. It is also possible that it had to do with the fact that, by the end of the second century, the family had become extremely rich. There were two ways in which a family could acquire a fortune at Rome. One was through warfare, but that required access to high command and a great deal of luck. The other was through public contracting. Given that only one Julius Caesar had held the consulship prior to the beginning of the first century, and that there is no record of military achievement connected with any of the Caesars, the most likely explanation for the family's wealth by the end of the second century is that it involved contracting. Even though senators were banned from direct participation in the contracting process, there was nothing to prevent them from using their personal connections to assist their associates and sharing in their profits.

Public contracting was very important because the actual Roman government was virtually nonexistent. There were some professionals who served as regular assistant to magistrates, usually as scribes or lictors (bodyguards), but there were not more than a few hundred of these people. Roads were built, armies supplied, and taxes collected by corporations led by "equestrians," people whose wealth would have allowed them to serve as cavalrymen in the Archaic Roman army but in the first century a group better defined as the wealthy who did not hold office. Equestrian contractors were known as *publicani* or "people engaged in state business." Every five years the Roman people would elect two magistrates (usually ex-consuls) who would serve as censors. Their task, aside from completing an official count of Roman citizens, was to issue contracts for public works during the next five years. If the contract for a building project turned out to be worth more than it cost to complete the project, the *publicani* kept the difference. If the contract was for provincial tax collection, the corporations would submit bids based on an estimate of the amount of tax that would be collected in the course of five years. The corporation that won the contract would then pay the estimated sum into the state treasury. It would keep any excess revenue that it happened to collect and would also be in a position to issue high-interest loans to enable a city that was short of funds to pay its taxes.[16]

Prior to the end of the third century, the Roman state had not managed large sums of money. That changed in the decades after Rome's defeat of Carthage in 202 BCE and subsequent victories over two of the major powers of the eastern Mediterranean, the Antigonids, the royal house ruling Macedonia, and the Seleucids, who ruled a kingdom that extended from western Turkey to eastern Iran and from Kazakstan and Uzbekistan in the north to the Red Sea, northern Arabia, and Israel in the south. In what is now Israel, their kingdom bordered the third great eastern realm that had emerged in the wake of Alexander the Great's conquest of the Persian Empire in the late fourth century BCE, that of the Ptolemies, whose power was centered on the Nile valley.

For Rome, the victory over Carthage brought with it a substantial war indemnity and control of Spain, whose rich silver mines had once financed the Carthaginian war effort. There was a substantial indemnity from the Antigonids as well in the early 190s, and a gigantic one from the Seleucids that started to be paid in the 180s. These new sources of revenue enabled massive new building projects and extensive payments to military contractors supplying what appear to have been deliberately inefficient campaigns against the Celtic peoples of Liguria in northern Italy. The next big increase in Rome's revenue would come in the third quarter of the second century when the king of Pergamon, an independent state in western Turkey, died and left his kingdom to Rome. The contract for the taxes from this new province, known as Asia, was the most profitable contract a corporation could win.[17]

Although we cannot know for certain, it is likely Caesar's grandfather had some connection with the Asian windfall. Caesar's father was governor of the province in 91, which is a sign that there was some sort of connection with the family's interests. By the time that he died, Caesar's grandfather had accumulated a fortune that would support extensive political careers for both of his sons, one of whom, Sextus, would be consul in 91. The other son was Caesar's father. He was praetor in 92 and would have been well positioned for a run at the consulship in 89 if chaos had not engulfed the Roman state. A cousin, Lucius, was consul in 90. No other Roman family was able to support three such careers in the decade of the 90s and certainly the Julii had not been able to do this in previous generations.

The pursuit of a political career required considerable expenditure. Not only were Roman politicians expected to provide financial gifts to members of their tribe before an election but they were also expected, if they wished to stand for the praetorship, to have displayed generosity as they passed through the earlier offices of the *cursus honorum*. In the case of a patrician the first elected office would be that of quaestor (essentially a financial assistant to higher magistrates), a post for which one would become eligible at the age of thirty. The second position would be that of aedile. There were four aediles each year, two patricians and two plebeians, who were expected (among other more practical tasks) to pay for elaborate games. As one noted Roman politician would put it: the Roman people loved public generosity and despised self-indulgence.[18] Former aediles would be remembered for the success of these games, and they would have no opportunity to recover the costs through a subsequent provincial command unless they later were elected to the praetorship.

The traditions of Roman politics were well established by the time Aurelia gave birth to Gaius Caesar. But now the validity of the system was frequently subject to question. Increasingly, people throughout the Italian peninsula, people who had been drafted into service to fight in Marius's campaigns, resented the fact they were cut out of the political process and the fiscal rewards of empire. The average Roman welcomed the handouts in election season but increasingly resented the unwillingness of the Senate to allocate resources to their well-being. At the same time, equestrian contractors expected some accountability from the senators with whom they worked. The underlying issue was whether the traditional aristocracy would continue to control the state or would have to share power with members of families newly enriched with the profits of Rome's empire—families whose interests might align with those of other people further down the economic ladder who felt the state owed them more than they were getting.

2

Rage

The crisis that would explode a few months after Gaius Caesar was born had been brewing for years. It stemmed from the question we outlined at the end of the last chapter: who would control the Roman state? Would it be the old aristocracy, or would it be members of the newly enriched classes in alliance with those excluded from direct participation, other than voting, in political life?

The two sides in this conflict tended to exploit different facets of Rome's constitution, which were defined by different ways of counting votes. The highest offices of state—the two consulships and six praetorships, which gave access to provincial commands—were elected through an assembly based on the ancient organization of Rome's army. This assembly was divided into 193 centuries (hence its name, the centuriate assembly) and further organized into five classes, with eighty of the centuries in the first class, for the wealthiest Romans, and another twenty in the second class. The poorest Romans, the so-called *proletarii*, were relegated to one century below the fifth class. Offices that did not give access to provincial commands were elected through a different system organized according to the thirty-five tribes into which Romans were also divided. Here there was no advantage given to the wealthy, and the most influential officials elected through this system, the ten tribunes of the plebs, could bring legislation to regulate the conduct of magistrates elected through the centuriate assembly.[1]

By the second half of the second century, the greatest generations of Rome's nobility, the men who had defeated Hannibal, crushed the kingdom of Macedon, and humiliated the Seleucids, were a distant memory. Their descendants were rather more notable for venality, ineptitude, and brutality. Those qualities had been amply on display throughout the two decades before 100 BCE. The tipping point for Roman politics had been the mass slaughter of the supporters of the ex-tribune Gaius Gracchus and the murder of Gracchus himself. Gracchus, who was from a very aristocratic family, had been motivated in his approach to politics by the murder of his older brother Tiberius, who had sponsored a bill to alter landholding throughout Italy. The Roman state had acquired a great deal of land from other Italian communities during the conquest of the peninsula in the fourth to third centuries and again during the later reconquest of portions of south-central and southern Italy that had gone over to Hannibal between 218 and 203 BCE. Most of this land had ended up under the effective control of wealthy individuals who hired it out to tenant farmers.[2]

Tiberius Gracchus had proposed that the state reassert control of this property and distribute it in roughly twenty-acre plots to members of the city population, a process that would be governed by a group of three elected commissioners from whose decisions there could be no appeal. Although Tiberius Gracchus's legislative program had passed and he had managed to finance it with revenue coming from the new province of Asia, he had been beaten to death by a mob led by an aristocratic cousin near the end of his year in office. Even though the person of a tribune was supposed to be immune from violence, Gracchus's cousin had not been prosecuted for murder. Instead, he was allowed to undertake an embassy to inspect Rome's newly acquired lands in the east.[3]

Gaius became tribune a decade after his brother's murder. He proposed far more wide-ranging reforms than had his brother, aiming to create accountability in government and improve the lot of the average Roman. The elements of his program, taken up by other politicians throughout Caesar's lifetime, included legislation that would make it easier to convict corrupt magistrates, improvements in provincial administration, distribution of subsidized grain to Rome's poorer citizens, further redistribution of state-owned land in Italy, and settlement of Romans in new cities where they might have a chance for greater prosperity. The places Gracchus selected for his overseas settlement program were Carthage and Corinth, cities Rome had destroyed in 146 BCE. The restoration of those cities would be symbolic of a new order.[4]

Gracchus carried out his program by holding the office of tribune for two years in a row. That was unprecedented, and he was defeated when he ran for a third term. One of the consuls who was elected for 121 BCE, Lucius Opimius, proposed repealing some of Gracchus's legislation, and when Gracchus's supporters gathered to protest, he brought archers into the city to shoot them down. Rome had no police force, and it was a basic tenet of Roman society that no person could be put to death without a trial. Opimius, however, introduced the novel principle that if the Senate declared a state of emergency, the consul could take any measures he deemed necessary to protect the state from harm, even if this meant killing lots of other Romans.[5] A couple of months after Caesar's birth, such a state of emergency would be declared and a consul would again oversee the slaughter of Roman citizens.

The decade following the murder of Gaius Gracchus saw the dominance of a conservative faction of the nobility led by members of the clan Caecilius. The exceptional incompetence displayed by the members of this group ultimately undermined their control of the state and opened the door for Gaius Marius.[6]

Marius's early political career had been a bit uneven. He had lost an election for local office before winning, in 122, the lowest office in a pre-senatorial career, that of military tribune, which is probably what landed him on the staff of Publius Cornelius Scipio, who was then leading Roman armies against the Spanish city of Numantia.[7] This was a plum appointment for an aspiring aristocrat. The time on Scipio's staff, and the connections gained there, helped him when he ran for the most junior senatorial office, the quaestorship, in which role he served as a financial assistant to a senior magistrate. He was then tribune of the plebs in 119 (having suffered a defeat in an earlier effort to gain the office). As tribune he had a fight with the consuls, whom he threatened to have arrested for opposing his proposed bill making it harder to bribe a jury, but he may have redeemed himself in the senators' eyes when he opposed a Gracchan-style bill to subsidize grain for the poor. Aristocratic support would have been necessary for him to achieve election to the praetorship in 115 and avoid trial for electoral corruption. In the following year, he demonstrated his ability as a soldier, again in Spain, as a provincial governor. And there his career would probably have ended were it not for some breathtaking scandals connected with a person he would have met while serving on Scipio's staff: Jugurtha.[8]

Jugurtha, the adopted son of King Micipsa of Numidia, a kingdom that extended from what is now Libya across Tunisia and into Morocco, was ambitious and homicidal. He secured power by murdering one half-brother and driving the other out of his realm. The Roman Senate ordered him to return a share of the kingdom to the surviving half-brother but took no punitive steps against Jugurtha. Jugurtha secured his place through massive bribes and observed that at Rome everything was for sale.[9]

Jugurtha got away with his thuggish behavior until 112, when he murdered not only his half-brother but the Italian merchants who had tried to protect him. Rome declared war and sent an army to North Africa. That operation became a farce when the commanding consul accepted a massive bribe to allow Jugurtha to "surrender" and retain his throne. The ensuing outrage at Rome led in 110 to the dispatch of another army, which was so badly led that it surrendered to Jugurtha.[10]

The surrender to Jugurtha was not the only embarrassment during these years. In 114, an army commanded by the consul Gaius Cato had been badly beaten in northern Greece by a Celtic group raiding southward from its home in central Europe. A year later a different Celtic group that had begun migrating westward crushed a Roman army in southern France. By 109 the situation in Rome was so tense that a tribune passed a motion to empanel a special commission to investigate people who had taken bribes from Jugurtha or had managed the war against him incompetently. This was not quite the revolutionary moment it might appear to be, for one of the men appointed to the commission was Aemilus Scaurus, an exceptionally powerful relative of the Caecilii, then the dominant political clan at Rome. Another Caecilius, Caecilius Metellus, was elected consul and was given control of the war in North Africa, appointing Marius as his second-in-command. The choice reflected his belief that Marius would be a loyal subordinate, and his hope that a bit more competence, along with theatrical expressions of outrage, would calm an increasingly angry public.[11]

The public that concerned a Caecilius or an Aemilius Scaurus was not that constituted by ordinary people on the streets of Rome. Rather it consisted of people who like themselves were largely in the first census class, members of the equestrian order and others with substantial property. These were people who could swing a consular election if they were annoyed enough, and failures in North Africa were creating a good deal of annoyance.

The war in North Africa started going better once Metellus (and Marius) took over, but descriptions of the ensuing battles demonstrate that Metellus's conservatism wasn't limited to politics. We're told that he organized his army according to an ancient system in which the basic tactical unit of a Roman army, the legion, was divided into *maniples*, units of about a hundred men armed according to their anticipated role on the battlefield—some were light-armed skirmishers, others were more heavily armed men who would fight with spears and swords. The preferred tactics involved wearing down an enemy through attrition. It had long been recognized by some of Rome's more able generals, including both Scipios, that this wasn't the best way to fight. They had organized their legions into ten *cohorts*, units of around five hundred men, all armed with swords and shields to deliver a powerful frontal attack while supported by units of light infantry and cavalry recruited from Rome's provincial subjects. But there was no staff college in Rome, and generals were still free to organize their armies as they saw fit, so Metellus could opt for the old-fashioned maniples.[12]

After eighteen months of only moderate success people were getting fed up with Metellus. It didn't help that he was an intense snob who believed that only people like him should be able to hold high office (he told Marius as much). Marius consulted with members of the equestrian order to see if there would be support for him if he ran for the consulship. He had a reputation as a competent soldier who could get things done if he was allowed to do so. He received an encouraging response. And so, in the summer of 108, he left the army in North Africa and declared his candidacy for the consulship. He was elected.[13]

There was a law on the books, passed by Gaius Gracchus, requiring that the provinces consuls received after their time in office would be selected before the consular election. This was to prevent consuls from selecting particularly lucrative provinces for themselves. But Marius, as soon as he took office, arranged to have a tribune pass a bill transferring the command in North Africa from Metellus to himself. This was nothing less than an electoral *coup d'état*.[14]

Marius won the war against Jugurtha by the end of 105. The person who was ultimately responsible for Jugurtha's capture was his quaestor, Lucius Cornelius Sulla. One of the more interesting observers of Rome's political history, and the author of an account of the war against Jugurtha, was Gaius Sallustius Crispus (hereafter Sallust). Introducing Sulla, he wrote:

> Sulla was a noble from a patrician family which had nearly become extinct through the sloth of his ancestors. Well educated in Latin and Greek literature, brilliant, desirous of pleasure and even more so for glory, he was never distracted by pleasure from public affairs, though he could have treated his wife with greater respect. Eloquent, subtle, jolly with his friends, he possessed an extraordinary ability to disguise his intentions. He was generous with most things, especially with money. Although he was the luckiest man alive before his victory in the civil war, the luck was never greater than his effort, so that many wondered if he was braver or luckier. As for what he did after his victory, I am uncertain whether discussion is more shameful or more lamentable.[15]

The civil war mentioned here, and Sulla personally, would have a profound impact on the life of Caesar, as we'll see in our fourth chapter. The story that Sallust tells of Sulla's family will put the story of Caesar's own family in some perspective since both families claimed great antiquity and had emerged from obscurity while the war with Hannibal was raging.

Even before Marius returned to Rome it was clear that his abilities would be needed again. In the summer of 105, the consul of that year had quarreled with the consul of the previous year when both were commanding armies in the south of France. They were supposed to confront a new movement by the people who had destroyed a Roman army in 113. The Romans were encamped near Arles when the consuls refused to cooperate, which enabled the Celts—there were now two groups, the Cimbrians and the Teutons—to annihilate both of their armies. The battle was the worst defeat the Romans had suffered since Hannibal had destroyed armies commanded by two consuls at the battle of Cannae in 216 BCE. In the aftermath of the defeat, the Romans were lucky the Cimbrians and the Teutons decided to raid western France and northern Spain instead of invading Italy.[16]

Marius was elected consul for 104 and immediately set about reorganizing and retraining his army, organizing his legions into cohorts with fresh tactics based on a new throwing spear, known as a *pilum*, that was designed to embed itself and bend when it hit an enemy's shield. When this happened, the enemy would have to drop his shield, leaving himself open to easy attack by the legionaries who would follow the volley of pilums with their swords. The process of reconstructing an army, getting soldiers into excellent shape and trained in the new tactics, took two years. Marius recognized that intense training was necessary to build the discipline and morale his men would need to face up to enemies who were described as huge, fierce, and invincible.[17]

Marius defeated the Teutons, who had now returned to southern France, in 102, and he destroyed the Cimbrians in northern Italy a year later. An experienced self-publicist, Marius advertised the divine assistance he had received, channeled through a prophetic woman from Syria who accompanied him on campaign, and dispatched enthusiastic reports of his triumphs to the Senate. In the campaign of 101, he met his self-promotional match in his consular colleague, Lutatius Catulus, who would claim that he, rather than Marius, had won the battle over the Cimbrians. To reinforce his point, Catulus erected a temple, still standing in the area of Rome called the Largo Argentina today, to *Fortuna Huiusce Diei* (The Fortune of This Day). Catulus had Sulla, who had decided to align himself with Marius's aristocratic rivals, on his staff.[18]

As the situation on the frontiers moved toward a resolution, the political situation in Rome became more difficult. The result would be mass slaughter a few months after Gaius Caesar's birth. While Marius was dealing with the Cimbrians and Teutons, various aspiring politicians had continued the effort to break down the nobility's control of the government. One of the tribunes of 103, Lucius Appuleius Saturninus, brought a bill rewriting the current treason law so it could be used to prosecute Mallius, one of the consuls responsible for the disaster at Arles, for "diminishing the majesty of the Roman people." He also proposed a bill conferring very generous retirement benefits on veterans of Marius's African campaign. The theory that linked these two actions was that the Senate was corrupt, and that Marius was a person whose needs had to be looked after. In addition to his legislative program, Saturninus engaged in a bit of theater when he convinced a man to pose as the long-lost son of Gaius Gracchus as a way of reminding people of the Senate's past repressive actions. In 101 another tribune, Servilius Glaucia, passed a bill restoring equestrian control of juries for the extortion court in order to make it easier to convict senators—they had been replaced by senators on these juries a few years previously when it appeared they were too ready to convict members of the Senate. Glaucia then oversaw the election of the tribunes for the next year, and when one of the candidates was killed, he ensured that Saturninus was elected in his place. Glaucia was also elected praetor for 100.[19]

Marius had returned to Rome at the end of 101 to celebrate a triumph for his victories. The triumph, a parade through the streets of Rome at the head of one's troops, preceded by displays of booty, prisoners, and images illustrating the commander's achievements, was the highest honor a Roman senator could win. Marius shared this honor with Catulus in order to mollify his ego and smooth the rough waters of Roman politics. Saturninus had other ideas. First, he sponsored a series of bills that were plainly in Marius's interest, including grants of land for his veterans and a guarantee of cheap grain for the people of Rome. Both these bills included clauses requiring senators to swear to uphold them. Then Saturninus tried to seize control of the government for the coming year by supporting Glaucia, then praetor, as a candidate for the consulship. That was illegal since there was supposed to be a three-year interval between the tenure of a praetorship and a consular candidacy. Meanwhile, Saturninus also sought to be reelected as tribune and to have the fake Gracchus elected alongside him.[20]

Violence broke out at the elections. Glaucia's rival for the consulship was murdered. The senate passed an "ultimate decree" ordering Marius to bring order to the city. Marius brought troops into Rome, besieging his former allies on the Capitoline Hill overlooking the Forum. When they surrendered, he brought them down into the Forum where they were imprisoned in the Senate House to await trial. The trial never happened. A mob murdered them first. Glaucia, who had escaped the initial round of arrests, was tracked down and killed. This was on December 9, 101 BCE.[21] Caesar was less than six months old.

3

Little Caesar

Immediately after his birth, the infant Caesar was inspected for defects, and given his first bath. Ideally his body would be rubbed with salt and honey or olive oil and fruit juice to remove the afterbirth, and then bathed in lukewarm water. He would then be presented to his father. No defect being found, his father, whose decision this was, determined he should be raised. On the ninth day after his birth, the baby received his name.[1]

The young infant would have been wrapped in blankets and placed in a cradle. Aurelia may have breastfed him for a time—that was not unheard of for an aristocratic lady—but the primary responsibility for his care would have fallen to a wet nurse. At about six months she would wean him gradually onto a diet of softened bread, soup, and porridge.[2]

The younger Gaius Caesar was his parents' second child. His older sister was probably born around 102, and his younger sister was most likely born a couple of years after him. The two girls were known simply as Julia the elder and Julia the younger. Roman women were identified simply by their family name and the order in which they were born. This naming practice represented their theoretical subordination within the family. Like most theories this one seemed increasingly nonsensical, for the women of Caesar's generation, while they could not vote and could not hold office, could still exercise enormous influence over the course of affairs and were not content to be pushed around by their male relations.

In the early years of Caesar's life, his mother would have overseen his upbringing along with that of his sisters. Until they turned five, Caesar and his sisters would likely have played with the other children in the household. These children would all have been slaves, for most slaves in Rome grew up in the household in which they would serve. Given the harsh demographic regime of the time, due largely to the total absence of antibiotics, about half the early playmates, even in this wealthy home, likely died before they reached the age of five. We don't know if Gaius and the Julias lost any siblings. The surviving biographical traditions don't suggest that there were more than the three children who grew up, but, as we'll see, time and again these traditions aren't very informative on important details of Caesar's early life. Often silences in this tradition will reveal as much as anything that is openly stated.

Formal education for a young Roman of high standing began at the age of seven. One thing we are told about Aurelia (interestingly, from a source that is outside the direct biographical tradition) is that she was a model mother, devoted to her son's upbringing. It is quite likely that she was equally devoted to her daughters' education, and that, in his early years, Gaius was educated along with his sisters, who would have been expected to participate fully in the cultural life of the elite when they were grown up. Aurelia supervised her children's education at the hands of a *paedagogus* (literally, "child guide").[3]

The *paedagogus* made sure that Caesar and the two Julias knew their letters and numbers. Discussions of early childhood education by ancient theorists on the subject enable us to have a decent idea of what young Caesar and his sisters went through. First the child would learn the letters from A to Z. There was debate about whether they should learn to pronounce the letters before or after they learned to write them. Learning to write involved tracing over letters that were written on a wax tablet, as we can see from some of these school tablets that have survived. Once they had learned their letters in order they would learn them in reverse, and then in different combinations. They would sing an alphabet song and play letters games; the *paedagogus* could reward them with little letter-shaped cakes.[4]

Once they'd learned the alphabet children would learn to combine consonants and vowels into syllables. They would not proceed, as children do today, to learning real words. This was because Greeks and Romans did not divide words on the written page. To learn to read was to learn which syllables went together to form words so that they could be read out loud. Theorists recommended that children work with long series of consonants to get them used to the idea of managing a page of actual writing.[5]

For a young person of Caesar's time and class a big question was whether to learn Greek or Latin first (there was no question but that both had to be mastered). Most theorists seem to have felt that Greek should come first, which would complicate things for a child who was learning to read a language other than the one which he or she was hearing spoken each day. Play and games aside, the theory was that the more challenging the learning process, the better.[6]

The rudiments of reading were taught along with some basic arithmetic. This had a practical aspect, for the Roman monetary system, like our own, required a basic understanding of multiplication and division. The principal bronze coin, the *sestertius*, was worth a quarter of the principal silver coin, the *denarius*, and was itself valued at sixteen *asses* (a much smaller bronze coin). Small children learned number rhymes rather like the alphabet rhymes their *paedagogus* used to teach them their letters—we can imagine Gaius and the Julias chanting "one and one is two, two and two are four." We are told this rhyme was taught at a later date, but it's unlikely teaching arithmetic was different then than at this point.[7]

When they weren't in school the children would have continued to play with the other children in the household, though now it's likely that the games they played reflected their different statuses and that, even at this very early stage, the children of aristocrats were taught to play at giving orders to others. Since the toys for Roman children which we have discovered through archaeological excavations show that children played at the occupations in which they were expected to engage when they grew up, it isn't too fantastic to imagine the young Caesar at the age of seven waving a wooden sword and ordering his playmates about. These slave children would also have been in school, being educated by their own *paedagogus*.[8]

The practice of slavery at Rome during Caesar's childhood was radically different from the American and Caribbean experience of slavery. The most important distinction between slavery in the Americas and slavery at Rome was that the Roman system was not based on race. While Romans were certainly capable of expressing contempt for people of different backgrounds (Caesar would rely on this in making his annual reports to the Roman people about his campaigns in Gaul), groups were generally defined by their cultural attributes rather than their physical appearances. Romans could certainly comment on the giant size of semi-naked Celtic barbarians, but when those barbarians learned Latin and started participating in Roman culture, they ceased to be barbarians and their "barbarous" appearance was no longer worth commenting upon.

A second major difference between Roman and American slavery was that Roman slavery was not seen as a driver of the economy. Despite the rhetoric of Tiberius Gracchus, who claimed the peasants of Italy had been driven from their farms to make way for giant slave plantations, there is no evidence that this was true. Like many politicians, Gracchus didn't mind lying to make a point. Ownership of large amounts of land was basic to the definition of aristocratic status—you had to have land valued at 400,000 sesterces to be a member of the senatorial or equestrian order. This land was usually held in the form of large estates spread around Italy. The bulk of the land associated with those estates would be leased to tenant farmers and there would be a central house with a slave staff which was expected to support itself from the land that had not been leased out. There would also be a house in Rome with a large domestic staff to provide the services necessary to keep up appearances.[9]

Two other major differences between Roman and American slavery were that many Roman slaves expected to be freed if they retained the favor of their owners, and many of them were brought up in the households in which they served. It is likely that owners decided what level of education a slave would receive before he or she was twelve. At that point, a basic education was complete and a child would move on to the more advanced education in literacy and math at the hands of the *grammaticus* (grammarian; the title is indicative of the fact literary education

was considered more important than math). Roman households operated on the basis of strict gender and class relationships. Slaves selected
for higher education would become their owner's secretaries or business
managers, while other slaves would be relegated to more menial tasks
such as cleaning the furniture, watching the door, or serving in the
kitchen, where the head chef, although also a slave, would be a person of
very great importance. Female slaves were relegated to household tasks.[10]

Male and female slaves did form relationships, and one job for a female
slave was to provide the next generation of slaves within the household.
If she was freed, she and her partner would leave their children as slaves
in their former owner's household. Female slaves were also subject to the
sexual desires of their owners. It is impossible to know how common
sexual abuse was in Roman households—it was certainly common
enough to be the source of some bitter jokes in Roman plays, and to
provide an undercurrent to the one book from antiquity that was written by slaves about their experiences. This book was the *Life of Aesop*,
and it offers a sense of the wisdom that slaves could pass on to each other.
Two of the major concerns in this book are physical and sexual abuse,
though in both cases it appears that there were understood to be limita-
tions on what the typical slave owner could get away with. Roman males
who were seen to be sexually dissolute (a charge that would be brought
more than once against Caesar) were people who could not be trusted in
public life. Likewise, men who were cruel were not to be trusted, and
people were watching. This didn't always guarantee good treatment. In
the *Life of Aesop*, the owner is depicted as a jerk who conspires against
Aesop to justify flogging him (though he is only beaten once in the
story). Aesop avenges himself on his owner by having an affair with the
owner's wife, who had earlier been described as a person on the lookout
for a young slave who would be more interesting than her spouse.[11]

In real life, the man we know best out of all the Romans—Cicero—
was told by his brother to recall that everyone in the Forum would ask his
slaves about his character. We also know he had a slave, Tiro, whom he
eventually freed, as his closest companion and in many ways his closest
friend. Tiro seems to have genuinely liked Cicero, which wasn't a univer-

sal feeling among Cicero's acquaintances. Tiro would spend his life after Cicero's murder in 43 BCE publishing his former master's collected works. Cicero also makes no reference in his writings to any woman who might have been his mistress. Things may have been a bit different in Caesar's household—Aurelia had no more children after the younger Julia, which does suggest that her husband, with two dowries and a senatorial career to pay for, may have decided against having further children with Aurelia and may have taken slave concubines instead. Such arrangements can be discovered in some surviving Roman wills.[12]

Slaves who were not selected for education or were born in rural areas had harder lives. A skeleton found at Pompeii, for instance—a young man in his late teens or early twenties—shows signs of severe overwork, with compressed discs in his spine. Conventional wisdom holds that he was a slave, and, generally speaking, hard labor for slaves was considered a punishment. Boredom, on the other hand, was a fact of life. Roman writers discuss people who held elaborate dinners while their slaves stood around and watched, treated like furniture.

The hierarchical structure of slave-owning households meant that slaves could be divided against each other. Aesop started off as a mute servant working in the fields of western Turkey. His muteness in the story is a metaphor for the condition of any field slave who did not have a way out of his situation. Then, through a divine miracle, Aesop is given the power of speech, a metaphor for what it would take to move into a position where he could flourish. His overseer sells him to a slave trader for fear that, now that he can speak, Aesop will reveal the overseer's dishonesty. This is a significant statement about the absence of class solidarity among slaves. Those who were better off would not see it as being in their interests to help a slave who was less fortunate. Masters were not expected to be any more compassionate. Some owners would turn older slaves out of their houses to starve in the streets when they were too old or sick to work any longer.[13]

Slave punishments could be brutal, and included flogging, torture with heated implements, and crucifixion. The remains of one former slave have been found wrapped in chains, and slave shackles have been discovered at a wide range of archaeological sites. In later times, the Roman state tried to intervene to restrict the abuse of slaves. Slaves who fled to a statue of the emperor were sold to new owners if they could make a case that they were ill-treated at home, and a text discovered at Pozzouli lists the brutal punishments that could only be inflicted by a public executioner—another effort to restrict what could be done within the household. Accounts of a slave revolt in Sicily during with the tribunate of Tiberius Gracchus state explicitly that cruelty on the part of owners was the proximate cause of the rebellion, and an account of the later slave revolt led by Spartacus states that it was ill treatment by the manager of the gladiatorial training ground where Spartacus was trained that sparked the revolt. Social constraint, which was the only protection for a slave, could only go so far; in Caesar's generation, the Senate was not about to pass legislation that would interfere with a slave owner's power over his or her property.[14]

We don't know if Caesar formed any close friendships with any of the slaves in his household along the lines of that between Cicero and Tiro. He worked in later life with a number of secretaries who were quite familiar with his habits, so it isn't impossible that some connections were formed at this stage. These secretaries were the people who enabled Caesar, as he grew up, to communicate with the wider world, producing the published versions of his speeches and books. His biographers would also stress that he was kind to his slaves. This may all be a legacy of his early years.

4

Teenage Years

At the age of twelve, the curriculum changed. Caesar's *grammaticus* would ensure he developed a good command of Greek and Latin literature so, when he turned fifteen, he would be ready to learn, with instruction from a rhetorician, how to produce literature on his own. This is also the point in Caesar's life at which the ancient biographical tradition gives us some indication as to who, other than Aurelia, was shaping his character.

We know about this period of Caesar's life because, shortly after his death, two of his good friends and subordinates, Lucius Cornelius Balbus and Gaius Oppius, wrote books about him. Those books are the source of the virtually identical accounts of key events in Caesar's early life preserved in the short history of Rome composed in the reign of Tiberius (14–37 CE) by the imperial apparatchik Velleius Paterculus, as well as in the much better-known writers Plutarch and Suetonius, close contemporaries who wrote at the end of the first century CE, in Plutarch's case, and in the second decade of the second century, in the case of Suetonius.[1]

After a visit to Rome, Plutarch spent most of his life at Chaeronea in central Greece, which is where he composed his *Parallel Lives of the Greeks and Romans*. The parallel for Caesar in Plutarch's book was Alexander the Great. For Plutarch they were the two greatest generals and administrators of all time, with Caesar being the slightly greater man because he was not given to drunken homicidal rages. Plutarch did not, however, see Caesar as the first Roman emperor. In addition to his *Parallel Lives*, he wrote a book about Roman emperors and, for him, the first emperor was Augustus. The last Republican figure in Plutarch's lives was Mark Antony, whose lack of self-restraint ruined him, making him also a figure whose career could be seen as being emblematic of his era. Suetonius, who probably composed his *Lives of the Twelve Caesars* under the influence of the emperor Trajan (98–117 CE), a huge fan of Caesar, took the very controversial view that Caesar was the first emperor. We'll return to the debate that these writers exemplify at the end of this book. For now, it is important that the version of Caesar's early life these authors repeat was an "official version" compiled once he had achieved great prominence. The point of the stories Balbus and Oppius told about Caesar's early life is that the personality their readers had seen in the 40s BCE was consistent with that of the young man—bold, talented, and controlling. Their other purpose was to refute the numerous slanders circulated by Caesar's enemies in the 60s and 50s. As we seek to find the truth behind the biographical tradition as we have it, it is striking that there are no fond reminiscences of Caesar's relationship with his father to pair with those of his relationship with Aurelia. There are, however, two other characters who emerge as being very influential in Caesar's life. One was his *grammaticus*, Antonius Gnipho. The other was his cousin, Gaius Julius Caesar Strabo Vopiscus.

Caesar Strabo was an accomplished poet and orator. He wrote three plays on mythological themes and was advancing toward the consulship when Caesar would have encountered him. One of Strabo's admirers was Marcus Cicero (plate 3). Strabo's oratory, Cicero said, was lacking in force but surpassed that of all his contemporaries in gaiety and wit. Cicero provided a striking picture of Strabo's views on humor in a book he wrote on Roman oratory. The scene is set in 91 as Cicero records how, in his youth, he traveled to Tusculum (modern Frascati), where he attended a gathering that included some of the great orators of the previous generation. Caesar Strabo shows up in the second of the work's three books to discuss humor. In Cicero's account, he is a man of great charm and prodigious memory, who believes (despite what Greek theorists on the matter had written) that humor is not something that can be taught. Rather it is the result of a person's natural cleverness and command of language. True humor stems from "an elegant kind of humor with a mixture of gravity and adapted to oratory as well as polite conversation." Cicero has Strabo recall how, after he told a rich man named Metellus that he (Strabo) couldn't serve in the army because of his bad eyesight, Metellus asked him if he could see anything. Strabo responded that he could see Metellus's huge mansion in the country from the walls of Rome. Strabo also tells how one of the heroes of the war with Hannibal responded to the commander of the garrison at Tarentum, who had preserved Roman control of the citadel even though the Carthaginians had taken the rest of the city. The commander wanted to be complimented for what he had done, to which the reply was "I will certainly remember it, I would never have recaptured the city if you hadn't lost it."[2]

In one of his early court cases, Caesar would quote one of his uncle's speeches, and his own writings betray the sort of irony Cicero praises in Strabo's work. When inventing an account of a meeting with an enemy leader in Gaul, he has the man open his speech with the words "I'm not such an ignorant barbarian" (*non tam ignarus barbarus*) before going on to make what Caesar knows his readers will see as ignorant claims about the nature of Roman policy. In describing one of his least favorite rivals in the civil war of 49, he would write that the man undermined the confidence of his own troops "when his appearance didn't match his words." Going to Spain later in the same year, he would remark that he was going to take on "the army without a general," then go after "the general without an army."[3]

The other great influence in Caesar's early life, his *grammaticus* Antonius Gnipho, had been born to Celtic parents in southern France who had exposed him because they could not afford to raise him. He was rescued by an Antonius, possibly a member of the aristocratic clan to which the Julii would soon develop an important connection.[4] His rescuer treated him initially as a slave, educated him, realized he was exceptionally bright, freed him, and sent him to Alexandria to complete his higher education. Returning to Rome, Gnipho's first job was as Caesar's teacher. This was around 88 BCE.

During that era, education chiefly consisted of mastering the Greek literature upon which Latin literature was based, and Gnipho ensured that Caesar knew the fundamental works of Greek literature, including the poems of Homer, along with various tragedies and comedies. Gnipho also introduced his pupil to canonical Latin literature such as Ennius's epic poem on the history of Rome from its foundation in the early second century, comedies by Plautus and Terence, and some prose works that the young Gaius could use as a model for his own compositions. Significantly for Caesar, Gnipho had definite views on the Latin language: he believed that the proper form of Latin words had to be determined by analogy with other similar words. Given the fact there was no standard dictionary of the Latin language or agreed-upon way of writing it, this was an important idea, one that Caesar would later endorse decades afterward in his own book, *Concerning Analogy*. Caesar's decision to write a book defending Gnipho's position is a sign of just how powerful an impact his teacher had upon him.[5] After leaving the household of the Caesars, Gnipho would go on to set up his own school, which attracted students who would become some of Rome's other leading literary figures, including Marcus Cicero. Although his name is Greek for "skinflint," Gnipho was remembered fondly as a charming person who did not charge in advance for lessons.[6]

As Gnipho was beginning his teaching of Caesar, the world around them was in flames. One terrible war was drawing to an end and an even more terrible one was just beginning. The first war was a sort of civil war within Italy, and its cause was the poor treatment of Italians who were not Roman citizens by those who were. In the first decade of the first century BCE the majority of people living in Italy were not Roman citizens, and most Italians were not even speaking Latin among themselves. They were still communicating with each other in their local languages, which included Greek around the Bay of Naples and throughout much of southern Italy generally, Oscan, Umbrian, and Etruscan in central Italy, and Celtic in the area of the Po valley. After the Roman conquest of Italy, completed in the early third century BCE, the peninsula's varied communities had been bound to Rome by treaties, with each individual city having its own treaty relationship with Rome. These treaties spelled out the various communities' obligations to Rome, which consisted mainly of contributing troops to Rome's armies. About one-half of a Roman army would consist of Italian allied troops who served under their own leaders under overall Roman command. By the latter part of the second century, some Italian communities had begun to do very well out of their association with Rome. These prosperous areas included Etruria and those parts of Campania that bordered the Bay of Naples. Other areas, however, were doing very much less well.[7]

In addition to the inequity in the division of the profits of empire there were two other major grievances among the Italians allied to Rome. One was that their former lands, officially confiscated by Rome to be "public land of the Roman People" but in practice left in the control of the local aristocracies, was now being taken away to provide farms for Romans who were benefiting from land distribution schemes such as that initiated by Tiberius Gracchus in 133 BCE. A second complaint was that Roman officials could behave in quite appalling ways when they passed through an Italian town whose inhabitants had none of the protections afforded to Roman citizens. The situation was exacerbated by the consuls of 95 BCE, who passed a law ordering all Italians who were then living in Rome to return to their home districts, essentially cutting them off from access to the wealth concentrated at Rome.[8]

In 91 BCE, when the consuls were Sextus Caesar, a cousin of Caesar's father, and Marcius Philippus, one of the tribunes was a man named Livius Drusus, whose connections in general were very much on the right wing of Roman politics. His father had been a major opponent of Gaius Gracchus, and he was the guardian of the young Marcus Porcius Cato, who would grow up to be the young Julius Caesar's most bitter rival. As tribune, however, Drusus pursued some policies that most Romans would have seen as reformist or radical. Claiming his actions would protect the authority of the Senate, he proposed doubling that body's size and restoring its control of juries in certain cases. At the same time, he proposed both a new land distribution bill and a bill that would give Roman citizenship to non-citizen Italians. The land distribution bill and the bill enlarging the Senate were passed. Then Drusus was murdered. No one was ever tried for the murder and Marcius Philippus, who had vigorously opposed Drusus's legislation, passed a bill invalidating his laws.[9]

The Italians were outraged by what they saw as the withdrawal of the equality with Romans they had long felt they deserved. Before the year's end, the people of Asculum (Ascoli Picino) in northwestern Italy murdered all the Romans resident in their city and a league of Italian states formed with the avowed aim of destroying Rome. Full scale war broke out the following year, when one of the consuls was Lucius Caesar, another of the elder Gaius Caesar's cousins. (Sextus Caesar, the consul of the previous year, had won some victories against the rebels in northwestern Italy before dying on campaign.) Although Lucius showed some ability as a soldier, he also pursued a political solution to the crisis by passing a bill which granted Roman citizenship to Italian communities that remained loyal to Rome and even allowed Roman generals to grant citizenship to particular communities after taking advice from their staff. In the long run, this law proved a diplomatic triumph, preventing the revolt from spreading from eastern Italy to the more prosperous west.[10]

Rome's situation was helped by the fact it could draw upon the services of men who had held significant commands in the past. One of these men was Marius. Another was Sulla, whose career had looked like it had ended with his praetorship several years previously. He returned to active duty in 90, serving first under Lucius Caesar and then under Marius before getting his own command in 89. It was also in 89 that Marius produced what may have been the best one-liner of his career in response to one of the leaders of the Italians who had challenged him, saying, "If you are a great general, Marius come down and fight us." Marius replied, "No, but if you're a great general, make me fight when I don't want to." When he did decide to fight, Marius inflicted a severe defeat on his Italian adversary.[11]

Another important figure during these years was Pompeius Strabo. He owned a great deal of land in Picenum, a district of northwestern Italy, and in 90 BCE, the first year of fighting, proved himself an able general, leading to his election as consul for the following year. Many of the young officers who made up Pompeius's staff were teenage aspirants to political power who would figure prominently in Roman politics over the course of the next generation. Chief among these young officers was Strabo's own son Gnaeus (plate 1). Gnaeus would become much more famous than his father, and we'll be referring to him throughout this book simply as Pompey, the form of the name Pompeius most common in English. Pompey's future would be tied inextricably to that of Caesar. Another staff member was Cicero, as well as his future rival, Lucius Sergius Catalina, referred to in English as Catiline. Others on the list included Gaius Rabirius, later a financial services tycoon and friend of Cicero, and Lucius Vettius, a thoroughly disreputable character, who would be at the center of a couple of scandals in his later life. The presence of so many future leaders in Strabo's orbit underscores for us the fact that the Roman governing class was really very small, and its members would have known each other for years before they competed for public office.[12]

While Pompeius Strabo was campaigning in northern Italy, capturing the city of Asculum, Sulla had command of an army further south, and his military successes pushed him into the political forefront, and he was elected consul for the year 88.

At that point, thanks to a combination of superior Roman generalship and the law of Lucius Caesar, the Italian war was winding down. But even as it was doing so, a new crisis exploded overseas, where a Roman ambassador, an ex-consul named Manius Aquillius, had encouraged the king of Bithynia—a region in what is now northern Turkey, extending eastward along the Black Sea from the sea of Marmara—to attack a neighboring king, Mithridates, whose kingdom of Pontus extended further eastward along the south coast of the Black Sea and inland across the mountains into central Turkey. Nicomedes, the king of Bithynia, had a bad army, and probably should not have taken Aquillius's advice. Mithridates, by contrast, was a highly competent general with a good army.[13]

The result was a total disaster for Nicomedes and the Romans. Mithridates chased Nicomedes back into his kingdom, occupying its territory and forcing Nicomedes to flee to Italy. Buoyed by success, Mithridates then decided to move against Nicomedes's Roman allies. The Romans controlled two provinces in the area: Asia, along the west coast of what is now Turkey, and Cilicia, along Turkey's southern coast. Both provinces were dependent upon relatively weak local militias for their defense. Gaius Cassius, the governor of Asia, tried to resist Mithridates's invasion of his province but failed and had to flee. Gaius Oppius, the governor of Cilicia, led his provincial forces into Asia, where he too was crushed by Mithridates. Manius Aquillius, the Roman whose advice had touched off this debacle, was captured and died an agonizing death when Mithridates had molten gold poured down his throat.[14]

Mithridates was said to own a cloak that had once belonged to Alexander the Great, and he now decided to play Alexander in the reverse, using his Eastern conquests as a base from which to take over Greece. He sent an army into Macedonia and a fleet across the Aegean to occupy Athens, promising the Greeks an end to Roman oppression and the domination of local politics by Roman puppets. Meanwhile, in Rome's now-threatened province of Asia, the poor, the debt-ridden, and the discontented rose in enthusiastic support of Mithridates's anti-Roman crusade, answering his call to murder all the Italians in their midst. There is no accurate count of those who died in the ensuing slaughter. Our sources give an estimate of eighty thousand, but, the numbers in ancient sources are often unreliable and probably this total is simply a rhetorical statement to the effect that a lot of people were murdered. Still, the massacre must have been horrific. Such an atrocity, coupled with the devastating loss of Rome's most important eastern provinces, demanded an immediate response. The senior consul for the year 88 was assigned to handle the job.[15]

Seniority for consuls was determined by the order in which they crossed the electoral finish line. Sulla had been the first candidate to win the required number of votes for consul and had been elected ahead of the other winning candidate, Pompeius Rufus, a distant relative of Strabo. Pompeius's politics aligned closely with Sulla's, and their alliance was strengthened in the year before their shared consulship when Rufus had married Sulla's daughter, who would later bear their only child before the end of the year. We'll be meeting her again in chapter 6.[16]

The consular election had gone smoothly, but the election of tribunes resulted in the election of Sulpicius Rufus, a powerful orator who was closely aligned with Marius. Chaos ensued. Sulpicius proposed a series of laws, including a crucial revision of Lucius Caesar's citizenship law that enhanced the power of the new citizens by integrating them into the existing thirty-five tribes where they outnumbered old citizens, and a law transferring the command against Mithridates to Marius.[17]

Sulpicius recruited gangs of thugs to intimidate opponents and ensure the passage of his laws. There was nothing the two consuls could do to stop passage of the bills, and Sulla, fleeing from a mob, took refuge in the house of Marius. The history of Rome would have changed forever if Marius had simply turned Sulla over to his pursuers.[18] Instead he protected his rival, and paid a price for his decency. Sulla took off for Capua, where the large army he had been commanding in the war against the Italians was currently stationed. The soldiers were expecting they would soon set sail to fight Mithridates—an attractive prospect, since Romans did not rate eastern soldiers highly (despite the evidence that Mithridates' troops were quite competent) and Mithridates was very rich, so the soldiers anticipated that a lot of plunder would be theirs. When Sulla arrived, he explained to his former soldiers that his removal from command would have negative consequences for them: they would be stuck in Italy, losing the chance to fight a lucrative war in the East. Sulla may also have asserted that, as consul, he had the duty to suppress riotous assemblies in Rome. In any event, he persuaded his soldiers to march with him to Rome and put a stop to Sulpicius Rufus's mischief. This was the first time in history that a Roman magistrate had led a Roman army against Rome, and it was a sign that the soldiers of Sulla's era felt greater loyalty to their comrades and general than they did toward the Republic itself.[19]

With the support of his soldiers, Sulla occupied Rome and sentenced his enemies to death. These enemies included Marius, who skipped town and made a dramatic escape to North Africa when he saw what was happening. Sulpicius was betrayed by a slave, whom Sulla duly rewarded with his freedom and then immediately executed for the crime of betraying his master.[20]

Sulla, who fancied himself a political theorist, now passed a series of laws intended to make the Roman constitution more functional. Summoning a meeting of the people—whose acquiescence to Sulla's demands was guaranteed by the threat of violence—he announced that the state had long been dominated by irresponsible demagogues. He claimed that, in the distant past, no bill could be presented to the people unless it had been approved by the Senate. Moreover, all laws had to be passed by the centuriate assembly, where the votes of the wealthy had greater weight. These rules, he said, had been made by the ancient king Servius Tullus before the foundation of the Republic. Now they were to be restored. Sulla also deprived the tribunes of the plebs of most of their powers—the main ones left were the power to bring public business to a halt and the power to protect a citizen from the arbitrary action of a magistrate—and he reintroduced Livius Drusus's former proposal to double the size of the Senate. All the measures passed by Sulpicius Rufus were declared null and void.[21]

Sulla's revision of the Roman constitution reflected both his personal style and the thinking of the Roman right wing. Old was good, change was bad, and the common people needed to be kept in line and had to learn to follow the lead of their social and economic betters. The ideal Roman state—which, contrary to Sulla's proclamations, had never really existed—was one in which there were no tribunes and the Senate controlled everything.

Sulla now held consular elections for the coming year and forced the two winning candidates, Gnaeus Octavius and Lucius Cornelius Cinna, to swear an oath to maintain the new constitutional order he had just created. Cinna was a distant relative of Sulla's whose branch of the clan Cornelius had been out of the public limelight until Cinna's father had become consul in 127. The family connection may have been the reason why Sulla thought he could trust Cinna. Thinking he had now settled matters in Rome to his advantage, Sulla took his troops south to

Brundisium (Brindisi) and landing in Greece before the year's end. He was so keen to depart that he ignored a flagrant sign that his political settlement was about to come apart. This was Pompeius Strabo's murder of Pompeius Rufus when the latter had journied to northern Italy to take over command of Pompeius Strabo's army.[22]

No sooner had Sulla and his army departed than his political settlement, based on an eccentric reading of Roman traditions and imposed by violence, was rapidly undone by violence. Pompeius Strabo was still an independent operator northern Italy when Cinna incited political controversy of his own and seized the forum with a gang of armed men. Though initially driven out by his fellow consul Octavius, he gathered troops from across Italy and invited Marius to return from Africa to support him. Assisted in their efforts by some good luck—a plague struck Rome, and Pompeius Strabo, who had agreed to support Octavius against Cinna, suddenly died—Marius and Cinna managed to take control of Rome after a brief civil war. Octavius was killed while attempting to flee the city, leaving Marius and Cinna firmly in control.[23]

The savage conflict between the followers of Marius and the supporters of Sulla naturally split the Roman aristocracy, creating unbreakable divisions even within individual families. Julius Caesar's father had sided with his brother-in-law Marius, but his cousins, Gaius Julius Caesar Strabo and Lucius Julius Caesar, did not, and both were murdered by the victorious Marian faction. We can only guess at the impact that the assassination of Strabo in particular had on the young Caesar.[24]

Caesar also had other things to think about as ordinary domestic life proceeded in the shadow of great events. Not long after the outbreak of the war against Mithridates—and the eruption of civil conflict at Rome—he had gotten married. He was not yet fourteen, a very young age to marry, even for a Roman aristocrat. His bride was a girl named Cossutia, who was from an equestrian family. His sisters too were finding matches. The older Julia had married a Pedius, who presumably came from a wealthy equestrian family (none of his ancestors had been senators). She would later marry a Pinarius, a member of a family that was astonishingly ancient and indolent, having done nothing for centuries other than manage the ancient shrine of Hercules near the Circus Maximus. The younger Julia married a man named Atius Balbus. It was not an especially aristocratic match, but it would produce two daughters, one of whom married a man named Gaius Octavius around 70 BCE; their son, Julius Caesar's great-nephew, would one day become his heir and, as a result, the first emperor of Rome.[25]

All these marriage arrangements were made by Caesar's father before he died (of natural causes) in 86. The spouses he found for his children suggest he had no great ambitions for them, and that perhaps explains why he seems to be such a minor figure in the official version of the younger Caesar's life.

Cinna had other ideas, however. He was now the virtual master of Rome. Sulla and his army was still in the East fighting Mithridates, and Marius had died shortly after assuming an unprecedented seventh consulship in 87, the year after he and Cinna had seized the city in the wake of Sulla's departure. Cinna, seeking a husband for his own daughter Cornelia, cast his eyes on Marius's nephew and decided the young man ought to be his son-in-law. Caesar apparently thought so too, or perhaps Cinna was not a man to be defied. Caesar divorced Cossutia and married Cornelia in 84. At the age of fifteen or sixteen, Caesar was already on his second marriage.

He was also already a participant in a very important aspect of Roman public life, having become a member of the priestly college of the Salii, whose members danced at public festivals. Now Cinna proposed that he take up a new religious office, that of priest of Jupiter. It was a very ancient position which would have conferred prominence, but it also would have excluded him from any further position in public life. Among other taboos reflecting the antiquity of the position as Jupiter's representative in the city of Rome, the priest couldn't leave town for more than twenty-four hours—a severe restriction given the growth of Rome's empire in the centuries since the job had been created. In the end, for reasons that are unknown, Caesar did not become priest of

Jupiter and no one else wanted the job, which remained unfilled for the next eighty-seven years.[26]

The year of Caesar's second marriage was also a turning point in the history of Rome. His new father-in-law, Cinna, was killed in a military mutiny. One of the challenges he had not been able to overcome was the poverty of his administration. Italy was essentially bankrupt in the wake of the Italian war and the subsequent civil conflicts. The same could not be said for Sulla, who after four years of war had made a peace treaty with Mithridates that would allow the latter to keep his throne in return for a massive payment to bankroll Sulla's prospective return to Italy. Sulla had levied five years' taxes on the reconquered province of Asia, the wealthiest of Rome's overseas possessions, on the grounds that the region's cities owed that much for the years in which they were ruled by Mithridates. The example Sulla set as a man who could assemble an army that was better financed than that of the Roman state would not be forgotten.[27]

Sulla returned to Italy in 83, winning a series of victories over the armies of the state and negotiating with Italian communities for their support. In 81 he finally fought his way into Rome, receiving some important assistance from the young Gnaeus Pompey, who had raised a private army to support Sulla. Pompey's father's plunder from his successful operations during the Italian war presumably provided some of the funds for this army.[28] The victorious Sulla was not inclined to mercy. He slaughtered prisoners taken in the final battle outside Rome in October of 81 and immediately posted a list of persons who were to be summarily executed and their property seized. What would this mean for Marius's nephew and the husband of Cinna's daughter?[29]

In later life, Caesar circulated the story that Sulla ordered him to divorce Cornelia, and that he refused. This much is certainly true, and it is also true that Sulla seized Cornelia's dowry. But did Caesar then have to go into hiding, and was he hunted by Sulla's assassins? He said so. He also told a story about how, when he was brought before Sulla, his mother's family, all staunch supporters of Sulla, joined with the Vestal Virgins—the most revered religious officials of the Roman state—in begging Sulla to spare his life. Against his better judgment, Sulla agreed to do so. "In Caesar there are many Mariuses," he is alleged to have said, and is said to have warned that Caesar would destroy the cause of "the best men," the *optimates*. That one word, *optimates*, gives away the story as a fake. The term came into common usage after Sulla's death. In Sulla's lifetime the word for these people was *nobiles*. Moreover, Sulla was not given to mercy and if he had really held the view he is supposed to have expressed, it is inconceivable that Caesar would have been allowed to live.[30]

While Aurelia's relatives surely did play an important role in Caesar's survival, convincing Sulla to spare Caesar may not have been a tough sell. Caesar was not yet the man whom he would become. The proposal that he be made priest of Jupiter suggests that even his own relatives didn't think the teenage Caesar had a bright future in Roman politics. A further sign Caesar wasn't seen as a threat was that he would soon be taken on as a staff officer by several of Sulla's lieutenants. If the general view had been that he was a potential menace, it is doubtful that Sulla's own supporters would have launched him on a political career. Another reading of the historical evidence is that Sulla saw Caesar as a young man of good family whom he wished to draw into his orbit. The demand that he divorce and remarry is very similar to the situation faced by Gnaeus Pompey, who did divorce his wife at Sulla's behest.[31] Caesar's refusal to divorce Cornelia suggests he genuinely loved her. That Sulla did not regard this as a fatal flaw is indicated by Caesar's subsequent employment by Minucius Thermus, Sulla's handpicked governor of Asia.

5

Early Adventures

Suetonius, who is well informed on this point, states that, after his meeting with Sulla, Caesar took off for the province of Asia as a staff member (*contubernalis*) to the new governor, Minucius Thermus. He also implies that Caesar was trying to stay out of Sulla's way, an implication which fits well with the overall tendency of the biographical tradition to depict Caesar as a diehard opponent of the settlement Sulla was imposing on Rome. As a matter of fact, however, it is impossible to believe. Caesar's commander had been praetor in 81 and was clearly well trusted by Sulla, who would have acquiesced in what was a very significant appointment.[1]

Thermus had a problem on his hands. His predecessor as governor had started a new war with Mithridates. Despite his claim to have won a smashing victory, compelling the king to make a fresh treaty, it appears he botched the operation and Mithridates had been willing to make a new peace merely so that he could continue to rebuild his forces as he recovered from the first war with Rome. Far from being straightforwardly crushed by the previous governor, Mithridates had, in fact, demonstrated unexpected strength. The brutality of the settlement Sulla imposed on the cities of Asia in the wake of that first war had created a groundswell of support for the Pontic king during the second war. And the city of Mytilene (modern Mitilini), on the island of Lesbos, which had joined Mithridates in the first war, was still in revolt as the second war technically came to an end.[2]

Thermus needed a fleet to transport his forces to the island. Some of the ships could be gathered from cities in his province, but he also looked to Rome's ally, King Nicomedes, who was now back in Bithynia. He sent Caesar to gather additional ships from Nicomedes. For Caesar this was a golden opportunity to make contacts at the king's court. An aspiring politician's standing in Rome was predicated, in part, on his ability to build a network of dependents in the provinces. Caesar did not waste his time on this occasion, for he appears to have charmed the king, befriended the king's daughter, and made other contacts in the kingdom that would lead to his being regarded as a potential patron for Bithynians in future years.[3]

A story was later spread that Caesar's relationship with Nicomedes had a physical aspect. According to the polite version, Caesar had played Ganymede to Nicomedes' Zeus. In other words, he had prostituted himself to the king. This story, widely repeated by Caesar's enemies in later years, has no foundation in reality. Caesar willingly advertised his Bithynian connections during the next decade, which he is unlikely to have done if actual scandal attached to them. Most likely, the story had its origins in a court case a few years later.[4]

We will come to the beginning of Caesar's legal career shortly, but for now we will follow Caesar and the Bithynian ships he obtained back to Asia, where he served with distinction at the siege of Mytilene under the command of Licinius Lucullus, another of Sulla's devoted lieutenants. In the assault on the city, Caesar saved the life of a fellow soldier, for which Thermus awarded him the civic crown (*corona civica*), one of Rome's highest military honors. The civic crown was woven of oak leaves, and a person who was awarded it could wear it for the rest of his life. When he appeared at games, the Senate would rise to greet him and, even if not a senator, he was allowed to sit in the front rows of the theater where members of the Senate were seated (seating in Roman theaters was based on social class). It is most unlikely that Thermus would have awarded Caesar the crown, even if he had earned it, if he thought he would be advancing the career of a future political enemy, or honoring a person who was tainted by recent scandal.[5]

Mytilene captured, Thermus returned to Rome. Caesar did not. Instead, he joined the staff of Publius Servilius, who had been consul in 79 and had now become governor of the province of Cilicia, which extended on both sides of the Taurus mountains in southern Turkey. The coastal region, excluding the broad plain around what is now the city of Antalya, did not support robust agricultural economies, with the result that those peoples living along the coast had taken to supplementing their incomes by raiding the trade routes passing along their coast. The by now dysfunctional regimes of the Ptolemies, who ruled Cyprus, and the Seleucids in Syria no longer had the capacity to patrol the region, so the task of suppressing piracy fell to Roman governors. Caesar only served in Cilicia for a year, but it is quite possible he picked up some experience of naval warfare that stood him in good stead in his later life. He may also have made the acquaintance of a man who would play an extremely important part in his life both as an ally and then as a bitter rival. This was Titus Labienus, the nephew of a man who had perished with Saturninus in 100.

Suetonius, who is the only biographer who preserves an accurate chronology of Caesar's life during these years, says Caesar returned to Rome when he learned of Sulla's death. Sulla had been dictator in 79, laying down his power prior to the consular elections for 78. The date of his retirement was thus likely to have been in June. Caesar would later observe that this showed Sulla didn't know what he was doing, but Sulla liked to party and liked to imagine he had safely reformed the Roman state. He believed he was the favorite of the gods, so the massacres he committed had been enabled by their assistance. As it turned out, Sulla's retirement didn't last for long. He moved down to the area around the Bay of Naples, continued to drink heavily, and now exhibited symptoms of a bowel disorder that may have been connected with colon cancer. He died early in 78.[6]

By the time Caesar got back to Rome, the city was in chaos. Marcus Aemilius Lepidus, one of the newly elected consuls, was trying to restart the civil war, threatening to overthrow Sulla's constitutional order. He tried, unsuccessfully, to prevent the massive celebration of Sulla's

memory at a publicly financed funeral, then proposed bills to restore the
powers of the tribunes which Sulla had eliminated, to subsidize reduced
grain prices for the people of Rome, and to restore land confiscated by
Sulla. He was successfully opposed in all these matters by his fellow consul, Lutatius Catulus, who was emerging as a stalwart supporter of
Sulla's policies, but Lepidus's opposition did not end there. Given command of an army at the year's end to suppress a revolt in Etruria, he
turned around to attack Rome. Trounced on the battlefield by Pompey,
he withdrew to Sardinia, where he died. Suetonius makes it very clear (as
Caesar's first biographers must have) that Caesar would have nothing to
do with Lepidus, despite being invited to join him in his revolt.[7]

Caesar had important things to do if he was going to pursue the public career to which he plainly aspired. Young men would often try to
make a name for themselves as defenders of the oppressed by prosecuting
senior magistrates for criminal acts in the provinces. In early 76, Caesar
took up the cause of the people of Macedonia, who claimed (probably
with good reason) that their last governor, Cornelius Dolabella, had
oppressed them. At his trial, Dolabella was defended by two of the leading lights of the conservative wing of the Roman legal profession. One of
these was Caesar's uncle, Gaius Cotta. The trial became a spectacle,
drawing aspiring orators to listen to the proceedings. Caesar personally
did very well, subsequently publishing his speech for the prosecution,
which found admiring audiences in later centuries. But he lost the case
and, in the course of the proceedings, Dolabella, who delivered his own
defense speech, got off the line that Caesar was the "rival of the queen,
on the inner half of the couch."[8] Thus was born the story about Caesar
and Nicomedes. No one much bothered about it at the time since Caesar
was not yet seen as a significant force in Roman politics, even if he presumably showed up wearing his civic crown while proving that he could
argue a case with the best Rome had to offer.

Not long after Dolabella's acquittal, the people of Greece asked Caesar
to represent them in a civil suit against Gaius Antonius Hibrida, a much
less powerful figure than Dolabella, for his conduct as a lieutenant of
Sulla in the war against Mithridates nearly a decade previously. The case

was a civil action for the recovery of stolen property and Caesar argued the case so effectively that the praetor, who decided the case on his own since juries were required only in criminal cases, held in favor of the plaintiffs. Antonius appealed to the tribunes to protect him from the judgment, which they appear to have done. That may have saved him some money, but the incident itself was not forgotten. Six years later, the censors removed Antonius from the rolls of the Senate, quoting from Caesar's prosecution when they did so. Antonius had stolen from the provincials and avoided the judgment of the court, but was now so deeply in debt that he no longer had the property to qualify as a senator.[9]

Having made a name for himself and annoyed powerful members of the senate, Caesar again decided to leave town, this time to study on Rhodes with the famous rhetorician Apollonius Molon. In the course of his journey to Rhodes, Caesar had an adventure his biographers rewrote and reinvented at length. He was captured by pirates. The simplest version of the story, which can be distilled from the varied versions that have come down to us, is that he was seized by the pirates on the island of Pharmakussa, near Miletus in what is now western Turkey. A ransom was collected, and he was freed. The story's full-scale version includes, in addition to these basic facts, Caesar's vengeance against the pirates, his correction of their ransom demands, and a fight with the governor of Asia about how the pirates should be punished. The point of the story, as one author makes explicit, was to show that, even at this very early stage in his life, Caesar was "the brightest star in the sky." His future greatness was predicted by his conduct on this occasion.[10]

According to the expanded story, when the pirates set the ransom at twenty talents, Caesar explained to them he was worth fifty. While a captive, with only three servants for company, he worked on the cultural improvement of his captors, reading them poetry and speeches he had written, while at the same time promising he would chase them down and kill them as soon as he was released. Upon his release he did gather a fleet and immediately set upon his former captors. The pirates who survived the attack were held in prison while Caesar approached the governor, Junius Juncus, demanding that he execute them. Juncus saw a potential source of profit for himself if he allowed the pirates to be ransomed, but, when he became aware of what Juncus was up to, Caesar took the pirates from their cells and crucified them—though he slit their throats before placing them on the crosses to spare them the agonizing pain of crucifixion. In another version, Caesar simply has the pirates decapitated.[11]

There is much here that is simply unbelievable. In the first place, the sums of money mentioned would have been next to impossible in the province of Asia at this time. We know from other sources that the cities of Asia were virtually bankrupted first by the payment imposed upon them by Sulla and then the interest payments on the sums they had borrowed from Italian financiers to pay what Sulla demanded. In the second place, Caesar was not an official, so there was no way he could legally order an execution. The vision of Caesar we get here is very much that of the hyper-controlling Caesar we meet later in his own writings. It was the image Caesar would project at the time when his biographical tradition was taking shape, and it made sense to retroject this aspect of his character onto a story that Caesar had likely been circulating for years in some form or other.[12]

While the story outlined above became a significant feature of the official biographical tradition, there was also a completely different version of the story which survived into the second century CE when it was preserved in a collection of stratagems assembled by a man named Polyaenus. In this version, Caesar was captured by the pirates near Cape Malea in the Peloponnese. When a wealthy Milesian named Epicrates showed up with Caesar's ransom, he also had with him some drugged wine, which he gave to the pirates. When they had passed out, he and Caesar slit their throats. Two especially interesting aspects of this story are that Epicrates was a real person, and that, well after his arrival in Rhodes, Caesar served briefly in the region where this story places him.[13]

Another story that was soon in circulation was that Caesar left Rhodes in the spring of 73 to rally local militias when Mithridates yet again invaded the province of Asia. It had become clear Nicomedes was going to leave his kingdom of Bithynia to Rome when he died, and Mithridates wished to forestall any further growth of Roman power in the region. In 74, Mithridates made a treaty with Quintus Sertorius, a Roman rebel who had been leading, from his base in Spain, what was effectively a continuation of Cinna's war with Sulla. Recognizing the renewed threat from Mithridates that this alliance represented, the Senate dispatched the consuls of 74, Licinius Lucullus and Aurelius Cotta, to the East. Cotta took charge of Bithynia, while Lucullus raised troops from Cilicia and Asia. While the consuls were thus occupied, Mithridates exploited a gap in the Roman defenses, sending his forces into Asia. Caesar, as we have mentioned, took it upon himself to shore up Rome's teetering position by assembling troops from various towns. Rallying forces from provincial cities was not above the pay grade of a Roman private citizen, unlike murdering a group of pirates, so the story may well be true. By the time Caesar's first biographers got to work, however, there was an obvious parallel with a man to whom Caesar's life would soon be inextricably linked. In suppressing piracy and defeating Mithridates' forces in Asia, the young Caesar was modeling the conduct that would soon make Pompey into the great man he was already claiming to be—a man famous for suppressing piracy and finally defeating Mithridates. At this point, however, Pompey's accomplishments were still a few years off; in the 70s Pompey was having difficulty managing the war with Sertorius in Spain.[14]

The final glimpse we get of Caesar at this stage of his life is in a text honoring some Roman businessmen, the brothers Cloatius, at Gytheum, a city on the southern coast of the Peloponnese. This text mentions a legate named Gaius Julius, who appears to have been serving under Marcus Antonius (the father of Mark Antony and husband of the Julia who was the daughter of the consul of 90). This Marcus Antonius was campaigning against pirates based on Crete, so here at least Caesar may have seen some actual action on the pirate front before returning to Rome, most likely at the beginning of 72. Was this also when he was captured?[15]

6

Becoming Caesar

There would soon be major changes in Caesar's approach to political life, and his personal situation. On the personal side, Cornelia had borne him a daughter just before he departed for his stint with Apollonius Molon. On the professional side, he continued to build on the publicity he had won from his two prosecutions.

A sign of his good repute with the establishment was that, when his uncle Gaius Aurelius Cotta, with whom he had clashed in the prosecution of Dolabella, died in 73, Cotta's fellow members of Rome's chief college of priests, the pontiffs (*pontifices*), selected Caesar to take his place (according to a law of Sulla, priestly colleges were treated like private clubs whose members selected new colleagues when old ones died).[1]

In 72 Caesar stood for his first elective office, that of military tribune. There were lots of military tribunes, but most were directly appointed by commanding officers. To be elected was a sign that a young man had achieved some public recognition, and Caesar was returned at the top of the poll. How could people not vote for a man who was campaigning for a military position with a civic crown on his head?[2] As a military tribune Caesar would have headed straight to the front, for there was a nasty war going on at the time he was elected. This was the revolt in the Italian countryside started by Spartacus, a gladiator, at the beginning of 73.[3]

There is a good deal more fiction than fact in modern reconstructions of Spartacus's career. Among Marxists he became the first of history's "revolutionists and community leaders." To see him as a revolutionary is perhaps not unreasonable, but *whose* revolutionary leader was he?[4] It seems that Spartacus's revolt began because the person managing a gladiatorial training ground outside of Capua was a bully. Gladiators were not normally poor or downtrodden. Although theirs was a dangerous trade, it was scarcely the only dangerous trade in the Roman entertainment industry. Many gladiators were free men who fought for substantial purses; slave gladiators were expensive, and not readily expendable. When not in the ring, gladiators of all sorts could find ample employment outside the amphitheater as bodyguards for the rich and famous and as essential "muscle" at times of political stress. So the decision of the head of the school near Capua to imprison the gladiators training there was out of keeping with standard behavior.[5] And what happened next was that a gladiatorial labor dispute morphed into a large-scale civil war when Spartacus and his comrades broke out of the gladiatorial school.

What followed upon Spartacus's protest in the gladiatorial school was *not* a slave revolt. Spartacus's army was dangerous precisely because it could fight as a Roman army. Our sources make clear that his people could engage toe to toe with Roman legionaries. A gladiator untrained in the deployment of large formations would scarcely have been able to build such an army from nothing. The men who followed Spartacus must already have been trained as legionaries. Dispossessed by Sulla's confiscations of land—he took land from its original proprietors as a way to reward his veteran soldiers—and embittered by the resulting economic injustice, these were people whose lives had been undone by rapid change. Spartacus himself must have been extraordinarily charismatic, but he was not a drill sergeant.[6]

The revolt's initial success owed more than a little to the fact that Rome's best generals were abroad fighting Sertorius or Mithridates, and its most experienced soldiers were either retired or joined the revolt. The Senate's first response was to dispatch two praetors at the head of hastily raised armies, which Spartacus either eluded or defeated with alarming ease.[7]

The war continued into the following year, with both consuls deployed in Italy to fight Spartacus. Spartacus's force had split in two and one consul, Gellius, succeeded in wiping out one of these forces. But Roman efforts to deal with Spartacus himself were dogged by failure. Moving from Campania across the Apennines and into Picenum, Spartacus defeated the joint forces of the two consuls, then the garrison of the province of "Gaul on this side of the Alps" (Cisalpine Gaul). If Caesar was in these armies, it's no surprise that he did not find it worth mentioning later.

Spartacus now turned south again, recrossing the Apennines and ravaging Campania before moving into Lucania, where he occupied the city of Thurii in Calabria. At this point, command of the Roman forces was taken from the consuls and given to the praetor-elect Marcus Licinius Crassus (plate 2), who had recently been acquitted of the charge of corrupting a Vestal Virgin, one of the six priestesses charged with maintaining the city's sacred hearth, which was dedicated to the goddess Vesta.[8] Before that, Crassus had served with Sulla, and he had become very rich through real estate speculation at Rome.

A veteran commander with experience in the civil war against Cinna, Crassus imposed strict discipline upon his troops, but with an unpleasantly old-fashioned touch. Claiming that the practice of decimation—the execution of every tenth man in a defeated unit—was sanctioned by ancient tradition, he proceeded to inflict it upon portions of his own army. He then set about transforming the conflict with Spartacus into one of positional warfare, the preferred style of fighting promoted by Sulla and currently being employed by Pompey and Lucullus to defeat Sertorius and Mithridates. Spartacus responded by planning to evacuate his force to Sicily, aided by a pirate fleet from Cilicia. The threat was deemed sufficiently serious for Sicily's notoriously corrupt governor, Gaius Verres, to take active steps to prevent the crossing. It may be that Verres' personal connections with these same pirates facilitated a negotiation ending their dealings with Spartacus, thus enabling Crassus to crush Spartacus's army in a major battle at Senerchia. Spartacus is said to have died fighting.[9]

In the wake of his victory, Crassus crucified six thousand captives along the Appian Way, the major Roman road running southward through Campania. This was an act of brutality which, when considered alongside his harsh treatment of his own men, may have made his fellow Romans less willing to give him full credit for ending the war. The credit instead went to Pompey, who had rounded up some of Spartacus's followers before returning to Rome to celebrate a massive triumph for his victory over Sertorius in Spain.[10]

The silence of Caesar's biographical tradition on his role in the war against Spartacus is telling. The revolt had been an embarrassment, underscoring the stupidity of Sulla's land confiscations, which had fueled support for Spartacus. The point was not lost on young Caesar, who would later participate in the development of some very different schemes to reward his own veterans for their service. Just as bad was Crassus's brutality. The thousands he crucified would have included a great many Italian peasants, now Roman citizens. The claim that Crassus's victims were all slaves was a lie concocted to cover up the reality of the situation. Their families would remember the truth. The story Caesar slit the throats of the pirates he had captured before crucifying them may have been invented to stress Caesar's disgust at the brutality of the punishment. Another point upon which the biographical tradition is silent concerns how Caesar first became a close associate of Crassus, an immensely important supporter throughout the next decade. The most obvious explanation of this omission is that it occurred during the campaign it was necessary to forget.[11]

And now there was Pompey to deal with as well. Pompey was recognized as a true patriot when he announced that he would dismiss the army he had brought back from Spain. Given the strength of that force and his growing popularity, he could have marched on Rome, as both Sulla and Marius had once done. Instead, he would stand for the consulship, an act that, while less aggressive than a military takeover, was nonetheless completely illegal because Pompey had held no previous office. Crassus, however, announced his support for Pompey, as did others who were agitating for an end to aspects of Sulla's regime, chief among them the restriction on the power of the tribunes. Pompey made this a centerpiece of his campaign and further announced that he would take steps to limit the corruption of provincial government. Crassus was willing to go along with this—and to overlook the fact that he and Pompey did not get along particularly well—in order to become Pompey's co-consul.

In the wake of the war with Spartacus it was clear that die-hard loyalty to Sulla's dispensation would no longer be the order of the day. Cicero said that Pompey's announcement, after he was elected, to the effect that he would restore the power of the tribunes and that the courts were wicked, elicited a great shout of approval. In the wake of Pompey's victory, Cicero himself undertook the prosecution of Verres, whose three-year administration in Sicily was notable for his abusive behavior towards the provincial ruling class, incompetence, and criminality. He had once been quaestor to Papirius Carbo, who had succeeded Cinna as leader of the anti-Sullan regime in the 80s. He had later deserted Carbo for Sulla, taking the army's payroll with him, and he thereafter became a Sullan apparatchik and thus a person whose misdeeds could be overlooked. But no longer. So effective was Cicero's presentation of the case that Verres skipped town even before the verdict was handed down.[12]

Cicero's politics were generally on the conservative side; even when he had taken on Sulla's regime to defend a man who had been placed on the proscription list, he did so at the behest of members of the regime, friends of Sulla's wife who were looking to clip the wings of another member of the inner circle. Cicero would be joined in distancing himself from Sulla he joined others with previously impeccable credentials as supporters of the Sullan regime. One of these was another of Caesar's Aurelian uncles, Lucius Aurelius Cotta, who would propose a new bill reforming juries so that two thirds of their members would no longer be senators. Pompey and Crassus, meanwhile, could agree to undo one of the hallmarks of Sulla's constitution by restoring the traditional political powers of the tribunes. Caesar, now looking to cozy up to both these men, delivered a speech in favor of their law (which passed). One other thing Pompey and Crassus achieved was the appointment of the first censors since 85, fifteen years before. Censors, who were responsible for drawing up and maintaining the list of citizens, sanctioning immoral conduct on the part of public officials, and issuing public contracts, ought to have been appointed every five years. The censors appointed for 70 were the two consuls of 72, and together they cleaned house, expelling sixty-four men from the Senate, including Lentulus Sura, one of the consuls for the previous year, and Antonius Hibrida. These were the censors who quoted Caesar's prosecution of Hibrida to justify his expulsion.[13]

Where did all this change leave Caesar? He had thus far made his way in the world as a loyal supporter of the status quo. And he'd done quite well, as his position in the college of the *pontifices* shows. But he was also Marius's nephew and Cinna's son-in-law. The next year would see him begin to establish a new identity.

There were no political parties at Rome as we would understand them in the modern world. The formal structure of Roman political life, which would seem to favor the wealthy over the rest, obscures a reality in which broad community relationships played a crucial role. Except for the Palatine Hill there was no pure "high rent" district in Rome. Many anecdotes have come down to us which assume that wealthy Romans were living in parts of town where people from all economic classes resided. As visitors to Pompeii or Ostia today will note, shops were built into the houses of the wealthy or occupied the bottom floor of a tenement, and the community came together in the taverns where most people ate. The graffiti that once filled the walls of Pompeii saying that "the neighbors" or groups of workers support a candidacy, or, conversely, stating that drunks or thieves support a particular person, reflect the role of the common people in shaping the city's political discourse and show us how individual districts and street corners were in dialogue on a host of issues. It was not enough to be rich to be successful in political life, you also had to be able to get along with the people you met on a daily basis. An aspiring politician could stake out a position in a law court or by giving a speech at a public meeting, but it was the conversations that followed that defined a person's place in political society. For all that he espoused a top-down view of political life in which people thought what their betters told them to think, Cicero admitted that elections could be shaped by "neighborliness," and that politicians learned the will of the people in the theater and public assemblies.[14]

In the graffiti that cover the walls of Pompeii that political life was determined by the consensus of the population, not just by those who might be voting. The same was true at Rome. What mattered most was not how far the human voice could be projected in the Forum, what those who had heard a speech decided to tell their friends at the taverna.[15]

Instead of political parties there were issues with which individuals could associate themselves to define their place on the political spectrum. Now that the rights of the tribunes had been restored and the juries reformed, a politician who wanted to be seen as progressive could advocate for other victims of Sulla's regime, for distributions of land to the impoverished, for more generous distributions of subsidized grain to Rome's population, or for greater efficiency in government. Success would lead to a person's acquiring supporters for whom he would act as a patron when they sought office or needed something from the state. The larger the group of supporters, the more powerful a person would be. That said, support might be fleeting if people were asked to choose between two possible patrons, and even a family relationship could not guarantee that people would stay on the same side. Perhaps the most obvious example of just how problematic a situation might be was the case of Caesar's own family. His father had stood by Marius while his uncles had been murdered by Marius's supporters in 87.[16]

One way Caesar could set himself apart from the conservative circle in which he had been running was through dress and deportment. He stood out physically. Tall and handsome, he wore his hair long and under his toga he wore a long-sleeved, ruffled tunic with a loose belt. The biographical tradition would later claim Sulla had "warned the conservatives about the badly belted boy." This style of dress would be the equivalent of an aspiring politician showing up nowadays at a public event with a flashy tie or scarf and casual clothing as a way of making the point that he or she wasn't part of "the establishment."[17]

The next thing Caesar did was to start advertising his connections with Marius and Cinna. In light of the murders of his uncles, this was a difficult move to get right, and Caesar would usually be seen to be at odds with his cousin, Lucius, who was a few years older and already launched upon the career that would take him to the consulship of 64. But there was no denying his marriage to Cornelia, or that their daughter was Cinna's granddaughter. How was Caesar to navigate the minefield of partisan ill-feeling that covered much of the Roman political landscape? As it turned out, the way forward would be not so much to discuss the glories of Cinna's career or of Marius's old age but rather to try to undo the damage that Sulla had done to these men's supporters. Advertising mercy and forgiveness as a political platform was a far better idea than asserting that mass homicide, on either side, was justifiable.

Caesar's first significant display of his connections with the Cinnan faction came in 70 when the tribune Plautius proposed a bill—the *lex Plautia*—restoring the citizen rights that had been lost by the supporters of Lepidus, the consul of 78 who had tried to seize Rome and undo Sulla's policies after the dictator's death. One of those impacted by this bill would be Caesar's brother-in-law, Lucius Cinna. A line from the speech Caesar gave in support of the bill has been preserved—"it seems to me in light of our kinship, I have not failed in efforts, pain or industry"—shows that he published the speech. The fact he published the speech suggests that it had a positive impact.[18]

In 70, Caesar was elected quaestor for the following year, marking his first big step up the Roman political ladder. At the beginning of his quaestorship, however, he was struck by two personal tragedies. His aunt Julia, Marius's widow, died, and so did his wife Cornelia, who was only in her early thirties. His loyalty to Cornelia in the face of Sulla's pressure to divorce her and the loss of her dowry are indications that the couple was genuinely in love. The deep affection for their daughter that Caesar would later display also speaks to the strength of the family bond.

Caesar arranged funerals for both women. It was not without precedent for the relative of an elderly woman to give a speech in her memory, as Caesar did for Julia. What was unprecedented, we are told, was for a widower to deliver a public funeral speech in the heart of the forum for a young wife. We have no quotations from this speech but are told he impressed the audience with his gentleness and affection.[19] This was in keeping with the persona he had exhibited in his speech in favor of the *lex Plautia*.

Loyalty to the family was also very much on display in the speech he gave for Julia. Sulla had tried to banish Marius's memory, taking Marius's ashes from his tomb and scattering them on the river Anio and removing all the trophies to Marius's victories at Rome. It was, however, traditional, at a family funeral, to have actors wear masks depicting famous relatives of the deceased, and Caesar saw to it that a mask of Marius appeared as part of the ceremony. Julia's funeral was the first occasion since Sulla's victory at which images of Marius were displayed in public.[20] That created something of a stir, but when some people complained the majority of those in attendance shouted their approval. Caesar's speech in honor of Julia was also remembered for the potted history he offered of his family. On her mother's side, he said, she was descended from Ancus Marcius, the fourth of Rome's legendary kings, while "the Julii, the clan of which our family is a branch are descended from Venus." The family thus had the "sanctity of kings who had the greatest power among mortals and the reverence of the gods, who are the masters of kings."[21]

Caesar's family now included just his daughter, Julia, aged five, and his mother, Aurelia, who had continued to live with Caesar in the allegedly modest house he had in the Suburra.[22] The Suburra was a district northeast of the Forum that extended from the slopes of the Quirinal and Viminal Hills on its northern side to the Esquiline on its south. Much of the area was regarded as dangerous. But not all of it. A near neighbor, in the Carinae district, was Gnaeus Pompey, who could have afforded any house he chose in the city. In Caesar's case the choice to live in the Suburra rather than with most of the Roman elite on the Palatine that overlooked the Forum from the south, was sending a message that this descendent of gods and kings was a true friend of the average Roman, with whom he didn't mind rubbing shoulders.

Shortly after the funerals for Cornelia and Julia, Caesar left Rome. Quaestors served as assistants for more senior magistrates, and Caesar had been assigned to assist Gaius Antistius Vetus, praetor in 70 and now governor of the southern Spanish province known as Farther Spain. No meaningful details are preserved of Caesar's time in this office, but the province was an important one. In it were the very large silver mines that had provided much of the wherewithal for the transformation of Italy's economy in the second century BCE. Caesar would later return to Farther Spain as governor in his own right after the praetorship he would hold in 62, and he appears to have educated himself quite thoroughly on the benefits that could accrue from that province.[23]

The only stories surviving from this time in Caesar's life in the official biography are both predictive of his future. One story is that he saw a statue of Alexander the Great in the Temple of Hercules south of Cadiz, a city in Farther Spain, and burst into tears. Caesar lamented the fact that Alexander had conquered the world by the age of thirty while he, as yet, had accomplished nothing. The other story is a bit stranger. It is that, the very next night after seeing the statue of Alexander, he had a dream in which he had sex with his mother. Interpreters of the dream assured him that it should not be taken as being indicative of Oedipal designs on Aurelia but rather meant that he would dominate the world, for the earth was the mother of all. Inspired by that interpretation, he asked Antistius Vetus for permission to return immediately to Rome. Permission granted.[24]

The dream interpreters' reading of Caesar's dream depended upon a view of sexuality in which the male was always the dominant partner. This understanding of sexuality seems to have featured in the upbringing of young Roman males but to have been regarded as generally ridiculous by the women of Caesar's generation.[25] Also generally disregarded was the accompanying notion that relationships were essentially transactional, with minimal emotional investment by either party. Caesar's younger contemporary, the brilliant poet Valerius Catullus, wrote passionately in denunciation of these ideas. He presents himself as being desperately in love with a woman he calls Lesbia—likely a pseudonym for a woman whose real name was Clodia, a member of one of Rome's most aristocratic families and the sister of a man named Clodius, who would soon play a disreputable role in Caesar's life. In one poem, Catullus writes about his relationship with Lesbia in terms of *fides* (good faith) and *foedus* (formal agreement)—words which Romans typically used for public rather than private relationships. But these terms, he learned, did not in fact apply. In another poem he writes that, as he came to understand her sexuality, he understood her very differently but, as a result, "I burn all the more fiercely with passion."

It is in terms of such a conflict between transaction and genuine emotion that we need to understand Caesar's personal life in the years after Cornelia died. In 68 he married the eighteen-year-old Pompeia. Remarriage to a woman who was just entering the marriage market was fairly typical—Caesar would do this one more time, and, as we've seen, the marriage between Caesar's father and Aurelia was probably made under similar circumstances. Pompeia was quite a catch. Her father was the Pompeius Rufus who had been Sulla's colleague in 87. She had been brought up in Sulla's household and must have been very wealthy. Her money would be immensely helpful to a politician entering upon an expensive phase of his career: Caesar would soon be buying up gladiators wherever he could in order to boost his popularity through costly public games. (That large troupes of gladiators were not considered a bad thing in the aftermath of Spartacus's revolt is a sign that people knew the real problems had nothing to do with gladiators.)[26] The marriage to Pompeia also suggests that, despite his recent affiliation with anti-establishment causes and celebration of his connection to Marius, Caesar was still seen as essentially an establishment figure. Quite possibly some people thought an alliance with the daughter of Pompeius Rufus would short-circuit any possible dealings between Caesar and Pompey, whose father had killed Pompeia's father. That would not prove to be the case, however, and in fact the bond between Caesar and his new wife appears to have been difficult from a very early stage of their marriage. One of the problems was that Caesar would soon fall genuinely in love with another woman, who, even more problematically, was married to another man. This woman was Servilia.[27]

What Catullus's verses help us to see is that, for all that he thought he was restoring some golden age of the mythic past, Sulla ended up creating even more space for women to exercise influence in Roman society. His confiscation of his dead enemies' property strengthened the position of aristocratic women who retained their own families' property when that of their husbands was confiscated. These same women, whose marriage partners had seen themselves as rulers of the world, were not raised to be merely subordinate to their spouses, and they are increasingly visible in accounts of the period as conduits for otherwise difficult conversations between men who could not deal directly with each other, or as independent voices whose wishes their husbands were expected to hear. It is perhaps because these women could now deal independently with men other than their husbands that adultery became the talk of the town.

Gossip would link Caesar romantically with the wives of several of his most prominent associates, including Pompey's third wife Mucia, Crassus's wife Tertulla, Lollia the wife of Aulus Gabinius, an active supporter of Pompey, and Postumia the wife of the noted jurist Sulpicius Rufus. There is no good reason to deny that these relationships may have taken place, though it does seem most unlikely that Caesar was one of Mucia's lovers.[28] Pompey would divorce her in 62 BCE, alleging infidelity, and he later reacted very angrily to the story Caesar had been one of her lovers. But during this early period of his career Caesar needed Pompey's support, just as he needed Crassus's help, and Pompey's later anger at the story about Caesar's supposed relationship to Mucia suggests that he took a less lenient attitude towards marital infidelity than many of his contemporaries. Presumably Pompey's intolerance for this sort of thing was generally known in aristocratic circles, which makes it unlikely Caesar would risk a fling with Mucia. Crassus too seems to have prided himself on his "traditional" marriage, so the story Caesar slept with his wife Tertulla is likely false as well. Really, the point of the stories about Caesar's liaisons seems to have been that he would readily betray those closest to him. But that, as we'll see, was not actually a feature of his character.

Still, even if he didn't have affairs with the wives of the men who would become his most important political allies, it is clear that Caesar had a reputation for sexual adventures, and there is no reason to think Servilia—about whom we'll soon have more to say—was his only lover. But Caesar's affair with her is the best-attested of his life—with the single, very notable exception of Cleopatra, queen of Egypt, who became Caesar's paramour in the years just before his death.

It is Catullus who once again comes to our aid as we try to envision the social world in which male and female members of the aristocracy, married and unmarried, would get together. Catullus writes of a friend who lent him his house so that he could meet his lover there, and he claims, in the same poem, that he has learned to live with the fact that he's not Lesbia's one and only (a frustration he often complains of elsewhere). Meanwhile, Sallust provides a vivid description of a granddaughter of Gaius Gracchus whom he says committed many crimes with "the spirit of a man." This woman, Sempronia, could sing and dance with more elegance than was expected from a woman of her standing, and she would more often make advances than await solicitation. She was married, had children, and wasn't divorced even though she was plainly active on the dating circuit. In yet another glimpse of unconventional gender roles in Rome's upper classes, Catullus also gives us a picture of a drinking bout hosted by a woman he calls Postumia, who could very well be among Caesar's alleged lovers.[29]

As for Servilia, she would not be divorced by her husband Junius Silanus despite her well-known relationship with Caesar. Silanus was in fact Servilia's second husband. Her first, Marcus Junius Brutus, had joined Lepidus's revolt and had been killed by Pompey in 77. She had had one child with him also named Marcus Junius Brutus—who would one day become the most famous of Caesar's murderers.[30] She also had three daughters by Silanus (who as a *pontifex* moved in the same social circle as Caesar). Among her relations was also a half-brother, Marcus Porcius Cato (plate 4).

In the years immediately after his marriage to Pompeia, Caesar was taking the first steps toward building a relationship with Pompey. He was also burnishing his credentials in the courts. Years later, defending a man who had picked the wrong side in the civil wars that would begin in 49, Marcus Cicero reminded Caesar of the days when they had argued cases together.[31] There is no other record of this collaboration, but it must have occurred in the early 60s, the only period when the political profiles of the two men would come into any sort of alignment. As Cicero's brother, Quintus, would write while Marcus was running for the consulship of 63 BCE, Marcus, when he was supporting Pompey, had not always been perfectly aligned with those who took a politically conservative stance.[32] It is quite likely that Cicero and Caesar, attorneys-at-law, formed a highly successful partnership. In later years, when their politics were often starkly opposed, Caesar retained a personal fondness for Cicero. For his part, Cicero would later write that Caesar, if he hadn't opted for military success, would have been one of the greatest orators of the age. He obviously had respect for Caesar's powerful intellect.[33] The fact that Cicero published none of the speeches he gave in these early years may suggest he didn't want his left-leaning sentiments remembered—unless, of course, they were expressed in behalf of Gnaeus Pompey.

Pompey was again being politically eccentric. Although it was typical for consuls to take up a provincial governorship as soon as their year in office ended, neither Pompey nor Crassus had done so. In Pompey's case the choice makes sense. Not only was he starting a family with Mucia—they had three children between 70 and 67—but he had been away from Rome for most of the previous decade. When he was consul, he had needed to have an associate, Terentius Varro, write a handbook for him so he could run a meeting of the Senate. Pompey needed to learn his way around the domestic political scene. Crassus, on the other hand, simply needed to keep making money. Meanwhile, there was a war on, still, but it was in the East, where Lucius Licinius Lucullus had been granted a command over all three of Rome's eastern provinces—Asia, Cilicia, and Syria—in order to finally eliminate Mithridates.[34]

Lucullus was one of Sulla's few true friends. He had been Sulla's quaestor in the first war against Mithridates, during which he had raised a fleet from Rome's allies to end Mithridates' command of the sea. He had also completed the gigantic twenty-book memoir Sulla had composed to justify his career. (The memoir has not survived, though we can gain an impression of what Sulla had to say from Plutarch's biography of the man. To judge from Plutarch, who says he read the memoir, Sulla's memoir reported a wide range of miracles which indicated divine favor for his cause.)[35] Now Lucullus, a good general, was succeeding in his eastern campaign, driving Mithridates from his kingdom to take refuge with his son-in-law, Tigranes, king of Armenia, a land that stretched roughly from what is now Turkey's northeastern border into the south central portion of that country. While he had endeared himself to the people of the Roman provinces with which he had been entrusted, Lucullus had also alienated the equestrian business community there by refusing to allow them to charge the outrageous 48 percent interest rates they had been collecting on the loans various cities had taken out to pay the fines Sulla had imposed on them.[36]

But while Lucullus dealt with Mithridates, Roman operations elsewhere in the Mediterranean, especially an effort to suppress endemic piracy on Crete, were proving less successful. The problem of the pirates would interrupt Pompey's life with Mucia before the end of 68, the year in which a pirate gang captured two praetors and held them for ransom. Scandal! Horror! The threat of terrorism represented by the pirates had to be ended forever. And what better way to do such a thing than to toss constitutional norms out the window? Early in 67, Aulus Gabinius, now a tribune, introduced a law to create a special command to suppress piracy. Major provisions of Gabinius's bill drew upon elements of previous legislation intended to solve the "pirate problem." The main difference between what Gabinius proposed and what had been proposed or permitted earlier (most notably in the case of the powers given to Lucullus) was the scale of the operation. According to Gabinius's proposal, the holder of this new command against the pirates would have a fleet of two hundred ships, fifteen legates, a very large budget, and the ability to give orders in provinces bordering the sea for a period of three years. The crucial aspect of the law was the concept, borrowed from another law that had been passed, also to deal with piracy, a few years earlier, of *imperium infinitum*. Ordinarily *imperium*, the power of a praetor or consul, was limited to the magistrate's year in office or limited to the province the person would govern after leaving office. *Imperium infinitum* meant that the power exercised by the holder of this new command would not be restricted to the territory of a single geographical province. The ability to select fifteen legates gave the person who would hold this office enormous influence simply because of his ability to dish out potentially lucrative commands.[37]

Although he was not named in Gabinius's law, it was clear to everyone that Pompey was the person who would hold this command. Caesar was the only senator who spoke in the bill's favor. One of his biographers would write that he was motivated by a desire to win popular acclaim, pave the way for a similar special command for himself, and to encourage jealousy of Pompey. This is all hindsight: at the time Caesar was most likely trying simply to gain attention as he prepared to move up the electoral ladder.[38]

Lutatius Catulus, the consul who had opposed Lepidus in 78, lined up two tribunes to veto Gabinius's proposal. When one of them, Trebellius, attempted to do this, however, Gabinius took a page from a playbook written decades ago by Tiberius Gracchus, who had a tribune who tried to veto his land bill removed from office on the grounds that he was opposing the will of the people. Gabinius now introduced a similar bill to remove Trebellius. As the votes began to come in, overwhelmingly in Gabinius's favor, Trebellius withdrew his veto. Then, when the law creating the command against the pirates passed, Gabinius brought forward another bill giving the new command to Pompey. The legates appointed under the first bill would thereafter describe themselves as "legates of Gnaeus Pompey *imperator*," the first time (as far as we know) that officials created by one law would describe themselves as being subordinate to an individual appointed under another.[39]

It took Pompey six months to accomplish a genuine reduction in the threat of piracy across the Mediterranean. While it would be something of an exaggeration to claim (as Pompey did) that piracy had actually been eradicated, it was the case that the wide-ranging pirate squadrons of previous decades ceased to exist. The means by which Pompey accomplished this are interesting. His administrative skills were well developed, and he was not a mass murderer. Recognizing that piracy was a lifestyle choice for people living in economically challenged circumstances in places like Crete and southern Turkey where the opportunities for profitable agriculture were few, he resettled former groups of pirates to areas where they could support themselves through farming. Some of these new communities were a long way from home. Traces of these former pirates have been detected in North Africa and even in northern Italy.[40] Aware they could get a better deal from Pompey than from their provincial governor, Cretan communities sent embassies to Pompey to arrange peace terms.[41]

Pompey's success against the pirates coincided with the collapse of Lucullus's campaign against Mithridates. Rome's army, weary after years of campaigning, had mutinied while encamped in the vicinity of Nusyabin in modern Turkey. Some of the troops had been held in service beyond the twenty-year maximum then established for legionaries, and[42] they had been encouraged in this mutiny by Publius Clodius, Lucullus's brother-in-law.[43] While Gabinius back in Rome passed a law to replace Lucullus in command of the East, Mithridates, of course, had taken advantage of the situation to recapture his ancestral realm in northern Turkey and routed another army that had been sent against him.[44] So, when news of Pompey's success arrived, reinforcing his reputation as a man who got big things done, a tribune of 66 named Manilius naturally introduced a bill to transfer the command against Mithridates to Pompey.

Caesar was now accompanied by his partner Cicero in supporting Manilius's legislation. An ancient writer says that Cicero, who was planning to run for the consulship, wanted to make it clear his support would guarantee success for whichever side he took. This is plausible enough, and Cicero was indeed already planning his campaign for Rome's top job.[45]

While Caesar and Cicero supported giving Pompey the command against Mithridates, some senior members of the Senate, chiefly

Lutatius Catulus and Quintus Hortensius, an older man who was regarded as the best orator of his generation and was as conservative as Catulus, spoke in opposition. With the polished hypocrisy of experienced politicians, they argued that giving Pompey the command would violate the traditions of the Roman people and might expose Pompey himself to danger. Whatever would the Roman people do if it had to rely upon just one indispensable man? Possibly Catulus also pointed to the extended commands that had built up the excessive power of Marius (but the source who gives us this information assigns the speech to the wrong year). Cicero, in response, pointed out that Catulus had benefited from Pompey's extra-legal command against Lepidus, and that in time of war the Roman people had often broken with tradition. How else would they have defeated Hannibal without the extraordinary command given Scipio Africanus, the Pompey of his time?[46] In the end, Manilius's bill passed, and Pompey took over the command against Mithridates. He would remain in the east until the late summer of 62 BCE. In the meantime, Caesar completed his ascent to the forefront of Roman politics.

Election to the aedileship was a key moment in Caesar's career. Success as an aedile was an important stepping stone to higher office, but the basic tasks of the position illustrate the fundamental weakness of republican government which necessitated the creation of extraordinary positions such as Pompey's. The aediles' tasks, for which they received some support from a professional staff, fell into three categories: care of the city, care of the food supply, and care of the games. In the first category were tasks like the repair of public buildings, maintenance of the sewer system, regulating traffic, taking precautions to prevent fires, and enforcing morals laws legislation such as those against offensive gluttony, loan-sharking, and gambling. Aediles also maintained the official list of registered prostitutes. It wasn't an easy job, given that there was no police force or fire department, since the Roman Senate regarded such institutions as potential tools for aspiring tyrants. The sheer stupidity of this view was best exemplified by the career of Crassus, an actual aspiring tyrant, who had his own private fire brigade, which would show up at burning properties and force owners to negotiate their buildings' sale to Crassus before extinguishing the fire.[47]

Care of the food supply included inspecting the quality of goods being sold, making sure that weights and measures were accurate, and buying food to be distributed to the public at subsidized prices in the event of a shortage. Care of the games involved the aediles putting on the regular state-funded festivals, and then special games of their own. State sponsored festivals would involve a combination of religious observations and chariot races. The races were organized by four clubs or "factions," which had come into existence by the third century BCE and were administered by equestrian corporations. These people were professionals, and the wise aedile would let them get on with organizing the races which took place in the Circus Maximus.[48] Other events in these festivals might include theatrical performances, and here the aedile could negotiate with a poet for a new play or simply stage well-established favorites. A complicating factor, however, was that there was no permanent theater. Theaters were regarded as symbolic centers of Greek culture and thus inherently un-Roman, even though Roman drama was largely translated from Greek or inspired by Greek literature, and Caesar, like most young Romans, had written a couple of tragedies on Greek themes as part of his education in rhetoric. Aediles would typically have to build their own temporary theaters, and this could become highly competitive as well as expensive.

Once a theater had been secured, the aedile had to hire the performers. For traditional tragedy and comedy, the performers would all be male, in keeping with an ancient Greek tradition. Tragedy and comedy were not, however, the only possible sorts of performance. There were now mimes—a sort of ancient sitcom—which were extremely popular, had female as well as male performers, and often treated overtly sexual topics (adultery seems to have been especially common). The social connections between members of the Roman elite and the entertainers they employed in these events could be quite close. Cicero took elocution lessons from a famous comic actor named Roscius, whom he would later represent in court, and famous actresses could become very close indeed with middle-aged senators (we'll meet one such pair later in this book).

Finally, there could be gladiatorial games and wild beast hunts. Typically, the beast hunts, involving often-exotic animals an aedile had imported to Rome, would take place in the morning, while gladiatorial combats would take place in the afternoon. Aspiring officeholders might begin to assemble their own gladiatorial troupes before winning elections and then continue to hold onto gladiators whom they could rent out to others. Cicero and his close friend Pomponius Atticus were gladiatorial investors. But no one invested more heavily than Caesar, who would still have a very large troupe, based around Capua, fifteen years after his aedileship. During his aedileship he was preparing for so many gladiators to fight at his games—he advertised that there would be 320 pairs of them—that people who were now becoming very suspicious of his political ambitions decided that something needed to be done. A bill was passed forbidding the display.[49]

Caesar didn't get to present the most excessive gladiatorial display of all time, but the Roman people would recall his desire to do so. As Cicero would later say, the Roman people loved public munificence, and it wasn't Caesar's fault the show didn't go on.[50] It's also unlikely he cared very much. He had made his point, and, by preventing him from putting on the games, his enemies had looked mean-spirited. This was probably no accident. Time and again from this point until the end of his life, Caesar would often present rivals with two choices, each equally undesirable to themselves and each yielding some benefit to Caesar. It would become a hallmark of his political style. People who later recalled his term as aedile attributed all the successes of the year to him. His colleague in the office, thoroughly overshadowed, was Calpurnius Bibulus.[51] Their shared year as aediles solidified Bibulus's abiding hatred for Caesar.

Another hallmark of Caesar's political style was the increasingly powerful advertisement of his relationship to Marius. One of the tasks he took up as aedile was the restoration of the trophies commemorating Marius's victories over the Cimbrians and Teutons, which Sulla had destroyed. The biographical tradition suggests the people of Rome woke up one morning to find these had suddenly reappeared on the Capitoline Hill. That is deeply unlikely as restoring the monuments was a non-trivial process. The huge project was a tribute not just to Marius but also to Caesar himself for seeing to the monuments' replacement. We don't know how this project aligned in time with the proposed gladiatorial exhibition, but by the end of his year in office some people were looking askance at the way Caesar was gaining attention. Lutatius Catulus, the consul of 78, who was censor in the year of Caesar's aedileship, stood up in the Senate to complain Caesar was no longer merely undermining the state but attacking it with his own siege engines. But Caesar convinced the Senate he was doing the right thing, thereby humiliating one of Sulla's closest associates.[52]

Other events of 65 revealed that the Roman state was approaching dysfunction. At the end of 66, the consuls-elect for 65, one of them Sulla's nephew, were convicted of bribery before they took office and were replaced by the third- and fourth-place finishers in the elections. Before the year's end, the two censors, Crassus and Catulus, failed to complete the census registration of Roman citizens, which was their job. They had quarreled about whether the people of northern Italy should be admitted to citizenship. Citizenship for northern Italians was an anti-establishment cause, which Caesar had been supporting. His continuing support for such causes appears to have led to a split with Cicero, who was trying to put his anti-establishment past behind him while he ran for the consulship of 63.[53]

Cicero's chief adversary for the consulship was Catiline. Catiline is a difficult character to understand because it is hard not to read all of his earlier actions in light of the harebrained conspiracy he would lead in 63. The end of his career meant he would go down in history as a villain, but even Cicero, his fiercest enemy, would later admit that some of his friends had been charmed by Catiline and that he himself had even considered acting as his defense lawyer when he was charged with murder during his term as governor of North Africa in 66.[54] Cicero even considered making a deal with Catiline so they could run for the consulship of the year 63 as partners, though that idea didn't pan out and Catiline seems to have aligned himself with Antonius Hibrida, Caesar's old enemy, instead. Shortly before his election Cicero delivered a blistering speech about the generally deplorable earlier careers of his major competitors (Antonius included) as servants of Sulla. In the end, Cicero was elected along with Antonius, with whom he would soon be making serious efforts to mend fences.[55]

Although he would never have admitted it, Cicero's campaign for consul may have contributed further to the discrediting of the Sullan establishment, a trend that would enable Caesar to move to the fore-front of political society. Caesar had already been gaining admirers because of his consistent support for people whom Sulla had victim-ized. Caesar was plainly going to run for praetor in 63, and a good way to keep himself in the public eye was through a well-publicized action in a law court. We know of one speech he gave for a Samnite named Decius who had lost his property in Sulla's confiscations and was trying to recover it. Such attempts to recover confiscated assets had been specifi-cally forbidden by Sulla. But Caesar had already made it plain that his political platform included the undoing of Sullan injustices. In this effort, he would be working with Marcus Porcius Cato, his future enemy, for the one and only time in his life. As quaestor, Cato had tried to clean up corruption in the public records office, and he then brought murder cases against people who were recorded as having taken rewards from Sulla for their role in the murder of prominent Romans and the confiscation of their property. Cato summoned those who had received these payments, publicly attacked them for "their illegal and unholy" actions, and brought them to court, where they appeared to have been condemned in advance.[56]

At the end of 64, Caesar's cultivation of Pompey bore fruit. He may also have benefited from an old friendship: Titus Labienus, who had served under Servilius Isauricus in southern Turkey, possibly at the same time Caesar had, was elected tribune for 63. A native of Picenum, he was also connected with Pompey. Tribunes took office ahead of the new year, on December 10, and immediately after entering into office Labienus proposed a bill to change the way members of Rome's priestly colleges would be selected. Since the end of the second century the priesthoods had been elective, chosen by vote of a majority of seventeen tribes who had been selected by lot to participate in the election. The theory was that priests should not be selected by the people in the same way that magistrates were, and the selection of tribes by lot implied that the gods were playing a role in the process. Sulla had restored an older selection process in which the pontiffs—members of the most important group of priests—would themselves select their own colleagues. Labienus now proposed restoring the electoral system, which was still used for electing Rome's chief priest, the pontifex maximus, to apply to the selection of all the pontiffs. At the same time Labienus introduced his bill, a tribune named Servilius Rullus introduced a separate bill to appoint a board of ten land commissioners who would have *imperium* and be allowed, using public monies and war plunder, to distribute land in Italy as well as in the provinces for the foundation of new colonies. Decisions by members of the proposed board would not be subject to challenge. They were explicitly allowed to buy out Sullan veterans and occupants of confiscated land, who seem to have become something of a problem as some substantial number were not natural farmers and were going broke. Suddenly a challenge to an archaic procedure for the selection of priests was coming to be associated with a whole range of anti-establishment causes.[57]

Then the current pontifex maximus, Caecilius Metellus, died. We're not told when this happened, but it must have been in the first part of the year 63 since the election to replace him is not recorded in the year's extremely well-attested second half. Ordinarily, someone who was already a senior member of the college of pontiffs would be elected to fill the position, and two such individuals, Servilius Isauricus—Caesar's old commander in Cilicia—and Lutatius, announced their candidacy. Catulus may have been the favorite because he had taken charge of the reconstruction of the Temple of Capitoline Jupiter, which had been incinerated nineteen years previously during the civil war that followed Sulla's return from the East. But in the end he was not elected: instead, Caesar declared himself a candidate and won.[58] To some it may have been a shocking result, but Caesar could sense that his anti-Sullan acts of recent years were meeting with a positive response. The man who had restored Marius's trophies was going to be a lot more popular than one who, like Catulus, had complained about that restoration and hadn't even managed to finish the work on Jupiter's temple, especially at a point when the tenor of political debate was distinctly anti-establishment. Also, Caesar had recently sponsored splendid games, was a lively character, and had shown himself to be a true friend of the people. His opponents were representatives of an establishment whose credibility was increasingly dubious.

At the age of thirty-seven, Caesar had solidified his position among the most potent politicians of his age. His election as pontifex maximus also suggests that even voting for priesthoods could have an ideological tinge. Catulus represented old-school Sullanism; Caesar was representing the idea that the mistakes of the past should be admitted. He would have a lot more to say on that theme as the year wore on.

7

Catiline

The historian Sallust wrote that the year 63 BCE was emblematic of the political dysfunction of the Roman state. The reason was Catiline's botched coup attempt, which drew upon the disgruntled and dispossessed in the countryside as well as corrupt members of the aristocracy. Cicero saw things a bit differently. According to Cicero, 63 was the year he saved the state. For Caesar, it was the year in which he solidified his position in the upper echelon of political society even as his contention with Cato hardened into an implacable hatred.

Caesar's ascent was based upon consistent statements about the injustice of Sulla's settlement and the illegality of the ultimate decree of the senate. Before turning to the first of these issues, which once again brought Caesar into alliance with Titus Labienus, we should look at who he had become as he moved with Aurelia, Pompeia, and Julia from his old house in the Suburra to the Public House, the official home of the pontifex maximus on the far side of the Forum from the Senate House.

While we have met the teachers and mentors who influenced Caesar's style, as well as the women in his life, what is notably absent from the biographical tradition is any record of who his close male friends were. Cicero would write at length and eloquently on the value of true friendship, and most of what we know today about the social world of Caesar's generation comes through Cicero's voluminous correspondence with his very good friend Pomponius Atticus, as well as with other associates, some of whom were also genuine friends. There appears to have been no equivalent to Atticus in Caesar's life. There would later be a substantial coterie of people who were devoted to him and found his company congenial, but these were people who served on his staff. For Caesar, relationships with other men were shaped by circumstance and, when not defined by relative status within his organization, largely transactional.[1]

Caesar's intensely competitive nature is underscored by the story in the biographical tradition that, when crossing the Alps once, he came to a tiny village. There, his companions wondered if there were the same rivalries there as there were in Rome. Overhearing these remarks, which were spoken in jest, Caesar responded that he would rather be the first person there than hold second place in Rome. This supposedly would happen on the way to Spain at the end of the praetorship to which Caesar would be elected later in 63. It was this competitiveness, which was by this time pretty obvious to anyone who knew him, that made close friendships with equals an impossibility.[2]

Another aspect of his life that was now well known was that he didn't drink and had simple tastes in food. People who didn't like him said that he was the only sober man who tried to ruin the state. But there was a political as well as a personal aspect to his sobriety. Sulla was a notorious drunk. For all that he might advertise his freewheeling sex life, Caesar wanted to make it clear that he was in control of himself and would be no Sulla.[3] Another way that Caesar distinguished himself from Sulla was through his understanding of the role of the divine in human affairs. In his massive memoir, Sulla had described numerous signs of divine favor and presented his actions as justified responses to divine guidance. A speech Caesar would make at the end of 63 underscores the difference he wanted to establish between his personal belief system and Sulla's. Perhaps the most remarkable aspect of this speech is that the titular head of Rome's state religion would state openly that he did not believe in Hades or divine punishment. Death, he would say, had been established by the gods not so much as a punishment but as a natural law or a rest from the labors of life. Such a belief was often associated with the philosophic school of Epicurus, who held that the gods were distant and paid no close attention to human affairs.[4]

Caesar's views on Hades do not necessarily mean that he was an Epicurean, and it is unlikely that this was the first time he had said something like this in public.[5] A belief that the gods were not deeply interested in the affairs of men did not mean that one couldn't also believe that mortals should not irritate the gods by failing to observe the public rites of the state, which the pontiffs oversaw. As pontifex maximus, Caesar was not required to espouse any specific doctrine. His job was to be chair of the college of priests and speak for his colleagues, albeit after consultation. His executive functions were limited to control of the calendar, determining when an intercalary month would have to be inserted because the calendar had fallen out of alignment with the seasons, and supervising of the Vestal Virgins, whose house adjoined his own.

In 63, aside from the bills connected with priestly elections, the first part of January had been consumed with the debate over Rullus's agrarian bill. Cicero opposed the bill with considerable vigor, and one of his arguments suggests he recognized even then, prior to Caesar's election as pontifex maximus, that the "establishment" to which he was now trying to attach himself was in trouble. Rullus's measure was too costly, so Cicero said, and would deprive the Roman state of crucial revenue sources. A true friend of the people did not seek to guarantee the welfare of Roman citizens through handouts but rather by enhancing the stability of the state and its financial resources. After a couple of public meetings in which he attacked the proposal, Cicero found a tribune who would veto the bill, and Rullus did not force the issue.[6]

Cicero may have won the day, but the logic behind Rullus's proposal was the same as that behind the laws granting Pompey his commands: nothing truly important should be handled through traditional constitutional structures. Effective action required officials unfettered by the constraints of conventional office-holding. Although he appears to have steered clear of any active role in the debate over Rullus's bill Caesar would return to the political fray sometime later, most likely once the pontifical election had been decided since the issue he took up was not an obvious winner even though it was connected with controversies over extrajudicial killing and the validity of the "ultimate decree." In essence, Caesar was trying to relitigate an event that had occurred a few months after his birth: the murder of Saturninus and his colleagues.

Labicnus's uncle had been killed with Saturninus, and Labienus brought an action for high treason, a crime known in Latin as *perduellio*. *Perduellio* was defined not as "the diminution of the majesty of the Roman people," as treason had been defined under the Sullan system, but rather as behavior that angered the gods and consequently threatened the very existence of the state. It was an archaic concept and an archaic procedure, which had to be reconstructed from what passed for the historical record. Trying a case of *perduellio* involved prosecution before two judges, one of whom would be Caesar, the other of whom was his cousin Lucius, who had been consul in 64 BCE. If the defendant was found guilty, he could appeal to the people in the tribal assembly, from which seventeen tribes would be drawn to cast their votes for his guilt or innocence, presumably because as a religious offense the gods should be involved in selecting the jury.[7] If a defendant was convicted, the mandatory penalty for *perduellio* was crucifixion. Labienus had brought his accusation against an elderly senator named Rabirius, claiming he was responsible for Saturninus's death nearly forty years before, and he publicized the trial by erecting a cross in the forum. The two Caesars found Rabirius guilty, but it appears that the Senate, on Cicero's urging, invalidated the verdict.

Legal oddities didn't end at this point. Labienus now brought the case against Rabirius before the people, with a praetor presiding. Cicero spoke for the defense, and it is clear from the speech he gave that the major issue in the case was whether or not the emergency decree of the Senate, which had justified the murder of Saturninus and his comrades, had legal validity. Cicero said that the decree remained a necessary tool of state security. Misrepresenting events with reckless abandon, Cicero suggested that the actual murder of Saturninus's followers was the natural result of the passage of the ultimate decree, which it wasn't: the mob which had torn the roof off the Senate House and dumped the wreckage on Saturninus and his followers was just a group of Marius's followers. Moreover, as Cicero pointed out, a slave had been rewarded with freedom for having been Saturninus's actual killer. In discussing Saturninus's opponents in his defense speech, Cicero asks Labienus if he intends to prosecute Gaius Marius, "who is truly called the parent and father of the country," and rather archly points out that the Julii of the previous generation had joined the crowd which had forced Saturninus's surrender. In presenting himself as the real supporter of Marius, who was a distant relative of his, Cicero adopts the same strategy as he had earlier in the year to oppose Rullus's bill, claiming he was a true democrat defending the long-term welfare of the Roman people.[8]

Cicero was proud of his performance in the trial of Rabirius. He would later publish the speech as part of what he called his "consular corpus." This collection consisted of revised versions of the extemporaneous speeches he had delivered. The speech for Rabirius was a necessary inclusion because Cicero would later need to show that he had been consistent in his defense of the "ultimate decree" and that there was a strong tradition of using the decree to protect the state. That said, Cicero's speech, largely an attack on Labienus, was not what saved Rabirius. He was saved instead by another politician's resort to an ancient tradition. The praetor, Metellus Celer, took it upon himself to lower the red flag flying over the Janiculum hill, an act which, in earlier times, had signaled the approach of an enemy army and therefore brought all public business to an end.[9]

Caesar may not have minded. He had made his point; the case was not brought again. Besides, by the time summer rolled around, he had a praetorship to win, and, it seems, another legal battle to fight with Cicero. The issue in this case was connected to the links he had been developing with the peoples of northern Italy, and to his relationship with Pompey. Gaius Calpurnius Piso, the consul of 67 who had vigorously opposed Gabinius's bill appointing Pompey to the command against the pirates, had gone on to be governor of the provinces of Transalpine Gaul, "Gaul Beyond the Alps," which consisted of southern France from the Alps to the Pyrenees, and Cisalpine Gaul, "Gaul on this side of the Alps," which ran from the Alps across the Po valley and had the river Rubicon as its southeastern border. While governor, Piso had suppressed a rebellion by the Allobroges, a state whose territory lay between the Rhône and the Alps. That was how *he* wanted people to remember his governorship. Others would point instead to the facts that he had prevented Pompey from recruiting men from the provinces for his campaign against the pirates, and that he had taken a bribe to murder an elite member of northern Italian society. Caesar, representing the provincials, brought charges of corruption and murder against Piso. Cicero, speaking for the defense, responded by playing up Piso's success against the Allobroges, and probably claimed that the good Piso had done outweighed any little problems like corruption and murder. Piso, acquitted, remained Caesar's bitter enemy thereafter.[10]

Meanwhile, big news now arrived from the East. Mithridates was dead, driven to suicide in the Crimea when his own son rebelled against him. Pompey, meanwhile, had been sorting out the complex politics of Syria, trying to ensure the Greek core of what would become a new province would no longer be raided by the Arabs from southern Syria and Jordan who had been plundering the region in recent years. In addition, he was drawn into the nasty civil war engulfing the Jewish state in Palestine. Two brothers were fighting over who should be the high priest of the temple cult and *de facto* ruler. Pompey marched on Jerusalem, made one brother high priest and arrested the other. He then found that supporters of the arrested brother had seized the Temple Mount in defiance. In response, Pompey captured the heavily fortified temple, massacred the defenders, visited Yahweh in the temple's inner sanctum, and went on his way, leaving the temple treasury intact. His restraint in not plundering the temple may be taken as a sign that he already had plenty of money. And indeed he did: having installed allied kings throughout what is now central and eastern Turkey—Armenia, Commagene, Cappadocia, and Galatia—he had built a massive financial network to support them with high interest loans.[11]

Meanwhile, while Pompey finished up his eastern arrangements, there was a major new addition to Caesar's extended family. His niece, the daughter of the younger sister who had married Atius Balbus, was now married herself, to an up-and-coming politician named Gaius Octavius.[12] On September 23, a son would be born to them. The young Octavius was the future emperor Augustus.

The elections for 62 BCE took place in the late summer. Caesar duly became a praetor. Catiline, having lost another consular election, proclaimed himself the champion of the downtrodden, promising a cancellation of debts which would provide relief both in Rome and the countryside and restoration of citizen rights to victims of the proscriptions.[13] He also began to plot a special revenge on those who had defeated him. Catiline's plot would indirectly involve Caesar and for a brief time would place him in great danger for reasons related to his family situation. Lucius Caesar's sister had married an Antonius—Marcus Antonius, a relative of the consul of 63 who was among Caesar's sworn enemies. Marcus was now dead, but the one son born from this union, also named Marcus and eventually known to history as Mark Antony, was now twenty years old and quite devoted, so he would later say, to his stepfather Gaius Cornelius Cethegus, who, for all his possible virtues as a husband and father, was a lousy politician.[14] Cethegus liked to quote what he claimed to be an authentic oracle uttered by the Sibyl, a female prophet believed to have predicted, long before, important things about Rome's future. The oracle supposedly said that there would be three men from the Cornelius clan who would rule Rome. Cethegus took this to mean Cinna, Sulla, and—someday—himself. Neither Sulla nor Cinna was fondly remembered anymore, so the oracle was not entirely encouraging. It was perhaps the fact that he couldn't seem to get anywhere in politics that encouraged Cethegus to join Catiline's conspiracy. He also seems to have hated Catiline's opponent Cicero. When the conspiracy was eventually exposed, Caesar's fondness for his niece and for young Mark Antony enabled people who didn't like him to claim that he was tied up with the conspirators through Cethegus.

In addition to Cethegus and a few other fellow travelers in Rome, Catiline had contacts with a man named Manlius who was gathering an army of dispossessed farmers in Etruria. Cicero would claim that these people were all former Sullan settlers, a particularly unpopular group. That's likely a lie: Manlius displayed a legionary standard that had once been carried in Marius's army, making it an unlikely rallying point for Sullans.[15] Most likely Manlius's followers, like those of Spartacus, were victims of the Sullan settlement. Manlius raised his standard in Etruria on October 27. Soon afterward, on the night of November 6–7, Catiline, still in Rome, sent Cethegus to murder Cicero at his home while other members of the conspiracy set fire to the city. But Cicero had been warned by a woman named Fulvia, the aristocratic mistress of one of the conspirators, that this plan was in the works. The assassination attempt failed, and Cicero had posted guards around the city to prevent the fires from being set. The next day he summoned a Senate meeting at which he denounced Catiline. Catiline's response was to say he had been cheated of the consulship, which he believed was his right thanks to his patrician ancestry. Then, casting aspersions on Cicero's parentage, calling him a "transplant," he departed the meeting in a huff. That night he left the city. His friends said he was heading into voluntary exile in Marseille, but it turned out he was heading to join Manlius. And, as soon as he left the city, he assumed the insignia of a consul. This was what election denial looked like in 63 BCE.[16]

In the weeks after Catiline's flight, another vanquished consular candidate arraigned one of the victors of the latest election (for 62), Lucius Licinius Murena, on a charge of electoral corruption. Cicero spoke for the defense. He admitted there might have been some minor irregularities (in fact, there had been blatant violations of a statute Cicero himself had sponsored earlier that year), but Murena, the consul-elect, had lived such an exemplary life that such little details did not matter. Most importantly, people liked him. He was a generous man and the "Roman people despise private luxury and love public generosity" (never mind that the heart of the prosecution's case was that this munificence amounted to electoral bribery). Moreover, Murena was a soldier, and "military glory is better than anything else."[17] So said Cicero, who had made a point of never leaving Rome for an extended period of time and had given up the province he would have been due in 62 as a way of securing Antonius's support.

At the time, Cicero's picture of the ideal political candidate as a generous warrior could easily have been taken as a description of Caesar. There were rumors that his generosity had become so extreme that he was in serious financial trouble. It was said that when leaving the house on the day of his election as pontifex maximus, he had said to Aurelia that he would either return as pontifex or not return at all. The story is inherently improbable in the context of his election as pontifex maximus rather than his more recent election as praetor, since a provincial command, and the opportunity to profit from it, would follow upon the praetorship. Frankly, the story is likely an invention. Caesar was from a wealthy family and had access to the resources of a wealthy spouse. Accusations of heavy indebtedness were the flip side of praise for his munificent spending.[18]

Murena's image as presented by Cicero is not the only aspect of Cicero's defense speech directly relevant to Caesar's position. Cato was prosecuting the case alongside the defeated candidate Sulpicius Rufus. Cicero contrasts Sulpicius's image as a learned jurist with Murena's more charismatic persona, saying that people found Rufus boring. As for Cato, who would be a tribune in the coming year, Cicero suggests that, although he "surpasses all of us in every good quality," his morality is so stringent that he doesn't live in the real world. Should the Roman people not enjoy gladiators like those Murena had presented to the voters as part of his election campaign? Is Cato seriously suggesting our ancestors were wrong to provide gladiatorial shows? If only he had chosen a different philosophic school, Cato might be more reasonable and better able to accept people as they are. The contrasting images of Murena and Cato drawn by Cicero anticipate the clashes between Cato and Caesar. One of the most notable of these was but a few weeks away, while another more humorous one occurred just around the time of Murena's trial. Cato was debating the ongoing conspiracy with Caesar in the Senate when all of a sudden a letter was delivered to Caesar. Cato demanded he read it out, assuming that it was some sort of treasonous communication. Caesar protested, warning Cato that the subject matter was not appropriate for a Senate meeting, but Cato insisted. Caesar handed him the letter and Cato turned red with embarrassment. It was a love note from Cato's half-sister Servilia. The event was classic Caesar.[19] He had anticipated an opponent's response to a situation and set up an event to humiliate him: there was perhaps nothing so painful for Cato as the laughter of his colleagues.

While events like this were going on in Rome, the military response to Manlius was desultory at best. Although the senate had passed "the ultimate decree" when news came to Rome of the insurrection, no new troops were raised, rather the soldiers who were already encamped around Rome to celebrate the several triumphs which the senate had not yet gotten around to approving were placed under the command of Cicero's co-consul, Antonius. Then, in early December, Catiline's remaining supporters in Rome did something stupid. Their leader's plan was apparently to take Manlius's army to southern France; wishing to help, his friends approached some ambassadors of the Allobroges, a powerful state in southern Gaul. But the Allobroges promptly notified Cicero, who arranged for two of the praetors to arrest the ambassadors with incriminating documents from the conspirators in their possession. On December 3, Cicero produced the documents and denounced the Roman conspirators in the Senate, which ordered their detention. On the following day, Caesar's connections to Cethegus gave his old enemies, Catulus and Piso, an opening to attack him as an unnamed co-conspirator. Cicero would have none of it, but Cethegus and Piso went around the senate claiming they had gotten information directly from the Allobroges and their Roman contact. Those allegations against Caesar inflamed the cordon of young, armed members of the equestrian order that Cicero had summoned to protect the Senate House while crucial debates were being held.[20] Caesar was lucky to make it home alive.

It may have been at this moment that a rumor circulated to the effect that the men who had been denied the consulship for 65, having been convicted of electoral corruption, had conspired with Catiline to murder their replacements as they took office, and that Caesar was the person who was supposed to give the signal for the assassinations to take place. This alleged connection with Catiline is as believable as the story about Caesar's sexual relationship with Nicomedes—but it *was* believed, by the very same people who had wanted to believe in that older story. The new story would place Caesar in peril during the days ahead.

On December 5, Cicero summoned another Senate meeting. Two motions were discussed. The first was whether the men accused of contacting the Allobroges, a group that included both Cethegus and the senior praetor, were guilty as charged. When the Senate voted that they were guilty, the next motion regarded their punishment. Lucius Silanus, the consul-elect, proposed the prisoners' execution with Cicero's strong approval. After Silanus, the senators spoke in order of rank: the order being ex-consuls, praetors-elect, praetors and ex-praetors, and so forth.

Agreement with Silanus's position was unanimous until it was Caesar's turn to speak as a praetor-elect. He delivered an eloquent plea to spare the conspirators. The contents of his speech may be reconstructed from the attack that Cicero launched as he saw support for Silanus's proposal unraveling. Having stated that the gods did not create death as a punishment, Caesar proposed that, instead of violating the law by executing the conspirators without a formal trial before the people, the Senate should confiscate their property and imprison them in Italian towns under close supervision, at the same time passing a decree to the effect that no one should bring a bill alleviating their punishment.[21] Caesar reminded the Senate of the law passed by Gaius Gracchus which forbade the execution of a Roman citizen without trial. The point here, as it had been in the case of Rabirius, was that a law trumped a decree of the Senate. The "ultimate decree" could not justify an execution without due process.

Caesar's speech struck a chord, and those who spoke after him supported his proposal, while those who had once supported the death sentence—including Silanus—began to change their opinions. Although Cicero intervened to oppose Caesar, claiming what Caesar was offering was nothing more than standard "popular" ideology—what else could be expected from a man who was, despite the "splendor of his ancestry," well set on the "popular path," the *popularis via*—but even he could not carry the day.[22] The tide only turned when Cato, as tribune-elect, gave his own very powerful speech in favor of the death penalty, and the Senate voted in favor of execution. Cicero led the condemned conspirators to the state prison in the Forum and personally oversaw their strangulation. He then escorted Caesar home, as the guards Cicero had assembled around the Senate House were once again threatening him for being insufficiently hostile to the Catilinarians.

The day after the executions, the Senate, acting upon a motion by Cato, declared Cicero the "father of the country." Cicero would come to see the events of December 5 and 6 as the culmination of his career. In a sense that is correct, since for the most part his career went downhill thereafter. As for Caesar, his position on the punishment of the Catilinarian conspirators was thoroughly consistent with his well-established opposition to the use of the ultimate decree of the senate to justify the extrajudicial killing of Roman citizens, and with his self-presentation as an heir to Marius, and a foe to the Sullan dispensation.

The conspirators in Rome were dead, but the revolt wasn't over. The new tribunes, including Cato, took office on December 10. Cato, to prove the Senate actually did care for the common people, almost immediately introduced a bill to subsidize grain distributions to the citizens of Rome. Another tribune, Metellus Nepos, who had served under Pompey in the East, introduced a bill to recall Pompey and give him the command against Catiline. Caesar supported this measure, which outraged Cicero since it implied he wasn't doing enough to handle the situation. In fact, it could also have been taken as a criticism of Antonius Hibrida, whose management of the campaign could reasonably be described as slovenly. It was unclear at the time whether Metellus's motion was part of an elaborate plan on Pompey's part to gain a second consulship outside the usual rules, which required a ten-year interval between tenure of consulships.[23] The reaction to Metellus's bill reflected considerable dread in some quarters as to what might happen when the fantastically wealthy Pompey came home at the head of a devoted army, and where there were leading members of the Senate, among whom Catulus and Lucullus were the most prominent, who wished to take Pompey down a few notches.

The fight over Metellus's proposal turned nasty. Metellus prevented Cicero from giving a speech about himself when he left office on January 1, which resulted in some bitter exchanges in the Senate. Metellus's brother, the praetor who had lowered the red flag to end Rabirius' trial and commander of the army in northern Italy that was looking to ensure that Catiline's forces didn't make their way further north to foment unrest in Gaul, was particularly irritated by Cicero's attacks on his brother. Caesar, meanwhile, caused a further stir just after taking office when he demanded that Catulus provide a public accounting for his supervision of the restoration of the temple of Capitoline Jupiter, which had been an issue during their contest to become pontifex maximus. Since the restoration was still incomplete, Caesar proposed that Catulus be removed from the task, which could then be awarded to Pompey.[24] For the modern historian, this does look like payback for Catulus's effort to associate Caesar with Catiline, and it didn't go down well with Caesar's senatorial colleagues any more than Metellus's conduct did.

The result of the fracas on January 1 was that the senate removed Metellus from office and suspended Caesar's praetorship. Both moves were of extremely dubious legitimacy, but Metellus fled east to rejoin Pompey rather than contest the point. Caesar's response was rather different. He insisted on holding court as praetor until he learned (so he said) that a plot to assassinate him was afoot, at which point he took off his magistrate's robe and went home, planning to stay out of sight. He changed his plan when a large crowd showed up outside his door the next day, insisting that he take up his official duties. The story seems almost too good to be true, and it is entirely plausible that the story of the assassination plot was invented so Caesar could make a point about the illegality of the Senate's procedure—he had been elected by the people and his authority derived from their vote.[25]

Antonius finally caught up with Catiline in mid-January of 62 and destroyed his army. On the day of the final battle, Antonius said he was ill and turned over command to a lieutenant named Petreius (whom we'll meet again in another role). Catiline died fighting in the front ranks of his forces. His army was virtually annihilated while inflicting heavy losses on Antonius's men.[26] But Catiline's defeat did not end the annoyances his conspiracy would cause Caesar. Two men, urged on by a quaestor named Novius, named Caesar as an associate of Catiline. Caesar, thoroughly fed up, called upon Cicero's testimony to the effect that he had provided information against the conspirators, thus ensuring that one of the two would-be informers didn't receive the reward that appears still to have been on offer for information about the conspiracy. The other informer, Vettius, whom we first met on the staff of Pompey's father, was fined and imprisoned. Caesar also imprisoned Novius (for how long we do not know) for interfering with a superior magistrate in the conduct of his duty.[27] That would be the end of the Catilinarian affair as far as Caesar was concerned. He had once again taken his stand in favor of the proper functioning of the government. The Senate, in his view, was subordinate to the people's will.

8

The Three-Headed Monster

For all the drama of the opening days of Caesar's term as praetor, the bulk of the year passed without controversy. Caesar did argue at least one case in another praetor's court—as we saw with Cicero in our last chapter, holding office didn't prevent Romans from representing clients in private cases. On this occasion, which was late in the year, Caesar argued on behalf of a North African noble, Masintha, who was claiming he should not be subject to King Hiempsal of Numidia. During the trial, Caesar made a dramatic (and insulting) display by tugging on the beard of Juba, the king's son. Given that the Roman aristocratic style was to be clean shaven, it is possible Caesar was making a point about the inherent barbarism of his rivals. When he lost the case, with consequences he could anticipate would be fatal for his client, Caesar hid Masintha in his house until his praetorship ended; then he departed for Spain with Masintha in tow. If there was any gain to Caesar in taking this case, it was as a further demonstration of his interest in protecting the weak from the brutally strong.[1]

At about the time this trial was taking place, Pompey returned to Italy. According to later traditions, people feared what would happen. Would he keep his army together and impose himself on Rome as a new Sulla? Such fears, if they existed, proved unjustified. When Pompey landed at Brindisi, he dismissed his men to their homes with instructions to reassemble the following year for his triumph. Later historians praised his devotion to the constitution. They also noted that he would never again be so powerful as he was on the day he set foot in Italy. This is all a bit overstated. Pompey had written ahead to see if the next consular elections could be delayed until he arrived so that he could lend his support to the candidacy of Marcus Piso. This hardly suggested an inclination to seize power for himself. If Metellus's proposal to bring Pompey home to chase down Catiline had aroused any suspicions that he was seeking a consulship (or more) for himself, those suspicions seem to have dissipated by the time Pompey actually returned. It is possible that, by declining to seek another consulship himself, Pompey was exhibiting some self-knowledge. On more than one occasion Cicero would remark that Pompey was a stilted orator and rather dull, lacking the verbal agility necessary to be a successful debater in the Senate. As we've already seen in discussing the passage of the Gabinian law, Pompey preferred to act through agents who could make his case for him. Still, Pompey was sometimes exercising considerable power in supporting those agents. Cato's observation that Pompey was weakening the consulship by making it something that could be bought rather than achieved through merit, though a repeat of what he had said about Murena, was not unreasonable; both Piso and Afranius, who got the office in 60 with Pompey's support, were ineffective.[2]

December of 62 was not just the season for Pompey's return, it was also the season for scandal. While he was on his way home, Pompey had divorced his wife Mucia, alleging adultery.[3] That move added Mucia's relatives to those who would be looking to obstruct ratification of his Eastern settlement in the Senate. Meanwhile, another potentially massive scandal took place in Caesar's household. The occasion was the rites of the Good Goddess (Bona Dea), which were celebrated twice a year, on May 1 and in mid-December. Pompeia hosted the December festival at the Domus Publica, the house of the pontifex maximus. It was a rule that no male could be present for the rites, so when the festival was to be celebrated in the house of a consul or praetor, that man had to depart, taking all other males in the household with him. The main rites were celebrated at night in what was said to be a party-like atmosphere with singing, dancing, and drinking.[4]

That December, the party would be wilder than usual. Pompeia, in response to her husband's highly public infidelities, was having an affair with Publius Clodius. During the rite of the Bona Dea, Habra, one of her slaves, let Clodius into the house dressed as a woman and told him to stay hidden until Pompeia was ready for him and the sacred objects of the Bona Dea, which Clodius wanted to see, were on display. Clodius was never good at taking instruction. He left his hiding place and was intercepted by one of Aurelia's slaves as he was hiding in shadows. She asked him who he was looking for. When he responded, the game was up. Aurelia, notified that a man was lurking in the household, hid the sacred objects and led a search of the house. Clodius was discovered and identified before he ran off into the night.[5]

When the news got out, much of Rome was shocked by the offense against religion that Clodius had committed. As pontifex maximus, Caesar convened the pontiffs, who ordered the interrupted rites to be celebrated again, this time by the Vestal Virgins only, and referred the issue of Clodius's impiety to the Senate. Caesar also divorced Pompeia, saying that members of his family needed to be above suspicion—that is to say, suspicion of participating in such impiety. All this was done by January 25, 61.[6]

February too was filled with controversy as Piso, the presiding consul, brought forward a bill to assemble a court to try Clodius's case. Piso then argued against his own proposal, but it passed anyway. Notably absent from the ancient accounts of the discussion of this bill and of Clodius's ensuing trial in the middle of the year is any reference to Caesar. He had a province to govern, and the campaigning season would begin in the spring. Moreover, as Cicero would soon discover, there was no point in tangling with Clodius, who had many friends. Caesar's statement in divorcing Pompeia made no reference to her adultery (not an issue for him to be complaining about anyway) and the decree of the pontiffs said only that "a man" had been found desecrating the rites. As pontifex maximus, Caesar's authority might well have been compromised if he acknowledged his wife's direct involvement in the scandal.[7] Caesar now believed he could become the first man in Rome, and didn't need the Clodius business to interfere with his ambitions. To realize those ambitions he needed some successful campaigning in Further Spain so he could claim a triumph in the summer of 60 BCE, when he would be standing for the consulship.

So, while the Senate debated impiety, Caesar traveled to Spain. There would be a nasty story that he had skipped town after having taken out a big loan from Crassus to pay off his creditors but, as with other stories of this sort, there is no reason to think it is true. Other accounts of Caesar's departure for Spain include his smuggling of Masintha out of town and a famous story about his visit to a small Alpine village, where he commented that he would rather be the first man there than the second man in Rome.[8] The Clodius affair, meanwhile, continued into May, when a jury, which had allegedly been heavily bribed, found him not guilty. Clodius had asked Cicero to testify that he was nowhere near Rome on the night of his interference in the Bona Dea festival, but Cicero had refused and testified instead that Clodius's alibi—absence from Rome—was a lie. Cicero thereby earned Clodius's life-long hatred.[9]

Caesar's governance of Farther Spain was a practice run for his subsequent administration in Gaul. The first thing he did was increase the garrison by 50 percent, using as an excuse aggression by a community on the border of his province; subsequently, he even added a fleet to support continuation of a Roman military campaign along the Atlantic coast of modern Portugal. The money to pay these forces would have to be extracted from the cities of the province—governors, in the event of an emergency, were allowed to raise money for this purpose in lieu of the use of civic militias—but, in order to make this palatable, Caesar asked the Senate to eliminate a surcharge that had been added to the province's tax burden at the end of the war with Sertorius. It is a sign of his influence at home that the Senate agreed to do this, a decision possibly made easier by the large quantity of plunder he was sending back from his campaigns. The report he sent to Rome of his deeds in the field during the summer of 61, a precursor to the books he would write about his Gallic campaign, resulted in the awarding of a triumph.[10]

Caesar also concerned himself with the management of the Spanish debt that resulted from the demands of Rome's provincial wars. In the province of Asia, Lucullus had found cities bankrupted by the demands imposed by Sulla, which the locals could only meet by borrowing money from Roman financiers who lent them the cash at a 48 percent interest rate. Lucullus had restricted the interest rate to 12 percent, which earned him the enmity of the financial corporations doing business in Asia. Caesar took a different tack by restricting the proportion of a person's income a creditor could claim to two-thirds, and by forbidding creditors to seize a debtor's property. As the numbers here suggest, Caesar was not addressing the problems of the poor with these measures. The people responsible for making up tax payments, and who ended up in debt as a result, were members of the local elite. These people could still live on one-third of their income. During Caesar's time in Spain, a member of one such wealthy family from Cadiz became his chief of staff (*praefectus fabrum*). This man was Cornelius Balbus. He would remain at Caesar's side for the rest of his life.[11]

Meanwhile, at Rome it was politics as usual: nothing was happening. Pompey did not formally enter the city until September of 61, when he celebrated his triumph over Mithridates. The Senate was stalling decisions on ratification of many of the arrangements he had made in the East. It was happy enough to accept the new province of Syria, along with the garrison Pompey had left there and the new taxes the province yielded for the treasury (which had also received a huge bonus from Pompey's abundant plunder). But it would not recognize the various deals he had made with kings in the wider region who were fundamental to the financial network Pompey had established for himself in the area. Lucullus played down Pompey's accomplishments, saying that the war had largely been won when Pompey took over (not a completely unreasonable position). The consul Piso, having thoroughly discredited himself in the Clodius affair through his failure to support his own proposal, could supply no leadership. The same was true of Publius Afranius, who had served under Pompey in the East. His political skills were such that Cicero would write that his consulship "was not so much a consulship as a blot on the name of the great man."[12] Afranius's co-consul was Clodius's brother-in-law, himself from a very powerful old family. Although also a former lieutenant of Pompey, he was now thoroughly opposed to him.

The decline in Pompey's political fortunes is perhaps best illustrated in a letter Cicero wrote to Atticus in March of 60. At the beginning of the year, a tribune named Flavius had proposed a land distribution bill which Pompey had supported wholeheartedly. Cicero opposed it on the grounds that it contained elements that were not favorable to "private individuals," by which he meant people whose wealth was tied up in their large landholdings. More opposition accrued from those who remembered how the Gabinian law had failed to include the obvious fact Pompey was envisioned as its beneficiary—they assumed that Pompey would be placed in charge of the land distributions, thereby enhancing his power on the domestic front.[13]

While Pompey's affairs stalled, it emerged that the corporation that had most recently won the contract to collect taxes in the province of Asia had wildly overestimated what those taxes would bring in. Instead of the windfall they had expected to realize from the extra revenue they thought they were going to collect, they were instead facing a huge shortfall and were in serious trouble. Crassus took up the tax farmers' cause, arguing that the Senate should reduce the obligations in their contract by 50 percent. The request was scandalous, but even Cicero thought his colleagues should hold their noses and grant the request since to do otherwise would be to open a wide breach between the Senate and the financiers the state relied upon to manage its business. Cato thought otherwise. He gave endless speeches opposing the bill. Cicero wrote his friend Atticus that he wished Cato would realize that he lived "in the cesspit of Romulus" rather than Plato's *Republic*, and would shut up.[14]

Against this background of political paralysis at Rome, events in Gaul were attracting less attention than they otherwise might have. The Aedui, a state in the area of what is now Burgundy and Rome's most important ally in the area north of the province of Transalpine Gaul, had been attacked and badly beaten by the Sequani, their neighbors to the northwest. The victory of the Sequani was the work of an aggressive

German mercenary chieftain named Ariovistus, who soon asserted his dominance over his former bosses. At the same time, the Helvetians, a community in what is now Switzerland, began raiding Roman territory. The Senate ordered the consuls to draw lots to see who would govern the two Roman Gallic provinces, hold a military levy, recall soldiers who were on leave, and send ambassadors to the Gallic states to make sure they did not align with the Helvetians. For a while those steps seemed to have calmed the situation, and the province of Transalpine Gaul was not an obvious place for a man who hoped to be consul in 59 to imagine as a post-consular destination.[15]

Caesar was one of those aspiring to be consul in 59. (The fact Pompey was eligible to run at the same time, and chose not to, shows that rumors a few years earlier about his ambitions for future office were no more than that.) But Caesar also had a triumph to celebrate, and this created a dilemma. According to a law on electoral corruption passed by Cicero in 63, a candidate for office had to declare his candidacy within the city limits. To celebrate a triumph, however, a person still had to hold the command he had been exercising when he qualified for the triumph—and Caesar's command would lapse as soon as he crossed the city limit to run for consul. Although he seems to have arrived at Rome a month before the usual period for consular elections in July and August, there was no time to celebrate the triumph before the election. No doubt Caesar wanted the triumph, but he knew that there would be more triumphs to come if he won the consulship and then succeeded, as he intended, in gaining a new province on special terms. Caesar therefore gave up his triumph and was elected consul for 59 at the top of the poll. He had hoped he would hold office with a man named Lucceius. They had campaigned together, but to no avail. Those who had come to view him as a menace—the same people who had prevented the confirmation of Pompey's settlements and Crassus's deal for the tax corporations—had now engaged in massive bribery to ensure Caesar would not have a cooperative colleague. Allegedly, even the virtuous Cato had supported this effort by declaring that bribery for the good of the state—in other words, to thwart Caesar—was not a crime! These efforts by Caesar's enemies had paid off, quite literally. Caesar would be stuck with Bibulus, his former colleague as aedile, who finished in the polls behind Caesar but ahead of Lucceius.[16]

Caesar now had several months to plan for the coming year. Cicero noted that he was "flying high," but he didn't think Caesar had a clear plan—he thought he might even get him to join the conservative faction. Cicero was rarely the best at reading Caesar's mind. Caesar's chief concern as consul was to get a province different from that which his enemies now allotted him—contrary to standard practice, which held that proconsular provinces were assigned to the new consuls before, not after, the elections for the consulship in the coming year (Bibulus seems to have said in advance that he didn't want one). The province they chose for Caesar was "hills and woods," which meant policing peninsular Italy. Caesar would need to build a coalition which would support a change in his proconsular province, preferably with an extended term since it would be a decade before he would again be able to hold an office that would give him another province. Such a coalition would require Caesar to promote major legislation in the interests of others, and building the coalition would not be an easy matter. Clearly Pompey didn't have the necessary pull on his own, and neither did Crassus. Both were being thwarted by the conservatives in the Senate. Besides, even if those men had been seen supporting Caesar in his run for the consulship, that does not mean there was a pact among the three of them—they were obviously not going to be supporting Bibulus, Cato's brother-in-law.[17]

In other words, what is often called—wrongly—the "First Triumvirate" did not immediately take shape. Despite claims in later tradition that the death of the Republic was set in motion "from the consulship of Metellus" (i.e., 60 BCE), and despite popular images of Caesar, Crassus, and Pompey swearing an oath to each other to create a binding alliance to end politics as usual, the construction of the coalition and the plan for the new year were not complete before the very end of 60, and even then the membership of the coalition was still in flux. At the very end of December, Cicero wrote that he had received an offer to become a part of it:

I've had a visit from Cornelius—that's to say, Caesar's friend, Balbus. He assured me that Caesar would follow my advice and Pompey's in all matters and that he would try to bring Pompey together with Crassus. This offers a close association with Pompey, and with Caesar, if I want it—a return to friendship with enemies, peace with the masses, and tranquil old age.

Cicero turned the offer down, but the letter is proof that nothing had been finally decided as January 1, 59, approached. Caesar was going to mix and match until he saw a clear way forward.[18]

Under any circumstances the new year promised to be lively given the strained relationship between the two consuls, though pretty much everyone would have recognized that Bibulus, notoriously bad tempered and not the brightest of men, was no match for his colleague. Cato was probably going to be a bigger problem.

January 1, 59 was a day for grand theater. Caesar would have been awake very early, reading the heavens so that he could announce, around dawn, that the signs were favorable for the opening of his consulship. He was dressed for the event. Over the red tunic he wore as pontifex maximus, he would now have on his new toga with red trim, the sign that he now held Rome's highest office. The civic crown completed the impressive ensemble. At the head of a procession of friends and supporters, Caesar would leave the Forum and head to the point on the Sacred Way where it joined the main street down from the Palatine. There Bibulus would show up with his own procession.

The consular procession then moved into the Forum, where it was joined by the twenty-four magisterial assistants, or lictors, who attended the consuls (twelve apiece). Their bundles of rods around an axe represented the powers of a magistrate with *imperium* to flog or execute a Roman citizen (albeit, in the case an execution, the offender had to be outside the city's sacred boundary). The consuls-elect with their lictors were followed by the Senate, members of the equestrian order, and ordinary people as they ascended the Capitoline slope and came to a halt before the recently completed temple of Capitoline Jupiter, where both consuls sacrificed white bulls to the god. Again, the signs were good.[19]

Religious matters attended to, Caesar addressed the Senate. He delivered a report on the state of the Republic, leading with religious matters before moving on to secular affairs, and possibly outlining the legislative program he would soon be bringing before the Senate. He set forth the ground rules for Senate meetings, including his decision to publish records of those meetings and the order in which he would be calling upon past consuls. He announced that Crassus would have the honor of speaking first in response to any motion (a position Cicero had coveted in the past).[20]

The publication of the record of Senate meetings was a significant departure from past practice. Cicero had had shorthand writers in the Senate meeting where the fate of the Catilinarian conspirators had been decided. That had been an ass-covering move, but a smart one given the controversy Cicero expected would surround the death sentence. Now, Caesar would be able to offer a documentary record of the obstruction he expected would confront the bill he would bring before the Senate in a few days. Finally, at the end of his speech, Caesar turned to Bibulus, saying that he hoped they would get along, since any differences between the two of them could have serious consequences for the good of the State.[21]

Within days of the opening ceremony, in the first week of January, Caesar convened the Senate's first meeting for the purpose of public business. At that meeting he introduced a land bill that looked a good deal like bills tribunes had introduced in 63 and 61. It provided for the distribution, to specified recipients, of all the land belonging to Rome, other than the valuable tract in Campania from which the treasury received substantial rent each year. Additional land could be purchased by the board overseeing the distribution, a group of twenty senators—a larger number than was usual in such legislation since Caesar wished to eliminate the objection he was creating an oligarchy to take control of Italy. This group would be advised on any legal issues by another board of five senators. The price for land to be purchased would be set at the value assessed in the most recent census, thereby eliminating the possibility of corrupt deals, and, to avoid reopening the wounds of the Sullan era, current rights to land would not be questioned. Recipients of the land would include, first, Pompey's veterans, and then other people living in Rome. They were required to retain the land for twenty years, which would mean they could not be pressured into selling to powerful neighbors. Caesar said this resettlement of Rome's urban population would enhance order in the city, where rioting was common.[22]

Having outlined his bill, Caesar, saying that he would retract provisions to which there was substantial objection, asked the senators for comments according to the set speaking order. On that first day, he was greeted with silence. In subsequent meetings, the obstruction began. Cato was in the lead, saying that, even if there was nothing really wrong with the bill, no such legislation should be passed because change was, in principle, bad. At this point, Caesar did something he didn't often do—he lost his composure and ordered Cato to be hauled off to prison. Many senators followed Cato, and Caesar relented. He may have done so in hopes the bill would have the support of the Senate when it was put before the people for a vote.[23]

In the end, Caesar did not get the Senate's support. Failure to win over the Senate didn't mean the bill could not pass, but it did mean Caesar would have to take the unusual step of calling a vote without senatorial approval. The first step would be to introduce the bill at a meeting of the people in the Forum, then have it voted on by the assembly. As precedent, Caesar could point to the example of his uncle Aurelius Cotta, who had moved legislation reconstituting juries to include equestrians and "treasury tribunes" (wealthy people not enrolled in the equestrian order) as well as senators, or to Pompey's successful restoration of tribunician rights in 70.[24]

At the meeting of the assembly, Caesar appeared on the *rostra*, the speakers' platform that faced the Senate House, with Pompey and Crassus by his side. Bibulus showed up too and told the crowd he would not allow any innovation while he was consul. Then Pompey spoke, addressing the contents of the bill in detail, asserting that the bill was not innovative, that there was a clear parallel in the bill that had granted land to the veterans of his Spanish campaigns in 70 BCE, though that bill had never gone into effect because his enemies had claimed there was no money. His veterans wouldn't be cheated this time around, because, thanks to the eastern campaigns, there was now plenty of money. To prevent future obstruction, however, this bill contained an oath clause, requiring every member of the Senate to support the bill if it passed. Such measures had been introduced in the time of Saturninus but do not appear to have been included in laws passed after his death.[25] When Caesar asked Pompey before the assembled crowd if he would support the bill if his opponents used violence to prevent its passage, Pompey said he would defend it with his sword and shield. Crassus then made a short speech in favor of the bill. The alignment of Pompey, Caesar, and Crassus was now public knowledge.[26]

Once a bill was put before the people, a period of twenty-four days had to pass before it could be voted upon. Bibulus tried to make sure it didn't happen by declaring that religious holidays earlier in January hadn't been properly celebrated and would need to be re-celebrated on days upon which voting assemblies could be held. Cicero thought this was brilliant. But Caesar ignored Bibulus and arranged for the bill to be voted on at the end of January.[27] Caesar could count on Bibulus to show up and obstruct the land law, most likely by claiming he had observed signs of divine displeasure, which would mean that a public assembly had to end, or else by having a tribune veto the proceedings. Caesar would be prepared for such obstructionism. Not only would Pompey be bringing large numbers of his veterans to Rome but the vote was set to take place in the Forum, which would restrict the number of potential voters and make it easier to get things over with. Caesar's understanding of democratic process is quite clear at this point. He knew what was best for people and he would make sure the proper forms were followed so that the people could get what was good for them. It was less important that the greatest possible number of voices should be heard. Caesar's selection of the Forum as the place to vote meant that there would be perhaps ten thousand voters, rather less than 10 percent of Rome's citizen population.

On the day of the vote, January 29, Bibulus appeared with a mob of supporters and a trio of tribunes. As Bibulus approached, Pompey's men drove his supporters back and made sure the tribunes got nowhere near a place where they could attempt to veto the bill. The bill passed.[28] In response, Bibulus summoned an emergency meeting of the Senate on February 1, asking his colleagues to condemn the legislation—not an unreasonable request given the violence he and the tribunes had suffered, and also given that such decrees, which had moral rather than legal force, had been passed on other occasions. But the popular vote on Caesar's bill appears to have been so overwhelming that no member of the Senate rose to support Bibulus on this occasion. He went home and appears not to have returned to the Senate, where he was supposed to preside for the next month.[29]

February was a month in which the Senate would hear business connected with foreign affairs. We have no direct information as to what precisely it discussed, but we do know that Diviciacus, leader of the Aedui, came to Rome that year to complain about the treatment of the Aedui by the Sequani and to ask for aid against their German allies. Cicero found him charming, and a man learned in the lore of druids. That was all well and good, but nothing came of it. At some point, Ariovistus, the leader of the Germans who had assisted the Sequani, also showed up in Rome, perhaps to short-circuit Diviciacus's negotiations. His Germans seem to have created a quasi-independent state alongside the Sequani (or perhaps allowed the Sequani to remain quasi-independent alongside themselves). Caesar sponsored a decree naming Ariovistus a "friend and ally" of the Roman people.[30]

Cicero's own voice was soon raised in protest against the dominant coalition. In the middle of March, he defended his old colleague Antonius Hibrida who was charged with corruption and incompetence as governor of Macedonia. He looked forward to his defense speech as an opportunity to embarrass Pompey. Whether it embarrassed Pompey or not, we can't say. But it did irritate him, and Caesar too. The repercussions for Cicero were serious. Publius Clodius, Cicero's enemy as a result of the

Bona Dea scandal, had been looking to become tribune of the plebs, but for that to happen this scion of Rome's most patrician family would have to become a plebeian. Cicero had no sooner shut up than Caesar and Pompey presided over Clodius's adoption by a man of plebeian status. He could now become a tribune.[31]

Caesar, in the meantime, continued to bring forth a series of bills, which were all passed in March. Votes were scheduled in rapid succession to ratify Pompey's eastern arrangements and to grant relief to the tax collectors in Asia. A further bill most likely included with this legislation dealt with extortion by provincial governors. Sponsoring such a bill, which we know Caesar must have done as it is known as the Julian Law on Recoveries (of things illegally obtained), was an assertion of Caesar's interest in honest provincial government, a subject perhaps made all the more relevant because of Pompey's additions to the empire. Since laws on this topic had been around since the second century, a new law would largely repeat the contents of those prior laws with the occasional addition of a new clause. In the case of Caesar's bill the new clause prohibited a governor from leading his army beyond the border of his province without the Senate's permission. It was probably also at this point in the year that Caesar got himself the new proconsular assignment he had been hoping for. The tribune Vatinius put forward a bill granting him the provinces of Illyricum (consisting of portions of modern Albania, Slovenia, and Croatia along the Adriatic) and Cisalpine Gaul for a term of five years. There is no direct evidence for the date for this bill, which would prove to be the most important piece of legislation passed in this year, but we find Cicero complaining that Vatinius was awarded a coveted priesthood in early April. That looks like payment for legislative action on his part.[32]

This mass of new legislation, and the obvious power of the alliance of Caesar, Pompey, and Crassus, inspired a man named Varro to produce the book that provides the title of this chapter: *The Three-Headed Monster*.[33]

At roughly the same time as he obtained his new provinces, Caesar broke off his daughter's engagement to a relative of Cato's half-sister Servilia and announced her new engagement to Pompey. He would himself soon remarry, to a much younger woman, Calpurnia, the daughter of a man seeking the consulship for 58.[34] Caesar's new father-in-law, Lucius Calpurnius Piso, was an interesting man. We can get some sense of him from his library, which forms part of the collection in the unearthed Villa of the Papyri at Herculaneum. Among the works he must have appreciated were books by the Epicurean philosopher and literary critic, Philodemus, now literally restored from the ashes by the brilliant work of contemporary papyrologists. Also present in his library, as visitors to the National Archaeological Museum at Naples can see, were busts of famous intellectuals, some spectacular bronze statues of male athletes and others of young women drawing water. It is here that we come face-to-face with the rich cultural life of one of Caesar's contemporaries who was *not* named Cicero, and indeed was a man who disliked Cicero quite intensely (one of the partially preserved texts in his collection is a speech attacking Cicero). Piso was devoted to Greek as well as Latin literature and perhaps saw himself in the context of the kings and philosophers whose busts decorated his house. One of the most remarkable of these is a bronze bust depicting a balding Roman with an intense glare who is identified as none other than Scipio Africanus, the victor over Hannibal. Inscriptions celebrating Caesar that have been found in the area of the villa may suggest that Caesar himself liked visiting the place.[35]

Caesar had accomplished what he had set out to do at the year's beginning, but at what cost? The only contemporary response we have to these events comes through Cicero's letters, which date from April to the late summer. Cicero blames Cato for what he sees as the destruction of senatorial control of politics, but he also stresses the increasing unpopularity of Caesar and Pompey. In one of the letters from April he says he expects to make a splash in a speech that he will be giving later in the month, and he remarks that while "the domination of the Senate was unpopular, what do you think the reaction will be when that power is now reduced to three grandiose individuals rather than to the people?" He mentions in passing that there is discussion of an embassy to Alexandria and the "settlement" of the affairs of Egypt's king. That would never happen, but Cicero's comment pinpoints another important moment in Caesar's biographical tradition. King Ptolemy XII of Egypt had a dubious claim to his throne and had come to Rome seeking support. He got senatorial recognition of his claim in return for a gigantic "contribution" to the cause of Caesar and Pompey, but he never seems to have made good on the promised payment, some major portion of which was still outstanding more than a decade later.[36]

At the beginning of May Caesar brought a second land bill to the assembly. This bill particularly upset Cicero because it made available for distribution land Rome had confiscated from Capua in the Second Punic War. Cicero had opposed this same proposal vigorously, claiming that Rome could not afford to give up the rental income from the land, when it had appeared in Rullus's land bill of 63 BCE. Caesar may have argued that, with all the new money Pompey was bringing in, Rome did not need the Campanian rents. In his new bill, seven-acre farms would be given to men who had at least three children. There would also be an oath clause. Bibulus, who had been hiding from view, now reappeared in public to oppose the bill. Caesar was ready for him. Caesar concealed a person with a bucket of feces near the Temple of Castor and Pollux, the temple on the far side of the Forum from the Senate House. When Bibulus approached, Caesar's man dumped the bucket over Bibulus.[37]

The new bill passed with no difficulty, but we're also told that many members of the Senate had stopped coming to meetings in protest of Caesar's high-handed approach. One elderly senator named Considius earned Cicero's admiration when he told Caesar that senators were staying away because they were afraid of Pompey's soldiers in the streets. When Caesar asked Considius why he himself had shown up, Considius replied that his old age made him fearless and the short time remaining did not allow him time for anxiety.[38] Chief among those who had stopped showing up was Bibulus. He now claimed that he could declare all legislation invalid on religious grounds even without leaving his house—from which he posted regular denunciations of his colleague, accompanied by florid discussions of Caesar's sex life that described

Caesar as the queen of Bithynia, a man who, having slept with a monarch, now wanted to be one. Also included in Bibulus's broadsides were nasty stories about Pompey, which appear to have produced a visible reaction.[39]

Bibulus's religious objections to Caesar's legislation were totally contrary to custom and would have no impact. His departure from the Senate House led people to joke that they were living in "the consulship of Julius and Caesar." In June a final piece of legislation would pass, one that has shaped the history of Rome and Europe ever since. The governor of Transalpine Gaul had died, and the Senate voted to add this province to Caesar's other provinces for the same five-year period, allegedly on the assumption that a bill would soon be passed giving it to him anyway. The stage was set for what would become the Gallic campaigns. Governing such a sensitive border province was not something Caesar had been planning on even a few months earlier, but he appears to have been ecstatic, and he said he would now be able to stamp on his opponents. At the same time, he showed that he could turn stories about Nicomedes on their head. When one of those present in the Senate said a woman wouldn't find managing Transalpine Gaul an easy task, he responded that Semiramis (a legendary queen of Babylon) had been supreme in Syria and that the Amazons had once ruled much of Asia.[40]

Toward the end of the summer, Cicero convinced himself that the power of the ruling clique was weakening. He noted that Pompey was booed in the theater and there had been wild applause for an actor who turned the line "to our misfortune you are Great," into a Pompey joke. Caesar, attending the same performance, was annoyed when he received no applause upon entering the theater while a young critic got a standing ovation. Beginning in late April, Cicero routinely refers to Pompey in his letters to Atticus as Sampsigeramus, the legendary last king of Assyria, noted for his corrupt habits. He even takes the opportunity to congratulate himself, saying that the result of Pompey's loss of popularity would be that his "salvation" of the Republic from Catiline would recalled more favorably than Pompey's conquests. The curious thing about these letters is that Cicero almost never mentions Caesar. In Cicero's view of

Roman politics, Caesar seems to be a secondary figure—and he seems to think Pompey saw things this way as well, quoting him as saying that, while he supported the land bill, Caesar had to take responsibility for the way it was passed for the violence connected with its passage.[41]

The problem with interpreting Roman politics through Cicero's eyes becomes ever more pronounced in further letters as the summer wears on. For Cicero, Bibulus is still in heaven, a hero to all "right-thinking" people, and Bibulus's manipulation of the electoral schedule so that the voting for the next year's consuls won't take place until October is a sign of his political acumen. Caesar's increasing unpopularity, and that of his colleagues, is evidenced in Cicero's correspondence by a public meeting at which Caesar tried to convince a crowd to attack Bibulus's house— and nothing happened. In August, Caesar called Rome's attention to a man named Vettius, who had once provided Cicero with evidence against the Catilinarians. Vettius claimed to have evidence of a conspiracy, on the part of a gang of young aristocrats, to assassinate Pompey. Caesar made a great show of this, having Vettius make a public statement, but Cicero said that people saw through the sham and that no one seems to have been heartbroken when Vettius turned up dead in a jail cell the next day.[42] Cicero doesn't venture an opinion as to who killed Vettius. If it was Caesar, this is a uniquely brutal moment in his political career, and it is more likely that some of the accused took justice into their own hands. The fact that Cicero doesn't call Caesar a murderer at this point suggests that the killer was working for those who opposed Caesar and his colleagues.

Caesar was now looking ahead to the coming year and to what would happen if Clodius realized his ambition to become tribune. It appears that Clodius's recently widowed sister Clodia, an experienced operative in the political world, had played a major role in negotiating some sort of platform for him to run on that would be acceptable to Caesar and Pompey, but he would not be acting as their agent. Caesar tried to warn Cicero that things would not be pleasant for him—one of Clodius's proposed laws would condemn to exile any Roman who had put Roman citizens to death without a trial, as Cicero had done in the case of

Catiline's co-conspirators—and offered him a position on his staff. This would have conferred immunity from prosecution, and is a sign that, for all their obvious differences, Caesar's soft spot for Cicero was still present. It's also clear that he didn't much like Clodius, who was something of a loose catapult on the heaving deck of Roman politics.[43]

Cicero's vision of Caesar's increasing weakness is belied by the results of the autumn's elections, which returned Caesar's father-in-law Piso, along with Gabinius, as consuls for the next year, and saw Clodius elected tribune. At the same time, the election to the praetorship of two of Caesar's firm opponents, Domitius Ahenobarbus and Gaius Memmius, underscores a fundamental aspect of Caesar's understanding of the political system. He was interested in power, and so long as he could get what he wanted he was not interested in trying to build consensus. In fact, the whole of the previous year had suggested that Caesar regarded efforts to build consensus as a waste of time when he could get what he wanted faster and more absolutely without it. Ahenobarbus and Memmius might want to bring legislation invalidating the acts of Caesar's consulship on the grounds that Bibulus's claims meant all public business had been brought to a halt on religious grounds. But Caesar was confident that they could be beaten, and he was right. The Senate appears to have convened outside the city's boundary in early January so that Caesar, now proconsul, could attend a meeting at which the two praetors brought their motion to inquire into the legality of his actions. After three days, the business was dropped.[44] And while all this was happening, Clodius was taking center stage.

Clodius had taken the political initiative as soon as he took office on December 10, introducing several bills. One proposed accepting the will of a dead Ptolemy that had left Cyprus, an independent Ptolemaic possession, to Rome. Other bills provided free grain to a large number of people in Rome, granted new provinces to Piso and Gabinius, and formally declared illegal any religious obstructionism of the sort Bibulus had attempted. In the long run, however, Clodius's most serious act was not a law but rather his restoration of the ancient crossroads festival called the Compitalia, and of the associations, *collegia*, through which the celebration was organized. The Compitalia had been banned in 64 for having become a venue for disruptive politics; the *collegia*, regarded as subversive, had been banned too. Now Clodius encouraged the celebration of Compitalia on January 1, preparing the way for the vote on his legislative program under the direction of the person who would become his primary agent in dealing with the *collegia*, Sextus Clodius. In the course of the next few years, this Clodius—whose connection to Publius, to whom he was not related, may have begun through his service as a public scribe—would mobilize the *collegia* as a political force, raising the level of violence in the Roman streets.[45]

After his first round of legislation, Clodius moved bills to get people he didn't like out of Rome. The business of taking over Cyprus was given to Cato, who was awarded the subsidiary task of restoring some exiles to Byzantium. This put Pompey's nose somewhat out of joint since it would allow Cato to exercise some power in a part of the empire Pompey saw as his fiefdom, but it also meant Cato would be away from the Roman political scene for a while. A second bill, in March, declared that any person who had put Roman citizens to death without a trial would be exiled. It does appear that Clodius had at some point told Pompey and Caesar he wouldn't do this—and they had promised Cicero that he would be safe in the coming year.[46] Now things had apparently changed, and Clodius was showing himself to be an independent agent. Cicero appealed to his friends for support in resisting this initiative but found little. He departed into voluntary exile after the passage of Clodius's bill and before a second bill directed at him personally declared him an exile and confiscated his property. Clodius had Cicero's house on the Palatine destroyed and dedicated the site where it had once stood to the goddess Liberty.[47]

By the end of 58, Clodius's dominance of the political scene had begun to wear on Pompey, who would begin to look for a way to rein him in. In the meantime, Caesar was building a new position for himself through massive victories in his province.

9

The Land of Opportunity

Gallia est omnis divisa in partes tres. "All Gaul is divided into three parts." That is most likely the first real Latin most students of the language will meet these days. Like all opening sentences from books in Greek and Latin, it tells the reader what the book will be about—something that happened in all of Gaul. To a Roman it implied something special, for no Roman had ever operated throughout *all* of Gaul. The book entitled *Notes Concerning the Gallic War* (henceforth the *Gallic War*) tells readers from the very beginning that this Gallic War is going to be different from all the others because it will take place throughout the whole area we now know as France, Belgium, Luxemburg, and southern Germany.

In the lines that follow, Caesar tells his readers that the peoples of this area include the Belgae, the Aquitanians, and those people who call themselves Celts but whom the Romans call Gauls. The three regions of Gaul are divided from one another by rivers. The Garonne in southwest France divides the Aquitanians from the Gauls; the Marne and the Seine, in the north, divide the Gauls from the Belgae. The Belgae, says Caesar, are by far the most warlike because they are the furthest separated from the civilizing habits of the Roman province. They are also the closest to the Germans, who live across the Rhine and with whom they are constantly at war.[1]

Caesar's discussion of the different qualities of Gaul's inhabitants is deeply deceptive. The Rhine will always be a cultural boundary for

Caesar, a function it can fulfill because he does not expect members of his audience to carry a map in their heads. Nothing resembling a modern map existed in antiquity, so there was no need to belabor the point that the Rhine divided Germans from Germans as well as Gauls from Germans. The reason for the distinction between the Belgae and the Gauls on the basis of their relative proximity to Germany and lack of Roman habits is to justify the act of ethnic cleansing that Caesar was engaged upon in what is now northern Belgium when the first five books of the *Gallic War* were given to the public in 53. The leading state in the region had slaughtered the garrison Caesar had installed in the winter of 54, and he required that they pay a dreadful price.[2]

Caesar was by no means the first person to describe the customs of the Gauls. The Greeks had a well-developed tradition of ethnographic writing, one that extended back in time to the first great historian, Herodotus. In that tradition, an ethnography would begin with a description of the lands a people inhabited, including the nature of the terrain, rivers, climate, and animals, followed by a discussion of the people's history and customs, and concluding with a description of the most fascinating things about the people and their country.

The earliest encounters between the Greeks and Gauls dated to the sixth century BCE, when Greeks escaping the Persian conquerors of western Turkey (home to many Greek communities) had founded the city that is now called Marseille. The Romans had first encountered the Gauls in a serious way when a Gallic war band had destroyed the Roman army and sacked Rome in 387 BCE (the next time the city would fall to a foreign adversary would be in 410 CE). In the fourth and third centuries BCE, Gallic soldiers had served both the Greek rulers of Sicily and their Carthaginian rivals. They had played a major role in the armies that fought Rome in both the first and second of the great wars with Carthage, and in the early third century they had swept into northern Greece, where they killed a Macedonian king, and tried but failed to loot the great oracular shrine at Delphi. After that, they had moved into central Turkey, where several bands settled in the region around what is now Ankara and went on to wage periodic wars against their Greek neighbors.

Prolonged contact between the Gauls and the peoples of the Mediterranean coasts had provoked various cultural responses which Caesar would play off of in the tale of his campaigns. One of the most notable Mediterranean representations of the Gauls can be seen on the great altar at Pergamon, now in Berlin, which makes the Gauls part of the gigantic forces of chaos who challenged the Olympian Gods at the beginning of time. Other works of art depict Gauls dying: these Gauls are wearing minimal clothing but are well muscled and appear courageous (plate 5). The ambivalence of such artistic portrayals was also reflected in Rome's continuing refusal to grant citizenship to the Celtic people of northern Italy, and it can even be discerned in a description of Gaul and the Gauls that had recently been penned by Posidonius, the leading Greek intellectual of Caesar's time, in the twenty-third book of his history, which ran from the destruction of Carthage in 146 down to 88. Posidonius had travelled to Gaul, and he described their habits firsthand, updating earlier accounts.[3]

"Physically the Gauls are terrifying in appearance," wrote Posidonius, "with deep-sounding and very harsh voices." They are "boasters and threateners and given to bombastic self-dramatization, and yet they are quick of mind and with good natural ability for learning." They are tall, their flesh is moist and white, and they are naturally blond. Noble Gauls wear large moustaches which cover their mouths and catch their food and drink. At their splendid banquets there is a lively tradition of honoring leaders with poetic performance and they hold their bards in very high regard. This does not, however, stop them from getting into fights that end in duels to the death. The poor drink beer while the wealthy drink wine—*lots* of wine. They are allegedly so fond of wine that they would trade a slave for an amphora of it. Their clothing is striking: "tunics dyed in various colors and trousers...and they wear striped cloaks, fastened with buckles, thick in winter and light in summer, picked out with a variegated check pattern." Archaeological excavation of major religious sites provides evidence for lavish public feasts of the sort Posidonius describes, as well as for a well-developed textile industry.[4]

As for the Gallic warriors, Posidonius says that their armor included large shields, decorated in individual styles, and bronze helmets with large projections which served to enhance the size of the wearer. Some men had chain-mail breastplates, while others fought in the nude. Nudity in battle was a habit that the Gauls had given up some time before, but Posidonius could not resist an allusion to that tradition any more than he could resist describing Gallic war chariots, which had likewise gone out of fashion everywhere but in the British Isles. In general, Gallic armies were divided between cavalry drawn from the social elite and an infantry force consisting of everyone else. When on military service, Gauls were given to promiscuous same-sex relationships, something that appalled Posidonius. He was also appalled by the Gauls' tendency to collect the heads of those whom they had killed in battle and to nail them to the doors of their houses, embalming the heads of especially famous enemies in cedar oil. Although Posidonius was disgusted by this practice at first, he claims to have then gotten used to it. The heads were everywhere.[5]

Posidonius's ambivalence about Gallic habits extends to their religious observances. He finds they have two classes of priests: the prophets, who interpret sacrifices and are natural philosophers, and the druids, who study nature and moral philosophy. The prophets supervise all animal sacrifices, which is very much in line with Greco-Roman practice. What horrifies Posidonius is that, "inquiring into matters of great import, they have a strange and incredible custom: they consecrate a human being." According to Posidonius, they would stab this consecrated victim in the diaphragm and then interpret the future from the way the victim writhed and bled. Other sacrificial practices included shooting people with arrows, impaling them in temples, or burning them in statues of straw and wood. Archaeology has confirmed the truth of what Posidonius wrote. A religious site at Ribemont-sur-Ancre in northern France includes a structure built of human long bones arranged around pits and a large deposit of headless human remains outside the main enclosure. A shrine at Corent in the Auvergne contains skulls but no bodies. The evidence from these two sites at either end of Celtic territory suggests a continuity of sacrificial practice throughout the region and suggests that the display of human trophies affirmed the power of the governing class.[6]

Not long after Posidonius published his book, Caesar would report that the druids presided over divine matters and retained knowledge of religious traditions which were not recorded in writing. They acted as judges in private and public disputes, and if people did not do as the druids decided, they would be excluded from the worship of the gods. Once a year, according to Caesar, the druids assembled in the territory of the Carnutes in the center of Gaul, and it was there that they handed down their decisions regarding various disputes. Like Posidonius, Caesar says the druids engaged in human sacrifice, thinking it was not possible to propitiate the gods unless a human life was given in return for a life that was to be saved. They offered massive public sacrifices in which they packed living people into large human images made from wicker, which they then set on fire. Thieves and brigands were the preferred sacrificial victims, but innocents could be included if they lacked enough of the former to fill the gigantic effigy.[7]

Having finished his grisly depiction of druidic habits, Caesar implies that, setting aside the tendency to practice human sacrifice, Gallic religion can be understood as an extension of Greco-Roman worship. He writes that the divinity most often worshipped by the Gauls is Mercury, the Mediterranean god of commerce, with Apollo, Mars, Jupiter, and Minerva—divinities associated with healing, war, the heavens, and wisdom—also being revered. This version of Celtic worship is vastly oversimplified. The material record reveals a far wider range of divinities with overlaps among their functions that do not occur in the classical world. Most notably, Caesar's scheme has no place for the tripartite mother goddess, the Matrons, who were routinely depicted as seated in the midst of symbols of fertility. Celtic art also presents hunting gods such as the horned figure Cernunnos, who appears on the Gundestrup cauldron along with images of animal sacrifice. The poet Lucan provides the names of three Celtic gods: Esus, Tarannis, and Tethrutes. In images found in the vicinity of Paris and Trier, Esus is depicted cutting branches in the company of wetland birds, which may suggest he was connected with bodies of water. Meanwhile, Taranis's name is connected with Welsh and Irish words for thunder, suggesting he was a sky god. The name Tethrutes is linked with the Gallic word for community, which may mean that he was seen as a community protector. In general, Celtic divinities appear to have been imagined as spirits who facilitated human connections with the natural world, and their pantheon was somewhat less hierarchical than the classical cult in which Jupiter reigned supreme.[8]

A crucial difference between what Caesar would say about Gaul and what Posidonius had previously said was that Posidonius saw no real difference between Gauls and Germans. As far as he was concerned, there were no notable cultural differences among the peoples of Gaul, Germany, and central Europe. Posidonius's observation of the cultural homogeneity throughout the Gallic lands is borne out by the archaeological record. Archaeologists have uncovered a continuum of practices stretching from Britain to central Europe, and have found signs that Celtic society was far more sophisticated than the hard-drinking, homicidal one that readers of Posidonius might have envisioned. True, Gauls liked to drink—there is ample evidence for large-scale importation of wine from the south even into the region of the Belgae, despite what Caesar has to say about their austere virtue—but the common elements of Gallic culture went well beyond tastes in alcohol. Celtic sites in mainland Europe include a wide variety of types, revealing highly stratified social organization throughout the region. On one end of the scale are small rural settlements where farming was the primary activity. Somewhat larger settlements, while primarily agricultural, were also home to craftsmen of various sorts, including exceptionally talented metalworkers who produced a wide range of implements and decorative objects in addition to the weapons carried by Gallic warriors. Finally, there were some very large urban agglomerations that were major centers of commerce and craft production. Ideally, these sites occupied a large hilltop, as may be seen today at the sites of Gergovie, Mount Beuvray Thuin, and Alise sur Reine, all of which would play a significant role in Caesar's campaigns. Major sites such as these could be found from the Atlantic coast to central Europe, and extended north into the land of the Belgae. Such continuity must further call into question Caesar's distinctions between the cultural attainments of various groups and his implication that these attainments varied purely as a result of different degrees of contact with Rome.

Caesar would admit that the Gauls were capable of impressive projects. The great hill forts of the region were surrounded by walls (plate 6) whose construction impressed even him. The typical "Gallic wall" began as a wooden frame which surrounded the area of the town. On the outside, the frame was supported by a wall of cut stone, while the inside often backed up onto the town's houses. The area inside the frame was filled with earth and rubble, making it impervious to Roman siege machinery. Throughout his campaigns Caesar had to either starve his enemies out or build siege equipment that could enable him to overtop these fortifications. Within the walls of these towns there are signs of extensive economic activity.

The hierarchy of settlement types, and the evidence for high level economic activity, does tend to confirm Caesar's basic picture of Gallic political society as being dominated by powerful oligarchies, whom Caesar refers to—again drawing upon the Roman model—as the "equestrians." The relative standing of the members of these ruling groups was determined by the number of retainers they could support. These retainers might be bound by an oath not to survive their leader.[9] Such aristocratic retainers would most likely be mounted and well armed, while the bulk of the infantry in a Gallic army would be made up of peasants, probably organized into bands according to the aristocrats who were their patrons. These peasants were individually responsible for showing up when needed, but communities or individual aristocrats seem to have kept records so they would know who was expected. According to Caesar, there was a law, common to all Gallic communities, according to which all able-bodied men were required to appear for an annual muster. The last person to show up was tortured to death. The timing of these musters was sufficiently predictable that, on several occasions, Caesar would ravage tribal territories before it could take place.[10]

The Gallic state Caesar described in the greatest detail, the Aedui, had a tribal council which selected annual leaders. Caesar suggests that, in the generation before he arrived in Gaul, some groups had longer-term leaders who were effectively kings, and, as we'll see, Caesar would attempt to stabilize his control of Gallic groups by making their aristocratic councils, which he regarded as highly unstable, subject to more permanent executive leadership. The annual leaders of Gallic communities, or those occupying more long-term administrative functions, seem to have operated in both the civic and religious spheres, but it is not altogether clear what decisions could simply have been made in the local "senate" and what sorts of decision required a larger assembly (Caesar refers to both sorts of decision-making). Archaeologically, it appears that aristocrats maintained bases in the countryside as well as in the main tribal centers.[11]

A further aspect of Gallic society was the existence of large-scale coalitions. Caesar writes that when he came to Gaul the most powerful factions were those of the Sequani and the Aedui. The Aedui were "the more powerful because they had the largest number of clients." As Caesar's campaign in Gaul developed, the more powerful communities would act as representatives for less powerful groups in negotiations with Caesar, who clearly found these regional associations useful. The high level of political organization within Gallic societies provided the structures upon which Caesar could ultimately base his own reorganization of Gaul, and aristocrats with mounted retainer groups could be directly recruited as Roman auxiliaries. Aeduan cavalry were already serving with cavalry raised from the province of Transalpine Gaul in 58 "Gallic" cavalry more generally would form an important part of Caesar's army by 56. Along with German units that were incorporated into the army by 52, they would play important tactical roles while also facilitating the incorporation of Gallic aristocrats into the Roman military organization.[12]

Caesar would write that local power structures depended upon a wealthy ruling class, and Posidonius had noted that the Gallic nobles had a great deal of gold. Archaeology shows the Gallic rural economy producing an ample surplus and reveals the existence of a viable transport network, including regular roads and bridges, to facilitate commerce. It

is perhaps somewhat ironic that, at the present time, the excellent scholarship on the coinage of the Belgic peoples, whom Caesar dismissed as
being cut off from the economy of central Gaul, shows a highly developed
coinage system typically based on four types of metal—potin (a combination of copper, tin, and lead), silver, and gold, along with some bronze
coins, which, like potin coins, were for day-to-day use. The coinage of
the Belgae is thus similar to very-well-studied coinage of the Senones,
whom Caesar would have termed Gauls. It is notable that, as Caesar's
armies in Gaul expanded in the course of the next decade, there is no
evidence for an increase in the production of coinage at Rome. This
allows for the presumption, true in other parts of the empire (and
expressly stated by Caesar in reference to troops who would come under
Pompey's command in Spain during the 50s) that legions were paid from
local resources. Caesar would use money raised in Gaul to pay legions he
raised without permission of the Senate on the grounds that crises were
breaking out in Gaul. The conquest of Gaul could unfold as it did
because Caesar was able to fund it from Gallic wealth.[13]

10

Caesar on Being Caesar

Our primary source for the next decade of Caesar's life will be the books he wrote about his campaigns in Gaul from 58 to 52 and then about the Civil War of 49–48. These books are anything but straightforward: as we've already seen, Caesar's description of the Gauls is shaped by his need to justify specific policies, and the process of composition varies from one book to the other. We'll deal with the commentaries on the Civil War when we get to that point in Caesar's life. For now, we need to look at how the story of the Gallic War came together and see what Caesar has to tell us about his vision for the future of Rome as well as Gaul.

The *Gallic War* as we have it is the result of an extended three-stage process of composition. The first stage would have been the reports Caesar sent the Senate during and after each campaign. We have a good idea of what these would have looked like because we have several reports Cicero wrote when he was governor of Cilicia (southern Turkey) in 51. These reports are all in the first person, as Caesar's would have been, and there may be a vestige of one of Caesar's reports at the end of Book 5, where he speaks in the first person to explain the revolutionary conduct of the Gauls in 54. Because these reports were the basis for senatorial action, some of the details they contained could not later be changed. Chief among these details would have been reports of enemy casualties, which would have been used to justify the awarding of a triumph or the celebration of days of thanksgiving. The fact Caesar reports votes of thanksgiving for his victories shows that the narratives have been updated from the original reports, but wild inconsistencies in accounts of enemy dead within those narratives show he had to leave intact the original claims of death and destruction which justified the celebrations. Hence the statement in Book 2 to the effect that the Nervii were virtually annihilated is followed by the presence of a powerful army of the Nervii in Book 5, where they are accompanied by forces of the Atuatuci, whom Caesar had claimed (also in Book 2) were all sold into slavery. Absurd claims about casualties—Caesar ultimately claimed to have killed and enslaved two million Gauls—were not a feature of Caesar's propaganda alone. Pompey had issued similar bulletins about his Eastern campaigns.[1]

The second phase of composition involved a shift from first-person to third-person narration. It is very likely that this was to facilitate performances of the works around Italy, and this phase will likely also have involved the addition of some new material. Ariovistus, for instance, is made to say in Book 1 that he knows that many members of the Roman nobility would be happy if he killed Caesar. That statement is hardly likely to have appeared in a missive to the Senate. Another likely addition—because of its inherent improbability—is Ariovistus's quotation of a famous passage of Thucydides' Melian Dialogue when he tells Caesar that "it is a law of war for the victorious to deal with the defeated in any way that they wish." Similarly, the evil Ambiorix, the villain of Book 5, which treats of the events of 54, is allowed considerable space to lie to Roman ambassadors, while Sabinus, the senior commander of the Roman garrison Ambiorix is deceiving, is presented as undermining the authority of his more cautious colleague at a meeting, then as losing his cool when Ambiorix ambushes his men. In this case Sabinus's actions define bad generalship, and contrast with his earlier good conduct, which suggests that, up to this point, he was a trusted subordinate. In Book 3 Sabinus even gives a speech to his soldiers, telling them that a legate must do as the general commands (which is exactly what he fails to do in Book 5). In the same vein, Caesar had reminded the assembled centurions, early on in the campaign, that it was not up to them "to inquire or conjecture as to the direction they were marching or the object of the campaign."[2] That was Caesar's business.

The third phase of composition is detectable through internal cross-references, typically in the first person and referring, through phrases such as "as I've said above," to the physical form of a book written on a papyrus scroll. These cross-references are typically within a single book, which make the backward reference to Book 1 that occurs in Book 5 especially striking. Caesar is about to order the assassination of one of the most powerful men in Gaul, and he mentions his ample discussion of this man's duplicitous conduct during the opening campaign of 58 against the Helvetians. The likely reason for producing a new version of the tale of Gaul at this point is that he had just suffered a major reverse—the destruction of Sabinus's forces by Ambiorix in the winter of 54. Ideally Book 5 would have ended with the subjugation of Britain and the receipt of so many hostages that it took two voyages back and forth between Britain and Gaul to transport all of them. Then Ambiorix intervened. Readers would now see how Caesar had restored the situation by the end of the book, and would still have the tale of his invasion of Britain at the book's beginning. Book 5, with its extensive praise for Publius Crassus, the son of Caesar's triumviral colleague, who had campaigned in southwestern Gaul (the area known as Aquitania) in 57, could also be read as a recommendation for the young man who was playing a major role in his father's Syrian campaign—and then as a memorial when that campaign ended in disaster during the summer of 53.

Books 6 and 7 form a coherent story, stressing how Caesar's cooperation with Pompey ensures the safety of Rome. Pompey gives Caesar troops at the beginning of Book 6 to replace those lost by Sabinus, and Pompey's intervention to calm the riots after Clodius's assassination in January of 52 frees up Caesar to begin his response to the Gallic rebellion inspired by news of the chaos at Rome.[3] As we'll see, the situation was a great deal more complicated than Caesar lets on here.

Another sign Caesar saw Books 6 and 7 as a pair is that he includes an extensive ethnography of Gaul and Germany in Book 6, far more substantial than anything in the first five books. That serves both as a justification for the policies he is carrying out in 53 and to emphasize the great importance of the events that are about to unfold in Book 7, which will be by far the longest of all the books on the Gallic War. His decision to include the ethnography at this point is similar to his decision to include a description of Britain in Book 5 rather than Book 4, when he initially invaded the island. Book 5 will be the book in which the British are decisively beaten, just as Books 6 and 7 will see the end of major conflict in Gaul.[4]

Another aspect of the ethnography in Book 6 is the opportunity it afforded Caesar to comment on the way a society could fail, wherein the majority of people "are held in virtual slavery, not daring to do anything on their own, consulted on no matters, oppressed by debt and taxes or by abuse of the nobles. They say they are in servitude to the nobles, who have the power over them that masters have over slaves." The result is that the "people" are easily misled by corrupt aristocrats seeking power in factional disputes while proclaiming an unwillingness to toe the Roman line. Aulus Hirtius, Caesar's former aide who produced the final version of Book 8, summed up Caesar's view of the political order when he wrote that Caesar told a Gallic community council that no one was strong enough to incite war with a lowly band of people if the leading men were unwilling, the senate resisted, and all the wealthy were opposed. We'll be exploring these situations in our next chapters, but Caesar's vision of Gallic society reads like a critique of the sort of oligarchic world Cato would have liked to live in.[5]

Having discussed Gallic society, Caesar moves on, as we've seen, to Gallic religion, offering an extended picture of the druids—who, to judge from Cicero, were regarded as interesting by Roman audiences—and then passing on to a highly literary picture of the Germans, expanding upon the description of German habits—their diet of animal flesh and avoidance of agriculture—to discuss the strange animals inhabiting their vast forests while referring to descriptions of Germany composed by "Eratosthenes and certain other Greeks."[6]

The central takeaways for readers of the *Gallic War* were stated clearly by Aulus Hirtius when he to wrote L. Cornelius Balbus about the work he had done completing Caesar's narrative for the years 51 and 50 in Book 8. Readers were struck, he said (and Cicero agreed with him), by Caesar's prose style and his skill in explaining his plans. Caesar made it clear that his well-oiled military machine was at the service of the Roman people. As has often been noted, he studiously avoids using the phrase *senatus populusque Romanus* ("Senate and people of Rome"), preferring *populus Romanus* ("people of Rome") throughout. When the Senate is mentioned, it is to point out that its members are engaging in treasonous communication with an enemy or encouraging rebellion through factional disputes which will distract Caesar from Gallic affairs.[7]

Caesar's own leadership is also a central theme. The commander-in-chief led by example. The proper conduct of a general who finds himself in unexpected difficulty is best illustrated by Caesar's description of himself in a battle "when everything had to be done at once." The Nervii had launched a surprise attack and, once Caesar had given the necessary instructions, "he moved to the front of the battle line, calling upon the centurions by name and encouraging the rest of the soldiers to advance the standards and loosen their ranks so they could use their swords more easily." Inspired by their officers, both the general before whose eyes they will fight and their immediate unit-level commanders, the soldiers respond with their own displays of disciplined valor. The role of centurions in communicating the general's value system cannot be overemphasized. Drawn from the regional aristocracy, the centurions had, in civilian life, already been leaders of the troops they later commanded, since military units in this period were raised community by community. Caesar's tipping of his cap to the centurions, men like Sextus Baculus, whose courage is singled out on several occasions, is also a compliment to their compatriots.[8]

Caesar considered regular communication with the rank and file to be crucial, although it was to be mediated by the centurions. The men needed to know why they were fighting and how. In the siege of Avaricum in Book 7, for instance, Caesar explains to his soldiers that he is not sending them against Vercingetorix because, although he knows that they would avoid no danger to further his own renown, it would be wrong for him to risk their lives unnecessarily. Similarly, in his account of the Civil War, Caesar offers several examples of the self-justificatory speeches he gave his men in the course of his invasion of Italy. Their interests are his interests. He is conscious that soldiers will look to the general for an example in hard times, so he makes sure people will see that he is, for example, sending away his horse before the battle with the Helvetians. In notes he made about the Alexandrian War in 47, later incorporated into the finished book by an editor, Caesar tells his men how a general will note every incident both of slackness and of courage. He later writes, before a major engagement in Alexandria's harbor, how he had repeatedly told the troops that the consequences of defeat would be far worse for them than for the enemy. Another one of Caesar's subordinates who produced a book about the campaign in North Africa, compares Caesar, instructing his troops in the best way to fight their enemies, to a gladiatorial trainer.[9]

Given Caesar's stress on the importance of communication between himself and his subordinates, it is perhaps not surprising that reference to Roman religion is notably absent from his books. Unlike Sulla, who mentioned signs of divine favor on a regular basis, and even Marius, who advertised the services of prophetic figures in his entourage, Caesar almost never mentions the gods or fortune. One occasion where he does do this is in Book 1 of the *Gallic Wars*, when he writes that, "whether by luck or the plan of the immortal gods," an opening victory in the Helvetian campaign avenged an ancient debacle. Another is in Book 5, where he tells his men that the beneficence of the immortal gods and their own courage have brought them victory. A third case is in Book 6, where he writes that "Fortune plays a great role in everything, but most of all in war," and that Fortune preserved Ambiorix in flight. But most of the time the word *fortuna* as used by Caesar implies "fate" or "chance" rather than an act of a divinity. For Caesar battles are won by generals, not by gods.[10]

Technology and logistics are more important than luck. Throughout the narrative Caesar draws attention to the high quality of his organization. Fortifications are erected at lightning speed to keep the Helvetians from crossing into the province; new legions are conjured up to meet new threats; masses of grain are deposited at Bibracte in advance of Caesar's arrival in 58; a fleet is built as needed in Book 3; and a "statement" bridge is constructed across the Rhine in Book 4. A regular theme of the early books is the way the Gauls are overawed by or unable to respond to Roman engineering. Two Belgic peoples, the Suessiones and the Atuatuci, surrender when they see the impressive siege works the Romans can build. The result of the decisive battle at Alesia is determined by Caesar's capacity to construct massive siege works at very high speed so as to dictate the tactics the Gauls must use.[11] The decisive naval battle over the Veneti in 54 is determined by Roman cleverness, which enables them to dismast the Venetian ships, and then there is the aforementioned bridge built over the Rhine in 55, which prompts perhaps the clearest statement of how Caesar understood these projects:

> He did not think that crossing in boats was sufficiently safe, nor did he judge it appropriate to his own distinction (*dignitas*) or that of the Roman people. Therefore, even if the very great difficulty of constructing a bridge was obvious due to the width, speed, and depth of the river, he decided that he must overcome this or otherwise not take the army across.[12]

An important aspect of Roman technology is the way it helps manipulate Gallic psychology.

It is the general's job to ensure that his men are confident in their chances for success. He sets an example through his conduct on the battlefield, sharing the dangers with his men as the situation requires. The general's example inspires further exemplary behavior from junior officers. Valiant centurions such as Sextus Baculus, or the eagle-bearer of the Tenth Legion who leads the landing in Britain, repeatedly encourage their colleagues to acts of courage. At the same time the general needs to be conscious of how the psychology of the enemy can be undermined. At the decisive moment in the campaign of 52, Caesar leads the charge that will fall upon the rear of the Gauls who are attacking his fortifications, visible in the red cloak that he wears, so that his men are encouraged while the Gauls are demoralized.[13]

The Caesar who appears in various rhetorical set pieces, passages in which he needs to explain Roman policy to the Gauls, is a traditionalist who presents his actions as in keeping with what Romans have done and suffered in the past. One reason he knows the Helvetians are a deadly threat is that they had once defeated a Roman army (albeit a half-century before the campaign in 58 which kicks off the Gallic wars). Ariovistus, however, needs to be lectured on Roman history. No, he is not, as he thinks, the first person to take control of Gaul. Quintus Fabius Maximus had fought the Arveni in 121 in the very territory Ariovistus was claiming, but had forgiven them and decided not to impose tribute. Ariovistus should be aware that the Senate wished Gaul to be free. In general, in his dealings with foreigners, Caesar is always prepared to defend or assert the dignity of Rome. He does not present himself as a radical expansionist. The Remi claim Caesar's assistance in 57 by surrendering themselves into the good faith of the Roman people, which requires Caesar to defend them against their aggressive neighbors (although we'll see that there's a bit more to the story than Caesar lets on at this point). The Britons, on the other hand, have been assisting the Gauls in all their wars against Rome, so Caesar had to invade their island, just as he needed to raid southern Germany after two German tribes had crossed the Rhine in 55. Caesar's rationality and restraint are on display throughout. Where he is harsh, he is harsh for good reason: the Gauls had broken agreements.[14]

A notable characteristic of Caesarian campaigns is the speed with which he and his armies move. Caesar says that in his first campaign in Gaul he dashed from Rome to Geneva by the longest possible marches to confront the Helvetians, and that he then returned to Cisalpine Gaul to lead the five legions from that province to central France, crossing the Alps in a mere seven days. In the second book, it takes him ten days to get the army from its quarters in eastern France to the border with the Belgae, "arriving more rapidly than anyone could have foreseen," and he speeds with similar alacrity to the rescue of Quintus Cicero in Book 5. The rapidity of his movement from Italy in 52, crossing the Cervennes despite deep snow, throws Vercingetorix off balance, allowing Caesar to rejoin the army and set in motion a campaign that will be marked by his men's hard marching.[15]

The Caesar who appears between the lines is a more interesting figure than the one who is carefully crafted to serve a narrative purpose. Perhaps most notable is Caesar's ability to adapt his own tactical schemes to his enemy's tactics and his willingness to abandon plans that put his army at greater than necessary risk. We'll see that the tactics employed in 58 do not reappear during the rest of the Gallic campaigns. Secondly, there is his obsession with logistics—every campaign begins with a brief statement that the supplies had been secured, and arrangements at the end of a year are likewise shaped by logistical concerns. Caesar was building a very substantial logistical operation, something which only becomes visible in brief sentences, such as when he mentions that he needed to make sure the central headquarters was protected before he took off to fight the Nervii in the winter of 54. The magnitude of Caesar's private bureaucracy was no secret: Cicero was quite aware of its development, but the construction of such a bureaucracy isn't a standard feature of ancient war narratives.[16]

Another topic that doesn't garner much attention in typical accounts of ancient warfare, yet upon which Caesar harps constantly, is the value of good intelligence. The longest single discussion he offers on the topic, in Book 4, is about the need to beware of the self-interested informant:

> Gauls are fickle in planning and eager for novelty. For this reason, [Caesar] did not think they could be trusted. In addition, there is this Gallic habit, which is that they compel travelers, even if they are unwilling, to stop, and they seek to find out what each of them may have heard or knows about some matter, and a crowd stands around merchants in towns and compels each one to speak about the areas they have come from and the business they know about. Moved by what they have heard, they often make plans about the most important matters, of which they have to repent very rapidly since they are beholden to uncertain reports and many people tell them false things according to their interests.[17]

In Book 1, Caesar briefly alludes to this theme when he writes that his soldiers were frightened by exaggerated reports from Gallic merchants about the frightening capacities of Ariovistus's Germans. What this passage also underscores is that Caesar's army, being recruited from the Celtic regions of northern Italy and southern France, contained a very high proportion of men who spoke some form of the native language, which would have enhanced their ability to interpret information as it came in from native informants. At a higher level, even before the first campaign began, Caesar was drawing information from well-placed individuals such as Marcus Mettius, associate of Ariovistus, in addition to Gallic leaders. Diviciacus the Aeduan is mentioned as the sort of person Caesar will talk to, the leaders of the Remi are identified as people who advise him at the beginning of 57, and Commius, the Artebatian, who would ultimately prove a grave disappointment when he joined Vercingetorix in 52, was selected for his intelligence as an adviser to Caesar in 56. Elsewhere Caesar says he changed what he was doing when he learned something new from "prisoners and deserters." Additionally, despite what he has to say about the role of merchants at Besançon who had caused momentary panic among the troops, he does allow that they may be useful sources of intelligence about overall conditions in areas he is planning to attack.[18]

Caesar did not suffer fools easily and demanded a high level of accountability from his subordinates. It is clear, for instance, that, since he knows that the Nervii came to understand his marching order, he must have launched an investigation into what had led to the near-catastrophe suffered in the ambush and how disaster had been avoided. Likewise, his discussion in Book 1 of how Publius Considius mistook Labienus's men for Helvetians suggests a similar sort of investigation was conducted, and Caesar appears to be justifying his choice of a person of dubious competence for an important task when he says that Considius had previously served under Sulla and Crassus. There are also signs of an investigation into the reasons for the defeat at Gergovia (plate 9) when Caesar says that the men could not have heard the trumpets that sounded the recall—but he also notes that they still disobeyed the orders of their officers who had tried to prevent their advance, as he had ordered. He then says that he told his men that their defeat stemmed from their failure to obey the signal and their officers. The obvious disconnect between what Caesar says he knew about the signal and what he says to his men is likely an indication of how he thought he should convey his thoughts about a failure to the troops. In discussing the near-catastrophe suffered by Quintus Cicero at Aduatuca in 53 Caesar observes that Quintus had followed the orders he had been given until he surrendered to the complaints of his men and allowed them to leave the camp. As he would write in his account of the Civil War, "the roles of legates and of the supreme commander are different. The one does everything as ordered, the other ought to be concerned with the most important matters." When things did not work out the commander needed to know why. Caesar seems to have been able to recognize a cover-up when he saw one, and created an environment where truth, even if uncomfortable, was preferable to self-serving falsehood.[19]

The author of the book on Caesar's campaign in North Africa offers a picture of what the culmination of an investigation would look like. In this case a tribune of the Tenth Legion had used the ship transporting him to Africa for his private property, not taking a single soldier with him. Caesar, who was looking for an excuse to make an example of some officers whom he thought had behaved improperly during a mutiny some months earlier, called all the officers from the army together and delivered a speech in which he condemned the tribune and three other men for their conduct and dismissed them forthwith from the army. Message sent and received.[20]

Although Caesar usually presented himself as a friend of the common people of Rome, in the *Gallic War* he often suggests that the common people of Gaul are easily led astray, becoming pawns of ambitious aristocrats like Dumnorix. Dumnorix, Caesar says, had become extremely powerful, so when he bid for control of the Aeduan revenues, no one dared bid against him, which enabled him to obtain the contract at a low cost and to maintain a private army. Prior to his arrival in Caesar's camp in 54, Dumnorix had allegedly told the Aedui—presumably to make trouble for Caesar—that Caesar intended to make him their king. In its context, the claim reflects a policy Caesar was beginning to adopt as early as 57 of replacing annually elected magistrates with leaders whom he could convince tribal councils to accept as "kings."

Dumnorix's claim also shows us why Caesar considered the sentiment of the Athenian speaker in the Melian Dialogue so stupid that it could be placed in the mouth of Ariovistus.[21] In the Melian Dialogue, the Athenians tell the Melians the powerful can do whatever they want and the weak have to deal with it. Thucydides himself presumably thought this view of Athenian policy, held by some of his contemporaries, was foolish, for the brutal treatment of the Melians was brought up by the allies of Sparta as a reason to treat the Athenians harshly once they had surrendered in 404 BCE. Moreover, in Thucydides' history, the Dialogue is juxtaposed with the beginning of Athens' catastrophic expedition to Sicily. What Caesar's policy recognized was the need to give people a reason to buy into the system he was now creating. By the time Dumnorix acted up, Caesar had already made Commius king of the Atrebatae and established a man named Tasget as king of the Carnutes. Presumably there were many others, since we know of these appointments only through chance comments in the narrative, and Caesar himself appears to joke about his policy when he wrote to Cicero saying that he would make a younger friend of his "a king in Gaul" in the spring of 54.[22]

The appointment of kings went hand in hand with a program of holding regular meetings of the tribes that appears to have begun in 55. The first we hear of such a meeting is in that year, when Caesar says "he summoned the leaders of Gaul" and told them to provide cavalry for his proposed invasion of Germany. By the next year, Caesar takes failure to appear at a meeting as an implicit violation of an existing agreement that needs to be dealt with immediately. In this case, he summons a meeting of the tribal leaders to build a consensus for his preferred candidate for tribal leadership, a man named Cingetorix who had earned his position through "outstanding good will toward himself." Caesar later says that, in the spring of 53, he summoned a meeting of all the Gauls "as he was accustomed," mentioning in passing that he addressed the group from his magistrate's platform. But the purpose of these meetings and appointments was not simply to build an administrative structure; it was also to give the Gauls a voice in the way things were being run. The Gallic leaders who served with the Roman army commanded their own men. The point of Caesar's policy was that Gallic aristocrats who were loyal to Rome should see genuine benefits.[23]

Caesar's personality and political program emerge with increasing clarity throughout the *Gallic War*. He is a demanding leader, keen on detail and accountability, flexible in his planning, and capable of responding to the unexpected—but also very clear that the response to the unexpected will come from the top down. His picture of the common people of Gaul as the victims of self-interested aristocrats who can easily deceive them raises the question of how he viewed the common people of Rome. His praise of Pompey is praise of a person like himself who owes his authority to laws of the Roman people which created extraordinary commands outside the usual political apparatus. What Caesar is offering, by implication, is what Rome had gotten in his consulship. It is the purpose of government to ensure the people's welfare by efficient management, just as Gauls who know their place in the system do for their people. The model he offers of good management is highly centralized and autocratic. For Caesar in the 60s, the *via popularis*, the "populist path" which Cicero claimed Caesar was following in 63, had meant the protection of the Roman people from arbitrary actions by Roman magistrates—above all through the "final decree of the senate," the *senatus consultum ultimum*.[24] Caesar's support for the laws granting commands to Pompey against the pirates and then Mithridates was likewise "populist" by this definition. What we see through the *Gallic War* is how Caesar came to redefine what it meant to be a populist.

For Caesar the protection of the Roman people depended upon efficient leadership. By implication, that was not the leadership provided through the annual electoral process. In Books 6 and 7 he draws attention to his alliance with Pompey. It is this which allows him to recover rapidly from the disaster at the end of 54, and to respond to the Gallic revolt in 52. The Roman state had long farmed out basic administrative functions to private corporations. We can watch the development of Caesar's own organization to support his army as the *Gallic War* proceeds, with the result that, by the end of the 50s he—and Pompey, who had continued to build his own organization—stood at the head of vast enterprises providing financial and administrative services across the empire.[25] Caesar's version of the *via popularis* is a path to better government through efficient corporate management. The program that emerges from the pages of the *Gallic War* is the transformation of the Roman state so that it can be governed by the holders of long-term commands who are not subject to the whims of factions.

11

Opening Phases

G iven the complicated political situation when he laid down his consulship, Caesar did not immediately depart for Gaul. There was no
need to do so. The campaigning season would not begin until the spring.
By the time he left the area around Rome, his legislative legacy was intact.
Even though he was not yet in his provinces, Caesar had begun assembling a staff of people with local knowledge. Two persons who show up
in the summer of 58 and must have been recruited well in advance were
Marcus Mettius and Valerius Procillus, both of whom Caesar says were
friends of Ariovistus. Pompeius Trogus, the son of a man who had been
granted citizenship by Pompey, was also taken onto the staff, as was
another man, Gnaeus Pompeius, who served as a staff translator. Valerius
Troucillus, whom Caesar describes as one of the most respectable figures
in the province of Transalpine Gaul and "a good friend," was also brought
on board at this time and would serve as an ambassador to the Aedui
during Caesar's opening campaign. Two Allobrogian aristocrats named
Roucillus and Aecus also signed up and would command a tribal unit of
cavalry throughout the eight years that followed.[1]

The rebellion of the Allobroges, suppressed by Gaius Pomptinus in
60, meant the province's administrators and logistical structures had
recently been tested. This would be helpful in the future, but despite the
emergency decree that had accompanied that rebellion there had also
been serious intelligence failures in Transalpine Gaul. It isn't clear
whether the embassy the Senate had sent to urge the Gauls not to join

with the Helvetians had ever set out, and the presence of rival embassies from the Aeduans and Germans at Rome in 59 makes it seem like not much of anything had been accomplished. If it had, it's unlikely that both sides would have been in the city looking for Senate support. Moreover, the attenuated terms of the most recent governors of Transalpine Gaul— Pomptinus, who left early to claim a triumph, and his successor, whose decease in the first part of 59 had opened the door for Caesar—had resulted in failure to keep an eye on neighboring peoples.[2] The result was that the Helvetian threat had been forgotten and Caesar anticipated he would be operating in the Balkans. Three of his four legions were at Aquileia at the western edge of Cisalpine Gaul.

The sudden arrival of the Helvetians, seeking permission to pass through the Roman province, came as an obvious surprise in March of 58. It is very unclear what connection, if any, this had with the events of 60, and it is also unclear how we are to understand the story Caesar tells us about the background to the situation he faced. This story begins with a complicated aristocratic conspiracy. In 61, according to Caesar, an ambitious Helvetian named Orgetorix had decided that he could obtain the chief position in his state if he could convince his people to migrate. He convinced them to make this move and then began to conspire with Dumnorix, leader of the Aedui, and a man named Casticus, a member of an influential family among the Sequani, so that they could obtain the joint kingship over all of Gaul. To this end, Orgetorix's daughter married Dumnorix. When the Helvetians found out what Orgetorix was up to, however, they summoned him to stand trial, and he ultimately commit- ted suicide; the implication is that this was in 59, since the Helvetians decided to migrate anyway and the next thing Caesar says is that they were on the border of his province.[3]

The difficulties with this story are many. First of all, there is no refer- ence in Caesar's version of these events to the raids in the summer of 60, which Cicero connects with the defeat of the Aedui by the Sequani and Ariovistus. The total absence of Ariovistus from the narrative is also deeply suspicious. It is especially hard to see what Casticius (whom Caesar never again mentions) was up to, but there were clearly leaders of the Sequani who disliked Ariovistus, which makes it possible that the migration of the Helvetians was planned by these factions to strengthen opposition to Ariovistus at a time when it looked like the Romans were not going to do anything about him—and, worse, had decided he was their "friend and ally."[4]

Whatever was going on with the Sequani, the one point of certainty is the existence of some sort of agreement between Dumnorix and Orgetorix, because there is no reason for Caesar to have invented the marriage between Dumnorix and Orgetorix's daughter. It is also significant that Caesar says the Helvetians, in their migration, were bound for the territory of the Santones, a region just north of Roman territory. The combination of the marriage and this destination make it conceivable that some among the Aeduan leadership saw an alliance with the Helvetians as a counterweight to the alliance between the Sequani and Ariovistus. Even so, the feeling cannot have been uniform among the Aeduan elite. Diviciacus, who was the chief magistrate of the Aedui in 58, supported Caesar's intervention to prevent the migration of the Helvetii despite his own brother's involvement.[5]

The campaign began when Caesar was told that the Helvetians would appear opposite Geneva—on the river Rhône, which formed the boundary of the Roman province—at the end of March. He left Rome and arrived as soon as he could, bringing with him the single legion based in Transalpine Gaul along with levies summoned from provincial communities. He cut the bridge over the Rhône and explained to the Helvetian ambassadors that they would not be crossing into Roman territory. At the same time, his men were building defensive works along the river—a wall nineteen miles long and sixteen feet high.

When the Helvetians withdrew, Caesar left Titus Labienus, who would be his most trusted lieutenant over the next nine years, in charge of the local defenses while he dashed back to Aquileia to summon the legions already there and to raise two additional legions from Cisalpine Gaul.[6] Legionaries had to be Roman citizens and, even though not all the inhabitants of this province were citizens, there were enough to satisfy Caesar's manpower requirements, or so he implies. With the two new legions added to the existing ones, Caesar would have an army of about 24,000 men. He would later write that the Helvetians had eight times that many people, citing a document, written in Greek, which he claims to have found after his final victory. That is frankly impossible. Caesar's own army required 72,000 pounds of food per day, and there is no possible way sufficient food was available in the spring to feed such a gigantic Helvetian force, even one that had started out with some provisions of its own, for the roughly six weeks of the campaign that followed. The likelihood is that the total Helvetian migration didn't number more than about 60,000 people, a number equivalent to the largest armies that operated in the pre-modern period.[7]

Moreover, given that many of those Helvetians would have been non-combatants, it's likely the actual size of the Helvetian army was around the same size as Caesar's. But the effective strength of Caesar's army was less than it seemed, for the newly raised troops would not have been much use until they had gained some experience. Basic training in the US army, for instance, is now a ten-week period to provide new soldiers with the physical and mental strength to carry out their duties. The first two weeks of the training period are designed to teach new soldiers core values and first aid while beginning the physical conditioning process which will continue throughout the ten weeks. Weapons training begins for recruits in weeks 3 and 4 and continues thereafter as troops familiarize themselves with a greater range of weapons and develop greater skill. What we know about basic training in the Roman army suggests the theory was very similar to that of a modern army: it was to develop physical conditioning and then train men to use their weapons. Killing in the Roman army was intensely personal. Once the *pilum*, the throwing spear that had been devised for Marius's army, had disarmed the enemy, it was up to the Roman soldier to kill him with a sword. Roman recruits therefore had to learn how to take a life by standing next to a person, feeling his breath, and thrusting a weapon into him. It took time for the new men to be able to do this and to get into the shape required for a combat soldier. Marching around with Caesar's veteran legions was just a start to their conditioning program, and by the time Caesar fought his final battle with the Helvetians in late June, it's plain he didn't feel they were ready to do more than guard the baggage—the task assigned them in that battle.[8]

On the Roman side the campaign began in earnest when the legions from northern Italy crossed the Alps through the Mount Genévre pass and arrived, by early June, in southern France.[9] The Helvetians were on the move, having been granted permission by the Sequani to pass through their lands so long as they did no harm on the way.[10] This was something allegedly negotiated by Dumnorix, though one has to wonder what Ariovistus thought was going on since he was the dominant political force in the land of the Sequani. By the time Caesar got his men across the Alps, the Helvetians, who had been joined by some other groups in the region, had moved well into Aeduan territory, raiding as they went, and even, according to Caesar, attacking the Allobroges, whose land was within the territory of the Roman province. If this was true, then Caesar could safely claim he was acting to defend the province and not blatantly breaking the clause in his own extortion law which forbade a governor to lead his men beyond the borders of his province. Given that he would later cite the Senate's decree of 61 that directed the governor of Transalpine Gaul in order to protect the Aedui, he seems to have recognized that he had some vulnerability on this point.[11]

By the time Caesar's army approached the Helvetians in mid-June, they had advanced as far as the Saône, a tributary of the Rhône. There he fell upon them as they were crossing the river, slaughtering one subgroup, the Tigurini. Caesar goes on to say this was especially gratifying since the Tigurini had been responsible for the destruction of an army under the consul Lucius Cassius in 107 BCE and had caused the death of his father-in-law's grandfather. Caesar reports some tentative negotiations in the wake of the battle, saying that the Helvetian leader was a man named Divico—the very one responsible for the Roman defeat fifty years earlier. That seems to be a convenient fiction, and this Divico plays the useful narrative role of reminding Roman readers that the Helvetians were an ancestral foe as well as very arrogant.[12]

The next phase of the campaign, as the two forces moved west from the Saône, opened with a cavalry attack, launched by Caesar's auxiliaries and some Aeduan allies, on the Helvetian column, which was repulsed. This was followed by a huge fight between Caesar and the Aeduan leadership about the provision of adequate supplies for the legions which could no longer be fed with grain shipped up the Saône.[13] The issue came down to Dumnorix's interference, which was preventing the Aeduan leadership from making good on its promise to provide the Romans with the necessary grain. The discussion of this problem takes up considerably more space than the descriptions of all the battles in the campaign, which makes it look like Caesar is using this moment to justify his assassination of Dumnorix five years later. In any event, the Aeduans did finally come up with the promised grain and Caesar had to turn aside from his pursuit of the Helvetians to collect the grain at Bibracte, the Aeduan capitol.

En route to Bibracte, Caesar tried to ambush the Helvetians by luring them into an uphill assault on two legions commanded by Labienus and then attacking them, with the remainder of his forces, while they were thus engaged. This operation failed when the commander of his cavalry, Publius Considius, wrongly reported that he had spotted the Helvetians occupying the hill that Labienus was supposed to hold. The people he had seen were in fact Labienus's troops and the Helvetians had already gone on their way. As suggested in the last chapter, there must have been considerable discussion in the aftermath of this blunder and Caesar likely sent a message about the accountability he expected from his staff.[14]

By now the two armies had reached the valley of the Arroux, the narrow river that flows south through Autun to the Loire. There is a line of low hills to the west of the river, and it was here, as Caesar turned away from his pursuit of the Helvetians just outside the modern village of Toulon-sur-Arroux, that the Helvetians attacked in full force.[15] Caesar placed his baggage train on top of a hill, leaving the newly raised legions and auxiliaries to guard it while deploying his experienced troops on the slopes of the hill and sending his own horse away before walking along the lines to encourage his men before the battle. The message he had sent by dismounting—that all would share equally in the danger—was clear.[16]

In the standard account of Marius's victory over the Teutons in 102, the Teutons had charged uphill, falling into disorder as the Romans hurled their *pila* and attacked with their swords. Both terrain and the *pilum* figure in Caesar's account of this battle. He writes:

> The soldiers, hurling their *pila* from higher ground, easily broke the enemy's phalanx. It was a great drawback for the Gauls that many of their shields were penetrated and held together by a single strike from a *pilum*. When the iron heads were twisted, they weren't able to remove them or to fight with their left arms impeded, so many of them chose to throw away their shields and fight unprotected.

With the Helvetians in flight, the groups which had formed the rearguard of their column suddenly appeared and threatened the flank of the Roman army as it pursued its enemy. The army was saved by the legion's standard formation, whereby it was drawn up in three lines. The third line turned to deal with the new enemies while the first two lines drove the Helvetians back to their camp. The Romans then returned to their own camp. After a four-day retreat, the Helvetians agreed to surrender and return home.[17]

In the course of this narrative, Caesar turned, both consciously and reflexively, to the example of Gaius Marius. The destruction of the Tigurini gave Caesar the chance not only to claim that he was exacting personal revenge but also to present himself as reenacting the opening encounter of Marius's campaign in 102, when Caesar's famous uncle had destroyed a Teuton subgroup, the Ambrones, at a river crossing. These people are explicitly described as having been responsible for the horrific Roman defeat at Arles a few years earlier.[18] Between this action (the destruction of the Tigurini) and the final battle near Bibracte, Caesar's effort to deploy Labienus's men and lay an ambush is a variation of Marius's tactics at his victory over the Teutons in 102, and the details offered in Caesar's description of his final battle seem to continue the Marian theme. The differences in those details should reassure us that Caesar has not simply repeated a narrative borrowed from the generation of Marius even if the events seem to parallel one another. On the other hand, the similarities do suggest that Caesar was exploiting an earlier story and presenting himself as the new Marius, Rome's new savior from the barbarian hordes—a continuation of his use of Marius throughout his personal political self-fashioning.

Caesar's reason for allowing the surviving Helvetians to return home was that Germans might otherwise move into their unattended fields. The fact the Aedui gave land to one of the subgroups accompanying the Helvetians points to ongoing confusion as to what the point of the whole migration by the Helvetii was in the first place, and to the possibility of genuine division among the leaders of the Aedui as to whether the Roman intervention to stop the Helvetii was desirable. Still, once the Helvetians were eliminated as a possible factor in settling the Aeduans' dispute with Ariovistus, the Romans were now very welcome to intervene if only they could be convinced to turn on their "friend and ally." Caesar offers the picture of a dramatic meeting in which the Aeduan Diviciacus reminds Caesar that he had sought assistance against Ariovistus in the past and introduces him to an ambassador from the Sequani who explains how his people are terribly oppressed by Ariovistus, their former ally, now master.[19]

Given that Caesar had named Ariovistus a "friend and ally" of the Roman people, the justification for going to war with him requires considerable explanation. This is provided through a series of diplomatic exchanges in which Caesar seeks to educate Ariovistus as to what the friendship of the Roman people means and Ariovistus makes it clear that his own understanding of power is at odds with that of Caesar and the Roman people. The quotation from Thucydides which we discussed in the last chapter introduces the second of these exchanges. In the first exchange, Caesar had sent ambassadors to ask for a meeting and Ariovistus had replied that, if he had wanted to meet Caesar, he would have to gather his army and enter those parts of Gaul which Caesar controlled, which he would find expensive. But since Caesar wanted the meeting, he should come to Ariovistus, although Ariovistus allows that he cannot imagine what business Caesar, or the Roman people generally, would have in his part of Gaul.[20]

The result of the first embassy was clearly unsatisfactory, so Caesar sent a second one. His ambassadors point out that Ariovistus has a personal obligation to Caesar because of the generosity Caesar showed him during his consulship. Consequently, Ariovistus needs to return Aeduan hostages he holds and to ask the Sequani to return any they may be holding. Caesar's ambassador further reminds Ariovistus of the Senate's decree of 61 BCE, which instructed the person governing Gaul to look out for the interests of the Aedui and other friends of the Roman people. Having quoted Thucydides, Ariovistus proceeds to point out that he doesn't tell the Romans what to do and they have no business telling him what to do. The Aedui, defeated in battle, are tributary to Ariovistus, and if Caesar were to try to change that situation he would be doing Ariovistus a great wrong. Caesar is also urged to recall that Ariovistus is an invincible warrior.[21]

The Aedui now complain to Caesar that they are being raided by the Harudes, subjects of Ariovistus. The Treviri, a state residing south of the Rhône in the area of modern Trier, send Caesar information about the prospective movement of large numbers of Germans southward across the Rhine. Caesar is appalled. He regards it as essential to prevent the arrival of new Germans (it is perhaps too good to be true that one of the leaders of the prospective arrivals is named Cimberius, so that Caesar can imply a connection between his own enemies and the menace Marius had faced).[22] Caesar now sets his army in motion. This would most likely have been in the first half of August. The modern road from the Aeduan capitol at Bibracte (where Caesar probably had his initial discussion with Diviciacus) to the city of Vesontio, modern Besançon, allows for a trip of just over two hours—the distance is 111 miles and the road briefly intersects with the southern edge of the Route des Grands Crus, the heart of France's Burgundy district. There would have been no fine wines in Caesar's day, and his own route would have run a bit to the south of the modern road since he would have used the river Doubs, a tributary of the Saône, to ship his army's supplies. Well over 700,000 pounds of food would have been required for a march that may have lasted about two weeks.[23]

Caesar reports a serious challenge to his authority at Besançon. His Celtic-speaking soldiers were talking to local merchants who had gathered there to supply the Roman army. They stressed the physical size of the Germans, their victories over the Gauls, their hideous appearance, and their military skill. Listening to all this, Caesar's men were scared. Caesar's army had only served under him for a few months, a third of the troops were new recruits, and even the veterans' experience had consisted more of police actions than full-blown combat. Many of the junior officers had come from Rome out of friendship for Caesar and didn't know much about soldiering. Their own fear spread downward through the ranks, illustrating the Caesarian principle that officers needed to set an example for their men. Soldiers could be seen writing their wills, a recognizable sign of incipient mutiny in a Roman army.[24]

Off the battlefield, Caesar didn't often communicate directly with the average soldier. Instead, he depended upon the centurions to keep the troops in order. So on this occasion he summoned a meeting of the centurions. First, he criticized them for questioning their general's authority— there was only one person who made decisions for the army. Second, even if Ariovistus, "driven by rage or madness," should forget his obligations to Caesar and choose to fight, they should remember the victories of Marius over the Cimbrians and Teutons and the defeat of Spartacus's men (now, by implication, German slaves). Moreover, the Gauls had not so much been outfought by Ariovistus as outsmarted by him. Their campaign had been long, and they had run out of supplies before the Germans attacked, but the Romans had only to look around and they could see they were well supplied. Finally, Caesar's troops needed to remember that the Helvetians, whom they had just defeated, had often beaten the Germans. Caesar was, by implication, rational rather than rash. If his men continued to complain, he knew the Tenth Legion would follow him anywhere and, if need be, he would depart the next day with just that one legion. Caesar's arguments prevailed. The unrest ended. Caesar led the army out to one final parley with Ariovistus before conflict became inevitable.[25]

This final meeting occurred a few days after the incident at Besançon. Caesar had led his army by slow marches to the area around Belfort where Ariovistus was encamped, and there Caesar and Ariovistus met face to face. Caesar reminded Ariovistus of his personal debt to him and told him that the Roman people had a longstanding relationship with the Aedui, that the Senate had passed many decrees in their favor, and that it was generally the policy of Rome not only to protect the interests of their allies but even to promote their welfare. Ariovistus should therefore return the hostages and not allow any more Germans to enter Gaul. In response, Ariovistus asserted he had defeated the Gauls after they had attacked him and that his own power in Gaul was older than that of the Romans. Moreover, he was not such "an ignorant barbarian or so ignorant of affairs" as to be unaware of the fact the Aedui had not assisted the Romans when they had recently been at war with the Allobroges, so it was clear that the only reason Caesar was keeping his army in Gaul was in order to attack him. He was also well aware that, if he should defeat and kill Caesar, "he would bring pleasure to many of the nobles and leaders of the Roman people." Ariovistus claimed to be in direct contact with these people.[26] Caesar's response was simply to set Ariovistus straight as to the date of Roman primacy in Gaul (121 BCE) and to break off the meeting when it looked like the Germans were trying to pick a fight with his escort.[27]

The extensive account of diplomatic engagement with Ariovistus which fills the second half of the opening book of the *Gallic War* serves both to establish Ariovistus as an "ignorant barbarian" and to show that Caesar's understanding of Roman diplomacy is entirely traditional and that he is only doing what the Senate had already said it wanted done. He is protecting allies whom Rome has a moral obligation to protect. As in Spain, he was taking no action on his own initiative. He is not being aggressive, he is simply there to help. He shows his readers how the conflict with Ariovistus arises from the latter's flat-out refusal to return the Aeduan hostages. He further justifies his position by putting into Ariovistus's mouth precisely the complaint that might have been heard in Rome—that Caesar really had no business in that part of Gaul—and by implying quite clearly that those who might have been complaining about him at Rome were traitors. (We have no other direct evidence on this last point because Cicero, whose letters might have told us something more, was in exile. But Caesar seems to be answering objections to his conduct on the home front.)

Despite the failure of negotiations thus far, Ariovistus offered a further round of discussion as soon as his army and Caesar's were encamped facing one another. This seems to have been a trick: when Caesar sent ambassadors, the Troucillus and Mettius we've met above, Ariovistus arrested them.[28] For the next week the two armies maneuvered around each other, with Ariovistus attempting to cut Caesar off from the supplies that were being sent to Caesar by the Aedui and Sequani, whose support bespeaks some significant contact that has gone unmentioned in Caesar's book. After several skirmishes, Caesar learned from prisoners that Ariovistus was avoiding a full-fledged battle because prophetic women in his camp had assured him that he would not win if he gave battle before the next new moon on September 25. Caesar decided to force the issue. Advancing on the German camp, located in what is now the commune of Andelnans, he launched a direct attack on the German position. The Germans responded with an advance which Caesar says was so rapid that there was no time for his men to hurl their *pila*.[29] Caesar says that he commanded the army's right wing, which routed the Germans opposite them, but that the battle was only decided when Publius Crassus (the son of his political ally), in command of the cavalry and therefore with a clearer view of the battlefield, committed the reserves to routing the Germans who had been pressing the Romans back on the left wing. The broken German army, defeated on both flanks, abandoned its camp and fled for miles with the Roman cavalry in pursuit. Among those left behind were two of Ariovistus's wives, one of whom was killed and the other captured. Ariovistus himself escaped.

News of Ariovistus's defeat, Caesar says, convinced the Germans already encamped on the Rhine, in preparation for joining Ariovistus, to go home instead. Then, with considerable understatement, he writes that "having concluded two exceptionally important wars in one summer, Caesar led the army into winter quarters in the land of the Sequani and placed Labienus in charge of the winter camp"[30] The decision to occupy the territory of the Sequani goes well beyond any reasonable interpretation of the Senatorial decrees Caesar has been quoting and it explains the tone of his negotiations with Ariovistus. The Roman audience was to understand that Caesar was not engaged in a novel act of imperialism which would create a massive military organization under his own leadership. This was simply the proactive defense of Rome's allies: politics as usual.

Caesar spent the winter, as he would do in the future, traveling in northern Italy to conduct the legal proceedings that were part of his business as governor. At the same time, he would be encouraging celebration of his victories and deepening his connections with the local leaders, whose support was crucial when it came to recruiting new troops and spreading the good word about him to Rome. A man named Varro, a resident of Transalpine Gaul composed a poem on the theme of the war with Ariovistus which seems to have compared well with other poems of its time. It may also have been at this time that Caesar developed a friendship with an important man in Cisalpine Gaul, the father of the poet Catullus—this despite his connection to Caesar's enemy, Gaius Memmius, on whose staff in Bithynia the younger Catullus would be serving in the coming year.[31]

While Caesar was in Italy that winter, it appears that the Belgae were distressed by the presence of Roman troops near their borders and began to plan (or so Caesar says) to attack the Romans. As soon as he received this news Caesar enrolled two more legions in northern Italy and ordered logistical arrangements to support a new campaign. He now had an army that was double the size authorized by the Senate. He could not use state funds to pay these troops, but he could use money extracted from cities in Gaul which had treaties requiring them to support defensive operations, and he could also request support from the Aedui and other allies. These troops would therefore be paid in the local coinage we discussed in our survey of Gaul.

The prospect of a war with the Belgae brought Caesar into contact with the Remi, whose leaders appear to have been on good terms with Diviciacus. An alliance with the Remi was operationally invaluable for a campaign against the Belgae, and, in the longer term, it gave Caesar access to the resources of the state that controlled most of the territory between the Rhône and the Atlantic. The Remi chose to enter the Roman diplomatic sphere by "surrendering into the good faith of the Roman people."[32] A "surrender into the good faith of the Roman people" was perhaps the oldest tool in the admittedly somewhat limited diplomatic tool chest of the Roman state. Such a surrender, which did not need to be accepted if the people making it were thought to be acting in bad faith, obligated the Romans to come to the rescue of those who surrendered. As governor, Caesar presumably had the power to accept the surrender, contingent on the Senate's later approval. The alliance was sealed when the Remi gave Caesar hostages. This was not a necessary aspect of a Roman treaty, but it certainly was an aspect of Gallic diplomacy, and is a sign of Caesar's ability to link Roman concepts with local custom.[33] This practice would also require him to start developing a base at which hostages could be kept.

The plan of campaign against the Belgae involved both the Aedui and the Remi. The Aedui were assigned the task of raiding the territory of the Bellovaci, the largest community among the Belgae. The Remi were to provide intelligence and logistical support for the Roman army, which advanced to their border on the river Aisne. The problems of transport for large numbers of men have meant that, over the course of history, major battles have often been fought in roughly the same places.[34] The opening round of Caesar's conflict with the Belgae involved an unsuccessful attack by the Belgae on the town of Bibrax, which sat atop the hill now occupied by Saint Thomas in northern France. Between Saint Thomas and the crossing of the Aisne stands the *Monument national des chars d'assaut*, a memorial to the first major use of tanks in combat by the French army in 1917 (the operation wasn't a success). A few miles south of that sits the Ville-aux-Bois cemetery for the British and Commonwealth soldiers killed in battle the next year. Remains identified as those of Caesar's camp during the decisive action against the Belgae (plate 7) are in the vicinity of the French war memorial and cemetery at Berry-au-Bac. The battles recalled by these modern memorials were notable for the lack of tactical sophistication showed by Allied forces. The same could be said of the Belgae who were fighting on this same ground some two thousand years before.

In 57 the Aisne river marked the boundary between the land of the Remi and that of the Belgae. Here the Belgae gathered under the leadership of Galba, ruler of the Belgic Suessiones. Caesar lists the various communities' contributions to this force with admirable precision, so that it amounts in total to just over 300,000 men. As elsewhere, this is a vast exaggeration (the armies concentrated in this region in 1917 didn't amount to that many people), but it is likely that the Belgic army was somewhat larger than Caesar's army of perhaps 32,000 men, which included the new legions and what appear to be newly raised auxiliary cohorts from various parts of Roman territory—slingers from the Balearic Islands, archers from Crete, and Numidian cavalry from North Africa. After failing to capture Saint Thomas, the Belgae encamped across the Aisne from Caesar's camp at Berry-au-Bac. At this point, Caesar says, he decided not to give battle immediately given the exceptional numbers and reputation of the Belgae. But once his men had gained confidence that their enemy weren't any more capable than they themselves were, Caesar began lining his army up in a defensive position in front of his camp, seeking to lure the Belgae into a frontal assault. Given that such an assault would have involved crossing a river and marshes, it was not going to happen.[35]

In setting up his army as he did, Caesar was taking a leaf out of Ariovistus's tactical handbook, since the German leader had won his big victory over the Aedui once their army, which could not reach him because he had encamped in a swamp, had dispersed.[36] After some time had passed, the Belgae attempted to cut Caesar's supply lines and were repulsed. Then, when they realized that Caesar wasn't going to budge and "their supplies began to run out, they summoned a council and decided that it would be best if they all went home, coming together again to defend those into whose territory the Romans first brought their army, making use of their own resources and food supplies rather than fight on foreign ground."[37] The withdrawal began in the middle of the night, and at dawn the next day, when Caesar saw the Belgae had departed, he sent his cavalry with three legions under Labienus in pursuit. The cavalry forced the men at the rear of the Belgic army to stand their ground, enabling Labienus to catch up and inflict severe casualties.

The agreement among the Belgae to come together wherever the Romans should show up first rapidly fell into abeyance. Caesar advanced into the territory of the Suessiones, who were terrified when they saw the siege works the Romans were building to attack Pommiers, located on a hill overlooking Soissons. At this point Caesar makes it clear that he is looking for a solution to the conflict which will make a point about the value of a Roman alliance. He has the Remi speak in favor of showing mercy to the Suessiones, who duly surrender into "the faith of the Roman people" and deliver hostages (including two of Galba's sons).

Caesar then advanced into the land of the Bellovaci, said to be the most powerful of the Belgae. There, he allowed Diviciacus to speak on that people's behalf, and he says that it was "to honor Diviciacus" that he allowed the Bellovaci to surrender, like the Suessiones, into the "faith of the Roman people" (albeit delivering 600 hostages as they did so).[38] The neighboring Ambiani, having gotten the message as to what was expected, also surrendered in the "faith of the Roman people." But the process through which negotiated settlements with Belgic groups was obtained came to a crashing halt when Caesar entered the land of the Nervii. The Nervii accused the rest of the Belgae of having violated their oaths, and they prepared to defend themselves, drawing support from some neighboring groups. The result might have been a catastrophe for the Romans were it not for the fact that Caesar (so he tells us) paid attention to local intelligence and changed his behavior in accordance with what he was being told. In this case, he was told that his line of march was all too predictable—each legion's baggage train followed its respective legion, creating substantial gaps between the various legions. As he moved towards the Nervii, whom he was told were based beyond the river Selle near the modern town of Saulzoir, Caesar changed the line of march so that the six veteran legions would march together at the head of the column, followed by the baggage train, and then the two newly raised legions.[39]

The change of formation saved the army. The Nervii, although they could not predict the change in the army's marching order, could predict that Caesar would look to place his camp near a source of water. The river Selle, a narrow, slow-moving stream in the hot summer months, was an obvious place for Caesar to stop. When Caesar began to make camp on a low rise on the river's west bank, his cavalry and light troops crossed the Selle and engaged with scouts of the Nervii. What the Romans had failed to notice was that the Nervii's entire army was hidden in some nearby woods, most likely behind the higher rise to the river's east. While the Romans began entrenching their camp, the Nervii burst from their hiding place, overwhelmed the Romans who had engaged their scouts, and dashed across the river. Caesar's dramatic description of the battle that followed occludes what was plainly a massive failure in scouting. There would be no such fiasco during future campaigns, and the fact that no one is mentioned as being responsible for the failure may suggest either that the person responsible did not survive to be chastised, as Considius had, or that Caesar recognized that the fault was his own. He had become predictable.

Whatever failures had led to the ambush, Caesar's account of the events that followed show that he now had a very good understanding of the way his men reacted to the heat of combat. He recognized that their eyes would be on him and it was his duty to model the calm, disciplined behavior he expected from his soldiers. For the Romans, the battle was complicated by hedges which broke up the space around the camp so that the legions could not form a single line. Instead, the action broke down into three separate conflicts, one on the left end of the line where the Ninth and Tenth Legions were stationed, another for the Eighth and Eleventh Legions in the center, and finally a third for the Seventh and Twelfth Legions, which were crowded together on the right, facing the strongest forces of the Nervii. When Caesar joined the Seventh and

Twelfth Legions, he saw that he first had to rally the badly pressed troops by advancing into the front line, and then, with the situation restored, resume his job as commanding general, taking his place with the legions' staff officers to reset the battle line since the soldiers were crowded too closely together to use their weapons effectively. All this was successfully accomplished, the line stabilized, and the Romans began to push their enemy back. Finally, Labienus, who had command of the troops on the left and had captured the camp of the Nervii, turned back to take the forces facing Caesar from the rear. The two legions that had been left with the baggage train arrived to complete the rout.[40]

Caesar claimed to have virtually annihilated the Nervii, and offered some bogus statistics to make his point. Of six hundred tribal councilors, only three remained alive and a mere five hundred warriors had survived from an army once numbering sixty thousand. Perhaps more realistic is Caesar's claim to have urged the Nervii's neighbors to leave them in peace once they had surrendered. That would be in line with his conduct with other peoples who had surrendered and were now under his protection.[41]

The final stop in that summer's campaign was near the modern Belgian city of Thuin, at the city of the Atuatuci, on a high rise in the lovely modern park of Bois du Grand Bon Dieu. Like the Bellovaci, the Atuatuci were amazed by the skill of the Romans in building siege works. Their amazement convinced them to surrender—or to simulate a surrender, for according to Caesar their actual intention was to use the truce to launch a surprise attack on the Roman camp. The attack failed and Caesar says he sold the entire population into slavery.[42] That is likely enough, even if the number of prisoners he gives—53,000—is totally implausible: the population of the town Caesar captured formed only a part of the Atuatuci (who reappeared in Caesar's narrative in subsequent years).

Caesar had not advanced into the territory of the Atuatuci with his whole force. After defeating the Nervii, he had dispatched Publius Crassus with one legion to visit the lands of coastal tribes to the southwest. These would likely have been subordinate to the Remi, and,

Crassus's report of their submission to the "power and dominion" of the Roman people may reflect their acquiescence to the earlier surrender by the Remi. It would otherwise be hard to see why only a single legion had been sent on this mission.[43]

The action against the Atuatuci and Crassus's expedition to the southwest were the final episodes of the campaigning season of 57, which probably ended in mid-September.[44] The year is significant not simply because of the victories won but also because of how Caesar was beginning to build a political structure through which the Gauls would be governed within a Roman alliance system. He was also seeking to show Gallic tribes that it was in their interest not to behave like the Atuatuci but rather to honor those alliances. This point emerges from the settlements with the Belgic tribes and is reemphasized at the end of Book 2 of the *Gallic War*, when Caesar mentions embassies arriving from tribes across the Rhine.

12

Setting Boundaries

The third book of the *Gallic War* introduces the theme of Gallic resentment at the loss of their freedom to the Romans. This theme will run throughout the rest of the *Gallic War* and relates directly to the case Caesar would soon be making to justify the continuation of his command. His audience needed to be aware that any perceived weakness on the Roman side could lead to Gallic rebellion, that the Gauls could not immediately realize the benefits of Roman rule. Caesar would need to stay in the region to help them realize how much better off they would be if they developed more stable political systems and remained loyal to Rome. For Caesar, *libertas*, "freedom," was not a quality to be enjoyed without Roman discipline.

At the end of the Belgic campaign, Caesar sent his legate, Servius Sulpicius Galba, to stabilize the passage of the Alps through the pass now known as the Grand Saint Bernard, which takes travelers from Italy up into the region of Lake Geneva, from which they follow the route of the Rhône into central France. Galba encamped at a place called Octodurus (today's Martigny in Switzerland) and collected hostages from the neighboring tribes, the most powerful of which were the Seduni. When this happened the tribes began to conspire to destroy his force for several reasons: first, because they thought his troops were understrength; second, because they thought the terrain favored them; third, because they resented the hostage taking; and, finally, because they "had persuaded themselves the Romans were not only there for the sake of securing the mountain route, but because they intended to take perpetual possession of the highest points of the Alps and join the area to the neighboring province."[1]

Galba fought a skillful action, probably in November. When Caesar was given this information, he decided it was time to visit his province of Illyricum he said he didn't know. It hadn't been a bad year, all things considered. The Senate had voted fifteen days of thanksgiving for his victories, and he wrote that he "thought Gaul was pacified, with the Belgae defeated, the Germans having been expelled, and the Seduni defeated in the Alps." In the next summer, however, he says that "a sudden war broke out in Gaul" and he gave orders to the younger Crassus to deal with the situation "because he was going to be away for a while longer."[2]

The new war in Gaul began when Crassus sent envoys to a number of tribes along the Atlantic coast to collect more grain, at which point the Veneti, the most powerful of the groups in what is now southern Brittany, seized the Romans as leverage for the return of their hostages. This encouraged other groups, the Esubii and the Curiosolites, to hold the ambassadors who had been sent to them. They then encouraged other groups to "prefer to reclaim the freedom they had inherited from their ancestors rather than to remain in slavery to the Romans" and sent an embassy to Crassus demanding the return of their hostages. Caesar here reminds his audience that the Gauls are very unpredictable and likely to change their decisions very abruptly.[3] At the same time, he is completely obscuring the reason he will be away "longer." The reason was the unstable political situation at Rome.

Even before the end of 58, Clodius and Pompey had been coming to blows, with Pompey accusing a supporter of Clodius of trying to murder him. Now, while Caesar was fighting the Belgae, Pompey backed a motion by the tribunes to recall Cicero from exile. At the same time, he was supporting a pair of thugs, Publius Sestius and Annius Milo, both tribunes themselves, who raised their own gangs to fight with Clodius for control of the Roman streets. Meanwhile, grain distributions under Clodius's bill were being administered by Sextus Clodius, who was plainly not up to the job. He lacked the clout to manage the grain dealers or to set up new supply lines. The treasury was strained by the need to pay the high prices charged by grain dealers, especially when people began freeing their slaves so that they could be fed at state expense.[4]

By the beginning of August, the centuriate assembly voted to allow Cicero's return from exile. He had been expecting this and arrived back in Rome on September 4, a month after the measure for his recall had passed. People crowded into the city to greet him, and also to vote on a new law which the consuls were sponsoring to "fix" Clodius's grain law by creating a new position, with *imperium* equal to that of a former consul and backed by fifteen legates, to organize the grain supply for a period of five years. This was a classic piece of Pompeian legislation. The "modesty" of the proposal that was passed on September 7 was underscored by an alternative bill, brought by a tribune named Messius, that would have added a fleet, an army, control over all public monies, and "greater *imperium*" (*imperium maius*) than that of all provincial governors. Messius's bill would essentially have created what was later the legal position of the Roman emperors. What lay behind both these proposals is the understanding that Republican government was essentially broken and could only be fixed by the creation of a dictatorship to manage basic administrative tasks. Cicero himself spoke in favor of the consular proposal creating Pompey's grain commission and moved a senatorial decree for a fifteen-day thanksgiving to celebrate Caesar's Belgian victories.[5]

Just as it looked like Pompey was now the dominant political force at Rome, everything came unglued. The reason was that the Egyptian king Ptolemy XII had been driven from his throne by mobs in Alexandria a month after the Roman annexation of Cyprus in 58. At the end of that year, he had presented himself at Pompey's massive villa in the Alban hills, where he would remain for nearly a year with a view to getting his host to reclaim his throne for him. He may have brought with him his daughter, Cleopatra, in order to begin her education in the ways of the Romans.[6]

Ptolemy's presence gave rise to a series of scandals. First of all, the king began borrowing huge sums of money which were certainly used to maintain the splendor of his retinue and were allegedly used to bribe members of the Senate. Ptolemy hoped Pompey would be assigned by the senators to facilitate his return. Pompey was interested, but a substantial military force would be required and this was currently in the hands of Gabinius, who had been given the province of Syria for five years. When the suggestion was made that Pompey be sent with two lictors to act as a mediator between the king and the people of Alexandria, he seems to have lost interest. Things unraveled even further in late December when a Sibylline oracle surfaced which stated that Egypt's king had been expelled from his kingdom through trickery and should not be restored with "a multitude."[7] The oracle was an obvious fake, produced by a friend of Clodius who was on the board of priests overseeing the actual oracles. But it was a convenient fake, and the Senate ultimately decided to do nothing.

While Ptolemy's presence gave rise to scandal, it also inspired two of the most memorable pieces of Latin invective to survive from any period of Roman history. The first was the speech Cicero gave defending his young friend Caelius Rufus in April of 56. Caelius had been charged with causing a riot in Naples, stealing the property of a relative named Palla, attacking the ambassadors from Alexandria who had come to Rome towards the end of 57 to ask that Ptolemy not be restored, and trying to poison Clodius's sister Clodia, with whom he had a sexual relationship. Caelius and Crassus dealt in their defense speeches with the first three charges, then Cicero treated the large audience which had gathered to watch the trial to a vigorous and vicious description of Clodia's sex life.

The other piece of invective is the work of the poet Catullus, coincidentally another of Clodia's former lovers. Catullus adapted a poem composed by the Alexandrian poet Callimachus in the third century BCE to commemorate a remarkable act of academic sycophancy—the declaration by the astrologer Conon that the lock of hair the Egyptian queen Berenice II had dedicated so that her brother would return safely from a war had become a constellation. Catullus, in his adaptation, turned this poem into a vivid discussion of Berenice's sexual relationship with her brother to reinforce the Roman perception of Ptolemaic sexual perversity which went hand in hand with the Egyptian kingdom's political instability. His other poems give us some sense of what educated Romans who were not enamored of aspiring dictators might have been saying. Pompey appears in his poetry as a patron of a man Catullus despised and as a person whose political career coincided with a great increase in adultery. Cicero makes a cameo appearance as a windbag, and Catullus's treatment of Caesar is vitriolic.[8]

Ptolemaic scandals, and Pompey's inability to immediately undo the mess Clodius had made of the grain supply, undermined both his own position and, coincidentally, Caesar's. Clodius, now an aedile, felt safer in attacking Pompey and prosecuted Pompey's agent Milo for promoting public violence, and when Pompey showed up for the defense, Clodius incited the crowd against him, suggesting that his habit of rubbing the top of his head while he was speaking signified his sexual attraction to men.[9] A few days after this, one of Clodius's supporters attacked Pompey in the Senate. Pompey suspected Crassus was behind this and told Cicero a plot to assassinate him was afoot. At this point Cicero began to backslide, supporting a bill to halt the distribution of Campanian land under Caesar's bill of 59 on the grounds that the state needed the rents it was still collecting there in order to pay for the new grain laws. He also had expressed pleasure when the consul presiding over the Senate in March had prevented a vote on a bill requiring the state to take over payment for the legions Caesar had raised in his provinces; while enhancing Caesar's capacity for patronage by giving him the power to appoint ten legates to command those legions. At roughly the same time as Caesar suffered this reverse, a tribune proposed recalling him to face charges for his actions in Gaul.[10] Also, Caesar's old enemy, Lucius Domitius Ahenobarbus, declared his candidacy for the consulship of 55. Clearly the days of thanksgiving were not the final judgement on Caesar's successes in the court of public opinion.

Decisive action was needed to deal with the political situation in Rome. Caesar met with Crassus at Ravenna and then headed to the seaside town of Luca, the southernmost town in Cisalpine Gaul, where he met with Pompey. It was agreed that Pompey and Crassus would stand together for the consulship of 55, and that Caesar would send troops to "help" with the voting at the end of the campaigning season. A final aspect of the agreement was that legislation would be introduced awarding five-year provincial commands to the two consuls and that Caesar's command would also be extended for five years. Although later historians would exaggerate the scope of this meeting, claiming that hundreds of senators descended upon Luca, the meeting seems to have been private, and to have involved only Caesar and Pompey. Cicero, for one, hadn't heard of the meeting at Luca until Pompey had explained to his brother, Quintus Cicero, who was one of Pompey's legates under the grain bill, that Cicero needed to remember who had brought him back from exile. Cicero got the message, stopped supporting the measure to repeal Caesar's bill on the Campanian land, delivered a speech in praise of Caesar's actions in Gaul, and voted for Caesar's legates and the payment for his army.[11] In the meantime, Caesar returned to Gaul.

Caesar's departure was in early June. Sometime later that month, Cicero delivered a speech in the Senate about the consular provinces of 55. Given his antipathy toward Piso and Gabinius, who had supported his exile when they were consuls in 58, he argued for the transfer of their provinces to the consuls of 55, proposing that Caesar, whose removal had been suggested by Domitius, should be left where he was. To those who asked why Cicero was so hostile to Piso and Gabinius, but now so friendly toward Caesar, he answered that it was because Cicero loved Rome, for which Caesar was doing so much good. Moreover, the recent vote for the thanksgiving showed that the Senate now viewed Caesar in a positive light, and thus it was only right for Cicero to give up his opposition.[12]

Cicero now seemed very much aligned with the messaging coming from Gaul. While previous wars in the area, even those of Marius, had been defensive, Caesar was now reducing all of Gaul to Roman domination. In his speech, Cicero declares:

A great war is being waged in Gaul, the most powerful nations have been defeated by Caesar, but they have not yet been bound by laws, or fixed codes, or a peace that can be thoroughly depended upon. We see the war has been fought, and to tell the truth, nearly finished, but we will only see it completed by the one who undertook it.[13]

If another person is appointed governor, Cicero says, then there is a grave risk the war will be restarted. Caesar has no reason to remain in the province other than his desire to finish the job.

When Caesar returned to Gaul he needed to deal immediately with the Veneti. Their actions meant that the campaign would have a different justification than those of the last two years. Those had been wars to defend Roman allies, now the conflict would be with people who had betrayed their oaths of allegiance. Caesar stresses the Veneti's treacherous seizure of Roman officials, claiming with considerable exaggeration that these men were official ambassadors and thus that their treatment was a violation of both the laws governing embassies and the understanding inherent in a surrender into the "good faith of the Roman people." The situation was especially dangerous because, if Caesar did not take strong action, this rebellion of the Veneti might inspire other Gauls, who, he writes, are all prone to revolt. If anyone wanted to know why Caesar required the resources he was requesting, this was the reason.[14]

While he had been away, Crassus had collected a fleet, but no one on the senior staff had much experience of war at sea. As the summer progressed there were signs that the campaign was going to be a learning experience for Caesar. The Veneti were coast-dwellers and seafarers, and Caesar points out that the usual Roman tactic of storming an adversary's strongpoint wasn't viable when these adversaries would simply hop on their boats and sail away. The boats themselves were also a problem. Caesar had ordered the construction of a fleet of Mediterranean-style war galleys, but they were going to have trouble functioning in the Atlantic. Caesar admits that, when the Roman fleet first encountered the Veneti, his officers did not know what tactics they should use. The standard one of ramming an enemy ship wasn't going to work against the strong hulls of vessels designed to contend with Atlantic storms. Nor would it be easy to board ships which were much higher in the water, especially as their height meant the Gauls had an advantage in any exchange of missiles. Then someone, whom Caesar doesn't name, discovered that if grappling hooks were placed on the end of long poles they could snag the rigging of enemy ships, which would then be torn down when the Roman ship rowed away. Then several Roman ships could surround and board their immobilized adversaries. This tactic worked well for the Romans. Seeing their fleet in ruins, the Veneti surrendered. Caesar decided that their punishment must be especially severe so "the protection of ambassadors would be more carefully observed by the barbarians in the future." He executed all members of the Veneti's governing council and sold the rest of the population into slavery.[15]

While the naval war was winding up in Brittany, a very different sort of campaign was coming to a conclusion in Normandy, in the territory of the Venelli, who had allied with the Veneti against Rome. The commander dispatched to deal with the "revolt," Titurius Sabinus, was very cautious, knowing a legate should not take risks in the absence of guidance from his general. His caution had the effect of encouraging the rank and file of the Venelli's troops to force a battle. Caesar's picture of their decision-making process is a complete reversal of the way he believed decisions should be made. The Venelli were short of food, confident the Veneti would be victorious, and subject to the "general tendency of people to believe that what they hope for is the case." According to Caesar, it was the rank and file who compelled the leadership to order an attack on the Roman camp. Sabinus held his men in camp until the Venelli had run a mile uphill and were trying to fill in the ditches in front of the camp walls. At that point, Sabinus ordered an attack with the fresh Roman troops, "so it came about through the enemy's inexperience and exhaustion, and the courage and experience in prior battles of our own soldiers, that the enemy could not withstand a single charge from our men and turned their backs in flight." Defeated and learning of Caesar's victory, the Venelli duly surrendered, since "the spirit of the Gauls is

rapid and eager to start wars, but their mind is weak and unable to withstand defeat."[16]

The third campaign of the summer, waged under the command of
Publius Crassus, was in Aquitania. The action is justified by Caesar not
in terms of any immediate provocation, but rather, in a manner reminiscent of Caesar's explanation for fighting the Helvetians, because the
Aquitanians had joined with a lieutenant of Sertorius to defeat a pair of
Roman armies twenty years before. Crassus had with him only about
five thousand infantry, as well as the cavalry Caesar didn't need to fight
the Veneti, and some veterans called up from Transalpine Gaul, which
suggests that the Aquitanians did not have vast forces at their disposal.
Indeed, Crassus appears to have outnumbered the first group he
encountered and was probably heavily outnumbered by the second
group he encountered, who also had the advantage of having leaders
who "had served under Quintus Sertorius during every year of his campaigns and were thought to have the greatest experience of military
affairs."[17] Despite this, Crassus managed to win a total victory and secure
the surrender of all but the most distant Aquitanians. The summer concluded with Caesar on a brief expedition in the territory of the Menappi
and Morini in southern Belgium, since "with all Gaul pacified" these
were the only people "who were in arms and had never sent ambassadors
about peace."[18] When the Menappi did not come out to fight him—the
implication being that they had learned something from the failure of
others—Caesar ravaged their lands before leading his army into winter
quarters in eastern Brittany.

While Caesar was bringing the campaigning season to a close in Gaul,
Pompey and Crassus were waging their own campaign in Rome. Taking
control of the streets with armed gangs, and, in the autumn, with soldiers the younger Crassus brought with him from Gaul, they prevented
the elections for 55 from taking place until January of that year, when
the consuls for 56, including Lentulus Marcellinus, who had strongly
opposed Pompey and Crassus, would be out of office. Cicero doesn't
seem to have been terribly sympathetic to Domitius Ahenobarbus, who

persisted in asserting his candidacy. He archly commented to Atticus that this gentleman, "who's been consul designate for as long as he's been alive," deserved his disappointment.[19] He mused further that Pompey and Crassus might have enough candidates who they'd be supporting in future years that Domitius would never hold the office to which he thought he had been born.

In January it would fall to an *interrex*, or temporary supreme magistrate, to run the consular elections and declare who the candidates could be. The *interrex* (we don't know who it was) duly declared there would be only two. Pompey and Crassus took office in the middle of the month and ran the elections for the other magistrates (excepting the tribunes, who had already been elected). Milo and Vatinius were among those who were elected to praetorships. Cato was excluded. Among the tribunes was a man who would later become Caesar's dedicated adherent. This was Gaius Trebonius, and, soon after he was elected, he made good on a promise Caesar had made at Luca, namely, that Pompey and Crassus would have five-year terms as governors in major provinces of their own. Pompey received both Spanish provinces, while Crassus was given Syria, replacing Gabinius. Crassus wouldn't wait until the year's end before taking off for the East. He had urgent business to attend to. He planned to take over the war that Gabinius had been hoping to start. This was a war with Parthia, the kingdom that included much of what are now Iran and Iraq as well as portions of central Asia. The war had been put on hold while Gabinius restored Ptolemy to his throne with his army— notwithstanding the Sibylline oracle. It is alleged that, in the course of that operation, one of the officers serving under Gabinius, Mark Antony, met, for the first time, the future love of his life: Cleopatra.[20]

In the wake of Trebonius's law, Pompey and Crassus made good on their own promise to Caesar, passing a law to extend Caesar's command in Gaul for five years. The wording of this law would be the cause of great controversy in a few years' time. It seems to have been extremely badly drafted. At issue would be the terminal date it established for Caesar's command—was it 50 or 49? It seems that what the law said was that Caesar's command would be extended for a five-year period "in accordance with this law." In 51 and 50 Caesar's enemies would take that to mean "from the passage of this law" rather than that the law extended Caesar's original command, due to end in 54, by five additional years. Caesar did not seem to think there was any problem when this new law was passed, but he would later be very clear that those who interpreted the law as setting the terminal date for his command in 50 rather than the end of 49 were depriving him of a command that was legally his.[21]

At this point, Caesar's political organization in both Gaul and Rome was strengthening and the group which would later form Caesar's inner circle was coming together. There was, first and foremost, Cornelius Balbus, who shuttled between Gaul and Rome, looking after the affairs of his friend while enriching himself. Also present was Gaius Oppius, the future author of Caesar's biography, likely from a family of public contractors (*publicani*). He was second only to Balbus in visibility. Another man from a similar background was Aulus Hirtius. A person who appears to have acted for Caesar primarily in the Italian sphere was Gaius Mamurra, the target of some of Catullus's most violent poetry. But Catullus's friend Asinius Pollio would also soon be joining Caesar's staff. These were all originally people of some means, and they would soon be among Rome's most ostentatiously wealthy. Very different was the origin of Publius Ventidius, who would take charge of Caesar's army's supply chain. He was from Asculum. As a child he had been taken captive and led in triumph through the streets of Rome by Pompeius Strabo. His ascent to Balbus's old position of *praefectus fabrum* bespeaks enormous energy in that he had to assemble sufficient property to attain the equestrian status which was a minimal requirement for the position. His fortunes would soon improve even more, making him eligible to serve as consul in 42. A few years after that he would celebrate a triumph of his own, the first Roman to win such an honor fighting the Parthians.[22]

The men of Caesar's inner circle were deeply devoted to their general. Oppius would stress Caesar's personal kindness and generosity, his lack of pretension, his incredible energy. The loyalty of Caesar's inner circle would ultimately determine, after his death, the disposition of his estate.

The organization which they shaped would eventually morph into the government of the Roman state under Caesar's heir.[23]

With Pompey and Crassus as consuls in 55, Caesar writes that he could leave earlier for Gaul than usual, and it was a good thing he did. The Germans were coming. In the area near the present-day Dutch villages of Kessel and Lith, where the Rhine now flows toward the sea, two tribes, the Usipetes and the Tenecteri, were gathering to cross the river into the territory of the Belgic Eburones. They had been driven from their lands by their powerful neighbors, the Suebi, but were now receiving embassies from various Gallic states inviting them to continue their progress.[24]

Caesar, who had composed a book setting out his linguistic theories, dedicated to Cicero while heading north, was deeply disturbed by the news of Gallic dealings with the Germans.[25] The legions had been gathered from their winter camps by the time Caesar arrived in the territory of the Belgae, and he now summoned a council of the Gauls where, "soothing and strengthening their minds, he ordered them to provide cavalry and resolved to move directly against the Germans."[26]

When he reached the area around Kessel/Lith, he entered into negotiations with the Usipetes and Tenecteri. When they sent him ambassadors, asking to be allowed to settle in Gaul, Caesar replied that this would not be possible and that it was unreasonable for people who could not defend their own land to expect to be given the land of other people. What Caesar could do, however, was negotiate on their behalf with the Ubii, the powerful German confederation which was centered around the modern city of Cologne.

When the German ambassadors asked Caesar to stay put while they discussed his offer with their people, Caesar, who knew their cavalry were raiding a neighboring state, thought this was a delaying tactic to give time for the cavalry to return. He declined their request. The reader of the *Gallic War* was expected to see how reasonable Caesar was being. These were untrustworthy barbarians, and they soon would prove that. As a new embassy arrived in Caesar's camp, the German cavalry launched a surprise attack which routed Caesar's Gallic cavalry and killed a member of a noble family from Aquitania. Caesar now had no choice, therefore, but to advance on the Germans' camp and massacre them. The detail Caesar offers at this point in his book betrays the controversy that surrounded the massacre when news of it reached Rome. It was interpreted by Cato as an attack, during a period of negotiations, upon a peaceful group of people in violation of the best traditions of Roman diplomacy. (Cato had clearly understood the message about Caesar the traditionalist in earlier communiques.) He recommended that Caesar be turned over to the Germans, following the example of what had happened to a disgraced Roman general during the Spanish wars of the previous century.[27]

Archaeologists have recovered evidence for this battle (or massacre). Human remains showing wounds caused by spears and arrows have been found in the area of Kessel and Lith. The skull of an older man appears to have been smashed with an axe, a woman's skull shows a wound from an arrow or a spear, and that of a younger male had been hacked by a sword. This mixture of ages and genders, as well as dental evidence and articles of clothing of Germanic origin, show that these are people who were not native to the area, while the nature of the injuries to the remains has allowed archaeologists to identify the bodies as being from Caesar's massacre of the Usipetes and Tenecteri, who had been trapped by Caesar on a sliver of land at the confluence of the Meuse and Waal. What the findspot also shows us is that Caesar, having trapped the Germans in a position from which they had little chance to escape, has overstated the level of risk they posed. Given Caesar's theme throughout the *Gallic War* that Germanness represents the antithesis of civilization, this should not be surprising, but it suggests Cato had a point about the brutality with which Caesar handled the situation. Caesar's response is, once again, that those who violate diplomatic norms can expect brutal revenge for their action. In this case, Caesar gave the Gauls a chance to participate in extracting that vengeance from people who were, at least in theory, their ancestral foes.[28]

Having massacred the Usipetes and Tenecteri, Caesar decided to cross the Rhine so that the Germans would learn to respect Roman capabilities and would begin to fear for their own possessions.[29] His decision was reinforced, so he says, when he received an embassy he had sent to another German state who were sheltering members of the Usipetes and Tenecteri who had been away from these peoples' camp when Caesar attacked. These Germans had the gall to tell him that "the Rhine was the boundary of Roman power," and asked him, "if he didn't think it was fair for the Germans to cross into Gaul, why did he think it was reasonable to claim power and control across the Rhine."[30] The tone of this embassy, highly evocative of Ariovistus's earlier conduct, reiterates the "arrogant barbarian theme" as a justification for aggression. That justification was strengthened when the Ubii asked for Caesar's help in resisting the Suebi, the most powerful German nation, and formerly supportive of Ariovistus.

This was the occasion for Caesar's construction of his great bridge across the Rhine, a feat that was probably as much a propaganda exercise, directed at Caesar's critics in Rome, as it was a military action targeting the Germans. Indeed, it took almost as long to build the bridge (ten days) as Caesar would actually spend in Germany (eighteen days). While in Germany, he says, he burnt some villages and destroyed the grain in the fields (he had not yet contemplated composing the passage in Book 6 in which he says that the Germans had no settled agriculture). Having done this, and having discovered the Suebi had withdrawn to the middle of their own territory, thus relieving pressure on the Ubii, Caesar decided "he had done enough to satisfy prestige and utility," so he returned to Gaul, destroying the bridge as he did so.[31]

It was now mid-July, so, in keeping with the summer's program of terrorizing neighbors who had stirred up trouble in Gaul, Caesar decided to make an expedition to Britain. In the previous summer, he said, British tribes had assisted the Veneti, and he now writes that "in almost all the previous Gallic wars they had provided aid to our enemies," and that, having a fleet to hand in the wake of the previous summer's campaign, he decided to raid the island, which, he admits, was virtually unknown to the Gauls. To make up for the Gauls' lack of information, he interviewed numerous merchants who had visited Britain and then sent both a scouting expedition under an officer he could trust, Gaius Volusenus, to select a suitable landing spot, and also a second, diplomatic mission under a Gallic leader, Commius, to negotiate with British groups which had already been in contact with Caesar.[32]

The Roman fleet was probably near modern Boulogne, and Caesar decided two legions would be sufficient for the expedition he was envisioning. There was still some work to be done in Gaul, and the remaining six legions of Caesar's army were entrusted to the legates Cotta and Sabinus.[33] The primary invasion fleet consisted of eighty ships, with a further eighteen detailed to bring a cavalry unit across once the landing was complete. The fleet departed from Boulogne on the evening of September 12, and made landfall in the vicinity of Pegwell Bay in Kent. There, seeing the high ground occupied by British tribesmen, Caesar summoned his senior officers to a meeting on his flagship, where "he told them what he had learned from Volusenus and what he wanted them to do; and instructed them, as military principle demanded, especially in naval matters, which are rapid and unpredictable, that they should carry out his orders instantly when the signal was given." The fleet moved along the coast to an area where it was possible to land, but the Britons on shore had followed the fleet and now filled the beach. As the transports could not approach the shore so the men could disembark directly on the beach, Caesar ordered his warships forward to bombard the Britons with their war engines. When the British, pelted by missiles, had backed off, the standard-bearer of the Tenth Legion leapt into the sea, urging his comrades to follow him so as not to abandon their eagle; as for himself, his comrades would see that he would not fall short of his "duty to the state and to the general."[34] This is one of the few places in the *Gallic War* where an ordinary Roman soldier gives a speech in his own words. In Caesar's account, the speech was successful. The men followed their standard-bearer and, fighting their way ashore under cover from the artillery on the ships, secured the beach.

Just as the description of the landing provides a vivid summary of the principles of Caesarian warfare—the general rapidly adapts his plan to new circumstances, his immediate subordinates follow orders, technology is effectively deployed, and the troops are valiant—so the rest of the campaign in Britain will be as much a political as a military exercise. Embassies of Britons arrive at the Roman camp as soon as it is established, even returning Commius, who had been imprisoned by the people to whom he had been sent as an ambassador. His captors apologize to Caesar and blame the "common people" for their actions.[35] Implicit in his blaming the "common people" is the suggestion that Caesar had received some useful information which had guided his planning of the invasion from local leaders. Now he forgives the British leaders and demands more hostages while he forages for grain.

Then it started to rain. Shortly after the landing, a storm had scattered the transports bringing the cavalry, then another storm had shattered the main fleet. Short of food, and desperate to fix his ships, Caesar did not move inland, but instead sent out foraging parties to make up for the supplies lost in the storm. The obvious weakness of the Roman position encouraged the Britons to attack again, and, again Caesar had to adapt, finding a way to deal with British tactics based on the use of war chariots which delivered men rapidly to the front and enabled them to escape when they needed to.[36] Caesar handled the situation successfully and again the Britons showed up up to negotiate. Caesar ordered them to deliver hostages to him on the mainland, saying he intended to withdraw as soon as possible, which he soon did having spent less than a month on British soil.

Although he had in fact accomplished very little with his raids into Germany and Britain, Caesar seems to have scored a massive propaganda victory at Rome. The Senate voted twenty days of thanksgiving in October to celebrate his expeditions, and more people seem to have looked for ways to join the expanding bureaucracy that was supporting his military and political organization. It appears that a permanent administrative base was now established at Amiens for detaining hostages and concentrating other resources. Plans were being made for a more elaborate invasion of Britain in the coming year, and it appears that Caesar advertised the possibility of obtaining enormous wealth as a result. Since the money didn't materialize, the profit motive doesn't appear in the *Gallic Wars* (though Caesar does mention private entrepreneurs who had sent their own ships along with the fleet to supply the army and profit from the anticipated victory in Britain). Instead, it is from references in Cicero's correspondence that we can discern these expectations of substantial returns. In the wake of the campaign he would make it clear that such hopes were exaggerated: in composing the fifth book of the *Gallic War*, Caesar includes a (rather inaccurate) picture of the Britons. With the exception of those living in the coastal region of Kent, he presents them as nomadic pastoralists living on milk and meat while painting themselves blue. Communities like this would not have the sort of money people in Rome expected from such an expedition.[37]

Money would certainly be on people's minds in Rome, where Caesar would soon be spending a huge amount of it to acquire land for a new forum adjacent to the city's traditional center. This land even included a portion of the Capitoline, which was leveled to make way for the new forum. Cicero, who was involved in these real-estate transactions, put the cost of the real estate at fifteen million *denarii*; later sources put the total cost of construction at twenty-five million. The forum would be centered on a new temple of Venus the Ancestress (Venus Genetrix). Visitors to Rome today will see the remaining columns of the temple rising behind the Senate House northeast of the Capitoline (plate 13). Visually and ideologically, the plan would place the Julii—and the family's claim to a connection with the city's foundation—at the very heart of Rome. The project may also have been intended to overshadow Pompey's theater and temple, completed in 55 in what is now the area of the Largo Argentina on the west side of the Capitoline and out of sight from the Forum.[38]

While building was getting started in Rome, there was also a construction project in Gaul, where a new fleet that could operate more effectively in Britain's coastal waters and transport a much larger army was being assembled. The invasion force would involve a far greater number of Gauls, who were now to be integrated more thoroughly in the Roman administrative system. The creation of a viable system of what Caesar would consider responsible Gallic leadership at the local level was clearly well underway by the spring of 54, when Caesar jokes about it in a letter to Cicero, thanking him for recommending a competent protégé and saying he'll make the next one a "king in Gaul." As the language of this letter suggests, Caesar was now looking to replace annual magistrates with people who would have longer term authority. Another aspect of this plan was to arrange for regular meetings with the Gallic leadership. So it was that one of the first things Caesar did, after his return to Gaul following a winter in which he had a brief encounter with a group which had been raiding his province of Illyria, was to summon a meeting of the Gallic leadership, presumably at Amiens. There, he must have addressed the Gallic leaders from the raised platform upon which Roman governors sat when dealing with their subjects. When the leaders of the Treviri did not appear, Caesar set off at the head of four legions to deal with the controversy that lay at the root of their non-compliance.[39]

The Treviri were a very large and powerful confederation that was split between two leaders, Indutiomarus and Cingetorix, the latter of whom was a keen collaborator with the Romans. Indutiomarus, much less enthusiastically pro-Roman, had gathered the portion of the Treviri's warriors loyal to himself, sending their families to safety in the Ardennes. When Caesar approached the Treveri's territory, a group of "the leaders of the community" met him to explain that Indutiomarus was preventing them from "doing what was in the best interest of their people," language that presumably echoes statements Caesar had been making to the Gauls about the value of political stability under Roman guidance.

As his colleagues were dealing with Caesar, Indutiomarus, realizing that his support was slipping, now changed course and wrote to Caesar, saying the reason he had not come to the meeting was that he was trying to ensure the loyalty of his people to Rome since he feared that if "the nobility departed," the common people would slide into rebellion.[40]

Caesar could recognize nonsense when he heard it, but he also wanted to get on with the invasion of Britain and not waste more time dealing with the Treviri. He therefore allowed Indutiomarus to retain his personal independence but ordered him to meet him in person and deliver two hundred hostages (including all of his male relatives) when he did so. He then met with the whole Treveran leadership to "reconcile them individually with Cingetorix, whose outstanding goodwill toward himself he had recognized. Caesar thought Cingetorix deserved his favor, which would make Cingetorix's influence with his people as strong as possible."[41] The story of Cingetorix offers a case study in the sort of political manipulation Caesar was now engaging in throughout Gaul. Not only did he feel positive personal relationships would be needed, but he also thought that the Romans should rely on multiple informants for their intelligence. Even now he remained very conscious of the highly self-interested nature of the information he was receiving from the Gauls. A second case study follows immediately upon this one: the murder of Dumnorix.

When he returned to Boulogne to begin the invasion of Britain, Caesar found "cavalry from all of Gaul…to the number of four thousand, along with the leaders from all the states." He planned to leave the leaders he could trust behind while taking the others with him so they could not foment revolt while he was away. In the revised version of his account of the Helvetian invasion at the beginning of his term as governor, probably rewritten to justify what now happened several years later, Caesar had stressed Dumnorix's hostile behavior both in helping the Helvetians find their way into Gaul and then in disrupting Aeduan logistical support for the Roman army.[42] Now, Dumnorix had distressed an Aeduan council by announcing that Caesar planned to make him their king. Upon arriving in the Roman camp as the invasion of Britain was being prepared, Dumnorix began to complain about being part of the expedition—partly because he was afraid of the sea and partly because of religious scruples.[43] During the twenty-five days that adverse winds prevented the expedition from sailing, Dumnorix approached other Gallic leaders, telling them Caesar planned to murder them all when they got to Britain. Then, when the winds at last turned in the expedition's favor, he left the camp with a few Aeduan cavalrymen before the fleet could sail. Caesar sent a large force of cavalry in pursuit, with orders to kill Dumnorix if he did not return. When the cavalry caught up to him, Dumnorix refused to turn back and was assassinated.[44] The men who had been accompanying him naturally returned to the Roman camp. The length to which Caesar goes in explaining this event is testimony to Dumnorix's influence. His murder needed to be set in the broader context of Caesar's relationship with the Gallic aristocracy. Pairing Dumnorix's assassination with the milder treatment of Indutiomarus was a way for Caesar to remind his audience that he preferred to avoid extreme measures unless confronted by an extreme provocation.

The Roman fleet left Boulogne and landed once again at Pegwell Bay, though this time there was no resistance. The size of the Roman fleet overawed the Britons, who had seen it approaching. After landing and building a camp to protect the ships, Caesar advanced inland, destroying a fortress now identified as Bigbury Castle near Canterbury. At this point he was recalled to the coast: another storm had wrecked the fleet. After setting the repairs in motion, Caesar resumed his advance inland, having been told that the Britons had united around a leader named Cassivellaunus who was based about seventy-five miles from the coast in the valley of the Thames just north of London. After Caesar battled his way across the river in the face of stiff resistance, Cassivellaunus withdrew to his fortified base, which, it turned out, was unable to hold out against a Roman assault.[45] As he withdrew further inland, Cassivellaunus urged four allied rulers in Kent to attack Caesar's base, which they did without success. That said, the fact the attack took place suggests a high degree of organization on the part of the British resistance, and a strong desire not to be drawn under Roman control as it became clear Caesar was quite willing to become involved in local politics. He had with him the son of a former leader of the Trinobates named Mandubracius, who had come to the Romans during the winter and whom Caesar now restored to leadership over his people.[46]

The determining factor in this campaign was quite possibly the time lost first in dealing with the Treveri at the beginning of the summer and then during the twenty-five-day delay at Boulogne. It was now late September and, with the assistance of Commius, Caesar entered into negotiations with Cassivellaunus. In the resulting treaty, according to which the Britons delivered hostages to the Romans, Cassivellaunus agreed to leave Mandubracius in power and to pay an annual tribute (none of which appears ever to have been paid). These terms enabled Caesar to claim victory.[47] Yet one of Caesar's legates, Cicero's younger brother Quintus, conceded that there had not been much reason for either fear or rejoicing in the campaign.[48]

Even as the campaign in Britain was wrapping up, Caesar had received news of a great personal tragedy. His daughter Julia, Pompey's wife, had died. Her death had stemmed from complications arising from the birth of her first child, who died shortly after she did. She was a popular figure in her own right, and after her eulogies had been pronounced in the Forum a crowd seized her body and buried it in the Campus Martius. Caesar, whose love for her was well known, is said to have borne the news of her death stoically.[49]

As the army settled into winter quarters, its senior officers engaged in various literary activities. Quintus Cicero was writing a poem on the British campaign and sharing his thoughts with his brother, who was composing his own poem on the same subject.[50] Another legate, Aurunculeius Cotta, seems to have finished a poem on the first British campaign of the previous year. Some poems of Catullus may have arrived in Gaul, including the poet's attack on Mamurra and his suggestion that Mamurra's relationship with Caesar was of a physical nature. When he arrived back in northern Italy, Caesar would talk to Catullus's father about this and would invite the poet to lunch. Another poem circulating in the Roman camp at this time, albeit in draft form, was Lucretius's *De rerum natura* (*On the Nature of Things*), a brilliant exposition of Epicurean philosophy. Quintus Cicero acknowledged that there were signs of genius in what he read, and Caesar would echo elements of the poem in the last three books of the *Gallic War*. He no doubt appreciated the allusion to his new forum and temple of Venus in the poem's decidedly non-Epicurean opening invocation of *Aeneadum genetrix, hominum divumque voluptas / alma Venus*: "Ancestress of the race of Aeneas, delight of mortals and gods, nurturing Venus."[51]

As Lucretius's poem was making the rounds of Caesar's camp, it became clear that Gaius Memmius, to whom the poem was dedicated, ought to have devoted himself to philosophy, as the poet advised. But he had not. Hoping to be elected consul for 53, he had conspired with another candidate, despite having Caesar's support, to bribe the sitting consuls with the promise of enhanced provincial commands or payment of two million sesterces each. Then, losing his nerve after months of rumors that something foul was afoot, Memmius read the agreement out in the Senate! The upcoming consular elections were put off into the next year. Cicero said that Caesar was not happy with Memmius, which may be an understatement.[52]

Blatant electoral corruption was not the only problem facing Rome. Crassus had departed for Syria (being cursed by a tribune on his way out of the city) before the end of 55. Now Crassus was preparing to invade Parthia with a substantial army he had brought with him from Italy even though the Senate had not approved the operation. Crassus's biographer does say that Caesar had written from Gaul to support Crassus's project, which is likely true since Caesar had sent the younger Crassus with some Gallic cavalry to join his father. In any event, the deal giving Crassus Syria for five years was plainly not intended as a vacation plan.[53] The catastrophe that ensued in the summer of 53 would go down as the worst defeat suffered by a Roman army since the destruction of two consular armies by the Cimbrians and Teutons at Arausio in 105.

13

Rebellion and Reconstruction

Caesar's political restructuring of Gaul did not please everyone, and the events of the months following his return from Britain showed there was much to be done if Caesar was going to be able to make the region a stable addition to the Roman empire. Caesar's decision, despite the political chaos gripping Rome, not to depart for northern Italy at the end of 54 as soon as his legions were distributed in their winter camps throughout the lands of the Belgae suggests he believed trouble was brewing. And he was right.

The first issue arose among the Carnutes, a state that had come under Roman influence because of the Remi's decision to join with Caesar. Their tribal center was around Orléans in the Loire valley, and Caesar had supported Tasget, a man he described as being of very noble birth, as the tribe's ruler. For three years, Tasget had provided "outstanding service" to Caesar and had a positive personal relationship with him. Suddenly, however, Tasget was murdered. Caesar dispatched a legion under his legate Munatius Plancus to investigate the situation and arrest those who were responsible.[1]

There was also trouble brewing among the Treveri, where Indutiomarus was still active, and it appears that he was in contact with other tribal leaders. His message, Caesar surmised, was that tribal leaders could only be secure in their traditional positions if the Romans were eliminated.[2] The distribution of Caesar's legions in separate camps over a distance of about ninety miles (because a poor harvest made it impossible for them

to be concentrated in a single base) meant that individual garrisons did
not have local superiority in numbers. Indutiomarus's messengers had
found an audience in Ambiorix and Cativolcus, leaders of the Eburones,
a state centered around the modern Belgian city of Tongeren, about
eighty miles east of the Rhine.[3] Of the two men, Ambiorix was certainly
the dominant partner and, these days, visitors to Tongeren will find a
statue of him in the town square (plate 8). In that same square, they can
also enjoy a beer named for him. He is today seen as a hero of Belgian
independence. That is one possible view. Another possible view is that
his poor judgement resulted in the destruction of his people. Whichever
view one wishes to take, he was an immensely clever adversary who thoroughly outwitted Sabinus and Cotta, the legates whose forces had been
assigned winter quarters in his territory.

Upon arrival among the Eburones, the Romans led by Sabinus and
Cotta had been greeted with a supply of grain, and all seemed well. But
after they had been in camp for fifteen days, a mass of Eburones had
attacked Roman troops who had been detailed to gather wood and had
then assaulted the walls of the camp itself. When the first attack was
driven off, the Romans sent ambassadors to Ambiorix to find out what
was going on. Ambiorix told these ambassadors how indebted he was to
Caesar, who had freed his people from the tribute they had formerly
paid the Atuatuci and had also returned Ambiorix's son and nephew,
who had been given to the Atuatuci as hostages. With these expressions
of gratitude, Ambiorix presented himself as the ideal local politician of
the sort Caesar was promoting—all the more so because it was the common people who had insisted on attacking the camp. Nor was Ambiorix
so stupid as to think his people had the capacity to defeat the Romans.
The problem, Ambiorix explained, was that other Gauls had made a
plan to attack the legions quartered in their territory on the same day,
thus preventing the separate Roman forces from supporting each other.
And they were bringing in Germans to help: the ones coming Ambriorix's
way would be there in two days! The Romans would be smart if they
took themselves off to join either Quintus Cicero, who was encamped in
the territory of the Nervii, or Labienus.[4]

The ambassadors repeated Ambiorix's statements to Sabinus and Cotta. A fight broke out. Neither legate could believe the "minor and weak nation of the Eburones" would dare make war on the Roman people. Cotta took the view that they should do nothing. They had plenty of food and could defend themselves in their camp against any number of Gauls and Germans. They shouldn't leave without an order from Caesar, and it was a bad idea to take advice from an enemy. In making these arguments, Cotta displayed the qualities of a good officer, insisting on proper evaluation of intelligence sources, consideration of logistics, and obedience to the general's instructions. It was important for Caesar's audience to be reminded that the legion had not actually been exposed to a dangerous situation.[5]

Sabinus responded there was no time to waste with the Germans on their way, and there was the prospect of another camp's being destroyed if they stayed put. Caesar was probably in Italy, which would explain the murder of Tasget and why the Eburones were acting up. The Germans were upset by Ariovistus's defeat, while the Gauls were distressed by their own repeated defeats, which had cost them their previous reputation for military virtue. Sabinus here summarizes the political situation Caesar had been trying to resolve. What he is saying answers the question of why Caesar's command needed to be extended. Unfortunately, his view as to how best to manage the immediate situation was catastrophically wrong. So too was his conduct. An army was not a democracy. Caesar had made that very clear when he addressed the troops at Vesontio. Sabinus, who raised his voice so he could be overheard by the troops when he predicted dire ruin if they didn't leave the next morning, was violating the basic rules governing the conduct of a senior officer. Cotta, unfortunately, was bullied into agreeing with him.[6]

Trying to withdraw from the Eburones' territory, the Romans walked straight into the ambush Ambiorix had set at either end of a valley through which the troops had to pass. In this crisis, the two commanders again form a study in contrasts. Sabinus behaved "as one who had foreseen nothing" and panicked. Cotta behaved as a general should, encouraging the men and responding to the difficult situation.

The troops were stretched out in a long line and encumbered by their baggage, so Cotta ordered the men to abandon their gear and form a circle—"a plan which, in a mess of this sort, must not be criticized." That Caesar should write this suggests someone had in fact criticized or questioned Cotta's judgement. His order, unfortunately, disheartened the Romans, who broke ranks to grab their favored possessions from the baggage train. This encouraged the Gauls, who showed remarkable discipline, having been told by their leaders to leave things be since they would be able to collect all the loot from the Romans once the battle was won.[7]

Through eight hours of fighting, neither side could win a decisive advantage. During that time, Cotta and the Roman force's two senior centurions were still on their feet. Once Cotta was wounded, and the senior centurions were killed, Sabinus spotted Ambiorix. Although Cotta declared he would not deal with an armed enemy, Sabinus and some of his military tribunes nevertheless went to speak with Ambiorix. Ambiorix told them to lay down their arms. They did. And then he killed them. The Gauls pressed the attack. Cotta died fighting, as did most of the soldiers. Others, who had fought their way back to the camp, committed suicide during the night. Only a few of the men managed to reach Labienus's camp.[8]

Aside from illustrating Caesar's views on the way an army should be run, Caesar's description of this battle would remind his audience of another battle that had occurred some months after this one. It took place outside Carrhae (Harran) in modern Turkey. There too the collapse of the Roman army had followed upon the treacherous assassination of its general. In this case the general was Crassus.[9] Someone would have to fix the resulting mess, but as of 50, when Caesar's book was published, the Senate had been incapable of finding a solution. The *Gallic War* would show its readers who could provide that solution. In the meantime, there was still a war going in Gaul. Ambiorix rode to meet his immediate neighbors, the Atuatuci (the ones Caesar had not sold into slavery) and the Nervii, urging them to join him in an attack on the camp of Quintus Cicero, which was in the Nervii's territory. The Nervii summoned forces from a number of client states and set out to attack Cicero before news of what had happened to Sabinus and Cotta could reach him.[10]

Caesar's illustration of the principles of leadership continues with his description of the conduct of Quintus Cicero. As soon as Quintus realized there was going to be trouble, he wrote to Caesar. At no point did he negotiate with the Nervii, who were besieging his camp with great vigor. The defense of the camp was complicated by the fact that the Gauls had learned about siege warfare by watching the Romans, and they also "secretly held some captives from the army," who showed them how to build Roman-style siege works. Still, Cicero's men resisted, even when the Gauls set fire to the buildings inside the camp. They also had before their eyes the example of superb courage offered by two experienced centurions, Vorenus and Pullo (competitors for the position of the legion's senior centurion), who sallied forth from the camp and protected each other in the combat that followed.[11]

Caesar was now on the way from Amiens at the head of two legions. He had hoped to have three, but Labienus, writing to inform him about what had happened to Sabinus and Cotta, also told him that the Treveri were acting up and that Labienus's garrison would be required to deal with them. "Caesar approved of Labienus' assessment of the situation" and continued to advance, though with an army that was only two-thirds the size he had hoped for.[12] When the Nervii heard Caesar was coming, they abandoned their siege of Quintus Cicero's camp and moved rapidly to intercept him. With only 7,000 men under his command, it is quite likely Caesar was seriously outnumbered even if the Nervii didn't have anything like the 60,000 men he claims they did. When the Nervii arrived in Caesar's vicinity, he did not lead his army out to form a line of battle but drew the Nervii into an attack on his camp. When they were disordered by their attack on the camp walls, Caesar had his cavalry lead a sortie from all four of the camp's gates, which routed the unprepared enemy.[13]

When Caesar reached Cicero's camp, he held a meeting to congratulate Cicero and praise the officers whom Cicero singled out for their outstanding courage (this presumably included Vorenus and Pullo). The next day he held another meeting in which

> he consoled and encouraged the troops. The damage had been caused by the folly and rash conduct of a legate. He said this should be borne with equanimity because, through the beneficence of the immortal gods and their own courage, the damage had been set right; there was no extended joy for the enemy nor further grief for themselves.[14]

News of the relief of Cicero's camp, brought to Labienus by the Remi, caused Indutiomarus to abandon his effort to attack Labienus's forces. Caesar returned to Amiens and remained there throughout the winter with three legions, looking out for signs of further trouble. He wrote that Gallic tribes were in constant communication about when a new war might begin and were "holding nocturnal meetings in deserted places." But nothing happened. "Caesar held the largest part of Gaul in obedience, summoning the leaders of each state to meetings with him, terrifying some, and encouraging others."[15]

The only place where there was still trouble was along the northern border. The Eburones and Nervii looked to the Treveri and were offering to help Indutiomarus eliminate Labienus. At the same time, the Senones, their neighbors to the southwest, chased out the leader Caesar had supported and looked to join forces with the Carnutes whose murder of Tasget had not yet been punished. Indutiomarus held a general meeting of the Treveri, which caused the pro-Roman Cingetorix to flee to Labienus's camp. But when Indutiomarus approached the camp, a sudden sortie by the cavalry scattered his forces. Indutiomarus was killed as he fled, and the situation throughout Gaul grew somewhat calmer.[16]

Caesar's conclusion regarding the cause of these events is that when a leader can be found who is willing to start a war this makes a great impression on "barbarous peoples." He felt that he could trust no Gallic people other than the Remi and the Aedui, the latter because of their longstanding allegiance to Rome, the former because of their service in the recent conflicts. "I think [the restiveness of the Gauls] is scarcely to be wondered at," he wrote, "for a number of reasons, but most of all because they used to excel through their courage in war, and were deeply upset at having so ruined this reputation that they had to bow to the commands of the Roman people."[17]

The fifth book of the *Gallic War* ends with Indutiomarus's death, and Caesar's discussion of the cause of Gallic discontent was most likely composed in the campaign's immediate aftermath in order to complete the tale of Caesar's first five years and show why there was need for him to stay on in Gaul. The sixth book, most likely completed, as we've seen, in 51, opens by stressing the crucial political theme of the moment. This was the value of Caesar's association with Pompey. By 51 that relationship was under stress.[18] People, Pompey included, needed a reminder that the alignment of the two men kept Rome safe, and only bad things could come from an open break between them.

As 54 turned to 53, Caesar plainly needed more men, having lost nearly a quarter of the army with Sabinus and Cotta. Remaining legions were understrength. Caesar sent three legates to raise new troops in the anticipation of further fighting in the new year. Happily, Pompey, "who was staying around the city with *imperium* for the sake of the state," sent the troops he had raised from Cisalpine Gaul for his Spanish garrison to support Caesar. They amounted to a legion, and Caesar writes it was immensely important for the Gauls to realize the vastness of Italy's resources, which could repair any damage the Romans sustained. With Pompey's aid three new legions were ready by the end of the winter— twice the number of men as had been lost with Sabinus.[19]

Unpredictability could be a good thing. Caesar was aware the Gauls could anticipate the beginning of a Roman campaigning season in the spring, and so he began his operations before winter ended, when the Gauls' preparations were still incomplete. Caesar notes that the Senones, still conspiring with their neighbors the Carnutes, did not show up at Amiens when he ordered them to do so. They were also in communication with the Treveri, who were themselves trying to get help from Germans, as was Ambiorix and the united group of the Aduatuci, Nervii, and Morini (the state which occupied the southern Netherlands).

The way Caesar divides these groups up shows the importance he attached to good intelligence: knowing they were still not coordinated with each other and still not ready to take the field, he would be able to deal with them in turn. The Nervii were the first group he attacked. Their lands were ravaged by the four legions quartered at Amiens. They submitted. Then, transferring the spring meeting of the Gallic peoples to Paris, Caesar would be able to move against the Senones and Carnutes when they didn't appear. They were still not ready to fight and sent ambassadors to offer hostages. The process was mediated by the Aedui in the case of the Senones, and by the Remi in the case of the Carnutes, driving home the point that loyalty to Caesar resulted in greater local influence.[20]

It was time now to deal with Ambiorix and the Treveri. The attack on the land of the Eburones (and, coincidentally that of their allies the Menapii) was a massacre. Archaeologists who have studied the region have uncovered a massive decline in population in the middle of the first century BCE. The population gradually recovered in the course of the century's second half or during the early first century CE, with the replacement of the departed population by settlers from beyond the Rhine. While it would be wrong to assert that every abandoned settlement was a victim of Caesar, the overall pattern of abandonment in this one area does look like a direct result of what Caesar himself says was a program of mass destruction justified by the attack on Sabinus and Cotta. There was no big battle that summer. The Menapii sent ambassadors to Caesar after he had ravaged their lands, while the Eburones and others, in no position to resist the enlarged Roman army, withdrew into the forests of the Ardennes. Caesar says that Ambiorix himself escaped across the Rhine. His colleague, Catuvolcus, committed suicide, cursing Ambiorix.[21]

While there were no big battles in Gaul, there was action in Germany. Germans had been coming to the assistance of the Treviri, still up in arms and now led by Indutiomarus's relations. Labienus, who had received reinforcements from the enlarged Roman army, routed their forces before they could fully muster their strength, meanwhile giving a speech that must have warmed Caesar's heart (which is presumably why Caesar included it in his book). Labienus told his men to show "the same courage to us as your leaders as you have so often shown the general. Imagine that he himself is here to watch you."[22]

Having finished the first part of his campaign against the Menapii, Caesar decided to follow up Labienus's action against the German allies of the Treviri with an invasion of Germany itself. There were two reasons to do this. First of all, the Germans had responded favorably to requests of help from Indutiomarus, even if nothing much had actually happened. Second, Caesar wanted to make sure they would not provide Ambiorix with refuge. Building a bridge close to the spot he had used for his previous bridge two years before, Caesar advanced into the territory of the Ubii. The Ubii assured Caesar of their loyalty, offered more hostages, and pointed to their neighbors, the Suebi, as the real problem. When the Suebi heard of Caesar's approach, they withdrew into their forest lairs. At this point Caesar decided it was time to go home. Given that the Germans didn't practice agriculture, pursuit would be a logistical nightmare.[23] The whole thought process as presented here is classic Caesar: the initial decision is a reaction to threats of aggression, the plan is changed on the basis of fresh intelligence, and Caesar understands that the key to a successful operation is adequate logistical support.

Returning from Germany, Caesar continued the devastation of northern Belgium. While this was happening, the army was barely spared another catastrophe at Tongeren—an example of the power in war of Fortune, who makes more appearances as an active agent in Book 6 of the *Gallic War* than in any other.[24] Caesar had left the baggage train at Tongeren under Quintus Cicero's command. Unbeknownst to the Romans, a large band of cavalry from the Sugumbri—very bad people, as Caesar reminds his readers, who had given refuge to the surviving Usipetes and Tenecteri—had crossed the Rhine, looking for easy plunder. Having intended to plunder the Eburones, they changed their mind when they heard the Roman camp was in their vicinity.

Cicero had been careful to follow Caesar's orders, keeping his men safely in camp. After eight days, however, the men complained they were being kept under virtual siege and demanded a chance to go out and collect food. Cicero gave in to their request and, suddenly, the Germans attacked. They would have taken the camp were it not for the valiant behavior of Sextus Baculus, who had been left in the camp because he was sick and who rallied the troops to keep the Germans out. Caesar commented on the illogic of the Germans, who, having intended to ravage the Eburones, had in fact done Ambiorix a great favor by diverting the Romans from pursuing him.[25] A greater diversion would follow during the following winter.

The political situation at Rome, chaotic ever since the bribery scandal had disrupted the consular elections for 53, took a turn for the worse on January 19, 52. Late in the day, Milo murdered Clodius when the two men and their entourages encountered each other near Bovillae on the Appian Way. That night, Clodius's servants brought his body to his house on the Palatine, where his wife Fulvia and supporters (including Sulla's grandson, Caesar's former brother-in-law) displayed it to the crowd gathering around the house. The next morning, having assembled a huge crowd in the Forum to view the body, Sextus Clodius carried the corpse into the Senate House, which the crowd then set fire to. The Basilica Porcia, which abutted the Senate House, went up in flames too. Mobs wandered through the city, finally appearing near Pompey's garden, adjacent to what is now the Villa Borghese, and asking for him to be named either consul or dictator to deal with the chaos in Rome.[26] The situation was complicated by the absence of elected magistrates for the year. Despite the crisis following Crassus's disaster at Carrhae and a subsequent Parthian raid into Syria, political squabbling had forced the elections to be postponed into the new year. This quarrel came in the wake of the electoral scandal in 54, which meant that no new consuls had taken office until July of 53. By that time, chaos reigned in the streets while Milo stood for consul and Clodius for praetor.[27] Now, before the elections could even be held, Clodius was dead.

Violence continued in the weeks following Clodius's funeral. After mobs had prevented successive *interreges* from naming new consuls for a whole month, the Senate convened on February 18 to pass a version of the "ultimate decree," asking Pompey, the tribunes, and the sitting magistrates to take whatever action was needed to bring order to the city. Pompey responded by calling in soldiers he had raised, in theory, to be part of the garrison in his province of Spain. Legal actions were brought against Milo for murder and against various Clodian supporters for promoting disorder. Caesar, meanwhile, used the emergency decree as an excuse to raise an additional legion.[28]

A solution to the trouble in Rome could not be reached without Caesar's input, and he stayed at Ravenna, where he discussed possible options with Cicero, among others. The issue, for Caesar, was that any solution giving Pompey a great deal of additional power should not be allowed to impinge too seriously upon his position. It took two months after Clodius's murder for an agreement to be reached. Pompey would be sole consul—a major constitutional innovation—and would introduce laws to end the political chaos of the past few years while at the same time protecting the interests of Caesar, who announced he would stand for election to the consulship of 48, when his second term in Gaul would finally be up. The first of the bills intended to settle things was brought by the whole board of tribunes, stating that Caesar could stand for election without giving up his *imperium*: in order that he could remain governor of his provinces until after his election as consul, he would be granted *ratio absentis*, or the right of standing for election *in absentia*. But the signs his relationship with Pompey was beginning to break down would start to appear within months. The opening of Book 7 of the *Gallic War*, wherein Caesar states that he departed for Gaul when he learned that "affairs in the city had been brought into a better state through the virtue of Gnaeus Pompey," was a reminder to his audience of better times between the two of them.[29]

While the political situation in Rome was being sorted out, a massive conspiracy was taking shape in Gaul. Caesar's description of what was going on fits all too neatly into his paradigm for Gallic unrest. The initial outbreak was inspired by rumors that unrest at Rome was detaining Caesar in Italy. Those rumors caused Gauls to speak more openly about their grievances, and members of the Gallic leadership began to start meeting in the woods. They expressed anger at the fate of Acco, the leader of the Carnutes who had murdered and replaced Tasget, and they feared they would suffer the same fate: Caesar had had him flogged and decapitated at the end of the campaign in 53. Caesar had plainly underestimated the hostility to Tasget and the level of resentment arising from his recent relocation of his headquarters from Amiens to Orléans, the chief settlement of the Carnutes. He had suddenly imposed a high level of Roman intervention in an area where there had not previously been any direct presence.[30]

The new circumstances facing the Carnutes might not have been such a problem if Caesar had been present, so his claim that the murder of Clodius was a factor in the outbreak is not altogether lacking in credibility. All the Carnutes could see was that their chief city was occupied by a lot of Roman bureaucrats and had become the logistical base for an army they might reasonably expect would become a bigger factor in their lives in the summer to come (why else would these people be around?). So it was that two of the Carnutes, Gutuatrus and Conconnetodumnus, men Caesar describes as "thugs," gathered a sufficient force to wipe out the Romans at Orléans. Caesar's appraisal of these two is not totally unfair, for they don't seem to have had a plan for what to do next. In that sense they were not very different from Ambiorix, whose plan for what would happen once he killed the Romans in his territory relied very heavily on magical thinking.[31]

Neither Gutuatrus and Conconnetodumnus reappear in Caesar's account of the year 52. Instead, we're told that their actions inspired Vercingetorix, a young nobleman of the Arveni (plate 14), the state immediately to the south, to seek the leadership of his people with an anti-Roman agenda. We'll be returning to the significance of what Caesar has to say about him when we turn to the complete breakdown of Caesar's relationship with Pompey in our next chapter. For now, it is significant that Vercingetorix succeeded in organizing a coup d'état, overthrowing the leaders of his state when they had rejected his claim to the kingship. He then built an alliance with other groups west of the Massif

Central who had not hitherto been engaged in direct conflict with the Romans. There was no reaction from the Roman garrison in Gaul, which was still based in Belgium and along the Rhine. Caesar's hierarchical organization did not leave space for initiative when the unexpected occurred. For there to be a response, Caesar needed to rejoin his army.[32]

For Vercingetorix to be successful, he would need more people in his alliance. To this end he advanced north into the land of the Biturges, a people subject to the Aedui in the vicinity of the Loire Valley. Now freed from the aftermath of the Clodian crisis, Caesar began his own campaign. Anticipating Vercingetorix's move towards the Biturges (it was an obvious move on Vercingetorix's part) he led a raid into the southern portion of Arvenian territory, counting on the element of surprise. He had crossed the Cervennes despite a significant snow cover (it was early March by our calendar) and he ordered his cavalry to range as widely as possible, setting fire to Gallic villages to give the impression that he had a much larger force than he actually had. He then recrossed the mountains to join the legions he had ordered to assemble near Vienne. In response to Caesar's raid, Vercingetorix halted his northward movement, and then decided to attack a city belonging to the Boii on the western slopes of the Cervennes. The Boii were tributary to the Aedui, and the move was in keeping with Vercingetorix's plan of detaching the Aedui from their longstanding alliance with Caesar.[33]

It was still early in the year for a Roman army to take the field. Caesar explains that he needed to balance political issues against logistical ones. It was April when he joined the full army near Sens, and he was concerned the supply train would get bogged down if he started a full-scale campaign in the early spring. On the other hand, Caesar says, if he allowed Vercingetorix to take over the Aedui's tributary states, it would be a great disgrace and would alienate his Gallic supporters. That was a greater danger than difficulties with supply, so Caesar asked the Aedui to send what grain they could, sent emissaries to the Gauls now threatened by Vercingetorix, and began marching in the direction of Orléans with eight legions, having detached two others to protect the base at Sens.[34]

Caesar reached Orléans well ahead of Gallic expectations, having captured the town of Vellanodunum along the way after overawing its defenders. On the evening of Caesar's arrival at Orléans, the population of the city tried to abandon it. Caesar, who had anticipated their action, stormed the city as the inhabitants were trying to leave it and then moved on into the territory of the Biturges, where he captured the city of Noviodunum (Neung-sur-Beuvron) virtually under the nose of Vercingetorix's advance guard.[35]

Caesar's strategy was very much a mirror image of Vercingetorix's, the point being to demonstrate that the Romans' new adversary could not protect his friends. Vercingetorix was indeed worried about the effect of this strategy, but even more worried about getting his army locked into encounters where the Romans would have the advantage of fixed positions. Caesar has Vercingetorix outline his own strategy, which was to abandon all towns "unless their fortifications and natural defenses protected them from all danger" and to concentrate on cutting off Roman foragers, which he said his Gauls should be able to do because they had superior cavalry.[36]

The operational soundness of Vercingetorix's plan—which does actually seem to have been his own creation and not something Caesar invented and put in his mouth—was proved by the course of the rest of the campaign as Caesar tried to pin him down to fixed positions in what became a series of sieges during the course of the summer. The first of these would be at Avaricum, near the modern city of Bourges, which Caesar captured after a difficult operation. After that came the siege of Gergovia, located on a steep hill near Clermont Ferrand, and finally there was the siege of Alesia, where Vercingetorix would finally be crushed.

The siege of Avaricum proved more difficult than Caesar had anticipated as a result of Aeduan incompetence. They had failed to provide sufficient grain, causing severe shortages in the Roman camp. So great was the suffering that Caesar approached each legion in turn and told his troops he would abandon the siege if conditions were too harsh for them. Despite the soldiers' hardships, "not a word was heard from them that was unworthy of the majesty of the Roman people or their own previous victories." When the army complained that Caesar had not ordered it forward into the swamp where Vercingetorix had hidden his troops away from the Romans, he had to explain that he appreciated their willingness to go to any lengths to win him glory but also felt that it would be a terrible injustice if he did not hold their lives more precious than his own. This army was very different from the one that had worried about the Germans at Vesontio. It was now the highly motivated agent of its general's ambition.[37]

When Caesar finally captured Avaricum in early June after a siege lasting nearly a month, he seized its large store of grain and remained there for a few days. He then found it necessary to attend a meeting of the Aedui, who were themselves in the midst of a political crisis as a dispute over the tribe's leadership had broken out between two men named Convictolitavis and Cotus. Caesar, deciding this dispute, pointed out that Cotus could not legally be elected to the leadership since his brother had been leader the year before and the laws of the Aedui held that a person could not succeed his brother in office or even serve on the tribal council at the same time as his brother. In explaining his resolution of this conflict, Caesar stresses he is simply preserving their traditions. He also says he feared civil strife among the Aedui would cause them to start listening to Vercingetorix. Clearly Vercingetorix was behind the malcontents. Unfortunately for Caesar, Convictolitavis would turn out to be one of those malcontents.[38]

Returning to the army, Caesar divided his forces so that Labienus, with four legions, could ensure the tribes in the vicinity of Paris would not join the revolt. Caesar would manage Vercingetorix with the other six. The armies of Caesar and Vercingetorix moved south, with the Romans keeping to the east bank of the Allier and the Gauls to the west, heading towards the great fortress city of Gergovia. The location of the heavily fortified city atop a high plateau was typical of major population centers, but Gergovia was (and is) more difficult to access than most (plate 9).

When Vercingetorix arrived at Gergovia, he built a camp to house a portion of his army outside the city walls so the Romans could not establish themselves on the plateau outside the city. Caesar writes that, when he saw the place, he knew he had no hope of taking it by storm. He prepared to lay siege, but held off building extensive siege works until he could secure the necessary supplies from the surrounding countryside for what promised to be a lengthy operation. He did, however, occupy a hill to the south of the plateau so as to cut the Gauls off from ready access to water and forage. That was when things started to go south with the Aedui.[39]

Convictolitavis had taken bribes from the Arveni, so Caesar says, to give his attention to a group of young men of anti-Roman disposition. Their leader was a man named Litivaccus. Convictolitavis met with this group, telling them that Aeduan loyalty to Rome was all that stood in the way of a great Gallic victory. He placed Litivaccus in command of a large detachment of cavalry that was to accompany Romans bringing supplies to the army. When the Aeduan column was about thirty miles from Gergovia, Litivaccus summoned a meeting of the troops and told them that the Romans had recently murdered two young members of the Aedui's tribal leadership, Eporedorix and Viridomarus, also killing the elite cavalry they had with them. In fact, this had not happened and both men were still alive. Still, the Aedui believed Litivaccus. Enraged, they turned on the Romans who were with them, murdering them all.

Eporedorix, who was in the Aeduan camp when all this was going on, fled to Caesar, urging him to prevent the permanent defection of the Aeduan cavalry to Vercingetorix. If that happened, it could result in the immediate defection of the rest of the state since those cavalrymen had many important relatives. Caesar set out with four of his legions to try and resolve the situation, which he did by sending Eporedorix and Virodomarus ahead to show their colleagues that they were still alive. This ended—for now—the Aeduan rebellion, and Litivaccus fled with his personal followers to join Vercingetorix, who had taken advantage of Caesar's departure to launch a vigorous, if unsuccessful attack on the Roman lines.[40]

Caesar was plainly not confident the situation with the Aedui was entirely resolved, even though he now had a substantial force of their cavalry with his own army at Gergovia. He therefore thought it was time to withdraw from Gergovia and rejoin Labienus in the region around Paris. But first he wanted to score a success so it would not look as if he was withdrawing for fear of an extended rebellion. The situation on the plateau offered an opportunity for just this sort of limited success.[41] Vercingetorix had established a line of camps outside the city walls on the plateau's western edge and had constructed a six-foot wall along the eastern edge, facing the Roman camp at La Roche Blanc. Caesar decided to launch a raid to destroy the wall and wreck the encampments. Five legions would attack from the south while the Aedui launched a diversionary raid on the plateau's eastern side.

Initially the attack went as planned. The Romans overwhelmed the defensive wall and the camps, but then did not hear the signal for withdrawal which Caesar had issued first to the Tenth Legion, which was with him on the right wing: there was a good deal of distance between the various Roman units. The Roman soldiers also failed to listen to their senior officers, who tried to restrain them as they were "carried away by the hope for quick victory, the enemy's flight, and the successful battles of the past." Eager to follow up their initial success, they approached the city walls but found they couldn't scale them, and the Gallic troops took advantage of the fact that the Romans had broken formation and were becoming tired; the Romans had also spotted the Aedui, whom they wrongly identified as a Gallic force advancing on the Romans' flank. The four legions still on the plateau were driven back with heavy losses, though the Gallic pursuit was halted when the Tenth and Thirteenth Legions, which were not on the plateau, came up to support their fleeing comrades. Caesar says that forty-six centurions and nearly seven hundred men were lost.[42]

Aware that the news of this reverse was likely to encourage an Aeduan revolt, Caesar first held an inquiry to find out what had gone wrong, and then, hoping to give the impression that he would not be leaving the area, challenged the Gauls to battle on the plain during the next two days. On the third day, however, he headed north to join Labienus. Shortly thereafter, the Aedui rebelled against Rome and joined Vercingetorix.[43]

Labienus, meanwhile, was still operating around Paris when news came of the withdrawal from Gergovia. At the same time, the Bellovaci, the southernmost Belgic state learned of the change in the Aedui's allegiance. As a consequence, they too decided to join Vercingetorix. Defeating his enemies around Paris, but avoiding contact with the Bellovaci, Labienus withdrew to Sens, picked up the army's baggage train and shortly thereafter joined Caesar.[44] The focus of the campaign would now shift east of the Cervennes.

As Caesar was linking up with Labienus, a meeting of Gallic states was held at Bibracte. Caesar implies that Eporedorix and Viridomarus now expected to take command of the operations against Rome, but the ambassadors who assembled at Bibracte insisted that Vercingetorix be given the overall command, ignoring Aeduan complaints that they were being ejected "from the leadership of Gaul." Absent from the meeting were the tribes bordering the Aedui to the north—the Remi, Lingones, and Treveri. While the Gauls reorganized, Caesar planned the next phase of the campaign. He needed to be able to match Vercingetorix's cavalry. Having lost many of his own Gallic allies, who had provided most of the Romans' mounted troops, Caesar recruited a substantial number of German mercenaries. Worried also about the security of the province of Transalpine Gaul, he gave instructions to his cousin, Lucius Caesar, who had joined him as a legate and was now in command of twenty-two newly raised cohorts, and took up a position south of the Lingones so he would be able to reinforce Lucius if Vercingetorix moved against him.[45]

It was not just the situation in Gaul that was moving against Caesar. Back in Rome, Pompey was now aligning himself more closely with Caesar's long-term rivals. In July, at roughly the same time as news of the failure at Gergovia and the defection of the Aedui would have come to Rome, Pompey remarried. His wife was the daughter of Quintus Caecilius Metellus Pius Scipio Nasica, a member of one of the Roman nobility's most ancient families and a well-known enemy of Caesar. Pompey also supported a law stating that all candidates for office had to make a personal declaration of their intent in Rome, thereby invalidating the law of the ten tribunes that would have allowed Caesar to stand for consul without returning to the city, and passed a law, based upon a proposal made by Cato in 53 and even more threatening to Caesar's interests, that there should be a five-year interval between a provincial governorship and the tenure of a magistracy at Rome. He also had his command in Spain extended for another five years.[46] On this model, there would only be one great provincial command once Caesar's came to an end—if Vercingetorix didn't end it ahead of schedule. Pompey's actions suggest he saw Caesar's defeat as a definite possibility.

Overconfidence, however, would do Vercingetorix in. After a lull in the action of several weeks, he summoned a council of war and ordered his cavalry to launch an attack on Caesar's army while it was on the march, hoping for a repeat of what the Eburones had done to Sabinus and Cotta. The battle, fought near Alise-Sainte-Reine, did not work out as he had hoped. Caesar deployed his cavalry behind his marching column and had the baggage placed within a square formed by the legions which could advance as needed to support the cavalry. When the German mercenaries defeated the troops facing them on the right and attacked the infantry around Vercingetorix, his army turned in flight, taking refuge around the town situated atop the hill where Alise-Sainte-Reine sits today (plate 10).[47] Caesar says that three leaders of the Aedui were captured. His stress on this point suggests that he was planning to use them to help repair his relationship with the Aedui once the campaign against Vercingetorix reached what was now its obvious conclusion.

Caesar immediately began to build massive siege works enclosing Vercingetorix's troops on the hilltop. There were a few days of skirmishes between the men in the town and the Romans manning the growing fortifications until Vercingetorix sent his cavalry away, telling them to approach allied tribes to ask for a relief force since there were a mere thirty days' supplies in the town. Caesar in the meantime swept up the region's available grain, specifying that his foragers were to extend their operations to some distance from the camp.[48] Logistics would set the terms for the final battle. Caesar could predict that any relief force would be compelled by insufficient food to attack the outward-facing defenses he was now beginning to build in addition to his inward-facing siege works. When these siege works, described by Caesar in immense detail, were complete, he had thirty days of rations available in his camp.[49]

Caesar describes the assembling of a vast force from all of Gaul. In practical terms the account is deeply unlikely: Caesar would have us believe that thousands of soldiers could be called up and could march from Brittany in a matter of weeks. A better indication of what was actually happening comes from his list of those commanding the relief force. They include the Aeduans Eporedorix and Viridomarus, Vercingetorix's cousin Vercassivellaunus, and Caesar's old agent among the Belgae, Commius. The participation of the latter clearly bothered Caesar, who reiterates the point he had made at the end of Book 5—namely, that the Gauls who opposed Roman rule did so out of a desire to recover their reputation for military glory:

> There was such a great consensus on the part of all Gaul in favor of the recovery of their previous military reputation that they were moved by neither favors nor memory of friendship; rather, they all threw themselves into the war effort with all their hearts and resources.[50]

As this relief force approached, the situation in Alesia grew desperate. While Caesar presumably invented the speech he attributes to a man named Critognatus, advocating that the defenders turn to cannibalism to alleviate their shortage of food, it was an observable fact that Vercingetorix expelled all the town's civilians, who were left to starve in the no-man's-land between the two camps.[51]

The relief force at last arrived and within a day launched an attack on the Roman defensive lines, coordinating with the Gauls inside Alesia. The Romans stayed within their fortifications and repulsed their enemy. When the attack was renewed a day later, it met similar results. A third assault, perhaps a day after the second one, targeted a part of the Roman fortifications that was somewhat weaker than the others.[52] The legions assigned to hold the post were hard pressed, but none of this passed without notice—Caesar had taken up a post at a fort identified as being on Mt. Flavigny, to the south of the town. From there he could watch the battle unfold and direct reinforcements as necessary. In a narrative fully informed by Caesar's understanding of generalship, he has first planned to place the enemy at a disadvantage; he then adjusts his plan when it looks like they may succeed, and he personally encourages the troops in difficult situations. Finally, he leads the decisive attack himself. Labienus had gathered eleven cohorts as a reserve to sally out if the fortifications looked like they were failing. This is how Caesar describes the action:

> Caesar hastened so he could take part in the battle, and the conspicuous color of the cloak he was accustomed to wear in battle announced his arrival. Then, because the downward slopes were in plain view from the heights above, the enemy saw the cavalry squadrons and cohorts which he had ordered to follow him and they joined battle. With the battle cry rising from both sides, the shout was picked up from the ditch and the fortification. Our men, casting aside their *pila*, engaged with their swords. Suddenly the cavalry was seen attacking from the rear. Other cohorts were advancing. The enemy turned their backs. The cavalry fell upon the fugitives. There was a great slaughter.[53]

The battle was over. The relieving army withdrew the next day, and, after summoning a council of war in Alesia, Vercingetorix agreed to surrender. He would remain a prisoner for six years.

The victory won, Caesar recognized the crucial task would be to rebuild the political system he had been trying to construct. To that end, he separated the Aedui and Arveni from among those captured so that they would not be sold into slavery but would rather serve as hostages to facilitate negotiations with their people. Caesar himself would spend the winter at Bibracte to engage in negotiations. A thanksgiving of twenty days was declared at Rome. For Caesar it was perhaps more important that Pompey emended his law requiring that candidates declare their candidacy in person, adding a provision specifying that this did not apply to Caesar.[54]

For Caesar the author, the *Gallic War* ends with the dramatic charge at Alesia and Vercingetorix's surrender. By the time Hirtius picked up the story, at Balbus's request, in the summer of 44, the world had changed. Caesar was dead, the civil wars which had begun with the crossing of the Rubicon in 49 had been over for more than a year, and a succession crisis loomed. All these factors influence the story Hirtius has to tell, and his discussion of Caesar's conduct towards the Gauls, based on notes Caesar left, is largely tangential to the unravelling of Caesar's relationship with Pompey. From a Gallic perspective the most important issue after Vercingetorix's defeat is Caesar's management of internal politics. Two themes run through Hirtius's account, one being Caesar's desire to avenge himself on the individual Gauls and communities that had most offended him, including the Carnutes, Commius, and Ambiorix. At the same time, the experience of 52 appears to have made him realize that selecting as leaders those who were most willing and able to humor him was not the best way of going about things. More agency needed to be given to the Gauls themselves.

Hirtius has nothing to add to what Caesar said in Book 7 about the Aeduan leaders captured in the battle at Alesia, but he makes it clear that Caesar moved to Bibracte until December and, referring to the end of 50, twice says that the Aedui were the most influential of the Gauls, which does suggest that the overall situation had stabilized. In December of 52, Hirtius writes, Caesar had left the Aedui, reacting to reports that first the Biturges and then the Carnutes were planning "rebellions." In the case of the Biturges, Hirtius said the speed of Caesar's advance kept his friends loyal and dissuaded from violence those who might be wavering. Hirtius tries to promote the view that peace and stability were the result of Caesar's mercy, a policy which he had pursued in the last few years as a centerpiece of his policy to reunite Rome after the civil war. In the case of the Biturges, he wrote, "when terms were given to them, the Biturges realized that a return to the friendship of Caesar was open to them through Caesar's mercy, and that neighboring states that had given hostages had been received into his friendship, they did the same." Beyond this, Caesar made no effort to meddle in their politics. A different situation obtained with the Carnutes, whom Caesar appears to have felt incorrigible given that they were still under the leadership of Gutuatrus, one of the villains of the incident at Carnuntum the year before. Their territory was ravaged and no peace offer was forthcoming.[55]

The next operation was against the Bellovaci in the early spring of 51. According to the Remi, Commius was now allied with Correus, the Bellovaci's leader, and they planned to raid the territory of one of the

Bellovaci's dependent tribes. The campaign was complicated by Commius and Correus's recognition that, since their troops were no match for the Romans in a straight-up battle, they would need to fight the Romans from ambushes in the forests in the hope of repeating Ambiorix's success. Caesar, as was his wont, scouted carefully and adjusted to new intelligence as it came in. His campaign was successful. When Correus died in battle and Commius fled, the Bellovaci offered to surrender. Their ambassadors said Correus had been a demagogue whose influence over the common people had compelled their leaders to follow him and the tribal council was thus not at all to blame. Caesar replied that it was all well and good to blame the dead, but he did not believe that, if the members of the council had stood up to Correus, he would have been able to influence the common people as he did. (This sounds rather like a summary, from Caesar's perspective, of Clodius's career as an aristocratic demagogue.) Still, Caesar would take no further action against them. It would clearly be up to the Bellovaci to get their own house in order. As if to drive home the point that a new day was dawning for the Gauls, Caesar then led a fresh expedition into the territory of the Eburones, spreading ruin in his path with the purpose, so Hirtius says, of convincing the people to hate Ambiorix.[56]

By the end of the summer of 51, the message that Gallic tribes were to select leaders the Romans could trust appears to have been getting through. The Carnutes, who had, in the earlier part of the summer, supported Roman troops passing through their territory now surrendered of Gutuatrus, Caesar executed him.[57] While this was happening, Labienus defeated those among the Treveri who had joined the rebellion the previous summer. The final major military activity of 51 took place at the city of Uxellodunum in the province of Transalpine Gaul. The city had been occupied by a band of what were at this point dedicated Gallic revolutionaries under a pair of leaders named Drappes and Lucterius. Caesar captured the city (whose inhabitants had not been happy to be occupied) and ordered that the right hands of those who had fought against him be cut off. Hirtius claims Caesar did this because "he knew that his leniency was known to everyone and that he was not feared for any cruelty of his character," and that, by a singular act of cruelty, he would dissuade others from conspiring against Rome. It would be hard to imagine that, in light of the events of the past year, Caesar's "leniency" was quite so obvious. This decision was very much in line with the message Caesar had been sending: subordination would be rewarded while resistance would be dealt with harshly. The success of that message was underscored when Lucterius was turned over by a leader of the Arveni who was judged "most friendly to the Roman people."[58]

With the campaigning season of 51 at an end, Caesar first journeyed to Aquitania, on the grounds he had never visited the area, and then moved back to the Roman province where he rewarded people who had shown particular support during the war of the previous year. Finally, he headed to Arras in the territory of the Belgae for the winter. There "he had one hope: to hold the Gallic states in friendship and give nobody any hope or reason to go to war." It was probably at this point that Caesar established the annual tribute, for what would now be a Roman province with a permanent governor, at forty million sesterces, not an insubstantial sum, but not an especially heavy burden. As a point of comparison, he had spent considerably more on the land for his forum of Venus the Ancestor.[59] Of more significance, perhaps, was the total annual cost of the thirteen legions he currently had under his command: around 23,400,000 sesterces. There would be a substantial reserve built up after the first year's tribute collection, and none of that money would be leaving Gaul until such time as the Senate formally ratified Caesar's decisions.[60]

It is testimony to Caesar's success at rebuilding Gallic society so that it would be loyal to Rome, and the importance of his recognition that his heavy-handed practices of the past now needed to change, that there would be no further Gallic revolt despite the decades of civil war Caesar was about to launch upon the Roman world. Gaul now felt that its interests were aligned with those of the new ruling power. In nine years, Caesar transformed the shape of Europe forever, uniting what are now

France and Belgium with the cultural world of the Mediterranean. At the same time, he had built a military organization of exceptional quality and provided a model for successful conquest that few have been able to match. On the field of battle, he proved that he was, and would remain, among the world's best generals. His particular genius lay in attention to detail, his willingness to adjust to circumstances, and his ability not to impose assumptions about what *should* be happening upon the realities he was faced with.

14

The Rubicon

The explanations Caesar would offer for his decision, on the evening of January 10 in 49, to cross the Rubicon—the narrow river between Cesena and Rimini which marked the southern border of his province—were the Senate's repression of tribunician rights, specifically their veto power; the actions of his enemies, which had resulted in the estrangement of Pompey from their mutual friendship; and the Senate's passage of the "ultimate decree" against him. The whole responsibility for the war lay with Cato and his friends. Those explanations rather oversimplify a complex period of negotiation between two sides whose positions had hardened over the previous year.

Caesar concentrates, in justifying his actions, on a particular Senate meeting which took place on January 3, 49, according to the Roman calendar—now badly out of alignment with the season (the date by our reckoning was November 3). His focus on that one meeting, however, conceals a year of intense preparation on his part for an invasion of Italy. The poet Lucan would later offer the truest cause for the Civil War: Caesar could not endure a superior, nor Pompey an equal.[1]

At the time he completed Book 7 of the *Gallic War*, Caesar appears to have still felt that he and Pompey could run the state as coequal partners, hence the significance of his complaint that his political enemies had estranged Pompey from their friendship. In a passage introducing Vercingetorix to his readers, Caesar pointedly rejected a political program that would yield a Sullan-style dictatorship, writing that Vercingetorix's father, Celtillus, had held the *principatus*, "primary leadership," of Gaul but had been killed by his own people when he sought *regnum*, "kingship." By implication, *principatus*, which involved recognition of a person as a leader in a political order, was a good thing from Caesar's point of view, while *regnum*, "tyrannical power," was a bad thing. Cicero, who had once described Pompey as the "undoubted *princeps*" of Rome and had written about how the political order would function better if there was a single "moderator of the state," would presumably have agreed. The breakdown in the relationship between Caesar and Pompey fits within this paradigm. Could power be shared between two equally powerful *principes*? Since 55, when the two friends, along with Crassus, had renegotiated their alliance, Caesar's answer had been "yes." Now, Pompey's answer was that it could not be, and that Caesar must be subordinate to himself. In the biographical tradition, Caesar is quoted as saying, in the months leading up to the war, that it would be harder to be moved from the top position in the state to second place than from second place to the bottom. And Cicero would later write that Caesar had labored for years so he could obtain the leading position in the state.[2]

Hirtius provides valuable clues as to what was going on in Caesar's camp during the summer of 50. Caesar had "wanted nothing less than to be compelled to fight a war just before his departure, lest, when he was about to lead his army away, some cause for war would remain and all Gaul would freely join in without any present danger."[3] To prevent this, Caesar dealt respectfully with the various states of Gaul and rewarded their leaders generously. Writing six years after the crossing of the Rubicon, Hirtius is effectively saying that Caesar was planning to take his whole army with him and there wouldn't be a garrison when his governorship ended! As his readers would by then have known, that army would be engaged in the Civil War which Hirtius is suggesting was in prospect by the end of 51. Although Hirtius soon returns to the party line, in which Caesar was the victim of a conspiracy on the part of a small but powerful faction of political rivals at Rome, this is an astonishing statement, and one that betrays his memory of the situation in Caesar's headquarters in the months leading up to the outbreak of the war.

When he returns to the party line, Hirtius does so with a bit of contemporary bias. He was writing in the summer of 44, when the big question in Roman politics was the role Mark Antony would play going forward. Even though Hirtius ultimately died in battle against Antony when he was consul the following year, in Book 8 of the *Gallic War* he reminds his readers of Caesar's affection for his nephew. He presents Antony's candidacy for a senior priesthood as the big issue at the beginning of the summer of 50. Antony had also been Caesar's quaestor, and his eventual election to the priesthood, in the autumn, reveals the generally positive disposition toward Caesar on the part of the Roman people—a positive disposition which a faction of "a few powerful men" struggled to undermine. When Caesar arrived in northern Italy to support Antony's candidacy, he detected exceptional enthusiasm for his own impending consular candidacy next summer. The evil faction, as Hirtius presents events, had already undermined the constitution when it perverted the consular elections of 50. By doing so, it had secured the consulship in 49 for Lucius Lentulus and Gaius Claudius Marcellus both staunch enemies of Caesar, in place of Servius Sulpicius Galba, who had been Caesar's legate for several years in the early 50s.[4]

As Hirtius's comment about the departure of the army from Gaul reveals, trouble had been brewing for some time before the summer of 50. On June 1 of the previous year, one of the consuls, Marcus Claudius Marcellus, had tried to raise the issue of a successor for Caesar who would take over Gaul in the next calendar year. This was more than a year before Caesar maintained his term was due to run out under the terms of the law extending his command in 55. Marcellus had also flogged a man who held a magistracy in the city of Como, which had been founded with the status of a Latin municipality under one of Caesar's agrarian bills of 59. Tenure of a magistracy in a municipality granted a person citizenship, and by inflicting this treatment upon the man from Como Marcellus was challenging the legitimacy of Caesar's law: a citizen could not simply be beaten. Marcellus didn't seem to win much support for his view, however, and Cicero said that his action was disgusting.[5]

Marcellus's colleague had opposed his effort to appoint a successor for Caesar, but debate over the issue had raged for months in 51, bringing all other business to a halt. Finally, in September of that year, Pompey said the issue could not be raised before March 1 of the next year. Pompey was presumably quoting from the law he and Crassus had passed extending Caesar's command back in 55, but he was interpreting the law as stating that Caesar could be replaced in 49. This interpretation was only possible because that law had been poorly drafted, and Pompey's statement seems to flatly contradict the obvious intent behind his revision of his own electoral law of 52 to allow Caesar to stand for the consulship of 48 *in absentia*. Caesar himself would state in no uncertain terms that his command extended into 49.[6]

Pompey's latest declaration held, but in October of 51, Caesar's enemies introduced other legislation, possibly more to see how Pompey was thinking rather than because there was any prospect that could pass. One, regarding Caesar's replacement, was vetoed, as was one that would have released soldiers in Caesar's army from the ranks if their term of service had formally expired. The point of that bill was to assert senatorial control over Caesar's army. Not vetoed, however, was a measure postponing debate over the assignment of provinces for the consuls of 50 to March 1 of that year. When Pompey was asked what would happen if Caesar tried to retain his army and stand for the consulship, he replied, "What if my son should decide to hit me with his stick?"—implying that such an eventuality was beyond consideration. We read about this comment in a letter that Marcus Caelius Rufus wrote to Cicero, who was then serving as governor in Cilicia. Caelius went on to remark to the absent Cicero that people now assumed there was some sort of negotiation going on between Pompey and Caesar. Cicero would have preferred not to be getting such information second-hand. In fact, he had never wanted a provincial governorship, but now he had to take one up. This was because of another piece of legislation in 52, which had established a mandatory five-year gap between tenure of a magistracy and a provincial governorship. As a result of this law, the Senate was having trouble finding enough former consuls and praetors to fill all the available governorships.

To man the governorships until 46, when magistrates who held office in 52 would be eligible for provincial posts, former consuls and praetors who had not governed provinces were drafted into service.[7]

Hirtius's picture of the year 50 is filled with the progressive ascent of the faction he says was corrupting the Roman state. Caesar had left Labienus in charge of Cisalpine Gaul so he could build up support for Labienus when he too would run for the consulship, presumably in 48. While he was away in Gaul, Caesar was told that his enemies were trying to detach Labienus from his support for Caesar. He didn't believe the rumors (although events would prove that he should have).[8] Meanwhile, the situation in Italy was a bit more complicated than Hirtius would later let on. One consul, Gaius Claudius Marcellus, was indeed Caesar's vehement opponent, but the other consul, Aemilius Paullus, had received a large loan from Caesar, enabling him to rebuild the basilica named after his family on the east side of the Forum. He generally tried to restrain his colleague. Another man who had once been thought to be Caesar's stalwart opponent, the tribune Gaius Scribonius Curio, had also received a very large loan, which transformed him overnight into a powerful voice on Caesar's side.[9]

Tensions increased as the year wore on. In April the Senate ordered Caesar and Pompey to give up a legion each so that they could be sent to Syria, where the Parthians were raiding the province and threatening Roman client states. Pompey's choice was the First Legion, which he had given to Caesar in the wake of Sabinus's disaster in Gaul. That was very unfair, said Hirtius. His horror is disingenuous. In August of the previous year, Pompey had been asked in whose army the legion served. He responded it was in the Gallic army, but that he would be withdrawing it.[10]

Throughout the summer of 50, the central issue in Roman politics continued to be whether Caesar would retain his army while standing for the consulship of 48. In early August, Caelius, writing to Cicero, compared the position of Pompey, who had decided Caesar could only become consul if he handed over his army, with Caesar's view that he would only be safe if he retained his army while he ran for consul. Caesar later claimed that what he was really afraid of was that he would be prosecuted in a kangaroo court surrounded by Pompey's soldiers, which would be a repeat of the scene at Milo's trial for murdering Clodius, so intimidating Cicero that he couldn't get through his defense speech. There is little possibility such a trial could ever have taken place—a tribune loyal to Caesar would simply have vetoed the prosecution. What Caesar really feared was giving up the military organization he had built up over the years while Pompey retained the Spanish organization he had been constructing since his consulship in 55. It was precisely for this reason Caesar had been pointing out, in the sixth and seventh books of *The Gallic War*, how his organization and Pompey's could work together for the protection of Rome. These books would now have been making the rounds of the reading public.[11]

Caelius continues his analysis of the situation, writing, "those loves and that odious union have not receded into secret bickering, but have exploded into open war." He further notes that while Pompey might have the support of the nobility, Caesar had the better army.[12] Caelius's comment raises the question of why Pompey didn't see the military situation as a problem. The answer, which lies at the heart of the march to war, is the same feature of Pompey's character which made it impossible for him to acknowledge that he and Caesar could be equals. He was exceptionally narcissistic. The quality had been on display since he started calling himself *Magnus*, "the Great," in the wake of the Sullan civil war. It had been on display in his inability to foresee the possibility his opponents in the Senate might derail his settlement in the East, and in his mismanagement of Rome's relations with Ptolemy XII. This is not to say he wasn't a very good general—we'll shortly be seeing quite a few signs he was—but he was exceptionally prone to seeing himself in the best possible light.

As Caesar continued to win victories in Gaul, Pompey began contemplating the possibility of a war with his former father-in-law. His erratic conduct in 52 suggests their relationship, from his perspective, was problematic. The later biographical tradition associated the origin of the split between the two men with Julia's death in 54. No doubt that event was important, but Pompey continued to hedge his bets for some time, openly professing friendship with Caesar while building his resources with an eye to the possibilities of conflict.[13] For several years he had been stockpiling silver from the Spanish mines he controlled as nominal governor of the two Spanish provinces. He had also been building up the Spanish army to seven legions. He would further increase his army in the wake of the senate's request for legions to serve in Syria. Once Caesar sent two legions to Italy—one of his own and one that had formerly been Pompey's—Pompey would have nine legions under his direct command. The decision to retain the two legions from the Gallic army in Italy rather than dispatching them to Syria is taken, not unreasonably, by Hirtius as a sign of the bad faith of Caesar's enemies. From Pompey's perspective, the final split likely occurred in the spring of 50, motivating the decision to keep the legions in Italy. It may have been at this point Pompey repeated the story Caesar had had an adulterous relationship with his ex-wife Mucia.[14]

Pompey's conviction he could emerge victorious from a struggle with Caesar was strengthened after he fell ill in the late summer of 50. Plutarch writes:

> After this Pompey was dangerously ill at Naples but recovered. On the advice of Praxagoras the Neapolitans offered sacrifices of thanksgiving for his preservation. Neighboring people imitated them, and the practice spread throughout Italy, so that every community, whatever its size, held festivals of thanksgiving for many days. No place could contain those coming from everywhere to greet [Pompey], and roads and villages and ports were filled with people sacrificing and feasting. Many people with garlands on their heads and torches in their hands welcomed and escorted him, pelting him with flowers, so that his return to Rome was a most beautiful and magnificent sight. But this is said to have been a significant cause of the war. For while the public rejoicing was great, Pompey's reaction to the greatness of the celebration was to throw away the caution which had always given security to his successful achievements and to indulge himself in unlimited arrogance and disdain for Caesar's power, feeling that he would neither need an armed force nor have any trouble at all, but would pull [Caesar] him down much more easily than he had built him up.[15]

Pompey would tell people that wherever he would stamp his foot in Italy, armies would spring up. He would have done better to pay attention to an incident in the Senate that autumn. Caesar had written to the Senate saying that it should not cancel a privilege granted him by the Roman people and that it should insist that all other governors lay down their commands at the same time as he did. The first part of this reflects his claim that his command did not terminate at the end of 50, while the second is a classic Caesarian move to present his enemies with two undesirable choices: Pompey did not want to lay down his command and he did not want Caesar to keep his. When the tribune Curio introduced a motion to the effect that both Caesar and Pompey should give up their commands, the Senate voted overwhelmingly in favor. The next step would be for it to be voted into law by an assembly of the people, but the consuls refused to allow the assembly to be summoned. Curio could have anticipated the vote's outcome, and the consuls' subsequent action, which would lay the blame for a war at the feet of Caesar's enemies. In one version of the story, the consul Marcellus left the senate house to put a sword in Pompey's hand and ask him to take up arms in defense of the state.[16] But the important point made by Curio's action was that any support Pompey might have for fighting a war was not enthusiastic. In December, on the eve of war, Cicero would write his family saying "peace is what is wanted."[17]

Suetonius mentions another proposal, which he attributes to Caesar, to the effect that Caesar would give up Transalpine Gaul and the eight legions in its garrison, retaining only Cisalpine Gaul with two legions or Illyricum with one legion. It is unlikely this proposal actually came from Caesar, but someone may have floated the idea; Cicero's letters from December indicate discussions wherein Caesar was suggesting that if people would just give him what he wanted, there would be no war. What emerges from Cicero's correspondence are Caesar's demands for his right to stand for the consulship *in absentia* and for a guarantee of "parity" with Pompey until he took up that office.[18]

A crucial point about this statement of Suetonius is that it understates the number of legions under Caesar's command at the end of 50. It also misrepresents their location. Possibly some people thought he only had ten legions, having already given up two legions earlier in the year. Cicero uses the number eleven in a letter to Atticus around the same time. But

Caesar in fact had thirteen legions, of which eight were in Gaul and five, including twenty-two cohorts raised in Cisalpine Gaul to replace the legions sent to Pompey, were in northern Italy. He had more than adequate force to overwhelm Pompey if war should begin. He also had the financial resources to hand to double the pay of his legions in the event of war.[19]

As the events of early January will suggest, Pompey had a pretty good idea of the odds. He was in communication with Labienus, whose early career he had most likely fostered, given that Labienus was from his own home district of Picenum.[20] It also appears to have been the case that the praise Caesar had heaped upon Labienus throughout the *Gallic Wars* had gone to his head and he now acted as if he were Caesar's equal, which strained the relationship.[21] Pompey thought Labienus would make a valuable ally for the war he was sure was coming. He would not concede Caesar's demands, and on December 10 Cicero wrote:

> He [Pompey] spoke with me about political matters as if there was no doubt but that there would be a war: there was no hope of an agreement; he had previously thought he was thoroughly alienated from Caesar, but recently he'd become quite sure of it. Hirtius, Caesar's closest friend, had been in the area on December 6, but had not called on him, and Balbus had arranged to visit Scipio [Pompey's father-in-law and co-consul in 52] about the situation before dawn on December 7.

Hirtius had left to rejoin Caesar the previous night.[22]

Hirtius and Balbus had been trying to drum up support for Caesar's position by visiting other members of the aristocracy, including Cicero, who felt his obligations to Pompey would outweigh those to Caesar if war came. Cicero concluded his letter by writing that he hoped that a man whose enemies had conceded him a second consulship and to whom Fortune had given the greatest power would not be so mad as to put these things at risk. Days later he wrote that the outcome of a war would be tyranny, and shortly afterward he noted that he hadn't met anyone who didn't think it better to give in to Caesar's demand than to fight. He wondered what good it did to resist Caesar now that his power had been built up over so many years.

The situation took a turn for the worse when Antony, now a tribune, delivered a violent attack on Pompey at a public meeting. On December 26, Pompey told Cicero he had no interest in peace. On the other hand, he thought that, if Caesar found energetic preparations were being made for war, that would be enough to end the crisis. Pompey believed that, faced with the prospect of fighting him, Caesar would give up his insistence on standing for the consulship and would prefer to keep his armies and his province for the time being. Pompey was living in a fantasy world of his own construction.[23]

The first meeting of the Senate at which business could be discussed in the new year was on January 3. Caesar had sent a letter which the now former tribune Gaius Curio presented to the consuls. It opened with a statement of all the good things Caesar had done for Rome. What followed was Caesar's offer to dismiss his army and lay down his office if Pompey would do the same, on the grounds that it would not be right for Caesar to be exposed to his enemies. In the end, the consuls finally gave in to the demands of two tribunes, one of whom was Antony, and had the letter read to the Senate. They then refused to allow discussion of its contents, preferring instead to have a debate on the general state of the Republic. Those who attempted to speak on Caesar's behalf were silenced. Scipio then introduced a motion to the effect that if Caesar did not relinquish his command by a certain date he would be judged to be acting against the state. He appeared to be speaking for his son-in-law Pompey, so Caesar later said. The validity of Caesar's point about the bad faith of his enemies would be plain to all who observed, or came to know about, the meeting.[24] Two tribunes, Antony and Cassius, who attempted to veto the proceedings, were prevented from doing so. On January 7 they fled the city. That day, the Senate passed the "ultimate decree" in response to the threat posed by Caesar. Caesar was now at Ravenna.[25]

On the night of January 10, Caesar addressed the men of the Thirteenth Legion. He reviewed the wrongs his enemies had done him: they had estranged Pompey from him, even though Caesar had always supported Pompey's honor and dignity and had minimized his own glory. Even

Plate 1. Pompey the Great, Museo Archeologico Nazionale, Venice. Wikimedia Commons.

Plate 2. Crassus, Louvre Museum, Paris. Wikimedia Commons.

Plate 3. Cicero, Musei Capitolini, Rome. Wikimedia Commons.

Plate 4. Cato the Younger, Museum of History and Civilizations, Rabat, Morocco. Wikimedia Commons.

Plate 5. Dying Gaul, with a characteristic Celtic hairstyle and torc. HIP/Art Resource, NY.

Plate 6. The walls of Bibracte as restored here are an excellent example of the fortifications Caesar describes as surrounding major cities in Gaul. Manuel Cohen / Art Resource, NY

(a)

(b)

(c)

Plate 15. 15a–b: This coin, minted by Brutus in 54 BCE, illustrates the importance he attached to the achievement of his putative ancestor. The obverse depicts Libertas, the ideal of the Republican constitution, while the reverse depicts L. Junius Brutus, the first consul, with his lictors (Crawford *RRC* 433/1 obverse and reverse. Private collection). 15c: Mark Antony (Crawford RRC 517/1. Private collection).

Plate 16. This bust of Caesar catches the determination and intense focus of his character. Vatican Museums, Rome.

Sulla had left the tribunes their veto power, but now Pompey, who had once championed the rights of the tribunes, had taken that power from them. As for the passage of the ultimate decree, that had, in the past, been reserved for a moment when there was violence in the city. Now, it had been deployed in a time of peace. Caesar urged the troops to defend his honor and dignity, remembering their achievements in Gaul and Germany during the past nine years. They, not the faction in Rome, were the defenders of the legitimate government of the state. When the troops shouted their acclamation of Caesar's words, he led them south to Rimini. In doing so, he crossed the Rubicon.[26]

In the first book of the *Civil War*, Caesar's carefully crafted account of the opening days of January, 49, Caesar, who is keen to stress the legality of his actions, plays down the moment at which he departed his province and thus overstepped the legal limits of his military command. Instead, he keeps the focus on his opponents' conduct, laying great stress on the unconstitutional actions of his enemies to justify the contents of the speech he delivers to the troops. He is not invading Italy; he is defending the constitution from those who would destroy it for their own selfish reasons. His rationale is strikingly evocative of the one Sulla had used when he led his first march on Rome forty years earlier.

Asinius Pollio, who wrote a history of the Civil Wars, beginning with the alliance between Pompey, Crassus, and Caesar, says he was with Caesar the night before he crossed the river. In this version there's no speech to the men of the Thirteenth Legion. Instead, Caesar spends the afternoon at a display of gladiators, then goes to dinner with his friends. Pleading indisposition, he leaves the party and mounts a chariot. Followed by some of his friends and some cavalrymen, he heads south. When he reaches the river, he pauses to think. After a while he turns to his friends and says, "Not to cross the stream will bring great misfortune to myself, crossing it will bring it for all mankind." But then he looked up, called out "let the die be cast," and crossed the river, joining the troops he had sent on ahead at Rimini in the morning.[27] A later writer, the poet Lucan, whose ten-book epic on the Civil War opens with the crossing of the Rubicon, has a weeping and disheveled vision of Italy rise up before Caesar and his men, telling them to stop if they approach as law-abiding citizens. Caesar replies by calling upon Jupiter and leading his men across the river.[28]

Suetonius has the most convoluted version of the story. When Caesar learned of the tribunes' flight from Rome, he first attended a theatrical performance, then inspected the plans for a new gladiatorial training ground and had a dinner party. At nightfall he went out with a few staff members, borrowed some mules from a bakery, and headed out in a small cart. The torches went out and the party got lost, wandering aimlessly in the night until it encountered a local guide who put them back on track. On the Rubicon's bank, they caught up with the troops who had been sent ahead. Caesar's words in this version are "we can still pull back, but once across the little bridge, everything must be fought out." At that point a superhuman apparition comes into view on the river-bank, playing a reed pipe. A group of shepherds gather around it, and then some of Caesar's men, including his trumpeters, approach it. The apparition grabs a trumpet and blows a great blast. Caesar now says, "Let us go where the signs of the gods and the evils of our enemies call us. Let the die be cast."[29]

As we've seen, divine apparitions are not typically in Caesar's propagandistic tool kit, and even if he is now echoing Sulla's religious propaganda, it is deeply unlikely this would go so far as to extend to divinities on a riverbank. Those additions show us rather what Romans thought should go into such a moment. But we can feel confident in saying that Caesar did halt before driving his cart across the river and did let his companions know that the die needed to be cast. There really wasn't a lot of choice in the matter. Men of the Thirteenth Legion were already on their way to Rimini.

The version of the ultimate decree passed a few days earlier by the Senate had ordered that the consuls, praetors, tribunes, and all those with proconsular powers in the area of the city should see to it that the state should come to no harm. But despite issuing what was in effect a declaration of war, the leaders of the Senate were unready for Caesar. At the news he had crossed the Rubicon they panicked, leaving the treasury behind when they fled the city. It would appear they were familiar with the image Caesar had created of himself throughout his accounts of the war in Gaul—that he was a man who moved with incredible speed.[30]

Cicero was technically in the group of those with proconsular powers, but no one was under any illusions as to what this meant. There would be no committee decisions. Pompey would be in charge, but despite the theatrics in early January he didn't technically have superior *imperium*. He was one among several proconsuls, and while the consuls who technically had *imperium* superior to his own were willing to defer to him, there was a general lack of direction. On January 17, Cicero, technically in command of the coastal region of Campania, was wondering if Pompey planned to fight or to leave Italy. Two days later he wrote that the decision to abandon Rome was irrational. On February 5, Pompey told the consuls they should go back to Rome to get the money from the treasury. That didn't happen.[31] In the intervening weeks, a final effort at negotiation had fallen apart.

Shortly after arriving at Rimini, and just about at the same time he learned Labienus had deserted to Pompey, Caesar had received two ambassadors from Pompey: his nephew, Lucius Caesar, son of the consul of 64, and the praetor Lucius Roscius.[32] Pompey wanted Caesar to know that he had acted in the interests of the state but had intended no offense against Caesar. Pompey placed the good of the state above his private interests, and he hoped Caesar likewise would not damage the state just because he was so angry at his private enemies. Caesar replied that he was willing to compromise despite all the wrongs done to him (which, in his account of this period, he once again lists). Caesar's proposed compromise was that Pompey would depart for Spain, both he and Pompey would dismiss their armies, he would turn over Transalpine Gaul to Domitius Ahenobarbus and Cisalpine Gaul to Considius Nonianus (an ex-praetor), he would campaign for the consulship in person, and everyone in Italy would lay down their arms. If all this should happen, Caesar said, then fear would be removed from public life, free elections could be held, and the state would be administered by the Senate and people. After meeting with the consuls, Pompey replied that once Caesar removed his garrisons from Italy, his party would return to Rome and conclude the negotiation. In the meantime, Pompey continued to levy troops and arranged for the arrest of Caesar's gladiators, based at Capua, after they had refused to serve under the consul Lentulus. They were distributed, two apiece, to local heads of households to be held in custody.[33]

Cicero had been hopeful a deal would be reached on the basis of Lucius Caesar's mission, but the deal Pompey had offered in response altered Caesar's proposal in a significant way, as Caesar was swift to point out. Pompey was insisting Caesar leave Italy and give up his army before Pompey halted his own levies in Italy and before he left for Spain. It is hard to imagine Caesar did not foresee this response. The important thing, as far as Caesar was concerned, was that he be seen by supporters and potential supporters to be willing to negotiate while Pompey could be presented as having been unreasonable. Cicero's last reference to the potential settlement was in a letter of February 3, where he mentions that Curio had ridiculed Lucius Caesar's mission. Perhaps it was also at this point that Pompey declared he had no further interest in negotiating, since the dispatch of ambassadors would enhance the authority of the person to whom they were sent and detract from the authority of those who sent them.[34]

For his part, Caesar was again on the march. The legions previously stationed at Placentia were now closing up with the troops he had at Rimini. He was also raising new units, and taking into service units raised for Pompey which had surrendered to Caesar upon his approach. In the meantime, Pompey's own efforts to mount an effective military resistance faltered. On February 8, Cicero wrote to Atticus, saying that Pompey was a wretched sight, "no courage, no forces, no plan, no energy," and that recruits were not showing up. On February 15, he wrote to Pompey, saying, "I am ignorant of your designs and plan of campaign." A couple of days later he was appalled to discover Pompey's was indeed planning to leave Italy. He was even more unhappy when Pompey summed up his plan with the line, "Sulla could do it, why can't I?"[35]

By the time Cicero had written to Pompey, the lack of coordination between senior officers was becoming deeply problematic. Domitius

Ahenobarbus had never been easy for Pompey to get along with, and now he was being stupid. He had raised an army of 10,000 men from client farmers on his estates and was leading it against Caesar—he was proconsul designate of Cisalpine Gaul and he was going to take on Caesar himself. He advanced to Corfinio in east central Italy (plate 11). There he received a letter from Pompey, dispatched on February 17, in which the general wrote:

> What I thought and warned you of is now happening—namely that, at present, he doesn't want to fight a battle but will surround you by concentrating all his forces so that you will not be able to come to me and join your forces, consisting of the most loyal citizens, with troops concerning whose loyalty I am doubtful. I am therefore all the more disturbed by your letter. I am not sufficiently confident in the loyalty of the troops I have with me to risk a battle involving the safety of the state, nor have the men recruited by the consuls come in. For this reason, do your best to come here as soon as possible if this can in any way be accomplished.

Pompey, it turned out, had predicted exactly what would happen. When this letter was written, Caesar was already south of Domitius, who was proving as much a comfort to his enemies as he was a disappointment to his friends.[36] Separated from Pompey, Domitius had no chance of success in an engagement against Caesar, whose veteran legions outnumbered Domitius's raw recruits. Probably Pompey's letter to Domitius, circulated widely by Pompey to prove that Domitius had failed to follow his advice and preserved for posterity by Cicero, was the very same letter Caesar would describe in his own account as sending Domitius into a visible decline. While telling his senior staff that Pompey was on the way to rescue them, Domitius was in fact planning to flee with a few servants at night. When his men recognized "that his expression didn't match his words" and he was locking himself away with a few people, the soldiers mutinied and sent Lentulus Spinther, the consul of 57 to negotiate their surrender to Caesar.[37]

Caesar accepted the surrender and staged a dramatic scene when the garrison emerged from the city. Domitius, Lentulus, and their senior officers were set to one side, the troops to the other. The aristocratic prisoners were then dismissed while the troops were sworn into Caesar's service. No Sullan massacre here. Instead, a clear message went out that those who saw the justice of Caesar's cause were welcome in his ranks, and that these supporters included the common people of peninsular Italy. They had only served Pompey because they had been misled by self-interested and incompetent aristocrats. Events would suggest that Caesar's message was widely and warmly received throughout Italy, where there would be no active support for Pompey's cause during the rest of the conflict. As for Domitius Ahenobarbus, he would soon take ship for Marseilles and cause Caesar considerable trouble. Lentulus Spinther soon left to join Pompey, who by then had evacuated Italy with his forces and established himself on the other side of the Strait of Otranto, in Greece. The new legions Caesar acquired at Corfinio proved immediately useful. Under Curio's command they were dispatched to take over Sicily, which Cato was occupying with no garrison to speak of.

Caesar's mercy, a pointed contrast with both Sulla's behavior and rather bloodthirsty things Pompey was saying, sent a clear message. Continued war, and any accompanying devastation would be Pompey's fault. Caesar was still claiming that he saw peace as a possibility. In a letter dispatched to Oppius and Balbus around March 5 (and clearly intended for general circulation) he wrote:

> I'm happy that you say in your letter that you strongly approve of what was done at Corfinio. I will willingly follow your advice, all the more so because I have decided that I should show myself as merciful as possible and do my best to reconcile with Pompey. Let us see if by this means we can win over everyone's goodwill and enjoy a lasting victory, since others, through cruelty, have not managed to escape hatred nor to hold on to victory for any length of time—with the exception of Lucius Sulla, whom I will not imitate. Let this be the new plan of conquest, that we will defend ourselves with mercy and generosity. I have some ideas in mind as to how it will be possible to do this, and many more can be found. I ask that you apply your thoughts to this.[38]

Even as he pursued Pompey to Brindisi (where the latter was embarking his troops for Greece), Caesar was trying to build up a party in the Senate. He was often in correspondence with Cicero, whose presence in the ranks of Caesar's supporters would have been a massive propaganda success, but he never threatened him. Not only was he not Sulla, he remained committed to a peace process, albeit more for show than with any realistic hope anything would come of it. Since Pompey had made it clear that there was no room for compromise and that those who failed to support him would be dealt with harshly—Cicero, in describing Pompey, even coined a verb, "to Sulla," to characterize this uncompromising rhetoric—this apparent moderation of Caesar's simply reinforced the differences between the two sides. Notably missing from Caesar's self-presentation was any reference to Marius. It would do no good to recall his own family's bloody record in 87.[39]

The issue underlying Caesar's correspondence with Cicero, and with many others, was his need to construct a civil administration in Italy while he continued the war abroad. Caesar was relying on the principle, to which he had adhered in his last few years in Gaul, of recruiting supporters who, whatever their past relationship to Caesar, could best serve their own interests by serving his. He was planning for a meeting of the Senate as soon as he had killed Pompey or driven him from Italy. Pompey slipped out of Brindisi on March 17, eluding Caesar, whose forces were looking to block the mouth of the harbor and prevent his escape. Caesar then sent his legions into camps around southern Italy. He also dispatched a senior legate, Valerius Orca, to secure Sardinia, which, like Sicily, was a critical source of grain for Rome.[40]

Even after Pompey's departure, Caesar wrote that all he wanted to do was talk with Pompey and sort out their difficulties. In the opening thirty-three chapters of the first book of his *Civil War* Caesar only ever refers to his opponents as *inimici*, the Latin word for purely personal opponents. This is consistent with his language in documents preserved in our collections of Cicero's writings and represents his official position in April. Pompey, meanwhile, had been calling Caesar's people "enemies" (*hostes*) ever since the crossing of the Rubicon, and, to Cicero's dismay, had declared that he would treat anyone who remained behind as an "enemy."[41]

Within weeks of Pompey's departure Caesar called a meeting of the Senate at Rome. He needed to establish a government since he would be departing almost immediately to take command of a military campaign getting underway in Spain, where the bulk of Pompey's veteran army was stationed since he was technically governor of the provinces there even if he administered them through men who were technically his legates. The party he assembled included men of all sorts. Some had joined Caesar through ambition, seeing him as an obvious winner; others simply deplored Pompey, or those in his train.[42] Among the young and ambitious in Caesar's camp could be found Pollio, Caelius, Trebatius, who had served Caesar in Gaul and Sallust, the future historian. Others included two grandsons of Servilia. One was the son of one of Servilia's daughters, who had married Caesar's old commander Servilius Isauricus. (He had previously aligned himself with Cato into the mid-50s.) The other was the child of another daughter, who had married Aemilius Lepidus before his ill-fated consulship in 78. This younger Lepidus was now a praetor and would take over the administration of Rome while Caesar was away. The younger Servilius Isauricus would be Caesar's colleague as consul in 48. Crassus's surviving son Marcus also stood with Caesar; he had won his spurs in the final Gallic campaigns, as had Gaius Fabius, who had been tribune in 55. A consul of 51, Sulpicius Rufus, who had opposed the passage of the ultimate decree, supported Caesar too, and his son became one of Caesar's legates. Another of Caesar's legates would be Publius Cornelius Sulla. He was a grandson of the dictator and son of the man who had been denied the consulship in 65 on grounds of corruption.[43] His rather surpising appearance on Caesar's side may have stemmed from his prior association with Clodius, which indicates he was not a great fan of people like Cato. In the ensuing campaign he showed himself an able soldier.

Calpurnius Piso, despite some initial hesitation, stood by his son-in-law, but the war divided even Caesar's own family. His nephew Lucius followed Pompey, while Lucius's father remained with Caesar. Servilia's son-in-law, Gaius Cassius Longinus, was serving with Pompey, having earned distinction by protecting Syria after the catastrophe at

Carrhae. Standing with Cassius was Servilia's son Marcus Junius Brutus. On the other side, Cornelius Dolabella, Cicero's son-in-law, remained one of Caesar's favorites even after Cicero himself departed for Greece toward the summer's end.[44]

The Senate met during the first three days of April, assembling just outside the city limit so that Caesar would not technically have to lay down his *imperium* to attend. Caesar opened the meeting with a justification for the invasion of Italy, again stressing his enemies' efforts to deprive him of rights granted by the Roman people, his willingness to compromise, and his defense of the rights of tribunes. He then asked for ambassadors who would be willing to travel to Greece to open peace negotiations with Pompey. He could find no volunteers since people were afraid Pompey would treat them as enemies.[45] Caesar finally called a halt to the meeting when he found that the tribune Lucius Metellus had been suborned by his enemies to veto all his proposals.

The situation was a good deal more complicated than Caesar lets on in his own writings. Metellus had tried to bar Caesar's representatives from opening the treasury. They broke in anyway, and Caesar evidently told Metellus he would be willing to kill him, a scene which rather undermined his claim to care about the importance of tribunes' rights.[46] The Roman people who had assembled to see Caesar seem to have been put off by what they saw—Caesar struck them as behaving in a dictatorial manner. After ten years in command of his army, Caesar was used to getting his way without an argument and the diplomatic skills he had honed early in his career were now attenuating; "everything will come from me" was now his motto. He knew what was best, and if people didn't agree with him, he would become angry. After the meeting, Curio told Cicero, Caesar hated the Senate more than ever and he was disturbed that his opening of the treasury had not met with public approval. That Caesar recognized he was at fault for what had happened is suggested by his decision not to hold a public meeting before taking off for Spain. He also seems to have felt that he needed to mend some fences, a conclusion which may be drawn from Cicero's statement that Caesar had written him to say he didn't mind the fact he hadn't been at the meeting.[47]

Behind the drama associated with Metellus and the treasury was a decidedly non-trivial financial crisis. The invasion had set off a credit shortage which would be getting worse in the course of the summer. Caesar planned to alleviate the impact on the city's population by distributing seventy-five denarii to all citizens, a distribution that would be managed through the offices of the thirty-five tribes in the city. He also needed to pay his troops, whose salaries he had doubled when the invasion began. The result of his extraction of silver from the treasury was that the mint officials working for him at Rome issued what was, up to that point, the largest single issue of denarii in the city's history. Caesar may have been losing his touch as a politician, but he still had a very clear view of the role money played in winning wars.[48]

As the coinage to pay his armies was being produced, Caesar left Antony in charge of the troops in Italy and Lepidus in charge of Rome. He headed for Spain.

15

Defeating Pompey

Pompey's veteran army in Spain, consisting of seven legions, was commanded by Lucius Afranius, Marcus Petreius, and Marcus Terentius Varro. Afranius, the consul of 61, and Petreius, the effective commander of the army that had wiped out Catiline, had long histories of service under Pompey. Varro had very little military service. He was Rome's greatest scholar and, along with the two legions under his command in Further Spain, would play a minimal role in the events of the coming summer. Afranius and Petreius, following orders sent by Pompey, concentrated their five legions in northern or Nearer Spain, along with substantial auxiliary units recruited from what are now western Spain and Portugal, the area where Caesar had campaigned as praetor. All in all, the total number of men under their command may have amounted to around 35,000. Before leaving Italy, Caesar had ordered his legate Fabius to take six of the veteran legions from Gaul, along with substantial numbers of auxiliaries, into Spain—just over 30,000 men in total, given that the veteran legions tended to be understrength. Meanwhile, Caesar's other legate, Trebonius, remained near Marseilles with three legions, one of which he must have raised while the Italian campaign was getting underway.[1]

Caesar's own journey to Spain, at the head of nine hundred cavalrymen, was interrupted by Domitius Ahenobarbus. After his surrender at Corfinio, Domitius had gone to Rome and then to Cosa. While he was at Rome, he had collected the Massiliote hostages who were there and

sent them home, urging them to convince their colleagues to side with
Pompey. Given Pompey's long contact with southern France and probable contact with these people while they were in Rome, this was not an
unrealistic plan. Indeed, when the former hostages arrived, they did convince their colleagues not to admit Caesar's men into the city. Speaking
to ambassadors after he arrived, Caesar told them they should not wish
to be responsible for the outbreak of hostilities; rather, they should follow the example of all of Italy. Their response was that they understood
the Roman people were divided into two parties and that it was beyond
them to decide who was in the right. Additionally, they had received
equal benefits from the leaders of each side, so they should not help
either one against the other. The ambassadors were lying about their
intentions. Immediately after returning to the city, they received
Domitius and the ships he had brought with him from Cosa. Caesar
ordered Trebonius to lay siege to the city with the legions under his command and headed off to join Fabius and the legions in Spain.[2]

The actions which decided the Spanish campaign were most often
psychological and logistical, as neither side wished to risk a full-scale
battle. Afranius and Petreius, having stockpiled substantial supplies,
had established their forces in a camp near the modern city of Lerida
(ancient Ilerda) on the western bank of the Segre in the modern province of Lleida. Fabius had crossed the Segre a few miles to the north,
building two bridges to facilitate the actions of his foragers. Combat
was limited to engagements between the cavalry on both sides. Then a
storm shattered the southernmost of Fabius's bridges, exposing the
two legions he had sent to gather supplies to attack the superior forces
Afranius dispatched when he realized that the bridge had been
destroyed. Munatius Plancus, who commanded Fabbius's two legions,
drew his men up in a defensive position on a hill, resisting the cavalry
attacks Afranius launched ahead of an advance by the four legions he
had with him. When the standards of two more legions which Fabius
had sent to relieve Plancus were spotted in the distance, Afranius withdrew. From Fabius's point of view, the message Afranius had sent was
loud and clear: he did not think his men stood a chance in a battle with

troops who had served in the Gallic campaign. Caesar arrived a few days later.[3]

Two points Caesar makes in his description of the early weeks of the campaign are, first, that his men were exceptionally enthusiastic for their shared cause, and, second, that his opponents are Romans in name only. Afranius's troops have been in Spain so long that they have forgotten how to fight like Romans, having adapted to the tactical habits of the Spaniards.[4] This is a rather nervy assertion, given that the majority of Caesar's men were recruited from the Celtic zones of northern Italy— and now, increasingly, from beyond the Alps—but for that reason it was perhaps all the more necessary to claim his men represented true Roman virtues.

Caesar's stress on the enthusiasm of his troops recalls incidents from the campaign against Vercingetorix. In an early battle outside of Lerida, involving only a portion of the forces on both sides, Caesar's men drove Afranius's forces back to the town wall. There the Ninth Legion, one of those that had served with Caesar since the Helvetian campaign, pressed on too enthusiastically and was caught up in a five-hour struggle from which it withdrew only with difficulty. That does sound a bit like Gergovia. At another moment, this one evocative of the siege of Bourges, Caesar describes the hardship his men suffered after yet another storm wrecked both of Fabius's bridges. Gallic auxiliaries traveling with a large supply column managed to drive off the men Afranius had sent to intercept it, but they still could not cross the river to deliver the supplies. Grain was very short in Caesar's camp until the troops built some boats "like those they had encountered in Britain," which they used to cross the river so they could drive off the troops Afranius had sent to prevent the construction of new bridges. The bridges were repaired within two days and the supply column could now reach Caesar's camp.[5]

While the bridges were down, Afranius and Petreius had written their friends and associates in Rome "more enthusiastically and richly than the facts warranted." Crowds gathered outside Afranius's house and a number of people took off for Greece to join Pompey, some wanting to bring him the good news, others "to avoid appearing to have awaited the war's outcome."[6] Cicero was among those who left Italy at this time, having decided, after months of soul searching, that his obligations to Pompey outweighed those to Caesar. What Caesar would later write about this turn of events would offer an excuse to people like Cicero, implying that they had done what they did because they were lied to, and because they were frightened by Pompey's threats. That message was presumably disseminated in the autumn, after the end of the Spanish campaign.

The success of Caesar's cavalry in bringing the supply column into camp depressed morale on Afranius's side. Also, the tactical superiority of Caesar's men enabled Caesar to press what was essentially becoming a siege. As in the past, superior engineering on his men's part played an important role. Since the bridge that had been built to bring in the supply column was miles from Caesar's camp, he now diverted the Segre to lessen its flow and enable his cavalry to cross closer to the scene of the action. Taking control of the countryside on the eastern side of the Segre, the cavalry could prevent extensive foraging by Afranius's men. News of the shift in fortunes around Lerida encouraged several Spanish communities to change sides.[7]

Afranius, now deeply concerned about his own supplies, decided to abandon Lerida and head south to the Ebro. It took him two days to get his four legions across his own bridge near the town. Caesar's cavalry immediately set off in pursuit, slowing the march with repeated attacks on the rearguard. Caesar's men begged their officers to convey to Caesar their desire to pursue their retreating rivals, saying they would endure any danger and difficulty to bring the war to a speedy conclusion.[8] This story, as Caesar tells it, does raise some questions about what Caesar himself was doing—presumably the cavalry did not act without orders, and the request from the troops sounds like a reverse Besançon moment in that here the troops are questioning Caesar's reluctance to attack rather than his eagerness to do so. But the point of the story is to stress that Caesar is at one with his army with respect to the war: his interests are their interests, and he will be careful with their lives.

The subsequent maneuvers would be the most brilliant operation of Caesar's career. Despite their opponents' having a substantial head start,

Caesar's men overtook Afranius's army, which had been slowed by the cavalry's harassment, in the late afternoon. Since Caesar didn't want to risk battle with tired troops, the two sides made camp. The crucial point now was who could reach the Ebro first. The preferred path would go through a pass between the hills rising on either side of the plain where both sides were now encamped. Afranius hoped to steal a march by departing at night. But Caesar's scouts had captured some of Afranius's foragers and learned of this plan, so Caesar had the call to arms sounded in his camp. This caused a mini-mutiny in Afranius's camp when his men objected to leaving on the grounds that Caesar could intercept them while they were burdened with their baggage.[9]

When dawn came, Afranius's army was still in its camp. Caesar now left his baggage train in his own camp, under guard, and took the bulk of his army up into the hills, getting around Afranius and occupying the pass that led to the Ebro. When Afranius sent four cohorts of auxiliaries to occupy a hill overlooking Caesar's position, those men were slaughtered by Caesar's cavalry. Caesar's officers urged him to attack, sensing that the morale on Afranius's side would be near collapse after witnessing the massacre of their comrades. But Caesar refused. He had cut Afranius off from his hoped-for supply line, so why risk the lives of his men—"especially since it was no less the business of the general to win through planning than by the sword."[10] Additionally, at his most anti-Sullan and anti-Pompeian, he felt pity for fellow citizens and wished to achieve victory without killing them.

Caesar's men were not happy. They said that if they were not allowed to fight when they had a clear advantage, they wouldn't fight when they were next asked to. Caesar stuck to his position. On the other side there was confusion. Should they somehow try to continue their march, or should they head back to Lerida? They did nothing. Building up the defenses of their camp, they began to extend the fortifications to link their position to a water source. With Afranius and Petreius out of the way supervising this operation, soldiers in their camp began to talk with Caesar's men, whom they thanked for sparing them the day before, saying they looked forward to joining Caesar's army and regretted they had not done so before the campaign began. In saying this they implicitly admit the war is Pompey's fault. But they asked if Caesar would spare their generals, and a group of centurions and tribunes went to see Caesar to negotiate terms of surrender while some of Caesar's men sought out old friends in Afranius's camp since "to some extent the two camps seemed to have merged into one." When Afranius, whose son had been negotiating for his safety, returned to camp, he seemed ready to give in. It was Petreius who "did not desert himself." Gathering his personal guards and slaves he seized the ramparts, driving Caesar's men away and killing those whom he could capture. He implored the men not to hand himself or their "absent general, Gnaeus Pompey," to their enemies for punishment. He then ordered the men to bring any Caesarians they had with them to the center of the camp for execution. There were a number of executions, some Pompeians disobeyed, spiriting their guests back to Caesar, who, in the meantime, welcomed any former enemies who had come into his own camp and even giving those who had been officers in Afranius's forces the same ranks in his own army.[11]

Petreius's defiance didn't change the strategic situation. The Pompeian army was still cut off from the Ebro, and it was now short of food, having brought only eight days' supplies, enough to complete the march to the river if things had gone as planned. Faced with mounting desertions, Afranius decided to head back to Lerida, but now his column, harassed constantly by Caesar's cavalry, could make little progress. They covered only four miles before making camp again, this time in a worse location than the one they had left. Caesar continued to avoid a full-scale battle and now began to construct siege lines. This lasted for all of three days before Afranius threw in the toga. Afranius excused himself to Caesar saying that he and his men had simply been serving Gnaeus Pompey, and now, facing great shortages, they would ask Caesar for mercy.[12]

Caesar's response was to point out how mercifully he had behaved in not attacking them. He lamented Afranius's conduct at the time of the previous negotiation and pointed out that Afranius was suffering the fate of the stubborn and arrogant in that he now needed to beg for that which he had previously rejected. But Caesar "would not now exploit their humiliation, nor the opportunity offered by the occasion, in order to build up his own resources; rather, he wished that the army which had been built up against him over the course of many years might be dismissed." The army had not been needed in Spain, which had already been pacified. Pompey had constructed all manner of unconstitutional positions for himself, passed a law changing the way provinces were awarded, deprived Caesar of the respect he was due, and refused a reasonable compromise. Having said all this, Caesar released Afranius's army from service. At the time, it looked like a good idea: he didn't need the men and the war in Spain was about to end. In the long run, it might have been a better idea to keep those forces under arms since the disgruntled veterans would support a revival of Pompey's cause a few years later.[13]

Sending the bulk of his army back to Italy, Caesar now advanced into the province of Further Spain at the head of two legions. Varro's actions as governor of Further Spain had so far been highly ambiguous. He had communicated with Caesar after the invasion of Italy, telling Caesar that his loyalty was predetermined by his appointment as Pompey's legate but also recalling his friendship with Caesar and telling Caesar that the province held him in high regard. Then, when news arrived of the difficulty Caesar was facing after the bridges were destroyed outside Lerida the second time, he began to gather his forces to support Afranius. He recruited thirty cohorts of auxiliaries from the Spanish population, relieved the temple of Hercules outside of Cadiz of its treasuries (this was the place where Caesar had allegedly burst into tears upon spying a statue of Alexander when he was quaestor), and gathered a vast quantity of silver from the Romans in the province—20,000 pounds, in addition to eighteen million sesterces of coined money. This treasure was presumably on hand because Pompey wanted it there so he could use it in the event of a war.[14]

When news arrived of the surrender at Lerida, Varro discovered that public opinion was rapidly turning in Caesar's favor. His effort to coordinate the two legions under his command at Cadiz failed when one of them marched off to Seville. When Caesar reached Cordoba, the city council of Cadiz announced its affinity for his cause. This effectively ended all opposition to Caesar in Spain. Varro surrendered, and Caesar held a public meeting at Cordoba to thank the people of the province for their support. He told the Roman citizens they would not have to make the contributions Varro had imposed, and he returned the property confiscated "from those who had spoken too freely" in support of his cause, and replaced the treasures taken from the temple of Hercules. Caesar does not directly mention what became of the 20,000 pounds of silver, but modern study of Roman coinage makes it quite clear what happened. The largest single issue of silver coins in the history of the Republic was produced on Caesar's behalf in the late summer of 49. The coins bore the image of an elephant underneath Caesar's name, thereby commemorating his family's history, and were minted from Spanish silver.[15]

While Caesar was dealing with Varro, the siege of Marseilles ended. The gradual collapse of the defense of this well-fortified city had involved a number of twists and turns. The city's fleet, along with Domitius's ships and a small squadron dispatched by Pompey, had been defeated by Caesar's fleet under Decimus Iunius Brutus. After the construction of elaborate siege works, the citizens of Marseilles and the city council offered to surrender. The ambassadors of the city painted an eloquent picture of their fear of the city's ruin, speaking "with pathos and tears, as might be expected of such learned men." Trebonius, who had been ordered to spare the city, agreed to a truce until Caesar's arrival. But when his men had relaxed their watch, the Massiliotes suddenly broke the truce, attacking and burning the siege works. They failed to break the siege, however, and the siege lines were rapidly rebuilt. As food grew short and the population began to despair, the city fathers again appealed to Trebonius, who again granted a truce. Domitius took this opportunity to flee with his three ships, ultimately reaching Pompey in Greece.[16] At last, Caesar arrived. He ordered the Massiliotes to turn over all their money and weapons but agreed to spare their city—an act of mercy "more in keeping with the fame and antiquity of the city than with what they deserved from him." Leaving two legions as a garrison in southern France, Caesar headed to Italy. It was now August (according to our modern reckoning).[17]

While all this was going on, Caesar's cause had suffered a pair of setbacks. The first was in the Adriatic. He had assigned the province of Illyricum to Gaius Antonius, Mark Antony's younger brother, who was to be supported by a small fleet under Dolabella's command. Antonius had occupied the island of Curicta, now Krk, the northernmost of the Croatian islands in the Adriatic. The whole enterprise seems to have been ill-judged. Pompey had a much larger fleet and, when it showed up, Dolabella's squadron was overwhelmed, with only a few ships escaping, along with their commander, to Italy. Cut off on the island and starving, Antonius's men were ultimately betrayed by one of their own centurions and forced to surrender.[18]

The second disaster, which occurred at about the same time, was in North Africa.[19] Caesar had told Curio, once he had occupied Sicily with the legions taken into service after Corfinio, to proceed to the Roman province in North Africa to occupy portions of modern Tunisia. The object of this operation was to secure adequate supplies of food, since North Africa, like Sicily, was a major source of grain for Rome.[20] There were two recently recruited Pompeian legions in North Africa under the uninspired command of an officer named Attius Varus, who had been governor of the province for the last few years. Curio arrived with two legions of his own, and was initially successful in confining Varus to the city of Utica. But then Juba, king of Numidia, showed up to support Varus. Caesar attributes Juba's hostility both to his personal relationship with Pompey, who had restored Juba's father to his throne in 81, and to a bill, proposed by Curio while he was a tribune, that would have annexed Juba's kingdom to Rome. Caesar might also have noted that his own relationship to the man was probably none too good in the wake of the beard pulling incident back in 62.[21]

Juba's army was advancing in several sections. Curio, who was not an experienced general, relied on bad intelligence, which he had not tried to confirm with his own scouts. This intelligence led him to think that what was only the advance guard of the Numidian army was the entire army. (He believed a domestic crisis had recalled Juba to his kingdom with the rest of the troops.) He sent his own cavalry to launch a night attack on the Numidians who, as Caesar points out, had not encamped in an orderly fashion. The initial assault was a complete success: the Numidians fled, pursued by Curio's cavalry, and Curio took fifteen cohorts to join the pursuit. By the time they unexpectedly encountered Juba's main force, the Romans were thoroughly exhausted. Curio died fighting; his infantry was wiped out, and only a few cavalrymen escaped with news of what had happened.[22] That led to a chaotic attempt on the part of Curio's surviving subordinates to evacuate the remaining troops from the province. Most ended up as prisoners and were killed by Juba.

News of Curio's disaster probably reached Caesar while he was settling the affairs of Further Spain. When he was outside Marseilles he would also have learned that the situation in Italy was becoming difficult. At Rome, there was a debt crisis, accompanied by severe food shortages, and, at Placentia, the Thirteenth Legion, which he had led across the Rubicon, had mutinied. In one version of events the ostensible reason for the mutiny was that the soldiers were tired of endless campaigning, but the actual reason was probably that they were not being allowed to loot the countryside. In another version of the story, the men were angry because they hadn't been paid the gift he had promised them at the end of the Italian campaign.[23]

The mutiny is not mentioned in any contemporary source, which is hardly surprising since it's not the sort of thing Caesar would want to advertise, and Cicero, our other major contemporary source for this period, was now away with Pompey and perhaps did not hear about it. Moreover, the later sources which do mention the mutiny leave out some important information—chiefly why, when Caesar showed up, the legion submitted despite the threat of large-scale executions as a punishment for the rebel troops. Presumably Caesar arrived with overwhelming force at his back. Cassius Dio, who offers the most extensive account of these events, provides Caesar with a long speech which may be based on something that was circulated at the time, for it is filled with classic Caesarian propaganda: Caesar's men are in Italy to protect the people from evildoers, so they must not do evil themselves. They had waged glorious campaigns in Gaul from which they were called away by Caesar's rivals before they could complete the conquests of Britain and Germany. Pompey had forced the war on an unwilling Caesar through his unwillingness to compromise.[24] After Caesar finished speaking, the troops drew lots to determine who would be executed. Caesar is said to have rigged the lots so that the dozen men most responsible for the mutiny were killed. And when he found that another person had been wrongly included in this group by a crooked centurion, he had the centurion executed as well.[25]

Arriving back in Rome, Caesar had to provide a display of constitutionalism if he was to continue to assert that he was protecting the state from those who would subvert its institutions and invalidate the will of the people. While he had been away the praetor Lepidus had passed a bill authorizing the election of a dictator and then held an election in which Caesar was chosen for the office. The power of the people was thereby asserted: they had chosen a dictator instead of having one imposed on them by brute force. The electoral process had been reminiscent of that employed in the days of the Hannibalic war and on earlier occasions when a dictator had been selected for the purpose of holding constitutionally necessary elections. As dictator Caesar did just that, overseeing the elections for the coming year and resigning after a mere eleven days in office. He himself was elected consul for 48, along with the younger Servilius Isauricus.[26]

Now Caesar had to turn his attention to the debt crisis. The outbreak of what he politely termed "civil dissension" had destroyed property values throughout Italy. It was usual for people who were taking out a loan to secure it with property; if they were incapable of paying their creditors, they would turn over the property that had secured the loan. Now that property values had collapsed, debtors were faced with the prospect of losing everything, and creditors with non-payment. Caesar ordered the creation of a board of arbitrators who would value property at the rates that existed before he crossed the Rubicon so that debtors would be able to pay their creditors as had originally been agreed.[27]

Having imposed what he hoped would be a solution to the debt crisis, Caesar moved on to helping the "victims" of Pompeian legal proceedings during the last few years. In doing so, he also returned to an old cause: restoring the rights of the children of those proscribed by Sulla. He passed a bill restoring citizen rights and confiscated property to both groups of victims. Those whose recent convictions for crimes were over-turned included Gabinius, convicted of extortion after his return to Rome in 54, and Marcus Valerius Messalla, the consul of 53, who had been convicted of corruption in 52. In describing these men's resto-ration, Caesar says they had already offered him their services but he felt "it was better for them to be rehabilitated by vote of the people rather than to be restored by his own generosity so that he would not appear ungrateful in repaying kindness or arrogant in depriving the people of the right to confirm a favor." Both Gabinius and Messalla would receive commands from Caesar. Another exile recalled to Rome was Cicero's consular colleague of 63, Antonius, whose grudge against Pompey seems to have outweighed his grudge against Caesar for his famous prosecution now more than two decades in the past.[28] The one person who was not welcome back was Milo. Not only was he seen as a violent supporter of right-wing causes but he had been in Marseilles during the siege and had done nothing to help Caesar.

In his account of this period, Caesar's self-presentation has shifted subtly from what it had been in the *Gallic War*. There, as we have seen, Caesar reveals himself as a talented general who almost never leaves any-thing to chance. Although the three books of the *Civil War* were most likely not given to the public in their present form until after Caesar had died, they do reflect communications to the public, once again in the famous third-person style of those that formed the basis for the *Gallic War*.[29] It is thus quite revealing that, having referred to his opponents as "personal enemies" (*inimici*) in his description of the Italian campaign, Caesar suddenly shifts, in what are now chapters 40 and 41 of the first book, to calling them "foes" (*adversarii*) and "enemies" (*hostes*).[30] The linguistic shift reflects his claim that he is now defending Rome and Italy from what are essentially "anti-Roman elements." So too "luck" (*fortuna*) assumes a very different role from what it had in the *Gallic War*. Fortuna as a divine force routinely shows up in the *Civil War*, as Caesar seeks to undermine Pompey's image, which he had cultivated for years, as the favorite of the goddess.[31]

In addition to turning himself into Fortune's favorite, it looks as if Caesar also fabricated a miracle to evoke his family's connection with Bovillae. According to legend, the town got its name from a bull that escaped being sacrificed at the nearby Alban Mount and had been dedicated to the gods on the site of the town. According to Cassius Dio, our sole source for this event:

> While Caesar was sacrificing to Fortune, the bull escaped before being wounded, rushed out of the city and, coming to a certain lake, swam across it. Consequently, Caesar took greater courage and hastened his preparations, especially as the soothsayers declared that destruction should be his portion if he remained at home, but safety and victory if he crossed the sea.[32]

The total absence of geographical specificity here (what lake?) and the improbability that a sacrificial bull would be dashing about in any area where Caesar was present is enough to show that that the story is both invented and of considerable ideological significance: the gods are directing him to set off after Pompey.

Caesar remained in Rome for only eleven days before departing to join the army he had ordered to assemble at Brindisi. This consisted of twelve legions, including the three veteran legions with which he had begun the invasion of Italy, four legions that had come with him from Spain, the three legions which had been involved in the siege of Marseilles, and two legions of recruits.[33] In theory this would have amounted to an army of around 60,000 men, but Caesar says the veteran legions were severely reduced in numbers as a consequence of years of fighting, the long march from Spain, and disease that set in when they were around Brindisi. The upshot was that seven legions would muster only 15,000 men and the whole army may have numbered only around 30,000.[34] That was still more than Caesar could transport at one time.

Pompey had not been idle. At a meeting of the senators who had accompanied him overseas, and with the agreement of the consuls, he had been officially appointed commander of the forces opposed to Caesar.[35] He had recruited four legions from Roman citizens living in the eastern provinces to go with the five legions he had extracted from Italy, and he had gathered a superior fleet from a wide variety of provincial sources, placing it under the command of Bibulus. In the *Civil War*, Caesar would list an enormous number of provincial allies who had rallied to Pompey's cause as a way of stressing the fact that Pompey was planning to attack Italy at the head of a barbarian horde. Pompey's legions, which did actually consist of Roman citizens, were training around Veroia in central Greece while Pompey and his senatorial colleagues spent their time in Thessalonica.[36]

Caesar had long advertised speed as a key quality of his generalship, and indeed he had clearly demonstrated this quality in his conduct of the Italian campaign. But Pompey seems still to have underestimated him. It was very much in Caesar's interest to get across the Adriatic before winter set in. The result was that, when Caesar perceived Bibulus was having difficulty managing his fleet, he set sail with all the ships at his disposal on the evening of November 6, landing near the modern Albanian town of Pelasë on the southern end of the Karaburan peninsula.[37] He sailed with light baggage so as to fit as many men as possible on board his ships; the rest of the supplies could be transported in the next crossing, which he expected would be in the near future.

That would not be the case, however. Learning of Caesar's crossing, Bibulus, who was based at Corfu, stirred himself into action. He managed to intercept thirty of Caesar's ships on their return voyage, executing the crews when he did so. His homicidal passion, which "exploded from his anger at his own sloppiness and frustration," completes Caesar's portrait of his enemies as being out of touch with Roman values— especially that of mercy, *clementia*, so well illustrated by Caesar's own conduct. Caesar, meanwhile, would soon burnish his own image with a well-publicized peace offer.[38]

After having seized several bases from which to supply his troops and taking over the city of Apollonia, a site near the village of Pojan in modern Albania, Caesar just missed taking Dyrrachium (now Durrës), a port city in modern Albania ideally situated for an invasion of Italy. Pompey had dashed to the spot by forced marches, having received information about Caesar's movements from a man named Lucius Vibullius Rufus. Caesar had captured Vibullius twice, first at Corfinio, the second time in Spain. Caesar hoped the man, in return for having been shown mercy, would be a trustworthy messenger for the new peace offer—though he is unlikely to have been surprised when Vibullius also passed information about Caesar's movements on to Pompey. The way Caesar describes Pompey's dash to Durrës—he marched "fearfully by night and day"— suggests that Pompey knew he was overmatched.[39]

The message Caesar had wished Vibullius to convey to Pompey began by noting that both sides had suffered losses: Pompey had lost the equivalent of thirteen legions in his setbacks in Italy and Spain, while Caesar lamented the loss of Curio and Antonius (losses on nothing like the scale of Pompey's). They should therefore avoid further conflict, avoid putting the future at the disposal of Fortune, and allow the Roman people to determine the terms upon which they would make peace. Given that the Senate and people Caesar was referring to were those in Italy, and thus largely favorable to himself, the offer was at best disingenuous. But it reflects Caesar's perceived need to distance himself from previous civil warriors by advertising his desire to avoid a bloodbath, and to present himself as the defender of the Roman constitution.[40] The primary audience for this performance would have been people like Cicero in Pompey's camp and inhabitants of Italy who were no doubt informed of what was going on. Caesar wanted to make it clear where responsibility for the continuation of the war lay.

Pompey rejected Caesar's offer out of hand at a meeting which included Scribonius Libo, one of his admirals; Lucius Lucceius, Caesar's former partner in the consular campaign of 60; and Theophanes of

Mytilene, "with whom Pompey was accustomed to discuss the most important matters." The last two of these men make an interesting pair. Lucceius was the author of a massive book on the earlier civil wars (having turned down a request from Cicero to write a book about Cicero's adventures, from his consulship to his restoration from exile) and Theophanes was the author of a massive history of Pompey's campaigns. Pompey's brain trust, so to speak, consisted of a failed politician and a foreigner—and it seemed that he needed the help of professional historians. Caesar, as everyone knew, required no such help to narrate his victories, and his closest aides were all Roman citizens.[41]

In rejecting the peace proposal, Pompey allegedly asked: "What good would my life or citizenship be, if I was seen to have them through Caesar's gift? It will be impossible to remove the impression that I have been brought back to Italy, from which I departed voluntarily, with the war over."[42] Perhaps Pompey actually did say this, but Caesar is telling the story in such a way as to make sure that the war will be seen as the result of Pompey's personal flaws. This was the message he wanted to send both at the time and, even more so, once the campaign was over and tens of thousands of men lay dead on two battlefields. For Caesar, in contrast to Pompey, the ultimate solution to a conflict required a path to reconciliation—a lesson he had learned in the later years of the Gallic War. He also wanted a record of reconciliation he could point to when he needed it later.

Set against Caesar's "good faith" efforts for peace in this account are the bad faith efforts of the part of his rivals. In the weeks before Pompey's arrival at Durrës, Caesar's troops had occupied the Albanian coastline, cutting off supplies to Pompey's fleet on Corfu. Bibulus, still raging, had sent Libo to negotiate a truce in the hope that this would allow him to gather supplies from the mainland. Caesar says he rapidly recognized that the appeal was bogus and brought no hope of peace. Shortly after Pompey's meeting with Vibullius, in a scene recalling the informal negotiations between the camps in Spain, Labienus broke up informal peace talks involving Vatinius, Balbus, and other Caesarian leaders in the presence of the troops, hurling weapons that wounded Balbus and others while screaming that there could be no peace unless someone brought in Caesar's head.[43]

Shortly after the failure of the various negotiations, Bibulus died. Pompey did not appoint a new commander for his fleet, which resulted in a lack of coordination that ultimately allowed Antony, late in January to load the majority of the troops still at Brindisi onto transports and set out across the Adriatic. A strong wind carried the fleet past Durrës, but when Pompey tried to prevent Antony from rejoining Caesar, whose army was based to the south around Apollonia, he failed. The scene was now set for the first full-scale encounter between the two generals. In late April, Caesar laid siege to Pompey's base at Durrës.[44]

Pompey could not allow the city to fall, nor could he risk a frontal battle which would expose his less experienced troops to Caesar's veterans. Caesar wrote that he realized, when he saw Pompey had encamped a short distance from Durrës, which prevented Caesar from storming or laying siege to the place, that the war would not be over quickly. What followed was an extended period of pseudo-trench warfare. To secure his supply lines, Caesar needed to bottle up Pompey's cavalry on the coast. He thus began the construction of an enormous line of fortifications. Pompey, meanwhile, built his own defenses, which he kept extending to force Caesar to build ever longer lines and spread out his forces ever more widely. Caesar noted that the situation was highly unusual because a siege was usually the result of a prior victory in the field and the object was normally to cut the defeated enemy off from provisions, "but now Caesar was containing a larger force with his own smaller number of soldiers, while the other side had an abundance of supplies" because Pompey was resupplied on a daily basis by his fleet.[45]

The situation dragged on for several months, with serious difficulties on both sides. Until he could manage to bring in fresh food, Caesar's troops were on short rations, having to make do with barley cakes, meat, and muskgrass, which they mixed with milk. On Pompey's side, the constricted situation in his camp became increasingly unwholesome. Caesar had cut off the streams running into the camp, causing a water shortage and making it increasingly difficult to deal with the sewage produced by his army.[46] As the confrontation dragged on, there were occasional fights around the fortifications, generally resolving in Caesar's favor, with Pompey refusing to draw up his army at any distance from his camp: he wanted them to be protected by his artillery if Caesar's men tried to attack.[47]

Suddenly Pompey gained new information which enabled him to turn the tide. Roucillus and Eggus, brothers from an aristocratic family of the Allobroges who, throughout the Gallic campaign, had commanded a unit recruited from members of their state now decided to embezzle the pay for their troops. The men complained to Caesar, pointing out that the brothers had also inflated the size of the unit in order to receive extra money. Caesar decided not to address the issue publicly, but he let the brothers know he knew what they were doing. The brothers, who feared their relationship with Caesar was now in danger, also noted that their own men were making it clear they despised them. They decided to desert. Pompey received them with pleasure—because, Caesar says, these were the first men to desert to him, while Pompey's men were deserting to Caesar on a regular basis. But the crucial thing was the information the Allobrogians provided about Caesar's siege works: they were unfinished at the south end.[48]

Although Caesar would blame his ensuing defeat on Fortune and the panic which more than once beset his own troops, Pompey in fact made clever use of the information he had received. He embarked a strong force at night and sailed it to the south of Caesar's lines. With his landing party attacking the Ninth Legion from one side, he also sent a powerful force to join the attack from the north. The legion suffered heavy casualties and withdrew in disorder. Pompey held his men back from pursuit since he did not want them to encounter Caesar's men in the crowded area between the two walls of Caesar's lines. He already had what he needed, a breach through which he could import fresh supplies and interrupt Caesar's own supply lines.

Although he doesn't admit as much, Caesar was now compelled to attack in a place of Pompey's choosing since Pompey was rapidly building his own fortifications and had occupied an earlier camp Caesar's men had constructed slightly to the north of the lines which Pompey had breached. After rallying the Ninth Legion, Caesar attacked his former camp, looking to cut Pompey's southern force off from contact with the main army. After initial success, Caesar's men became disorganized—the effect of Fortune, so Caesar says—when they pressed the assault through the old defense works. Pompey counterattacked and drove Caesar's men headlong in flight. Caesar would later write that the only thing that saved his army from destruction was Pompey's fear of an ambush. He was completely surprised by the success his men had achieved. Truth be told, Pompey had achieved his objective, and, as the events of the day showed, even veteran soldiers did not react well when their formations broke down, as they easily did in the constricted space within Caesar's lines. Pompey was well advised to hold his men back, and his decision-making after the repulse of Caesar's counterattack was consistent with his cautious behavior after the initial breach. The siege was broken, and Caesar would have to either attack fortified lines, which Pompey knew he didn't want to do, or withdraw.[49]

The defeat had been the worst of Caesar's career. He admits to the loss of nearly a thousand men, more than the losses at Gergovia, and he recognized he could no longer maintain the siege. He addressed the army, telling his men they should not be disappointed by a minor setback but should rather be grateful to Fortune for their successes in the war so far: the conquests of Italy and Spain. They would be leaving Durrës for areas where there would be an ample supply of food. Fortune may have just deprived them of victory but they should now give Fortune a nudge in the right direction by working hard.[50]

The withdrawal from Durrës, even allowing for the admittedly biased perspective of our primary source, was a masterful operation. Caesar had his army leave at night, getting the jump on Pompey's men. Pompey soon realized he could not catch up, and, while Caesar headed south into central Greece along the Aous river valley through the Albanian mountains, Pompey moved in another direction, taking the great Roman road across the central Balkans, the Via Egnatia, in the direction of

Thessalonica. He probably hoped to intercept a subsidiary Caesarian force which had been dispatched to win over Greek communities while Durrës was under siege. This force of two legions was under the command of Domitius Calvinus.[51]

Caesar ordered Domitius, who had been operating along the Via Egnatia, to meet him along the line of his southern march. They met up around Kalabaka on the northern edge of the Thessalian plain. Caesar says Pompey's exaggerated reports of his success at Durrës encouraged Greek states which had formerly aligned themselves with Caesar to shift sides. One of those places was Gomphoi, whose people had previously "sent ambassadors of their own accord and invited Caesar to make full use of their resources."[52] Now, urged by a regional magistrate, they closed their gates to him. Caesar destroyed the place. The next city on his line of march, Metropolis, which had initially followed Gomphoi's lead, chose to surrender before Caesar took it by storm. The resources of these two cities provided sufficient logistical support for Caesar "to wait for Pompey and transfer the whole reckoning of the campaign to that region."[53]

By now Pompey had joined forces with a couple of legions from Syria commanded by his father-in-law, Metellus Scipio, and had moved to Larissa at the eastern end of the Thessalian plain. He was under increasing pressure to bring the war to an end. Many of the senators who accompanied him had not been enamored of him in the past, and they now accused him of prolonging the war so he could continue in his role as supreme commander. The battle at Durrës had convinced them that their troops were a match for Caesar, and they were already divvying up all the goodies they expected to come their way when the final victory was won.[54] This included the property not only of Caesar's most prominent supporters but of all those who had remained in Italy. Cicero confessed to being horrified by the brutality of the conversations.[55] Pompey would have to fight when next his army encountered Caesar's.

In early August the two armies faced each other on a plain near the modern town of Farsala, between the Enipeus river on the south and a range of low hills to the north. As is traditional, we'll call the battle by the ancient name of the site—Pharsalus. Pompey had about 40,000 men. Caesar's army numbered 22,000 infantry and one thousand cavalry.[56] For several days Caesar led his army out of camp, challenging Pompey to fight. Pompey didn't stir. Given the atmosphere in Pompey's camp, it is quite likely Pompey was telling people that he wanted to see if Caesar could be lured into attacking uphill (where Pompey was positioning his own forces). When Caesar broke camp, however, Pompey was forced into action. He advanced away from the walls of his camp, where he had been drawing up his troops on the previous few days. Caesar then turned in his tracks and drew up his own battle line. The date was August 9, 48 BCE (June 7 by modern reckoning).

Caesar and Pompey were both aware that, despite what Pompey's supporters were claiming, Caesar's veterans were infinitely superior soldiers if it came to a straight up encounter. Pompey's one hope for victory would be if his far more numerous cavalry could overwhelm Caesar's cavalry, outflank his battle line, and take it from the rear. He told his council the battle would be won by the cavalry before the two lines closed. The plain was sufficiently wide to make this a possibility, and Caesar recognized what Pompey's plan of action would be. He therefore withdrew six cohorts from his own third line, forming them up to support his cavalry. Plutarch adds the detail that, knowing the young aristocrats who made up Pompey's cavalry were vain, Caesar ordered his men to aim their *pila* for the faces of their enemies in order to demoralize them.[57] Both generals addressed their men. In response to Caesar's speech, Crastinus, a re-enlisted veteran of the Tenth Legion, called out to his comrades that they had just this one battle left. When it was over, their general would have the standing he deserved and they would have their liberty. "Today, I will make sure, general, that you will owe me thanks, dead or alive."[58]

Pompey held his main battle line stationary while Caesar's men advanced. He did not want to engage the infantry before his cavalry could do their job. For a time, it looked like his plan was working. His cavalry drove Caesar's men back, and Caesar's soldiers had to stop and catch their breath when they saw Pompey was not advancing. In his account of the battle, however, Caesar remarks that Pompey was foolish to hold back his men as he did, "since there is in all of us an innate zeal and excitement which is fired by eagerness for battle. Generals ought not to repress this, but rather enhance it." Caesar would rather not admit there was something to Pompey's plan.[59]

When Caesar's men at last collided with Pompey's line, Crastinus broke through the ranks in front of him, driving deep into Pompey's formation before he was killed. Pompey's line began to give way. At the same moment, just as Pompey's cavalry had driven off Caesar's cavalry and were turning to attack the main body of Caesar's force, Caesar ordered his six reserve cohorts forward. Pompey's cavalry, already disordered by the earlier fighting, were routed. The battle was as good as over when Caesar's reserve, having vanquished Pompey's cavalry, smashed into the left flank of Pompey's army.

Pompey knew he was beaten. He did not wait for the infantry battle to run its course but rode off to his camp. He told the men stationed at the gate by which he entered that he was going around to see to the rest of the defenses. Instead, he went to his headquarters tent, and, though despairing of the outcome, still awaited the results. When he heard Caesar's men entering the camp, he mounted his horse and, removing his general's insignia, rode away from the camp, heading for Larissa. Picking up a few associates and thirty cavalrymen along the way, he eventually boarded a grain ship on the coast.[60]

Caesar's men, meanwhile, had driven the remains of Pompey's army from the camp and surrounded them on a waterless hill. They surrendered the next day. Caesar says Pompey's army had suffered 24,000 dead and that 15,000 were now taken captive. The numbers are plainly exaggerated, but even if we accept instead the figure of 6,000 casualties that Asinius Pollio, who was at the battle, provides, the total is very large. It represents the catastrophic effect of the collapse of Pompey's line, which enabled Caesar's men to cut down adversaries who were defenseless once they had broken ranks. Caesar says that his own losses amounted to no more than three hundred men.[61] That too seems improbable. All that can be said for certain is that the victory was total.

Throughout the conflict, Pompey showed a very good appreciation of what Caesar could and would do. He accurately put the fate of Domitius's adventure at Corfinio down to Caesar's ability to interpose his troops between Domitius and a possible relief force. Although he appears to have been surprised by Caesar's crossing of the Adriatic, he retrieved the situation through his speedy march to Durrës, moving faster than Caesar predicted. He and Caesar shared an appreciation of the relative capacities of their armies. The only time Pompey took the initiative was at Durrës, when he had good intelligence regarding the situation on Caesar's side and could force a battle in which Caesar's troops could not deploy in a standard formation.

The poignant picture Caesar offers of Pompey's conduct on the day of Pharsalus also reveals how well both men understood the situation. The battle was fought because Pompey was losing control of the political situation in his own camp. This was something Caesar did not have to fear, even when things were not going well. The one area where Caesar shows himself clearly to be Pompey's master is in the management of the public relations campaign. By stressing that he would show mercy to those who surrendered he laid the groundwork for the peace that would follow upon ultimate victory. What Caesar could not foresee was that the passions which forced Pompey into battle at Pharsalus would not abate once Pompey was no longer on the scene. Caesar badly misread the strength of the opposition to himself, and thus he allowed it to assume a new form. While that was happening, he would be in Egypt, and with Egypt's queen—Cleopatra.

16

Cleopatra

Pompey left Larissa for Mytilene. There he collected his wife Cornelia and gathered some warships. He was uncertain what to do. His first instinct was to head to Syria. The province had been a mainstay of his regime during the war, and the kings in the region were beholden to him. They had all contributed troops to his army. Did he also think of doing a deal with the Parthians? Caesar doesn't mention the possibility, but the later tradition suggests it was a serious option.[1] The Syrian expedition soon collapsed. Although Pompey had gathered some more ships and reunited with some senior members of his "Senate" whom Caesar had released, the Roman business community in Syria wanted nothing to do with him. They seized control of Antioch and barred the gates. Pompey decided to move on. The next stop would be Egypt.[2]

Egypt was in chaos. When Ptolemy XII had died in the early part of 51, he left the kingdom to the two eldest of his four children. Cleopatra, his oldest child, was eighteen at the time; her younger brother, Ptolemy, was fourteen. Their sister, Arsinoe, was possibly in her early teens, while their youngest brother, also Ptolemy, was about twelve. Cleopatra (plate 12) was not interested in sharing power with her little brother. A document surviving from the year after Ptolemy XII's death is dated according to the Egyptian style, which measured time according to the number of years a king was on the throne, to "the Year 30, which is also the Year 1." Cleopatra is identified on another document as "the queen, the Lady of the Two Lands, the Father-Loving Goddess." There is no mention of her brother.[3]

Despite the chaos, Egypt was an important place. The last surviving kingdom of Alexander the Great's successors, it was very wealthy. Pompey, moreover, had plainly been important to Cleopatra's father, and the surplus grain Egypt produced would become, if it was not already, an important source of food for the population of Rome. Egypt also had a fleet strong enough to make a difference to one side or the other in the Civil War. It was the fleet, as well as the large number of soldiers left behind by Gabinius when he restored Ptolemy to his throne in 54, which drew Egypt into the conflict between Caesar and Pompey. There was also the question of money still owed to Caesar and Pompey for the Roman recognition of Ptolemy XII back in 59.

Cleopatra's situation had changed when Bibulus arrived in Syria to take up the governorship at the end of 51, not long after she had become queen. The Parthians were still raiding Syria and he was short of experienced troops, so he sent his two sons to Egypt asking for the return of the nearly two legions Gabinius had left there in 54. Gabinius's men were not interested in rejoining the Roman army. They murdered Bibulus's sons, and, when Cleopatra sent the ringleaders of the crime to Bibulus, a mutiny seems to have taken place, even though Bibulus ultimately returned the prisoners. A document dated to the end of 50, or Cleopatra's Year 3, reveals a regime change. Her brother was now her co-ruler. Events would soon show that the former legionaries were staunch supporters of the new king, Ptolemy XIII, whose affairs were managed by a eunuch named Pothinus, by Ptolemy's tutor Theodorus, and by Achillas, the commander of the royal guard.[4]

When Pompey abandoned Italy, ambassadors had been dispatched to summon troops from Egypt on the grounds that the "Senate" with Pompey was Rome's legitimate government and Egypt was an ally of Rome. The most important of these ambassadors was the older of Pompey's two sons, also named Gnaeus. He gathered a supply of grain, five hundred cavalrymen (formerly Gabinius's men), and sixty fully equipped warships. The "Senate" then recognized Ptolemy XIII as Egypt's legitimate ruler. The affinity of Pompey's "Senate" for Ptolemy should put paid to the story, spread later, that Cleopatra had seduced the young Pompey while he was in Alexandria.[5]

The war between Caesar and Pompey was not the only civil war to get underway in 49. In Egypt, Cleopatra and her sister Arsinoe left Alexandria. Although the course of events has not been preserved in detail, it looks as if Cleopatra fell out with Ptolemy's advisers, particularly Achillas. Taking off to Syria with what must have been a considerable amount of money, she raised an army with which to take back her throne.[6]

While Cleopatra was advancing on Egypt, Pompey hove onto the scene. Ptolemy was then at Pelusium, a site about twenty miles south of Port Said in today's Egypt, preparing to fight Cleopatra. Pompey sailed first into the harbor of Alexandria, sending an ambassador to request that the king receive him on the grounds of his friendship with the king's father, and protect him. The diplomatic tone of this message was undone by Pompey's messenger, who fell to chatting with some of the Gabinian troops still in Alexandria, suggesting they might want to come over to Pompey. When Pothinus and his associates found this out, they decided Pompey had to die. That, at least, was the version they later offered Caesar, Caesar suspected they might simply have decided to kill a man who was down on his luck, and Plutarch says Ptolemy's advisers decided to kill Pompey to make Caesar happy. Whatever the truth may be, kill him they did.[7]

Achillas, together with Septimius, who had once been a centurion under Gabinius and, before that, an officer under Pompey against the pirates, were chosen to be the assassins. Pompey was invited to come to Pelusium. When his ship appeared offshore, Achillas and Septimius asked him to join them in their own boat, which would bring him ashore. Pompey remembered Septimius, and, against the advice of those around him, he boarded the boat, taking with him Lucius Lentulus, one of the consuls of 49. He never reached shore. Septimius stabbed him, cut off his head, and left the body on the beach. The date was September 28, by Roman reckoning (July 25 by ours). That was the anniversary of Pompey's triumph over Mithridates. Lentulus was imprisoned and later died.[8] Cornelia retrieved Pompey's body, cremated it, and took the ashes with her when she returned to Italy, where she interred them in Pompey's tomb outside San Marino. But Ptolemy kept the head. That was the beginning of the end for him and his gang.[9]

Caesar's actions after Pharsalus were complicated, and the way he introduces them in his *Civil War* suggests he was aware later that he hadn't handled things very well. Although he could not have predicted Pompey's assassination in Egypt, he admits he was fixated on Pompey and determined not to allow him to raise a new army.[10] The upshot was that he took a relatively small force with him to chase Pompey down, leaving the rest of the army under the command of his legates to go back to Italy and wait for him. He gave no detailed instructions as to what those legions were to do if Pompeian forces began to rally or if he himself were delayed. His subordinates were all too aware that policy initiatives were not within their purview, and the result was that they did not take steps necessary to manage the increasingly mutinous army that returned to Italy from Greece or to solve the economic crises that were then plaguing Italy. Nor were they able to prevent a resurgence of the Pompeian cause in North Africa.

The saving grace for the Caesarian cause during what would prove to be Caesar's extended absence was the chaos among the Pompey-less Pompeians. The Pompeian fleet, which had been raiding Italy's coast, disintegrated when news arrived of the battle at Pharsalus. After an initial meeting on Corfu to decide what to do—Cicero presided as technical commander-in-chief—the various survivors of Pharsalus went their own ways. Some, like Cicero, went back to Italy. He had no interest in taking command of the losing side and now had a very dim view of his associates. Others went into exile. Some would join the diehard Cato, who took off for North Africa to reignite the anti-Caesarian cause in association with Juba. Another person who adopted this course was Afranius. It would be eighteen months before they could assemble an army. By that time Caesar had finished with his Eastern adventures.[11]

When he set out in pursuit of Pompey, Caesar had with him two under-strength legions, amounting to 3,200 men and 800 cavalry. One of these legions, the Sixth, had been raised in 52 and now mustered barely more than a thousand men; the other was a legion originally recruited from Greece to serve Pompey. When Caesar arrived in the province of Asia, he was greeted with stories of astonishing miracles that had occurred to announce the victory at Pharsalus: in Minerva's temple in Elis, the statue of the goddess Victory had turned to face Minerva, the sound of drums had been heard in a temple at Ephesus, and great shouts as if of armies were heard at Antioch in Syria. Caesar's decision to report these events suggests that, as he was drafting the *Civil War*, he may have been looking to change his public image. He also stresses how he returned money collected by Pompey's agents to the people of Asia. That could counteract charges that he himself played fast and loose with public moneys. He was looking for a new message now that Pompey was no longer available as a foil.[12]

One person who was absolutely not going to be part of any new messaging (though she may have been a reason why the new message was needed) was Cleopatra. The relationship Caesar was about to form with her, while plainly the result of a very deep attraction on his part, was profoundly embarrassing to his own side. He mentions her name exactly three times at the end of the *Civil War*, never placing her in the palace, while the editor who assembled reports from a variety of hands to create the *Alexandrian War*, which describes the events of 47, mentions her name only once. The editor never suggests Caesar might be fighting in her interest. This editor was quite possibly Aulus Hirtius, compiler of the last book of the *Gallic War*, who was very aware of Caesar's image problem.[13] Hence the importance of explaining how the war in Egypt was forced on Caesar by a collection of homicidally inclined courtiers of Ptolemy XIII who were seeking to exploit, for their own advantage, the dominance they exercised over a dimwitted child.

The trouble started as soon as Caesar landed in Alexandria at the end of July. It was only then that he found out about Pompey's assassination. It is from others that we learn how Theodotus had presented him with Pompey's head and how Caesar had turned away, in tears. He would later arrange for the head's burial in a shrine.[14] Meanwhile, Caesar says, people in Alexandria objected to the fact that he was accompanied by lictors, taking the presence of these magisterial assistants as an infringement on Egyptian sovereignty. Sensing that things would soon get worse, he immediately sent orders to the province of Asia: legions had been raised there to support the Pompeian war effort, and they were to come posthaste to Alexandria.

Caesar also offered to mediate between Ptolemy and his sister, "being anxious, as a friend of both sides, to settle disputes in the royal family." Once he had made this offer, he was told Achillas was advancing on Alexandria at the head of the royal army. Ptolemy was then in the palace, so Caesar suggested he send an embassy to Achillas to find out what was going on. Achillas murdered these ambassadors, at which point Caesar took the king into "protective custody," preparing to defend the palace and the dockyards. When Arsinoe escaped the palace to join the attacking force, Caesar occupied the shipyards nearest the palace, setting as he did so a large fire which destroyed the Ptolemaic fleet in the harbor and demolished storehouses connected to the Great Library. He also occupied the island just off the coast on which stood Alexandria's famous Lighthouse, intending to keep communications open with Syria and Asia, from both of which he had now summoned support.[15] When he discovered Pothinus was encouraging the attackers, he had him killed. On this note the *Civil War* comes to an end. No Cleopatra anywhere in sight.

How and when did Caesar and Cleopatra actually meet? Plutarch writes that Pothinus was plotting against Caesar, encouraging the revolt in the Egyptian army by giving the troops inadequate rations and serving people in the palace off cheap dinnerware, saying Caesar had taken all the gold and silver. Caesar does seem to have demanded payment of the uncollected bribe promised by Ptolemy XII back in 59, but Pothinus told him to go away and come back again later, at which point the money would be available. It was at this point, Plutarch says, that Caesar sent for Cleopatra.

There are two stories of their meeting. According to Cassius Dio, Cleopatra, who had been communicating with Caesar through her agents, heard that he was susceptible to the charms of a beautiful woman, sought a meeting, and completely enthralled him. According to Plutarch, the meeting was rather more dramatic:

> She set out with just a single companion, Apollodorus of Sicily, and embarked on a tiny boat. It was dusk when she came to the palace. There was only one way to come in unobserved, so she got into one of those sacks that are used for bedclothes and stretched herself out full length. Apollodorus rolled up the sack, fastened it with a strap, and brought it through the doors to Caesar. And that, they say, was the beginning of Caesar's captivation: the trick showed such style, and he was overcome by all the charm and grace with which she behaved towards him.[16]

Perhaps the most significant thing about this story is that it fits precisely into the context that Caesar provides for the outbreak of war in Alexandria. That is to say, it comes before the death of Pothinus, whose watchful eyes Cleopatra was trying to evade. It also answers the question a reader might raise in looking at what Caesar has to say: how could Caesar mediate between Ptolemy and Cleopatra if Cleopatra wasn't around? The month is August of 48, which fits well with the evidence for the pregnancy resulting from their contact. Cleopatra bore a son on June 23 of the following year.[17]

The *Alexandrian War* covers not only events in Egypt during the autumn of 48 and the first six months of 47 but also Caesar's actions in northern Turkey at the end of the summer of 47. Additionally, the editor gives some information about events in subsidiary theaters, Croatia and Spain. The Spanish narrative provides background for Caesar's final campaign in 45, and we can be quite certain from the way the editor obfuscates Caesar's relationship with Cleopatra that he was writing after Caesar's assassination. By that point, Cleopatra and her son by Caesar had been resident in Rome for more than a year. The child was by then a real problem for Caesar's advisers, who were asserting that Caesar had one heir only, and that this heir was his grandnephew Gaius Octavius. Caesar's friend Oppius is on record asserting there was no way Cleopatra's boy was Caesar's.[18] But the timing of her pregnancy speaks against him.

The emotional aspect of Caesar's relationship with Cleopatra is summed up very well by Plutarch's biography quoted above. She was wickedly bright, a younger version of Servilia, with whom Caesar still had a relationship even if it was no longer physical. (He had ensured her son, Marcus Junius Brutus, who had served with Pompey, was not killed at Pharsalus and released immediately after the battle.)[19] But what set Caesar's relationship with Cleopatra apart from his earlier relationships was that it was a stupid thing to do. By taking up with her as he did he virtually guaranteed there would be a war in Alexandria. The caution and careful planning that had informed his political conduct for decades, his constant ability to wrong-foot opponents and predict their reactions will from this point onward be less and less in evidence. He had defeated Pompey, was now the most powerful person in the Roman world, and he became increasingly careless of what people outside his immediate circle thought. And Cleopatra clearly enchanted him, and she appears to have been charmed by him too. Although he would never recognize the child she bore as legitimate, she advertised their liaison even though it wasn't politically advantageous to either of them. He wouldn't keep it a secret either. They were in love.

After Caesar and Cleopatra's first night together, Caesar summoned Ptolemy to their presence. He was shocked. He dashed out of the palace, tore off the diadem that was the symbol of kingship, and complained loudly to the crowd gathering around him that he was ruined. Caesar had him returned to the palace where he convened a meeting to announce his intention to uphold the original terms of the will of Ptolemy XII. Cleopatra and Ptolemy XIII would rule together. Caesar added the provision that Cyprus would be returned to Ptolemaic control and be ruled jointly by the two younger siblings, Arsinoe and the younger Ptolemy.[20]

The solution looked diplomatic, and the return of Cyprus was a surprising development. Given that it had been Cato's prize, following from a law of Clodius, Caesar may have been making a statement that he didn't consider it a necessary part of the empire.[21] In any case, this proposed arrangement didn't solve the problem in the palace. It did not so much mean Ptolemy was sharing power with his big sister; what it really meant was that Pothinus would again be subjected to Cleopatra's authority. Pothinus could reasonably think that this was a bad position for him to be in and thus determined to start a new war. He contacted Achillas, asking him to move his troops back to Alexandria. It was now that Caesar had Pothinus killed and Arsinoe fled the palace to take up with Achillas.[22]

The *Alexandrian War* opens with preparations on both sides. Caesar, who controlled the royal quarter in the eastern part of Alexandria, immediately realized he had a problem on his hands, sending for ships and auxiliaries in addition to those he had already ordered up from Asia. At the same time, he enhanced the fortifications around the royal palace, which the Alexandrians were preparing to storm. While this was going on, Arsinoe quarreled with Achillas, whom she then murdered, thereby assuming, along with the palace eunuch Ganymede, personal command of the anti-Roman faction. Their inexperienced leadership saved Caesar. The most effective thing his opponents could think to do was to attempt to pour massive amounts of seawater into the palace's water sources. Caesar's men simply dug new wells.[23]

Shortly thereafter a convoy arrived from Asia, bringing the first reinforcements. It consisted of supply ships and a legion of former Pompeians dispatched by Domitius Calvinus, the consul of 53 who had commanded the center of Caesar's line at Pharsalus and was now Asia's governor. Adverse winds drove the convoy past the royal harbor, controlled by Caesar, to a spot about seven miles west of Alexandria. Caesar led a daring expedition of his own warships to bring them in.[24] The next problem Caesar had to face was control of Alexandria's harbor. The harbor lay between the city and the great island of Pharos (not to be confused with the smaller island to the east on which the Lighthouse stood). It was divided in two parts by the causeway linking the island to the mainland. Caesar's ships were to the causeway's east and Arsinoe had gathered a fleet to the west. To control the harbor, Caesar needed to take control of the causeway, and, ideally, the whole island. Again the relative inexperience of his opponents would be a crucial factor in Caesar's survival while fresh forces made their way south from Asia, this time overland.

There followed a series of naval actions through which Caesar, now acting as an admiral, first attempted, with considerable success, to neutralize the fleet the Alexandrians had built on their side of the harbor. He then tried to launch an amphibious assault on the island of Pharos, which failed. When he tried to land troops from small boats on the causeway connecting the island to the mainland, he had succeeded in getting three cohorts ashore when sailors and oarsmen leapt from the ships to join them. The Alexandrians routed these less experienced fighters, and, in their panic, they disrupted the legionaries, who now had to fall back to their transports. Chaos ensued. Too many men were jumping into the closest boats, which sank under their weight. Caesar was on one of those boats. Realizing what was happening, he leapt into the sea, making for another boat a bit further off. The story goes that, multitasking as always, he held documents over his head with his left hand as he paddled through the water with his right. He reached the boat safely, but he had shed his purple cloak on the way. This was recovered by the Alexandrians, who delighted in displaying it.[25]

The mishap on the causeway cost Caesar at least four hundred men, and both sides settled into their positions. At this point ambassadors from the Alexandrians came to Caesar requesting the return of Ptolemy, saying he could provide the leadership needed to negotiate a peace. Caesar suspected they were lying, but he let Ptolemy go anyway, saying it would be more honorable to defeat a king than a rabble. The rabble hadn't been doing too badly, so the return of Ptolemy, whom Caesar must now have known quite well, may have been a subtle move on his part. With Ptolemy in command, the Alexandrians would not do better than they had already been doing. When Ptolemy left the palace, he immediately assumed titular command of the Egyptian forces, possibly doing away in the process with the eunuch Ganymede, who now vanishes from the narrative.[26] That was in November of 48 and, as Caesar may have anticipated, Ptolemy's leadership did nothing to enhance the efficiency of the besieging forces. Their ineffectiveness was to prove fatal. In March, the reinforcements Caesar had sent for, months ago, from Asia, were now approaching Pelusium under the command of Mithridates of

Pergamon (no relation to Mithridates of Pontus). These were joined on the march by 3,000 Jewish soldiers under Antipater, father of the future king Herod of Judaea, and some Nabatean Arab soldiers, dispatched by their king Iamblichus as the local dynasts now sought to make an alliance with Caesar.[27]

Mithridates took Pelusium by storm and moved rapidly on Alexandria. Ptolemy withdrew troops from the city to try and prevent Mithridates' arrival. When Mithridates defeated the blocking force, he wrote to Caesar, telling him he was approaching the westernmost, or Canopic, branch of the Nile. The king led more troops south to stop Mithridates, establishing a camp on the river's west bank. Caesar followed him, placing his men in a fleet of shallow-drafted vessels, and stormed the camp and routed the army. Ptolemy drowned trying to escape. Arsinoe was captured. The people of Alexandria threw down their arms.[28] Caesar reimposed the terms of Ptolemy XII's will insofar as it had provided for two rulers, who would now be Cleopatra and her surviving brother. Arsinoe was imprisoned.

The story of what happened next is complex. In keeping with his usual tendency to obscure Cleopatra's connection to Caesar, the editor of the *Alexandrian War* says Caesar remained in Egypt for a while to strengthen the position of the rulers who had just been installed. He implies the stay was not long. Suetonius and others suggest that it was months. Suetonius reports the two lovers routinely were partying late into the night and took a tour down the Nile which ended only when Caesar's troops refused to follow him any further. This seems to be a version of a story Appian reports in which the pair sail down the Nile in four hundred ships. This story, which also appears in Lucan's poem on the Civil War, wherein the portrait of Caesar is quite negative, seems connected with a version of Caesar's life, quite possibly created by his assassins, in which the victory over Pompey enabled Caesar to realize his inner tyrant. Who better to help him than the Egyptian queen, with whom he would show himself enamored when she came to Rome? The truth of the matter is likely a great deal less dramatic. Cassius Dio knows a tradition in which

Caesar didn't stay in Egypt long, and modern scholarship bears this out. By our reckoning, the final battle with Ptolemy took place on January 15 and Caesar departed Alexandria on February 18, taking with him only the Sixth Legion; three legions which had accompanied Mithridates were left behind to support Cleopatra.[29]

When he left Alexandria, Caesar had another war to fight. While the events in Egypt were unfolding, Pharnaces, the son of Mithridates of Pontus, had left his kingdom on the north side of the Black Sea and moved into the territory of two Roman client kings, Deiotaurus and Ariobarzanes, on the sea's southeastern edge. Ariobarzanes and Deiotaurus had appealed to Domitius Calvinus for assistance. Although, as governor of Asia, Calvinus was raising troops to be sent to Alexandria, he did his best to help. He wrote to Pharnaces, warning him that he was going to make trouble for himself by harassing allies of the Roman people. Pharnaces replied that he would not depart from lower Armenia, now Ariobarzanes' territory along the Black Sea, because it was his ancestral land.

The editor of the *Alexandrian War* seems to be very much on message when it comes to what followed. Calvinus was a favorite of Caesar, so no matter how badly things went, he was not going to be at fault (a stark contrast with some other passages, where less favored subordinates are heavily criticized). Although he had limited forces at his disposal, and was worried a lengthy engagement with Pharnaces would prevent the dispatch of more troops to Caesar, Calvinus realized he could not negotiate with the king. The result was a disaster. In October of 48 Calvinus attacked Pharnaces near the ancient city of Nicopolis ("Victoryville," modern Koyulhisar in eastern Turkey). Pompey had founded the city to celebrate his victory over Mithridates. It was now the site of a victory by Mithridates' son.[30]

Thoroughly trounced at Nicopolis, Calvinus withdrew to his province. Pharnaces took advantage of his victory to reoccupy more of his father's old kingdom. Caesar says he was only informed of these events, which had occurred months before his victory over Ptolemy, after he had left Egypt and arrived in Syria. The author of the *Alexandrian War*, again mindful of what were likely significant criticisms at the time, writes that Caesar was now informed of Pharnaces' ravages, learning at the same time that Italy was being run "badly and ineptly" and that indiscipline in the army was rife.[31] The person running Italy at this time was none other than Mark Antony, and the sharp criticism of his conduct looks like it was penned at a point in 44 when Hirtius had abandoned hope of a settlement with Antony and was looking ahead to the new civil war which would break out in 43.

Back in 47, however, Caesar recognized there was nothing he could do about the situation in Italy until he had dealt with the situation in the East. This was an area with which Pompey had had deep connections and from which he had received substantial support in the Civil War. Caesar needed to establish or deepen his own connections with regional leaders before going home. He also had to deal with Pharnaces. The claim, repeated in the *Alexandrian War*, that he would leave the region "free from internal conflicts" sounds very much like an official communiqué.[32]

Caesar had reached Syria from Egypt by late March. Caesar arrived on the border of Pontus at the end of July. He had four legions. One was the Sixth, two others had served under Domitius at Nicopolis, and the fourth was from Deiotaurus. Pharnaces decided to negotiate, sending ambassadors to present Caesar a gold crown and remind him that, unlike Deiotaurus and Ariobarzanes, he had not sent troops to Pompey. Caesar replied that the only person Pharnaces had helped was himself, since by failing to send Pompey assistance he had avoided being beaten. Caesar would allow him to depart in peace if he returned everything he had stolen from the provincials (especially those working for Roman business interests) and withdraw to his own territory. Then Caesar would accept the gold crown. Pharnaces, in response, began to drag his feet.[33]

Caesar marched into Pontus. Pharnaces met Caesar near the ancient city of Zela, which stood at some distance from the modern city of Amasya.[34] Mithridates' victory over a Roman army there in 67 had been the proximate cause for the *lex Manilia* conferring the command against him upon Pompey in the following year. Facing Pharnaces, Caesar's men began to dig in at the top of a steep hill. On the second day of the confrontation, when Caesar's men were working on the fortification of their camp, Pharnaces ordered his men to attack. The battle was over almost as soon as it started—a total defeat for Pharnaces. He fled as his camp was captured, evaded pursuit, and returned to his ancestral kingdom, where he subsequently died in battle with the son-in-law who had seized power in his absence.[35]

Caesar erected an enormous trophy on the battle site to overshadow the one erected years earlier by Mithridates. By Caesar's reckoning, the war had begun when he arrived within striking distance in late May. The decisive battle was fought on May 21. The message Caesar sent to Rome to report the victory was perhaps the most famous of all his missives. It consisted of three words: *veni, vidi, vici*—"I came, I saw, I conquered."[36]

17

Dictator

It was mid-July when Caesar arrived back in Italy. The situation he had to deal with was a mess. Veteran legions in the vicinity of Rome were demanding discharge and cash bonuses for their service. At the same time, the economic crisis, which Caesar thought he had solved with his debt legislation, had reignited. Another cause for distress was that it was now clear the Civil War hadn't ended at Pharsalus. Powerful Pompeian forces were now assembled under the leadership of Metellus Scipio in North Africa.

The cause for the domestic crisis, which had been sputtering for the better part of a year, was Cicero's friend, Caelius. He had joined forces with Milo, who at Caelius's invitation had returned to Italy, despite Caesar's desire that he not do so, to spark a rebellion in early 48. Caelius had tried to turn the terms of Caesar's debt law into a populist cause by setting up his own tribunal to which people could appeal the valuation of their property. When this didn't get much attention, he proposed a law to eliminate interest payments for people repaying a loan within six years. Servilius Isauricus, Caesar's consular colleague, who had remained in Italy, refused to allow the bill to come to a vote. So Caelius proposed two more laws: one that would eliminate rent, and another that would cancel all debts. After these proposals led to a riot in the Forum, Servilius had the Senate remove Caelius from office and ban him from any public function. When Caelius tried to summon a public meeting, Servilius had him forcibly removed from the Rostra (the speakers' platform in the Forum) and had an "ultimate decree" passed that would enable him to take further action as needed.[1]

Confined to his house, but not under guard, Caelius fled Rome to join forces with Milo. Returning to Rome, Milo had gathered a collection of thugs and tried to reoccupy one of his old houses in the city now owned by a man serving with Pompey in Greece. The man's wife mounted a vigorous defense of the property, driving Milo and his men away.[2] Milo then put on a large gladiatorial display, after which he took his gladiators into Campania where he attempted to start a rural revolt. The parallel with Spartacus's rebellion was presumably non-coincidental, as Milo was entering territory which had supplied numerous soldiers to the army Pompey had just taken overseas and could be imagined to be of anti-Caesarian disposition. As Caelius moved south to join Milo, Sulpicius ordered the troops who were stationed in Rome's vicinity to deal with the incipient trouble. A battle was fought somewhere in Campania, and Milo was defeated. He and Caelius were subsequently killed trying to storm different towns in southern Italy.[3] This was all in the months leading up to Pharsalus.

The problems in Italy after Pharsalus stemmed from Mark Antony's greedy incompetence. He was appointed "master of horse," or second in command to Caesar, who after Pharsalus had assumed the office of dictator. Antony's job had been to bring nine of Caesar's veteran legions back to Italy from Greece. Following his return to Italy Antony appears to have seen his job as limited to managing festivals and the property confiscated from deceased Pompeians, which he passed out, free of charge, to his friends. He himself moved into Pompey's former house in Rome. At the same time, he began a very public affair with a famous actress, with whom he paraded around Italy in an elaborate procession featuring displays of gold and silver dinnerware and a chariot drawn by a pair of tame lions. Such displays didn't go down well at a time when economic uncertainty prevailed.[4]

While Antony partied, Dolabella, one of the tribunes and another former legate, revived Caelius's debt legislation. He was opposed by two other tribunes, one of them Asinius Pollio, the future historian who corrected Caesar's casualty figures for Pharsalus. They pointed out to Antony that he needed to do something to stop Dolabella, otherwise it would look like he was being told what to do by his wife, who was allegedly Dolabella's lover. Dolabella then occupied the Forum, erecting a statue of Clodius. The Senate voted that Antony needed to suppress Dolabella, by force of arms if necessary. There was violence in the Forum, which unraveled the discipline of the troops who had returned from Greece and were stationed in Campania. Antony left Lucius Caesar in charge of the city and went to deal with the troops. The result was further chaos, which Antony compounded when he suddenly decided that Dolabella was in the right. Seeing that he had not won any credit for his change of heart, however, he once again set himself against Dolabella and found some soldiers to break up an assembly Dolabella had summoned to vote on his laws. This was the situation when Caesar arrived.[5]

Riots in Rome were not the only problem. The mutinous legions not only refused to deal with Antony, but they had also refused to receive three legates Caesar had dispatched when he was on his way to deal with Pharnaces. The continuing mutiny was a serious problem not just for the present, but also looking ahead since the troops involved were the veterans from the Gallic campaign, including the men of the Tenth Legion. Caesar was going to need them for the campaign he was going to have to fight in Africa. The author of the next book dealing with Caesar's campaigns, the *African War*, suggests the problem was not limited to the legionaries but that indiscipline was the result of discontent among the officers. It is possible he is echoing Caesar's belief that soldiers mimic the conduct of their commanders, but it is also possible this was indeed the situation: mid-grade officers who had been serving for a number of years were looking for a payout so they could go home and take up influential positions in civilian life.[6]

Caesar was aware of the problems he would face upon his return. On his way to Egypt, he had reformed the tax collection system in the Eastern provinces, eliminating payment of the principal taxes collected from cities through the *publicani*. Those taxes would now be paid directly to governors. This was an extension of the system he had imposed in Gaul, and quite likely in Spain. This had several effects, one of which was to curtail powerful corporations he did not control. Another was to make collection more efficient—it was claimed that the removal of the *publicani* reduced the tax burden on the cities of the East by a third; presumably this was the money the *publicani* had formerly pocketed when they passed on the contracted taxes to the state. Caesar was less generous on his way back home, however, collecting substantial payments from people and places that had shown loyalty to Pompey's cause.[7]

Upon his arrival in Rome, Caesar first addressed the question of debt. He announced that any interest that had accrued since January of 49 would be forgiven, and that there would be a year-long moratorium on rent. His program, which once again assisted Rome's less fortunate while enhancing the prospect that the principal on outstanding loans would actually be paid, brought peace to the streets. As the value of property used as collateral for loans had also collapsed, Caesar introduced a program to reset those values to prewar levels now that the war in Italy was over. [8] Debt was not only a problem for Roman landholders. Caesar was seriously short of cash himself. He demanded gifts from the municipalities of Italy to support the ongoing war effort on the grounds he had sacrificed his own fortune for the state. Then he insisted that those who had occupied former Pompeian properties must pay for them at their prewar valuations. This announcement was important, for it drew a line under his assertion that he was no Sulla. His subordinates were still servants of the state and accountable for their actions.[9]

It was time now to deal with the legions. Caesar sent Sallust, the future historian who was then praetor-designate, to negotiate with the troops, offering a substantial bonus if they would return to service. Sallust's mission nearly ended in his death, since the troops didn't want to hear from him any more than they had been interested in hearing from the legates earlier. The legions, led by the Tenth, now began to move on Rome, killing two envoys of praetorian rank as they advanced.[10]

When the Tenth Legion arrived on the Campus Martius, Caesar went to greet them. The men demanded release from service and retirement bonuses. In one version of what happened next, Caesar only had to utter one word: *Quirites!* (fellow citizens!)—indicating that the troops were no longer his "fellow soldiers." In another version, Caesar told the men he would give them what they were owed once the wars were over but that he would be celebrating his triumph with men who still served him: by implication, the mutinous legionaries were now dismissed. In both versions, the troops were stunned. The men of the Tenth Legion said they would volunteer to serve with him in the coming war if he readmitted them to his service. Caesar said he would be very happy to do this, guaranteeing them lots from the public land and giving them some of the money they were owed and promising they would get the rest with interest when the war ended. He offered a similar settlement to the rest of the troops. The negotiations at this point are obscure, but it seems that a substantial number of men—four of the nine veteran legions—opted for retirement. It was time to get the army to Africa before further trouble broke out in Italy and Caesar's enemies became better organized. Arranging his men's retirements, Caesar made it clear that he would be giving them farms from *existing* public lands; there would be no mass confiscations and settlements on the Sullan model.[11]

The anonymous author of our primary source for the North African campaign, although not a member of Caesar's inner circle, is at pains to defend Caesar from charges that he was off his game for pretty much the whole event. Critics claimed he had botched the initial landing, that he had paid insufficient attention to logistics, and that he had lost control of his men in the final battle at Thapsus (near Bekalta in modern Tunisia). The army itself was of dubious quality, mingling too many recent recruits with the surviving veterans. There was some truth to what people were saying, but the situation on the other side was worse.[12]

The Pompeian army was large but consisted mostly of recent recruits and had a divided command. Pompeian leaders who had gathered in Africa included Afranius, Petreius, Metellus Scipio, Labienus, and Cato. There was also Juba, who was not going to be taking orders from any Roman. Just what Roman would be giving the orders was also a problem.

Afranius and Petreius were still suspect to many Pompeians because of their defeat in Spain, Labienus because of his long service with Caesar. Metellus Scipio obtained the nominal command along with Cato, since their anti-Caesarian credentials were impeccable. But they also hated each other: Metellus had written a book a few years before on the topic of Cato's impossibility as a human being. So it is perhaps not surprising that, when Metellus took the field, Cato remained in Utica, the ancient city located about twenty miles' distance from modern Tunis.[13]

Caesar joined his fleet at Marsala in Sicily in early October. He set sail almost immediately to a staging area off the beautiful island of Favigena in the Egadi Islands. From there he directed his fleet to sail toward eastern Tunisia without giving clear directions as to where they should rendezvous should the fleet become separated. High winds then scattered the fleet. Caesar himself landed near Sousse with 3,000 infantry and 150 cavalry, encamping in front of the city, which refused to admit him. He did not have a strong enough force to take the place, and so moved east to Monastir a day later. Here, four days after his initial landing, he was joined by the rest of his transports.[14]

Was this poor planning on Caesar's part? Maybe not. The crossing of the Adriatic in 48 had been in stages, with multiple landing spots in the face of an enemy with a vastly larger fleet. In this case, Caesar directed his ships to a part of Tunisia well removed from Metellus Scipio's base at Utica, where he was coordinating his forces with those of Juba. He did have all the ships that had set out from Favigena in the same port within a week of their original departure—all in all, not bad for a large fleet sailing in the autumn. There would also be three more convoys sailing at one-month intervals. The first two delivered another four legions, all of them veterans (including the Tenth).[15] Until those legions arrived, Caesar would have to adopt a defensive posture around Sousse. The fourth convoy, with troops who had been convalescing when the first three departed, joined Caesar just before the decisive battle at Thapsus on February 7.[16] The timing of the campaign, late fall to early winter, suggests Caesar preferred facing some difficulty in transport to campaigning in the heat of the summer.

What the author of the *African War* leaves out was a dramatic moment when Caesar landed for the first time. Metellus Scipio may have had minimal command experience, but he was a Scipio, and there was a belief in some quarters that no member of a family whose ancestors had defeated Hannibal and destroyed Carthage could be defeated on North African soil. Caesar had already ignored one bad omen, the escape of a sacrificial animal before the departure of the first convoy. Now he slipped and fell as he was landing. This he transformed into a good omen, crying out to his men, "I've got you, Africa!," and he found a member of a less fortunate branch of the Cornelian family (and thus a relative of the Scipios) whom he added to his staff. Although Caesar plainly didn't believe in conventional religious practice any more than he had in the past, he was sensitive enough to the sentiments of his men to look like he was taking their concerns seriously.[17]

The arrival of the veteran legions determined the course of the campaign. Scipio had collected a substantial army from the Roman citizens living in the province of Africa, and he had the support of Juba's army, which may have numbered 20,000 men, giving him a total force of around 50,000. He had also trained many elephants. But despite what may have been a clear superiority in numbers at the beginning of the campaign, Scipio was unwilling to press an attack on Caesar, who in turn was plainly concerned about the quality of troops he was leading. In the one significant action, in which Labienus commanded his Pompeian opponents, Caesar is described as setting an example of calm for his novice soldiers even as they formed a circle to prevent Juba's Numidian cavalry from launching an effective attack. At another point, Caesar is described as playing the role of a gladiatorial trainer, telling his men how to fight the light troops deployed by their enemy. In order to acclimatize the troops to elephant warfare, Caesar ordered up a number of animals from Italy and trained his men in best practices for dealing with them.[18] Much of the time was otherwise spent marching and countermarching between towns along Tunisia's north coast. Caesar was in no hurry to fight before his full army was assembled and it looks as if his primary concern was to get his new troops into good physical condition while gradually exposing them to combat operations.

With the veteran army fully assembled and the new troops having gained several months of experience, Caesar marched east from the region around Sousse, which thus far had been the primary focus of the campaign, to Thapsus. Caesar's camp there was inside a line of marshes. On February 6, Scipio attempted to lay siege to Caesar's camp by establishing fortifications at either end of the swamp. In doing so, he committed the fundamental military error of dividing his forces in the face of the enemy. Caesar struck the next day.

Scipio had occupied an area due east of Thapsus; Petreius, who was serving as his chief subordinate, and his ally Juba were encamped south of the city. Accounts of the decisive battle differ in one important regard: the degree of control Caesar exercised over the outcome. The author of the *African War* says the battle started by accident. When Caesar was trying to restrain his men, who were calling upon him to launch an immediate attack, a bugler on the right wing, where the Tenth and Thirteenth Legions were stationed, sounded the charge and began to advance. Caesar gave in and ordered the rest of the army forward. His light-armed troops panicked the elephants which Scipio had stationed in front of his lines. They trampled their own men, and the battle line collapsed. When Caesar's troops pursued Scipio's men, they seem to have rounded the marsh and captured the other two camps. Cassius Dio adds the detail that Juba fled when he saw what had happened to Scipio's men. Dio, however, does not allow for the accidental advance, though he has the same detail about the defeat of the elephants, which makes it seem like someone had corrected the version of the story that appears in the *African War*. More significant is that, while the author of the *African War* says the soldiers slaughtered their enemies and even turned on some of their own officers while Caesar begged them to spare their defeated foes, Dio makes Caesar responsible for the massacre. Plutarch has a version in which Caesar was ill and returned to camp after drawing up his lines. Plutarch says the total casualties suffered by Scipio's army amounted to 50,000, while the author of the *African War* has the number at 10,000.[19]

Plainly the aftermath of the battle had been bloody. Was Caesar responsible? The efforts in various traditions to suggest he was not should most likely lead us to the conclusion that he was. The veterans, when they had mutinied, had complained that Caesar's willingness to spare his enemies was lengthening the war. Although in this campaign's aftermath Rome would be drenched in propaganda asserting Caesar's merciful nature, it is clear opposition losses were very high. Scipio's army was essentially wiped out, as was Juba's. Caesar had tempered mercy with savagery in the past—the case of the Eburones is the most obvious parallel. Scipio had prolonged the war that should have ended at Pharsalus, and it was important to Caesar for the war to be over now. There are also other signs that policy was different in the aftermath of Thapsus. When Publius Sittius, who had led an anti-Juba movement among the Gaetulian tribesmen on the Sahara's rim, encountered the Pompeians Faustus Sulla—Sulla's son—and Afranius, both fleeing towards Spain, he killed them. The author of the *African War* blames restless soldiers for the act, but Dio says Caesar ordered their deaths. The same fate befell Scipio and a number of his companions who had escaped with him by sea and settled in near Utica. The exact circumstances of their demise remain uncertain: in one version they were killed in a naval action; in another, Sittius killed them. Cato, meanwhile, had committed suicide rather than surrender. It would prove to be his most successful political statement.[20]

Cato had put on a display of arranging the defense of Utica in constant consultation with the city council. When Caesar's army approached and it became clear no defense could be offered, Cato entrusted his son to Lucius Caesar's care. (Caesar's nephew had remained committed to Pompey's cause despite his father's allegiance to the family brand.) Cato then had dinner with his closest companions before withdrawing to his bedchamber where he read Plato's *On the Soul*. When he saw his sword had been taken away, he sent his servants for it. It was clear what he planned to do, which is why his servants had removed the sword. Then, after resting for a while, Cato stabbed himself. Being, according to his biographer, infirm, he did not kill himself with the first stroke, but he resisted treatment and then died. He had made his statement about what life under Caesar's rule would be like. It would not be possible for the political world to return to normal in the foreseeable future.[21]

When Caesar arrived at Utica, he is said to have regretted not being able to spare Cato's life. That was an easy line to take now that Cato was dead. Lucius Caesar was killed shortly thereafter, which should tell us what Cato's fate would have been. Cato's son, a teenager, was spared.[22] Two other deaths that followed in short order were those of Juba and Petreius, who killed each other in a duel.[23] Caesar annexed a portion of Juba's kingdom as the province of New Africa and appointed Sallust as the governor. Juba's family were taken as hostages to Rome.

It may have been while setting the boundaries for the new province that Caesar met with Bogud, king of Numidia's western neighbor Mauretania, who would receive those sections of Numidia not annexed to the new Roman province. It was said Caesar also entered into relations, albeit of a more personal nature, with Bogud's wife Eunoe. The area around Cirta (Kasantina in Algiers) was given to Sittius as a reward for his labors. After making these arrangements and having imposed heavy fines on places which had supported his enemies, it was time for Caesar to return to Italy. The return took twenty-seven days, including a stop on Sardinia, where he also imposed a fine on the city of Sulci, in the vicinity of the modern town of Sant'Antioco. The city had supported Pompeian naval operations.[24]

The journey from Sardinia to Rome took nearly a month as storms delayed Caesar, who was now made dictator for the third time. He had with him the veteran legions from Africa, which were scheduled for demobilization. The recently raised legions were sent on to Spain in the hope that they would nip a further civil war in the bud. Labienus had joined Pompey's sons, Gnaeus and Sextus, to raise a fresh army there from districts where Pompey's memory still carried weight.[25]

Back in Rome, for Caesar it was time first to party and then to demonstrate he could serve the interests of the Roman people better through a government centered upon himself rather than the state's traditional institutions. Enormous wealth had been gathered in Rome's immediate vicinity, a combination of plunder and the fines imposed upon the recalcitrant. This wealth would soon be on display when Caesar celebrated four triumphs—one more than Pompey had celebrated when he returned to Italy in 62. These would all technically be for foreign wars: Gaul, Alexandria, Pontus, and Africa. The view Caesar had promoted of the African War was that Scipio had been the agent of Juba, the true brains behind the operation. The triumphs would drive home the essential point that Caesar had achieved more than any Roman in the city's history. They would also mark the official end of a period of enormous stress for the average Roman, showing everyone how Caesar valued their pleasures. The triumphs and accompanying celebrations would last for most of the month of September.

Before entering the city for his first triumph, over Gaul, Caesar summoned a public meeting at which he told the assembled people he had vastly increased the revenues of the state. Pompey, upon his return, had stressed the same point, so Caesar was once again demonstrating that he had outdone his dead rival. But he was also sending a message that the state had the resources to do better by Rome's people. Caesar also met with the Senate, reassuring those present that he had no intention of acting like Sulla. Earlier in the year, Hirtius had sponsored a law banning former Pompeians from holding public office, and that might have been taken as reflecting Caesar's attitude. Now Caesar was suggesting Hirtius had gone too far. He let it be known he had burnt, unread, the correspondence of Pompey, seized at Pharsalus, and of Scipio, taken after Thapsus.[26]

The Senate now declared Caesar dictator for the next ten years and gave him the post of "supervisor of morals" for three years. The implicit message, with whispers of resistance still coming from Spain, was that people who accepted Caesar's victory would be able to get on with their lives—perhaps not as they might once have planned, since Caesar's favor would be necessary for any advancement, but at least they did not need to worry about Sullan-style death and destruction Pompey had promised. Caesar, it seemed, still defined himself in terms of his rivals—he could not define his own success or program without reference to them.[27]

The general celebrating a triumph was, for that glorious day, Jupiter's representative on earth. His clothing was modeled on the attire of Jupiter himself as he appeared in his great temple on the Capitoline. This included a purple-dyed toga with gold embroidery, red boots, and a laurel crown. Possibly the general would have his face painted red as well. He would ride a four-horse chariot from the Campus Martius into the city and then through Rome's streets to the Capitoline, where he would drive the chariot up the road from the Forum to Jupiter's temple, dismount, and offer thanks to the god. Prisoners and plunder would be displayed in the procession ahead of the general, along with pictures of great moments in the war and an accounting of all the people who had been killed. The general's soldiers would march behind him. This was the only time armed men were supposed to be inside the city limits. According to some descriptions of triumphs, a slave would stand behind the general, whispering in his ear the words *memento mori*, reminding him to remember that he was still human.[28]

The Gallic triumph lasted all day as prisoners and plunder were marched through the streets along with pictures illustrating great scenes from the wars. Caesar's ascent of the Capitoline from the forum was by torchlight—forty elephants bore the torches alongside him. That was quite spectacular, but the day had not been without some miscarriages. Caesar's chariot had broken when the procession moved from the Forum Boarium into the Forum, pitching him out into the street, and he had to complete the journey in a fresh vehicle. And the soldiers sang lewd songs. One doesn't seem to have bothered Caesar:

> City dwellers, watch your wives, we're bringing the bald adulterer.
> In Gaul he fucked away a fortune, which he borrowed here.

Another one infuriated him:

> Caesar conquered Gaul, Nicomedes conquered Caesar.
> See: Caesar, he who conquered Gaul, now triumphs,
> Nicomedes who conquered Caesar does not triumph.

Caesar was really upset by these verses and would later swear an oath that Nicomedes had not raped him. As for the broken wheel, that could have been seen as a bad omen but, since the accident occurred opposite the temple of Fortune erected by Lucullus, it was interpreted as a good sign.

Still, Caesar tried to correct for it by ascending the steps of Jupiter's temple on his knees. Before this, the Roman people had seen Vercingetorix. He had been kept alive for this moment and marched along with the other prisoners ahead of Caesar's chariot. He was executed when his part in the procession ended.[29]

The triumph for the Alexandrian war went more smoothly, though the Roman people took pity on Cleopatra's sister, Arsinoe, who was paraded much as Vercingetorix had been the previous day. A teenage girl should not be treated as a Gallic chieftain. Caesar spared her life, which may not have delighted Cleopatra. She had come to town with her younger brother (now also, according to Egyptian tradition, her official husband) as well as her son. Caesar installed her in a villa west of the Tiber.[30]

The Pontic triumph was next. This was a big success. The crowd delighted at a painting of Pharnaces in flight and took up Caesar's post-battle message (displayed on placards): the air was filled with cries of *veni, vidi, vici*. The triumph for the African war, however, raised questions about Caesar's judgement. Included were paintings of Scipio's and Cato's deaths. Caesar's point was they were no longer Romans but servants of an African tyrant (whose death was also depicted). But many thought Caesar was celebrating the triumph as a victory over fellow Romans; many also thought Caesar had made himself look foolish in protesting about Nicomedes.[31]

After the African triumph, Caesar dedicated the Temple of Venus, the centerpiece of the new forum he had begun in 54. Again, he was accompanied by his torch-bearing elephants and a massive crowd of spectators. The other leftover business from 54 was the celebration of Julia's memory. There were massive banquets and other entertainments. A new wooden theater had been built in the Forum for gladiatorial combats and beast hunts. And giraffes were displayed at Rome for the first time! Another first, possibly intended to reflect the importance of Caesar's role in governing public morality, was a loosening of rules around who could participate in the spectacles. Traditionally, people who performed in public were excluded from polite society. So it was notable that Caesar allowed members of the equestrian order to fight as gladiators, and controversial when he paid the famous poet Quintus Laberius a huge fee to appear on the stage, which would ordinarily have cost him his own equestrian status (only an author who stayed off the stage was considered respectable). But after Laberius recited some lines about bowing to necessity when compelled by the "man of merciful mind... who towers above us," Caesar gave him a gold ring, restoring his status as an equestrian. By doing this, Caesar showed people that he could deal with criticism, which was important in the wake of his reaction to the songs about his relationship with Nicomedes.[32]

In addition to the gladiatorial and theatrical events, Caesar had arranged for battles to be fought in the Circus and for a mock naval battle in an area he had dug out and flooded on the Campus Martius. Unlike gladiatorial combats, which were rarely fought to the death, the people engaged in these battles were prisoners who had been condemned to die. The bloody spectacles were not popular with everyone. Dio tells us some people said that the events were an extravagant demonstration of Caesar's undiminished bloodlust.[33]

When the parties were over, it was time to get down to business. The troops being demobilized needed their retirement benefits, set at the extremely generous level of five thousand denarii, roughly double the total salary a man who had served for twenty years would have received. Caesar now also settled them on the land he had promised prior to the African campaign. To the people of Rome who were on the lists of those who received free grain, he gave substantial gifts of grain and olive oil in addition to four hundred denarii. This was a victory for all the less fortunate.[34]

Gifts given, Caesar set about making fundamental changes. Among the powers the senate had granted him was the right to nominate candidates for election in the coming years. He would nominate half the praetors, aediles, and quaestors each year. The other half would not have his direct support, placing those who did not achieve his favor at an expensive disadvantage. An increase in the number of praetors made it possible for him to decree that no person would hold a provincial governorship as an ex-praetor for more than a year, or as an ex-consul for more than two years. Rome's dealings with its neighbors would now be dictated from the center—Caesar would abolish his own example. He increased the number of senators from six hundred to around nine hundred to reward his followers, among whom were quite a number of Gauls and even some men from Spain. He also reformed the courts, eliminating the "treasury tribunes" who had made up a third of each jury since the jury reforms of 70, so that only senators and equestrians would now serve.[35]

As official in charge of public morals, Caesar had the powers of a censor, which he used to create new citizens and pass a law making families with three or more children eligible for land distributions. He reduced the number of Romans eligible for grain distributions from 300,000 to 150,000, presumably on the grounds that enrollment on the list had been managed incompetently by Clodius so that people who should not have been eligible had been included. He then founded two new colonies, at Carthage and Corinth, and other colonies at less notable sites in southern France as well as in Italy. In all, he dispatched 80,000 people, both veterans and members of Rome's lowest class, to inhabit his new colonies. While it might appear that he was undoing two atrocities of the previous century—Carthage and Corinth had both been destroyed by Rome in 146—the main effect of the new colonies was to establish large populations beholden to Caesar in areas that had recently come under his sway. He also sent new settlers to towns throughout Italy whose constitutions he had reformed to make government work more efficiently, and he ordered that one-third of all persons employed on large estates must be free, a law that was likely more rhetorical than practical as the typical estate was already farmed largely by free tenant farmers. Caesar also appears to have enforced laws against extravagant expenditure quite severely. On the one hand, this policy recognized the fact that Rome's less fortunate inhabitants were offended by lavish expenditure; on the other hand, it also sent a message to Caesar's subordinates that behavior such as Antony's the year before would not be tolerated.[36]

The combination of effective gain distributions and settlement programs, especially those at Carthage and Corinth, looked back to programs advocated by politicians of a *popularis* stripe since the time of Gaius Gracchus, who had attempted to initiate the refoundation of Carthage and Corinth in 123—a program cut short by his enemies two years later. It took a dictator, not a democrat, to make such a program work—a point that Caesar had been making for some time. The recipients of all these benefits could be expected to be grateful and loyal to the regime which had provided them. As Sallust would later write, Caesar's career was devoted to creating gratitude toward himself.[37]

The most lasting of Caesar's reforms was his change in the calendar. The official year was now badly out of alignment with the seasons: in order to prevent people he didn't like from having longer terms in office, in recent years Caesar had not inserted the "intercalary" months that were the usual way of rectifying this problem. Now he made use of calculations by an Alexandrian mathematician who had accompanied him home from Egypt to create the 365-day year, including a leap year every fourth year, which is the basis of our calendar today. To give the new system its proper starting point, he had already inserted one intercalary month after February, and he now inserted two more before the end of the year, making 46 the longest year on record, at 445 days.[38]

As the long year continued, Caesar needed to move on his promised policy of reconciliation in order to alleviate the memory of the African massacres. He had written to Cicero after the Alexandrian War, telling him he was welcome to come home. It was now time for some theatrical forgiveness in which Cicero played an active part. At a meeting of the Senate in October (our reckoning), Calpurnius Piso requested Caesar's forgiveness for Marcellus, the brutal consul of 51, who had been living on the island of Lesbos ever since Pharsalus. Caesar acquiesced. Cicero rose to offer thanks. Some, he said, might think the honors of war were shared between a general and his army, and that Fortune played a role in a general's success. But in this case Fortune bowed to Caesar, and the policy of forgiveness was Caesar's alone. He thus surpassed through equity and compassion all other victors in civil wars and he thus showed the superiority of his cause. For, while Pompey had threatened those who failed to follow him, Caesar was looking to rebuild a fractured society, restoring its moral fiber as he did so. But he did need to take care: his safety was crucial for the well-being of all, and he could not go around saying that he had lived long enough for glory or nature.[39]

Cicero appears to have been genuinely pleased with the course of events, writing shortly after Caesar's decision in favor of Marcellus that things were looking up:

> No one is so hostile to the course Pompey took up with more spirit than foresight as to dare call us bad citizens or evil men. In this regard, I admire Caesar's responsibility, justice, and wisdom. He never refers to Pompey in any way other than respectfully. He did do some harsh things to him, but those were the deeds of war and victory, not of Caesar. And look at how he has received us. Cassius is a legate; he has made Brutus governor of Gaul; Sulpicius, of Greece; and he has restored Marcellus, whom he was really angry at, to his full dignity. It would be inconceivable under the circumstances if other people were not treated in the same way.[40]

The irony of the fact that the first two people mentioned here as beneficiaries of Caesar's mercy—Cassius and Brutus—were to organize the conspiracy against Caesar just over a year later may be obvious to us in a way it would never have been to Cicero.

Cicero was not done with the business of Caesar's clemency. A few months after Marcellus's restoration, a privilege he was slow to take up and was never to fully enjoy, since he was murdered on his way home, Cicero took up the cause of Quintus Ligarius, who had served under Scipio in North Africa. Ligarius's brothers had approached Cicero about their brother's situation since, although he had been pardoned, he remained in exile. But a man named Quintus Aelius Tubero obtained permission to oppose the recall and charge Ligarius with treason.[41] Tubero disliked Ligarius because the latter had prevented his father from taking up the governorship of Africa in 49, refusing even to let him, or any of his family members (including Quintus himself, who had been sick on the ship), come ashore. The family had then sailed for Greece to join Pompey before Pharsalus. Tubero had been pardoned after the battle, and another aspect of the prosecution was his desire to demonstrate his loyalty to the regime by prosecuting an opposition loyalist.

The case was heard in the Forum. Caesar in his role as dictator presided at the hearing in person. His position was a complicated one as Cicero points out while representing Ligarius. On the one hand, Cicero suggests that Tubero was undermining Caesar's clemency. Were it not for that clemency, many members of the victorious party would be doing just what Tubero was doing—seeking to work out private vendettas. On the other hand how could Caesar do well by the state if he allowed criminals to flourish? In fact, the genius of Caesar's position was that his enemies were no longer to be seen as criminals. The Civil War had been a conflict in which both sides had the best interest of the state at heart, even if one of those two sides was deeply mistaken. The generosity of this view is a sign of Caesar's humanity and clemency. Cicero asks Caesar to honor the passion of Ligarius's neighbors, Sabines all, "the flower of Italy," who have come to support his cause. Can Caesar not see that, if Ligarius had been allowed to remain in Italy, his view would have been identical to that of his brethren? Like so many others, he was an unwilling Pompeian. Just as Caesar had restored Marcellus to the Senate, he could now restore Ligarius to Italy. He must show mercy to all, not just to the rich and famous.[42]

Caesar wept as he listened to Cicero—so says Plutarch—and he acquitted Ligarius. The whole business may have been judicial theater which took place only after a significant period of negotiation, but it was theater which made a point. Despite the many deaths in Africa, Caesar was genuinely committed to a policy of reconciliation, and what better place to show that than in the middle of the Forum? His life experience had taught him that peace without reconciliation would be no peace, and was he to be seen to treat Gauls better than Romans? Caesar was continuing to translate to Rome the policy which had finally worked in Gaul. It was a logical step, but its implicit equating of the Roman aristocracy to defeated Gauls had the effect of stressing that traditional aristocratic values such as dignity, achieved through competitive personal accomplishment, should be subordinate to gratitude.[43]

The acquittal of Ligarius took place against the background of preparations for a new campaign. This would be in Spain, where Pompey's
sons, Gnaeus and Sextus, along with Labienus, had assembled a genuine
threat to Caesar's position in the peninsula. Before he could set out,
however, Caesar needed to give some thought to the future. Now in his
mid-fifties, an age few reached, he had no heir. In addition to his child by
Cleopatra, there were sons to whom various women in Gaul had given
birth, or so rumor had it. But he had no children with Calpurnia. Despite
his persistent infidelities she appears to have loved him, and he loved her.
That they could not have children together was grounds for divorce
under Roman law, and the absence of a child after a decade of marriage
would certainly have afforded grounds for divorce if Caesar did not
value her. Her value may have had a political as well as a personal dimen-
sion. While Oppius, Balbus, Hirtius, and other members of Caesar's inner
circle saw to the management of public policy, especially in connection
with the settlement of veterans, Calpurnius and Calpurnia may have acted
as intermediaries with the Senate—hence Calpunius's role in Marcellus's
restoration.[44]

Given that a biological heir was plainly not forthcoming, and the
paternity of Cleopatra's child was firmly denied, who would be the heir?
Caesar's estate was enormous, and whoever inherited it would ascend to
instant prominence. The most obvious candidates were Caesar's four
grandnephews. One was Antony, who had clearly blotted his copybook
through his lifestyle choices. Another was Quintus Papius, who had
served as a legate in Gaul and was about to be employed in the same role
during the Spanish campaign. While a good subordinate, Papius seems
not to have impressed Caesar as successor material. A third grandnephew
was the much younger Pinarius Scarpus, whose absence from the record
of these years suggests Caesar's low opinion of his capacities. That left
one last nephew. Gaius Octavius. He was seventeen years old in 46. It
was time for him to become acquainted with his uncle. A contemporary
biographer paints a picture of him as being Caesar's constant companion in the second half of that year. This may even be true: something
between the two had plainly clicked.[45]

Caesar's thoughts about the future may have been given a special urgency by issues of health. The visibility of such issues may have been the reason why the author of the *African War* had stressed that Caesar really hadn't been losing his touch, explicitly denying the story that he had lost control of the battle of Thapsus. It is likely Caesar had been suffering a series of "mini-strokes," also known as transient ischemic attacks. Effects of these events include depression, apathy, and notable mood swings. As we'll see, there would be increasing evidence for these symptoms during the next year of Caesar's life, but since there was no classical diagnosis of transient ischemic attacks Caesar appears to have responded to his difficulties by putting about the story that he was suffering from the "sacred disease," or, in our terms, epilepsy. At least if he had a "sacred disease," the symptoms people were observing meant that Caesar was in contact with the divine.[46]

Even as his health declined, there was once again need for Caesar to take the field. The problem in Spain had been festering for some time. Having removed Varro as governor of southern Spain, Caesar appointed in his place Gaius Cassius Longinus, a cousin of his future assassin and Antony's associate as tribune in January of 49. Cassius had been quaestor in Spain under Pompey a few years previously and thus might reasonably have been thought to know the territory. The appointment turned out to be a terrible mistake. After winning a minor victory in Portugal, Cassius began looting the province, alienating both the leading men and his own soldiers, many of whom had been recruited during Pompey's governorship. Cassius survived an assassination attempt only to find half the garrison mutinying against him under the leadership of his own quaestor. Failing to calm the situation and provide the support Caesar had requested for the African campaign, he had been removed from office by Lepidus, governor of Nearer Spain, at the end of 47. Gathering his ill-gotten wealth, Cassius attempted to leave the province by sea. He drowned.[47]

Cassius's successor was Gaius Trebonius, one of Caesar's more experienced legates, but he was incapable of bringing order to the province where the memory of Pompey was still very positive, and where people were looking to North Africa in hopes of a Caesarian disaster. When news came of Caesar's victory, the pro-Pompeian leadership learning that Caesar's clemency was now running very thin, elected commanders for their men and started raising new legions. Trebonius was driven out and Pompey's sons, Gnaeus and Sextus, who had escaped the disaster in North Africa, now appeared in their midst, with Gnaeus now taking command of the army.[48]

Caesar now knew that the forces assembled by the Pompeys were substantial—eleven legions in all, combining recent recruits, survivors of Thapsus who had accompanied Pompey's sons from Africa, and men who had been discharged after Afranius's surrender in 49. Caesar sent three legions from the reformed army in Italy to join his five legions already in Spain. The veteran army was now being settled in various colonies, so this would not be a force with the quality of the one that had fought at Thapsus. Still, the soldiers recruited for the African campaign had now acquired significant experience of battle and would certainly be in good shape by the time they completed the march to Spain. The legions in the garrison of Nearer Spain, meanwhile, included three which had been raised before the crossing of the Rubicon. It may have been a smaller army, but it was better prepared for battle.[49]

Caesar's decision to go to Spain in person was taken after the departure of the three Italian legions, possibly as a result of reports about Trebonius's failure to contain the growth of support for the Pompeian cause. He left without having completed the elections for the coming year. He did not want a repeat of the conduct of Caelius in 48 or Dolabella in 47. Political life would therefore be under the control of appointees rather than elected magistrates. Lepidus, as his consular colleague, ran a curtailed election in which one consul (Caesar himself) was elected for the coming year. No praetors, patrician aediles, or quaestors were elected. While Caesar was away Lepidus would be in titular control of Rome as Caesar's master of horse. Actual administrative authority was in the hands of a group of six appointed prefects (a novel office) who would manage the government of Italy, which would chiefly involve the settlement of veterans. An additional pair of prefects would manage the treasury in place of the quaestors. The prefects had all the trappings of magistrates with *imperium*: lictors, the right to a purple stripe on their togas, and the official chair (*sella curulis*) of a high-ranking magistrate. What they did not have was the power to act independently: Cicero would write to one of these officials, saying he understood that "Gaius Caesar has assigned you a task, not asked you to exercise your discretion." The lines of communication ran back to Caesar through the inner circle. Balbus appears to have overseen the reorganization of municipal government in Italy, in which role Cicero communicated with him. Caesar, Cicero observed, rarely changed a decision made by Balbus or Hirtius, and Cicero therefore referred to the two of them as "the kings." It wasn't an unfair assessment. The government of Italy for the next ten months would look an awful lot like Cleopatra's in Egypt, with day to day administration being the business of the absent ruler's chosen agents.[50]

Caesar arrived in Spain in January, having written a poem about his journey during the twenty-four days it took him to make the trip from Rome to Sagunto. Even his own men were astonished by the speed of the journey. Then things slowed down. Caesar fell ill. That this was noticed and had an influence on the campaign is another sign that his health was becoming an issue.[51] Once he had recovered from his illness, Caesar united the troops from Italy with those already in Spain. The forces joined up at Porcuna, a small town about thirty miles from Córdoba. The Pompeian forces were concentrated around Córdoba, the leading city of southern Spain.

Our primary source for the campaign is very different from any previous narrative of Caesar's wars. The author of the *Spanish War* observes day-to-day events and is keen to emphasize the staggering brutality of the pro-Pompeian factions in Spanish communities toward their pro-Caesarian neighbors. In this, the narrative confirms suspicions about the younger Gnaeus Pompey's inherent brutality. As the campaign was getting underway, Cassius had written to Cicero, "You know what a fool Gnaeus is, how he thinks cruelty courage." But, while he gives a strong sense of the experience of the conflict our author cannot give a clear picture of overall strategy. His vision of the war is from the ground up.[52]

It gradually emerges from the *Spanish War* that Caesar's first objective was to send a message to his supporters in the province promising his support. After that, he wanted to force the younger Pompey into a frontal battle. Once Caesar had received a substantial force of horsemen from Bogud in Mauretania, he would have a clear advantage in the number of his cavalry, and it seems that both he and the young Gnaeus Pompey agreed there was a qualitative advantage in Caesar's infantry to offset Pompey's superior numbers. Pompey did all he could to avoid the type of battle Caesar was trying to force.

The opening action of the campaign was Caesar's relief of the besieged city of Montemayor (ancient Ulia), twenty miles southeast of Córdoba. He then moved to the area around Córdoba, where he found he could not gain control of bridges across the Guadalquivir. He therefore moved southwest, laying siege to the city of Ategua (there is no modern town on the site) at the end of January. The siege lasted until February 19, when the people of Ategua realized Pompey had abandoned efforts to relieve them and surrendered. Action shifted then southeast of Córdoba to the area around Espejo. After some low-level combat, Pompey burned the place down and withdrew to the area around La Lantejuela (ancient Munda) in the modern province of Seville. On March 16, Pompey drew his men up on the top of a hill next to the town. Caesar stood his ground without attacking, but on the following day, when Pompey deployed his troops on the same hill, Caesar ordered the army to attack. The order given, Caesar's men "began the battle, raising the war cry. Even though the courage of our men was superior, the enemy defended themselves fiercely from the higher ground. Both sides shouted, threw their weapons, and clashed so fiercely that our men almost lost confidence in victory." Caesar later said that this battle was the only one in which he felt he was fighting for his life. Both he and Pompey's son joined the fighting in person.[53]

The battle was decided by accident and exhaustion. The Tenth Legion, with Caesar fighting in its ranks, held the right wing and was pushing the Pompeian forces back, at which point Bogud led an attack around the left wing of the Pompeians, aiming at their camp. Seeing this, Labienus withdrew troops from his reserves to face Bogud's men, and when his men saw their support moving away they assumed Labienus was retreating. The line collapsed. Caesar's victory would be completed the next day, when the troops who had fled to La Lantejula surrendered. Dio claims they had been blocked in by piles of corpses Caesar's troops had heaped up around the town. The moment of Labienus's death is not recorded, only that his body was discovered on the field.[54]

While the author of the *Spanish War* concentrates on the pursuit of various Pompeians after the battle, culminating in the death of Gnaeus Pompey, it appears Caesar had other issues to concern him. The Pompeian success in rallying support from cities of Further Spain might conveniently be blamed on the venality of the deceased Cassius, but it was in fact a sign of a deeper problem that would have to be faced both here and elsewhere. Pompey had had deep roots in Spain, as he also had had in the Eastern provinces. Caesar may have thought that he had substantial connections of his own, but these were clearly not sufficient to guarantee loyalty to his regime. The author of the *Spanish War* includes a speech in which Caesar berates the people of Seville for their failure to appreciate all the nice things he had done for them as quaestor and governor in the province and later as consul. They have instead, he says, assaulted the magistrates of the Roman people and opened their gates to his enemies.[55]

It was one thing to remonstrate with people for disloyalty, it was another to fix the situation. The process of rebuilding the province took longer than the campaign. There are signs that a number of Spanish cities now received veteran settlements and promotion to the status of Roman colonies or municipalities as rewards for loyalty to the regime. At Caesar's side during these months was the young Octavius, who had come to join him when the fighting ended and who appeared to be increasingly influential in representing various Spanish communities to Caesar.[56]

Caesar finally headed back to Rome in September. His relationship with Octavius now deepened. Octavius had plainly impressed Caesar by his conduct in Spain, and Caesar had found his heir. As soon as he reached Rome in October, he wrote his new will. Octavius was named principal heir and would be adopted as Caesar's son upon his death.[57]

18

The Ides of March

Two incidents occurring toward the beginning of the Spanish campaign illustrate problems that would prove far less manageable than
the Pompeians. The issues were professional jealousy and ideological
insufficiency. The first incident was connected to an encounter between
Antony and Trebonius at Narbonne; the second was illuminated by a
book Cicero wrote on the subject of Cato.

Rumors would later spread about the conversation between Antony
and Trebonius. The alleged topic of the conversation, asserted by Cicero
and others in the wake of Caesar's assassination, was a plot to kill Caesar.
Trebonius, despite all his years of service under Caesar, would join
that conspiracy, and the suspicion was that Antony, smarting from his
removal from the center of affairs, was himself thinking about joining a
plot to kill Caesar. That suspicion, which arose after Antony's meeting
with Trebonius in 45, seems to have been an invention on the part of his
enemies, who sought to blacken his reputation with Caesar's supporters.[1]
But conspiracies, actual or anticipated, had been in the air since Thapsus.
In his speech for Marcellus, Cicero had asked Caesar to be careful. His
style, outside the charmed circle of his closest aides, was beginning to
annoy people. The high standard of accountability he demanded made
subordinates wonder if their careers were in jeopardy if things didn't go
well, as they had not of late for Trebonius or Antony. There was no
process for judging merit. The question of whether a career would
continue could be answered by Caesar alone.[2]

Meanwhile, Cicero's new book *Cato* portrayed the man as a repository of traditional Roman political virtues. Never a man to seek popularity for popularity's sake, Cato had sought a state that would be honest, one in which magistrates acting with integrity in the community's interests would preserve the order handed down from their ancestors. The good of the common people would be ensured by the actions of officials who had an eye to what the state could accomplish rather than what would make them look good. As his legislative proposals of the late 50s made plain, the wealth of the empire should not be allowed to corrupt domestic politics: Cato had died rather than surrender his principles and live in a state in which the traditions of the past could no longer be maintained. He was a symbol of integrity. In sum, Cicero's Cato probably looked a great deal like the character whose conduct had been summarized by Sallust a couple years later in his account of the Catilinarian conspiracy: upright, austere, a scourge to the wicked, restrained, moderate, and a model of rectitude.[3]

One must wonder, given the often frosty relations between the two men, how much of this portrayal of Cato was tongue-in-cheek on Cicero's part. The Cato he described was an ideal rather than the actual person. And that ideal had been illustrated by the gruesome image of the deceased Cato carried in the African triumph. As an ideal figure of the past, Cato dead was more dangerous to Caesar than the living Cato. Caesar recognized what Cicero was up to, and throughout the Spanish campaign he worked on his response to Cicero's book. His two-volume *Anti-Cato* was finished a day or so before his victory at Munda. The book opened with lavish praise for Cicero: his career was comparable to the great Athenian statesmen Pericles and Theramenes, his style was incomparable, he was the father of Latin letters, his cultural achievements exceeded those of all Rome's generals. Cato, on the other hand, was, according to Caesar, a greedy, drunken jerk with a strange sex life. Drawing explicitly from Metellus Scipio's attack on Cato a few years before, Caesar offered a vision of Cato not as an ideal politician but as a grim figure who no one could really get along with.[4]

Despite the riposte to his book, Cicero was pleased by Caesar's flattery. He was much less happy with the request that followed immediately after the *Anti-Cato* was distributed at Rome. This was that he compose a letter advising Caesar on the ideal constitution. The request came at a very difficult time for Cicero, who was dealing with the death of his beloved daughter Tullia. She had passed away in March, and Cicero withdrew from public life in a state of profound depression. Even if he had been at his best, it is unlikely he would have succeeded with the assignment, which he was to run by Oppius and Balbus before sending it on to Caesar, who would decide if it should be read by a wider public.[5] Cicero complained that the models that were suggested to him by Caesar were useless. These included books composed by the Greek philosophers Aristotle and Theophrastus, advising Alexander the Great when he took the throne of Macedon in 336 BCE. Caesar was now a mature statesman, not a twenty-year-old. Also, given that Alexander had been a temperamental alcoholic, prone to fits of rage resulting in the death of some of his closest advisers, the philosophers' advice didn't seem to have done a lot of good.[6]

A more essential point emerges from Cicero's complaints. One was that Caesar was looking for a book that could offer a theoretical justification for his top-down style of governance. He had rejected Sullan-style massacres, but he had also remarked that Sulla hadn't a clue when he had resigned the dictatorship. What would the Roman state look like with Caesar as its permanent head? It appears Caesar didn't have a clear idea himself, which is why he was asking for Cicero's help. So far, his experiments in finding a new style of government hadn't been a great success. He could not continue with a system in which there were no traditional magistrates, such as had been in place from January to September of 45. Magistracies conferred status within the aristocracy, and even Caesar's followers were not going to stand for a continuation of the current situation. But how would the magistracies function with a permanent dictator who could overrule any decision a magistrate took? And how would the dictator govern once he took off for the war against the Parthians which Caesar announced, during the summer of 45, as his next big operation? It was clear some solution had to be found that would not lead to a recurrence of the chaos of 48 and 47, but the new system also had to look enough like the traditional system to satisfy the former Pompeians whom Caesar was still trying to reconcile to his regime.[7]

Cicero failed to produce something satisfactory. Oppius and Balbus weren't any happier with his work than Cicero himself had been. Caesar was polite, but he also recognized that what Cicero had submitted to him in May was a nonstarter. Still, he wanted to be on good terms with him. He had sent Cicero a letter of condolence for Tullia, which Cicero described as kindly. He also expressed genuine pleasure at the published version of the speech for Ligarius, which Cicero gave to the world in June.[8] Caesar understood there was no ideological precedent for the system he was proposing: perpetual dictatorship on top of the traditional form of the constitution. And, as the summer gave way to fall and Caesar returned to Rome, there was a series of public relations fiascos. Underlying all of them was the issue which had bedeviled Cicero as he tried to compose his letter earlier in the summer: could Caesar act as a king without formally being one?

As we saw in connection with Caesar's discussion of Vercingetorix's father Celtillus, *regnum*, "kingship," was one of the dirtiest words in Roman politics. Another dangerous word was *rex*, "king." A *rex* could be tolerated in religious contexts: some of the rites of the Roman state were believed to have descended from the period in which there had been a king, and so one member of the college of pontiffs was designated to play the role of "king of the sacrifices," whose job it was to announce the monthly festivals and conduct a public sacrifice on the first day of each month and on March 24 and May 24. The "king of the sacrifices" was a vestige of a bygone era before the political freedom, *libertas*, which defined the republican constitution established when Lucius Brutus had expelled Rome's last king. *Regnum* was the polar opposite of this constitution. Sulla's choice to be a term-limited dictator rather than a *rex* for life had represented an implicit recognition of the ideological impossibility of recreating the archaic monarchy.[9]

When Caesar arrived back at Rome in September, his failure to articulate a vision of his position without using the word *rex* became ever more of a problem. It didn't help that the Senate voted him honors modeled on those given to the rulers of the Eastern kingdoms. In recent years, such honors had been awarded by provincial communities to Roman governors, including Cicero, who joked about his deification in communities of Cilicia, and many governors of Asia, including Cicero's younger brother. Typical of divine honors in the East would be the inclusion of a statue of the human honorand in processions that otherwise consisted of divine images and in temples. But what was done in the provinces stayed in the provinces. When Cicero came back from Cilicia, he did not want to be called a god; what he wanted was a Roman triumph. That, not provincial deification, would be the pinnacle of his career. (Cato, unfortunately, blocked the triumph.)[10]

Now, at Rome, however, Caesar had been given honors and privileges smacking of ruler cult. He may not have been consulted about all these decisions, many of which had been taken while he was in Spain. One was to grant Caesar the consulship for ten years in addition to the dictatorship. Another was to give him control of the plebeian magistracies—the only offices which had been filled by election in 46. Yet another was to include his statue among the statues of the kings of Rome and Lucius Brutus on the Capitoline. Then there was the decision to include another statue of Caesar in the procession held to open the games celebrated to mark Rome's official "birthday" on April 21. News of the victory at Munda had arrived the day before the festival, and Caesar's statue, in triumphal attire, was carried next to that of Rome's founder Romulus, to whom Caesar, as a fellow descendent of Aeneas, was related. The statue of Caesar, with the inscription "to the invincible god," was then placed near Romulus's cult statue in his temple. Still another statue of Caesar, made of ivy and placed in the temple of Capitoline Jupiter, was included in the procession opening the games in honor of the goddess of victory in July. These games had once been held in honor of Sulla's connection with the goddess; after his death they had become simply the celebration of Victoria. In 46 they became the games in honor of the

Victoria of Caesar. Cicero was not alone in being appalled by the sight of Caesar's statue in the procession.[11]

The celebration of Caesar's recent Spanish victory was also probably a mistake. Caesar wished to celebrate a triumph, which was duly voted by the Senate. He insisted that the campaign had not been a civil war. The younger Pompey's army had been Spanish, so the war, according to Caesar, was a foreign war. But this nicety was lost on people like Cicero who saw the campaign as a continuation of the war that began in 49. It was one thing (albeit not a thing everyone thought tasteful) to have displayed images of the deaths of Scipio and Cato at the African triumph, but that war had added a new province and had featured a genuine foreign king. There was no Spanish king, no new province to be won in Spain. The point people could take away from the Spanish triumph was that Romans who fought Caesar now ceased to be Romans. It did not improve matters when a tribune named Pontius Aquila did not rise from his seat to salute Caesar as the procession passed the benches upon which the tribunes sat. Caesar asked if Pontius wished to take the Republic from his hands. This claim to rule was a bit too overt for many people's comfort.[12] A further issue with the Spanish triumph was its celebration on September 27, just before the opening of the festival in honor of Venus the Ancestress (Venus Genetrix). The association of the triumph with the festival looked like another assertion of Caesar's divine ancestry.[13]

Another false step was the decision to grant triumphs to Fabius Maximus and Pedius. These were celebrated a few days after the festival of Venus. While there were no hard and fast rules governing the circumstances under which a triumph would be granted, one constant was that the general had to be fighting under his own auspices and so responsible for channeling the divine favor that enabled their victory. That was not really the case for Fabius and Pedius, who were serving as legates, and the implication was that a triumph depended not upon achievement but upon Caesar's patronage. And the fact Caesar already had a large staff meant that few opportunities were available for others who might want to get ahead through his favor.[14]

The situation grew ever more complicated as additional privileges showered on Caesar by the Senate set him further and further apart from his fellows. One of these privileges was the right to wear on all occasions the clothing a man wore only when celebrating a triumph. To this impressive ensemble Caesar added reddish footwear, which he said was the attire of the ancient kings of Alba Longa, his ancestors. Because of this alleged Alban connection Caesar also received the right to enter the city on horseback after the annual Latin Festival, celebrated on Monte Cavo outside of ancient Alba—traditionally, on this occasion, all magistrates entered the city on foot. Caesar was also honored as "the liberator," and a new temple to Freedom was dedicated in connection with this title. He was even given a new house, and it was decreed that a thanksgiving should be celebrated in his name whenever a victory was announced, even if he was not present at the battle. Other gifts to Caesar included the title of *imperator*, "victorious general," as an additional cognomen which would pass down to his heirs; a golden chair for public functions; and statues on the Rostra which would display the awards for valor Caesar had won back in his youth at Mytilene. Taken as a whole, all these honors stress Caesar's military success within the Roman tradition. Some of them—the right to wear special clothing in public—echo honors granted to Pompey when he returned from the Mithridatic war, thus continuing Caesar's implicit competition with his deceased rival that had been so noticeable when he returned to Rome in 46. Caesar's excuses for his Alban apparel and the title of "liberator" may have been intended to deflect talk about *regnum*, but the total effect of the honors was to underline Caesar's departure from the position occupied by any traditional magistrate.[15]

The celebrations of Caesar were not accompanied by any major new programs that could be used to showcase an attractive model for the future. On the other hand, the key elements of the programs announced in 46 were still being carried through: soldiers were being settled around Italy and in some provincial centers; people from Rome were also now getting land allotments, and work on new colonial settlements for Romans was beginning at Corinth and Carthage. New projects were underway at Rome, including the construction of a massive new building in the Campus Martius—"the Julian pens"—that would serve to shelter voters at elections. Further self-commemorative construction projects included a new Senate house aligned with the temple of Venus Genetrix, and some projects around Italy such as the draining of the Pontine marshes.[16]

Between the building projects and the divine honors, it was growing hard to reconcile the public reality of Caesar with the image he appears to have wanted to project as an affable person who still enjoyed the company of his fellow men. Still, Cicero offers a powerful picture from this period of the person Caesar still hoped to be. On December 19, Caesar came to dinner at Cicero's house, near modern Pozzuoli. Cicero was concerned about how the visit would work out. He had noted the large armed escort that had accompanied Caesar when he was staying at Marcius Philippus's house on the previous night. Philippus was Octavian's guardian, and Cicero plainly had someone at his house watching what was going on. He knew that Caesar, after spending the night, had had a long talk with Balbus in private. Then, around two in the afternoon, he had taken a bath and was told something about his old associate Mamurra. This news may have been bad, since Cicero found it worth observing that Caesar's expression didn't change when he heard it. Then it was on to dinner at Cicero's place. Caesar was in good form, something Cicero attributes to his following a program of induced vomiting, which ancient medical theory recommended people pursue during the winter months. Their conversation turned to literary matters, and Cicero said Caesar enjoyed himself. He concluded that the dinner had not been a disagreeable occassion.[17]

This nice literary dinner with an old friend, albeit one with whom Caesar had quite a few disagreements, shows us Caesar as his closest associates will also have seen him—unchanged by his great success, capable of treating others as equals, trying to entertain rather than insisting upon being entertained, restrained in his personal habits, and following his doctor's orders. And, shortly before the dinner party, Cicero had delivered the last speech he would give before Caesar on behalf of a former

Pompeian. The defendant was King Deiotarus of Galatia, with whom Caesar had previously reconciled during the campaign against Pharnaces. Now, however, Deiotarus's grandson charged him with having plotted to murder Caesar on his way back from the decisive battle at Zela. Cicero used the occasion of Deiotarus's trial to discuss Caesar's forgiveness of people who had "preferred their friendship with Pompey" to their friendship with him, and he ridiculed as street gossip the criticism of Caesar for allowing his statue to be placed with those of the kings. He dismissed the rumors that people thought Caesar was a tyrant and deeply unpopular. Caesar didn't immediately decide the case, but the fact Cicero was already circulating a draft of his speech before Caesar's decision strongly suggests that Caesar had indicated which way he was leaning. His presence at Cicero's house for the dinner party was an additional clue.[18]

The difference in tone between Cicero's defense of Deiotarus and his speeches for Marcellus and Ligarius just a year before shows how Caesar's management style had become an issue during the intervening months. While Caesar could be thanked for his mercy in 46, Cicero now had to address his unpopularity and accusations of tyranny. In 46 Cicero could ask Caesar to beware of conspiracies on the grounds that his death would wreck the state. Those conspiracies may have been hypothetical. But by the beginning of 44—the year that began not long after that agreeable dinner party—that was no longer the case, and Caesar's public behavior was playing into the hands of his enemies. Even though Caesar could exchange pleasantries with Cicero—at one point he even apologized for keeping Cicero waiting by saying he understood why people hated him—he actually talked to very few people.[19] And those he did talk to were people who had a vested interest in agreeing that Caesar had created a new regime even if he could not offer a coherent ideological framework for it. The old system was dead.

Three incidents in December of 45 and January of 44 illustrate Caesar's increasing clumsiness in dealing with the vestiges of Republican government, and, in two of these incidents, his realization he was getting things wrong. The first occurred as he was overseeing construction in his new forum, sitting on the platform of the Temple of Venus. He was approached there by the consuls and a group of other senators, bringing him honorary decrees just voted him by the Senate. Caesar did not rise from his seat to greet them. His failure to do so was taken as a sign of regal arrogance. A variety of stories were later circulated to excuse him. According to one he was sick, having experienced diarrhea. According to another he did not notice their approach. According to a third story, it was Balbus who advised him to stay seated to remind the Senate of the new order. The excuses acknowledge the severity of Caesar's error.[20]

The next incident was the one for which Caesar made no apology. Fabius Maximus, who had taken up the consulship with Trebonius in October, died suddenly on December 30, the day before he was supposed to hold the elections for the quaestors of 44 and two days before the new consuls would take office on January 1. When his death was announced, Caesar summoned the centuriate assembly (*comitia centuriata*) to elect a new consul, as opposed to the tribal assembly that had assembled to choose the quaestors. At one in the afternoon, the assembly finished voting and Caninius Rebilus, a former legate of Caesar, would be consul for the rest of the day. Rebilus, from a family which, although senatorial, could boast of few office holders, was perhaps thrilled to be able to live out his life with the dignity of an ex-consul. Others thought Caesar was desecrating the office. Cicero could joke about it, saying that no one had breakfast in the consulship of Caninius, and that Caninius was so vigilant that no crime was committed during his term as consul and indeed he had not even slept. But he was also outraged by what he saw as the denigration of the office, writing: "It is incredible how wretched I make myself by being a part of these things.... What if I should describe the other things like this? There are countless things of this sort." Caesar's failure to understand just how upset people were appears from a letter he wrote to a friend saying that the state was nothing more than a name without body or form. He should have kept that to himself.[21]

The third incident occurred in late January of 44. At some point, a person had placed a royal diadem on one of Caesar's statues on the Rostra. Two tribunes, Marullus and Flavus, removed the diadem, arrested the person who had put it there, and praised Caesar for not wanting to be king. Then, when Caesar was entering the city after the Latin Festival on January 26, some people shouted out that he was king. The tribunes arrested the first person who had done so. At the next meeting of the Senate Caesar attacked the tribunes for their actions, saying they were stirring up sedition against him. They replied he was preventing them from doing their duty. Caesar then supported a motion by one of their fellow tribunes to remove them from office and used his power as censor to expel them from the Senate. The incident made his protestations of disinterest in a royal title more difficult for some to take seriously.[22]

Talk of kingship was enhanced by another exceptional series of honors which the Senate voted Caesar in the new year. These included the title Father of the Country, which would appear on the coins soon to be minted with his portrait. Although coins depicting Marius and Sulla in triumphal chariots had been issued in their lifetimes, these had not carried portraits: a portrait coin was characteristic of Eastern kings. In addition, sacrifices would hereafter be offered on Caesar's birthday, and the fifth month, the month of his birth, would be renamed Julius (hence our July). The Senate also now created a cult of Jupiter Julius, appointing Caesar's consular colleague Antony to be his priest. In addition to these divine honors, Caesar would also be censor without colleague, and the Senate swore an oath both to protect his life and to uphold his decisions as if they had the force of law. Finally, in late January or early February, he became dictator in perpetuity. It is not clear Caesar asked for or desired all of this. His friends would later suggest that many of these measures had been proposed simply to annoy people and justify the conspiracy that was now beginning to take shape.[23]

For Caesar, it seems, what mattered most was the imminent Parthian war. Preparations for the war were on a very large scale and must have consumed much of his time. There were six legions in Syria, six in western Greece, and three in Illyricum. One more legion was sent to the East via Egypt. The war plan, which called for a long march through the highlands of eastern Turkey and northern Iraq, then a descent into central Iraq, most likely following the Tigris, was essentially the same war plan followed by later Roman emperors in their successful invasions of Parthia, and it must have required significant logistics work and depended on the exploitation of information gathered during Pompey's campaigns in the 60s. It was expected that the war would last three years, and Caesar designated magistrates for the period he would be away.[24]

This Parthian campaign, whose planning suggests Caesar hadn't lost any of his essential instincts as a general, would take him out of Rome and away from the increasingly fractious political scene where his instincts as a politician do seem to have been failing him. His sense of the irritation he was causing through his dismissal of the traditional political system was severely lacking. His assassins, who by this time were beginning to assemble under the leadership of Gaius Cassius, would later publish a list of events justifying their action. These included his failure to rise for the senators, his clash with Marullus and Flavus, and a third event—now very famous—that would occur at the festival of the Lupercalia on February 15.

The Lupercalia was an extremely ancient fertility festival through which the gods were implored to protect the flocks from wolves and to encourage female fertility. To this end a group of male priests sacrificed a goat and a dog and, after a sacrificial feast, cut thongs from the skins of the sacrificed animals and ran through the streets striking women they encountered so as to promote childbearing. The women were topless, and the priests tended to wear only a loincloth. On this day in 44 Antony was the leader of the priesthood conducting the festival.

Caesar was seated on the Rostra when the priests dashed into the Forum. A person, either one of his inner circle or a praetor (the tradition is uncertain on this point), had placed a royal diadem inside an ivy crown at Caesar's feet. The crowd called upon Lepidus, who was again serving as master of horse, to place the crown on Caesar's head. When Lepidus hesitated, Gaius Cassius, one of the praetors for the year—and even then conspiring to kill Caesar—placed the crown on Caesar's lap. Now Antony arrived, nearly naked. He ascended the Rostra and placed the ivy crown on Caesar's head. Caesar removed it, throwing it into the crowd. Then Antony produced another diadem, which he again placed on Caesar's head. The crowd yelled "hail, King!" But Caesar again removed the diadem and ordered that it be given to Capitoline Jupiter, as it was more appropriate for him.

What was the point of this bit of theater? Was it to prove that Caesar didn't want to be king? Was Caesar listening to the crowd to see which way the sentiment was swinging? Was this just a dumb piece of flattery dreamed up by Antony? Whatever it was—and I suspect the first option is the correct one, since I doubt Caesar would have allowed for something this elaborate and public to happen by chance—it didn't do anything for him. It did do a great deal for Cassius and his accomplices, for "this deed, as much as anything else, served to unite the conspirators, since it supplied manifest proof of the suspicions they harbored."[25]

We can't be sure when Cassius initiated the conversations that led to the assembling of a group of conspirators, but the author of the description of the Lupercalia incident just quoted makes it clear that he was already busily at work before February 15. Plutarch's biography of Brutus, the most famous man to join the conspiracy, gives us a sense of the way Cassius operated. Plutarch shows him approaching people he thought would be sympathetic to his view and urging them to join the group of the like-minded. Parts of Cicero's book, *On Obligations*, written after the assassination, may give us a sense for what was said in these conversations: Caesar was a tyrant who had crushed the state by force. His current style was at odds with the natural order of society, in which people selected leaders who had a reputation for justice and prudence. Caesar's agrarian legislation and debt laws had undermined the state by destroying unity between classes and fair dealing. And so what if Caesar was a friend? If a man murders a tyrant who is a friend his act will be seen as noble rather than wicked; nature does not forbid one from killing such a person; even a son who kills his father is justified in his act if his father is a tyrant.[26]

Caesar was aware of the possibility that a conspiracy or conspiracies were afoot. Rumors to that effect had been current since at least 46, when Cicero told Caesar that he needed to look out for himself, but gossip was, of course, hard to analyze. Had Antony really plotted with Trebonius? He was now providing exuberant displays of loyalty, albeit somewhat excessive ones. Dolabella, who was also loyal, had been linked to an alleged plot around the time that Caesar had dined with Cicero. Caesar was sufficiently satisfied that this allegation was false that he supported Dolabella's claim to the consulship when he himself laid down the office to set off for the Parthian war. Should Caesar pay attention to the graffiti painted on a statue of Lucius Junius Brutus, the man who had cast out the kings and established the Republic almost five hundred years before? "Would that you were alive," someone had scrawled. Could such words really inspire Servilia's son, who claimed descent from the ancient Brutus (plate 15a–c), to take action? Surely no sane conspirator would circulate lines of verse contrasting the ancient Brutus, chosen Rome's first consul after ejecting the kings, with Caesar, who was now king after having ejected the consuls? No one—certainly not Brutus— could be so stupid as to call attention to himself as a conspirator. And Cassius had seemed ever so loyal during that scene during the Lupercalia. Surely any claim that these men were organizing an assassination plot was just nasty gossip. Caesar knew he was indispensable and he assumed that the people around him recognized that, if he was murdered, another civil war was sure to follow. He dismissed his bodyguards.[27]

The actual conspiracy that would lead to Caesar's assassination seems to have come into being only when Brutus agreed to join Cassius, who was married to one of his sisters, some time after the Lupercalia. Caesar would leave for the Parthian campaign in just over a month. The topic of kingship had reared its head yet again in the first meeting of the Senate after the Lupercalia incident, when a member of the board overseeing the state's collection of Sibylline oracles said the collection contained an oracle stating that only a king could defeat the Parthians. The people who had convinced themselves that Caesar was effectively a king needed to act fast.[28] There would be a meeting of the Senate on March 15, the "Ides" or midpoint of the month, just three days before Caesar would be leaving for the Parthian campaign. The meeting would be held in Pompey's Theater, one of the few places where the enlarged Senate could assemble while its new meeting house was still under construction. The night before the meeting, Caesar had dinner at Lepidus's house. The topic of death came up. Caesar said he thought the best death was sudden and unexpected.[29]

Plutarch comments that famous people do not just die. Their deaths are accompanied by portents of all sorts: blazing lights in the night sky, terrible sounds at night, frightful dreams. Calpurnia is said to have woken from a dream and begged her husband not to attend the meeting of the Senate. Inauspicious sacrifices also supposedly deterred Caesar. There may be something to the story that he genuinely wasn't feeling well, because several accounts of the assassination agree that Decimus Brutus, who was in on the plot, had to come to his house and convince him to show up.[30]

Caesar arrived at the Theater of Pompey and entered the curia, or hall, in which the meeting would be taking place. Antony should have been seated with him when the meeting began, but Trebonius, who was now part of the conspiracy, called him aside out of the meeting to discuss a gladiatorial show. Antony was a strong man, and loyal to Caesar, so the conspirators wanted to make sure he would not be there to protect him.[31] When Caesar entered the meeting, the Senate rose in respect. Caesar seated himself near a statue of Pompey. The conspirators gathered around him on the pretext of supporting a request by Tillius Cimber for Caesar to restore his brother from exile. In mid-request, Cimber grabbed Caesar. Servilius Casca stabbed him. The rest of the conspirators then crowded around Caesar, stabbing him and occasionally each other. At first Caesar resisted. Then he stopped and covered his head. Was that because he saw Brutus in the crowd? In the end, he fell, stabbed twenty-three times. Pompey's statue stood over his body.[32] The senators witnessing the scene fled. The assassins, waving their daggers, went up to the Capitol to announce their deed. Sometime after the murder, some of Caesar's slaves collected his body and brought it home.

Caesar was dead. But not gone.

19

Caesar's Legacies

The hasty planning of Caesar's murder and the fantasies of the primary actors became clear in the days following the Ides of March. Brutus, Cassius, and their associates genuinely believed that with Caesar dead they could restore the Republic's traditional government. Like Cicero, who had no part in the conspiracy, they believed the excesses of Caesar's last months had turned people away from any form of monarchic regime. Two days after the assassination, the assassins made a temporary peace with Antony and Lepidus. They would retain their offices and receive amnesty for the murder, at the same time the senate declared that all Caesar's official decisions (including those not yet published) should remain valid, and that Caesar would receive divine honors.

A day later the situation changed. The terms of Caesar's will, making generous gifts of cash and parkland to the people of Rome, had become known. A huge crowd gathered in the Forum on March 20 for Caesar's funeral. The event was heavily stage-managed, with a chorus singing poems in Caesar's honor and a wax statue displaying the twenty-three wounds he had suffered twirling on a machine above the corpse. Antony capped the performance with an emotional speech. The crowd seized the body, scheduled for cremation in the Campus Martius, and burned it on what is now the site of the temple of the Divine Julius in the heart of the Forum.[1]

The Roman people had spoken. Caesar's generous will had reinforced his image as a friend to the common people, but it was Caesar's memory they cherished more than his money. He had not lied to them; he had not told them that their welfare was bad for the state as a whole. He had protected people from economic ruin and had provided for his veterans without impoverishing others. His actions had promoted the well-being of the average person in ways the government of the Republic had not. An efficient ruler who looked to their interests was more important than democratic institutions which had failed them while further enriching the wealthy.

Within months, Brutus and Cassius had departed Rome, taking advantage of divisions among Caesar's followers—the distrust of Balbus, Hirtius, and others in the inner circle for Antony and Lepidus. They would ultimately take advantage of the positions they retained to raise armies in the East, where their cause could still be seen as Pompeian. Affection for Caesar among the majority of Romans had made their position in Rome untenable. Things had not worked out as they had hoped. Cicero describes a family conference at Antium in June at which Brutus and Cassius regretted lost opportunities and Servilia had to intervene to demand practical action.[2]

Soon after the departure of Caesar's leading assassins, his nephew and heir Gaius Octavius—now called Octavian to reflect his new status as Caesar's posthumously adopted son—had arrived in Rome. At the end of July, Octavian celebrated games in honor of his dead uncle. Stage-managed by Matius, another member of Caesar's inner circle, these celebrations established Octavian's prominence in Rome.[3] Supported by Caesar's true friends, Octavian managed first to come to terms with Antony, who had failed to seize effective control of Caesar's legacy, and then survived an unimpressive showing in the battles at Philippi at which the forces of the assassins, assembled from former Pompeians, were destroyed. With the continuing support of Caesar's most devoted loyalists, he built up the organization he had inherited until, years later, in a campaign whose attention to detail Caesar would have appreciated, he crushed the joint forces of Antony and Cleopatra at Actium, completing his victory in 30 BCE when he captured Alexandria and the two lovers committed suicide.

Later generations would debate the significance of Caesar's career. Was he destructive or creative? Had he ruined the democracy or created the monarchy? Lucan in his *Pharsalia* presents Caesar as a thoroughly menacing figure throughout the bulk of the poem, which breaks off with his arrival in Alexandria and hints at further corruption. Writing as he did under the reign of Nero, a biological descendent of Caesar's rival, Domitius Ahenobarbus, this may not have been quite the anti-establishment line it seems at first glance: Caesar is being contrasted with Nero, whom Lucan presents as thoroughly delightful. But unlike Lucan, the majority of classical accounts see Caesar as a great figure, and ultimately a Republican one, but undone in the end by his own arrogance. He was immensely talented, a great general, but he lacked the vision to build a new system of government. Only Suetonius presents him as the first emperor, the first of the rulers whom history would know as Caesars.[4]

Suetonius was right. The formation of the monarchy depended upon Caesar's organization of a powerful military whose troops were loyal to himself and an experienced officer corps which understood that its job was to inspire the troops through exemplary behavior while executing their general's commands. In addition, the Roman imperial monarchy would need both a high-powered logistical team working with local communities to support the army and an administrative apparatus with the competence to manage both the military and civilian populations. The historian Tacitus would later recall the power of Oppius and Balbus in setting the direction for the administration of the imperial household, writing that they, "with Caesar's resources, were the first [equestrians] to set the conditions of peace and the terms for war."[5]

Octavian, who later took the name Augustus, depended upon Caesar's organization to secure his future. And he had the example of the Ides of March before him. He recognized the need to articulate a government which combined the institutions of the Republic with a bureaucratic state to support the army upon which the regime based its power. Was the creation of a bureaucratic monarchy a good thing? It is hard in this day and age to suggest that a monarchy might be a better form of government than a democracy, but a corrupt democracy which fails to serve the interests of average citizens has betrayed the social compact upon which it depends. When, after the assassination of a truly dreadful monarch, Caligula, the question arose of whether democracy should be restored, the people of Rome rejected the notion. They remembered how their ancestors had been betrayed.[6]

The memory of Caesar that was passed down to the modern world comes largely through the biographical tradition. The opportunity to meet the man himself through his own memoirs has largely been missed. A Caesar simplified by his biographers has proved easier to think with than the complex figure whom we have met in his own words. And it has been his ultimate fate that has shaped later judgements. Dante hung Brutus and Cassius from Satan's snout together with Judas Iscariot.[7] Shakespeare, aided by Thomas North's eloquent translation of Plutarch's *Lives*, offered a more complex vision of the Ides of March. The original audience for Shakespeare's *Julius Caesar* in 1599, especially those members of Elizabeth's court, were themselves living with an aged monarch who had no obvious heir and had often been threatened with assassination. The play's conclusion, relying on Plutarch's biography of Brutus for a scene in which the ghost of Caesar haunts his assassins to their deaths, encourages the audience to see Caesar's murder in negative terms: the assassination was wrong. Or was it? Was Caesar a tragic figure, or was Brutus? Was Caesar a king? For Shakespeare, who highlights the Lupercalia incident, he explicitly was not. In the play, it is Brutus who convinces Cassius that "our course would seem too bloody" if they should kill Antony as well as Caesar. They stand up only "against the spirit of Caesar" and Brutus wishes "that we then could come by Caesar's spirit / And not dismember Caesar." Caesar, meanwhile, is a victim of his own self-regard: "The things that threatened me / Ne'er looked but on my back. When they shall see / The face of Caesar, they are vanished." For "cowards die many times before their deaths; / The valiant never taste of death but once."[8]

Shakespeare's Caesar, self-confident to the point of arrogance, speaking of himself as if in the pages of his commentaries, has shaped modern perceptions of the man who once was. We lose the sense of humor which comes through in the commentaries and can lose sight of the man who knew he didn't always get things right, who knew how to correct his course. Shakespeare's Caesar, frankly, is not the man who could inspire the loyalty of Caesar's followers. He is too much the colossus. But Shakespeare's question of the effect of political assassination remains potent to this day. Whether Caesar is portrayed as Barack Obama (as he was in Bob Melrose's 2012 production) or as Donald Trump (as he was in Oskar Eustis's 2017 production, to the horror of conservative commentators who had not seen the production or appeared not to know the play very well), the result is still that the assassins ruin themselves and the society they had thought to preserve.[9]

Even before Shakespeare enshrined Caesar-the-colossus in modern consciousness, Caesar had become emblematic of sovereignty. In the Roman world his name became a title designating the heir apparent to the reigning Augustus, a curious reversal of the actual relationship, but one which reflects the general perception that it took Augustus to finalize the political process Caesar set in motion. The connection with the idea of supreme power was similarly enshrined in the titles of *kaiser* and *tsar*. In medieval Rome, monuments falsely attributed to him, including the Vatican obelisk, defined a Roman civic identity in opposition to the papacy.[10]

As the eighteenth century turned into the nineteenth, Caesar's image began to change, though it was still colossal. For Voltaire, Caesar was an ideal leader; for Frederick of Prussia he was a role model, a great soldier, and a man of culture. Claiming the mantle of Caesar, Frederick could strip away the claims of the Holy Roman emperor to be Caesar's spiritual descendant. Napoleon Bonaparte saw himself as Caesar's superior as an emperor, but in his final days on Saint Helena he penned a series of notes on Caesar's life and works in which a spirit of competition alternates with a very cool and intelligent assessment of Caesar's aims.[11] For Napoleon's nephew, Napoleon III, who presented himself as "the tutelary and democratic power of the plebeian hero who ensured the independence of peoples and was the true representative of our revolution," Caesar was an object of genuine fascination. Napoleon III laid the foundation for much modern scholarship on the Gallic wars even as he commemorated Vercingetorix as the spiritual father of France. The image of Vercingetorix on the monument Napoleon III erected at Alise-sur-Reine, is graced with Napoleon's features (plate 14), and the inscription reads "Gaul united, forming a single nation, animated by a common spirit, can defy the universe." Less successful was Napoleon III's effort to achieve what he understood to be Caesar's style of charismatic military rule. His connection with Vercingetorix seems especially apt given his catastrophic defeat and capture by the German army at the battle of Sedan in 1871.[12]

Napoleon III's vision of Caesar corresponds to some degree with that created by Theodor Mommsen in his great *History of Rome*, which ends in 46 BCE with Caesar's realization of the dream of the Gracchi, preserved through the "political party" they had formed and of which he assumed leadership. This Caesar corresponds with Mommsen's own political sympathies (he was a supporter of the revolution in 1848) and was admired by Mommsen's contemporary Karl Marx.[13] In light of Marx's appreciation, it is perhaps ironic that another person who admired Mommsen's Caesar was Benito Mussolini. In more recent times, Italian film versions of Caesar's career have been employed in contexts of aggressive nationalism. In France, Caesar as the enemy of the nation remains both opposed and linked to fascination with him as a role model. In the United States, Caesar's image as a dictator can be used to represent the antithesis of democratic leadership, but Caesar may also appear more positively in works that share the vision of him presented in George Bernard Shaw's *Caesar and Cleopatra*. In Shaw's play, Caesar appears as a teacher and mentor for the young queen, and he can also be seen in this light in Rex Harrison's portrayal in the 1963 movie *Cleopatra*.[14]

The multivalent traditions concerning Caesar today are a fitting tribute to the complexity of the man and his achievement. His abilities were amply attested by those who knew him; his extraordinary capacity as a leader is revealed page by page in his own writings. But so too is his fundamentally authoritarian approach to all issues. Caesar found that he grew up in a dysfunctional society. He saw solutions to the misery encompassing the lives of many of his contemporaries, and he was genuinely sympathetic to those born in very different circumstances from his own. He plainly understood the importance of incorporating the defeated within his victorious organization. He destroyed the political order in which he grew up, and provided a framework for his successor to create a new political system that would endure for centuries. But he could not, himself, discover that path forward.

Caesar's success was as much the product of the failure of others as it was of his own considerable genius. The final question his career leaves us is this: How and when can democracy that has lost the faith of its citizens regain their trust? Caesar's career models the way that an alternative state can be constructed on the basis of corporate structures that are inherently autocratic. Democracy cannot coexist with Caesar.

The Cast

(All dates BCE)

Aemilius Lepidus, Marcus: Consul of 77 who attempted to overthrow the Sullan regime; defeated by Lutatius Catulus and Pompey, he died in Sardinia.

Aemilius Lepidus, Marcus: Son of the preceding; *interrex* in 52, praetor in 49, governor of Nearer Spain in 48–47, consul in 46; and master of horse in 46–44. After Caesar's death he was a member of the triumvirate formed in late 43.

Afranius, Lucius: Long-serving lieutenant of Pompey in the 70s and 60s, he was consul in 60 and Pompey's legate in Spain from 55 until 49, when he surrendered to Caesar at Lerida. He also served under Pompey in 48 and was killed after Thapsus.

Ambiorix: Leader of the Eburones, responsible for the destruction of the force commanded by Sabinus and Cotta. He escaped Caesar's effort to kill him in 53 and later disappeared in the aftermath of the revolt of 52.

Annius Milo, Titus: Tribune of the plebs in 57, he championed Cicero's return from exile, organizing armed gangs to support his program. Praetor in 55. His gang was responsible for the murder of Clodius on January 19 of 52, after which he was convicted of violence and went into exile at Marseille. He returned to Rome in 48 without Caesar's permission, formented rebellion, and was killed.

Antonius Gnipho, Marcus: Freedman who was Caesar's *grammaticus*; his views on language influenced Caesar's own.

Antonius Hibrida, Gaius: Legate of Sulla in Greece, later prosecuted by Caesar for corruption and expelled from the Senate in 70. He was praetor in 66(?), consul in 63, and governor of Macedonia in 62–60.

Antonius Creticus, Marcus: Praetor in 74; assigned to campaign against the pirates around Crete in 73–71.

Antonius, Marcus (Mark Antony): Son of the preceding, he served under Gabinius in Syria in 54, was quaestor in Gaul in 52, legate in Gaul in 51–50, tribune in 49, master of horse in 48–47, and consul in 44. He was Caesar's nephew, being the son of Julia (1), daughter of Lucius Caesar (consul in 90).

Aurunculeius Cotta, Lucius: Legate of Caesar from 57 to 54; killed in action against the Eburones.

Antony, Mark: see Antonius, Marcus.

Appuleius Saturninus, Lucius: Tribune of the plebs in 103 and 100. Although he presented himself as an ally of Marius while the latter was on campaign, sponsoring a law to give land to his veterans, his overall program, which included elimination of senatorial control of jury courts and a law providing subsidized grain for Rome's population, was supported with a high level of violence, leading to the passage of the *senatus con-sultum ultimum* in 100 and his arrest by Marius. He was later murdered by a mob.

Ariovistus: Leader of the German mercenaries who defeated the Aedui on behalf of the Senones in 62. He was named a "friend and ally" of the Roman people in 59 but was defeated by Caesar in 58.

Arsinoe IV: Sister and dynastic rival of Cleopatra VII.

Asinius Pollio, Gaius: Served under Caesar in 49–48; tribune of the plebs in 47; legate of Caesar in 46–45. Friend of Catullus and the author of an extremely influential history of the period from 60 onward, known now only through quotations in later authors.

Atia: Caesar's niece, the daughter of Julia (4) and Marcus Atius Balbus. She was the mother of Gaius Octavius (Octavian), the future emperor Augustus.

Balbus: see Cornelius Balbus, Lucius.

Bibulus: see Calpurnius Bibulus, Marcus.

Bogud: King of Mauretania, he initially ruled in conjunction with Bocchus, by whom he was expelled after Caesar's murder.

Brutus: see Junius Brutus, Marcus.

Caecilius Metellus, Quintus: Consul in 109, he was replaced as commander in the war with Jugurtha by Marius, his former subordinate, in 107. He briefly went into exile in 100 when he refused to swear the oath required of senators in Saturninus's land bill. He returned in 99. Cicero claimed his exile and return as models for his own.

Caecilius Metellus Nepos, Quintus: Legate under Pompey in 67–63, tribune of the plebs in 62, praetor in 60, and consul in 57.

Caecilius Metellus Pius Scipio Nasica, Quintus: Praetor in 55; *interrex* in 54, consul in 52, and governor of Syria in 49–48. Father of Pompey's fifth wife. He was commander of anti-Caesarian forces in the Thapsus campaign, and was killed after the battle.

Caelius Rufus, Marcus: Friend and correspondent of Cicero. Tribune of the plebs in 52, he supported Milo. Aedile in 50. As praetor in 48, he supported a program of debt reform. Removed from office, he was killed assisting Milo in his rebellion against Caesar.

Caesarion: Son of Caesar and Cleopatra VII.

Calpurnia: Third wife of Julius Caesar; daughter of Lucius Calpurnius Piso.

Calpurnius Bibulus, Marcus: Aedile in 65, praetor in 62, consul in 59, governor of Syria in 51–50, and commander on Pompey's fleet in 49–48, in which office he died.

Calpurnius Piso, Gaius: Consul in 67 and governor of Transalpine Gaul in 66–64. Prosecuted for corruption by Caesar in 63.

Calpurnius Piso, Lucius: Praetor by 61, consul in 58, and governor of Macedonia in 57–55. Patron of Epicurean philosophers and owner of the library discovered at the Villa of the Papyri in Herculaneum. Father of Caesar's wife Calpurnia.

Cassius Longinus, Gaius: Quaestor in Syria in 53 and served in Pompey's fleet in 49–48. Legate of Caesar 47–46 and leader of the assassination plot in 44.

Cassius Longinus, Quintus: Quaestor of Pompey in Spain in 52, tribune of the plebs in 49, and governor of Further Spain in 48–47, departing which office he died.

Catiline: see Sergius Catilina, Lucius.

Cato: see Porcius Cato, Marcus.

Cicero: see Tullius Cicero, Marcus.

Cleopatra VII: Queen of Egypt, 51–30.

Clodia: Influential member of the Claudian family; sister of Publius Clodius and probably the Lesbia of Catullus's poetry.

Clodius Pulcher, Publius: Legate for Lucullus in 68, involved in a scandalous relationship with Pompeia (Caesar's second wife) in 62, and tribune in 58, when he passed bills annexing Cyprus and exiling Cicero for the execution of the Catilinarians. He was killed by followers of Milo in 52. His name is a dialectical variant of the name Claudius.

Clodius, Sextus: Leading assistant of the preceding.

Commius: Installed by Caesar as king of the Atrebatae before 55, he joined the revolt of 52 as a senior commander of the relief force at Alesia. In 51, he escaped to Britain, where he founded a dynasty.

Cornelia (1): Daughter of Lucius Cornelius Cinna, she married Caesar in 84, was mother to his daughter Julia, and died in 69. Caesar refused Sulla's order to divorce her.

Cornelia (2): Pompey's fifth wife, she is Cornelia rather than Caecilia because her father was adopted into the Caecilii.

Cornelius Balbus, Lucius: Served under Pompey, who conferred citizenship on him, in the war against Sertorius. He then served under Caesar in his term as governor of Further Spain (61–60). He accompanied Caesar back to Rome and was already acting as Caesar's go-between with Cicero by the end of 60. During the years of Caesar's Gallic campaigns, he alternated between service on Caesar's staff in Gaul and representing Caesar back in Rome. After 47 he and Oppius managed the operation of Caesar's government in Italy. His support for Octavian after Caesar's assassination was crucial to the Octavian's success. As consul in 40, he was the first provincial to hold that office. He contributed to the biographical tradition about Caesar.

Cornelius Cinna, Lucius: Consul in 87, he seized power in Rome, establishing an anti-Sullan regime with Marius as a colleague. He died in 84. His daughter Cornelia was Caesar's first wife.

Cornelius Dolabella, Gnaeus: Consul in 81 and governor of Macedonia in 80–77. He was prosecuted in 76 by Caesar for corruption in the latter office.

Cornelius Dolabella, Publius: Legate of Caesar, probably in 49–48 and tribune of the plebs in 47, in which office he introduced radical debt legislation. He was consul after Caesar's assassination in 44. Third husband of Cicero's daughter Tullia.

Cornelius Lentulus Sura, Publius: Consul in 71 but expelled from the Senate in 70. He was praetor in 63, in which office he joined the Catilinarian conspiracy and was executed.

Cornelius Sulla, Lucius: Quaestor to Marius in 107, legate for Lutatius Catulus in 101, praetor in 97(?), and legate in Campania in 89. As consul in 88, he marched on Rome when removed from the command against Mithridates VI, massacred his enemies, and reformed the constitution. Declared a public enemy by Marius and Cinna in 87, he defeated Mithridates by 85 and returned in 83 to Italy, where he was victorious in the subsequent civil war by the end of 82 and was appointed dictator. As dictator, he instituted in 81 a program for the mass murder of his political enemies through the proscriptions and a series of political reforms. He was consul and dictator in 80 and was still dictator in 79, when he laid down the office to retire to private life. He died in 78.

Crassus: see Licinius Crassus, Marcus.

Curio: see Scribonius Curio, Gaius.

Deiotarus: King of a district in Galatia; appointed by Pompey in 63(?) after the defeat of Mithridates, he ruled until 41(?). He was tried on suspicion of plotting to assassinate Caesar in 45 and was defended by Cicero.

Diviciacus: Leading figure among the Aedui during Caesar's early years in Gaul; famous also as a druid.

Dolabella: see Cornelius Dolabella.

Domitius Ahenobarbus, Lucius: Praetor in 58, consul in 54, and legate of Pompey in 49–48. Died at Pharsalus. Notable for his mismanagement of operations around Corfinio in 49 and his surrender of his army to Caesar.

Domitius Calvinus, Lucius: Tribune of the plebs in 59, praetor in 56, consul in 53, and governor of Asia in 48–46.

Dumnorix: Leader of the Aedui whom Caesar presents in the *Gallic War* as being especially problematic. Caesar had him executed in 54.

Fabius, Gaius: Tribune of the plebs in 55. Legate of Caesar in Gaul and then in Spain, 54–49.

Fabius Maximus, Quintus: Aedile in 57, praetor in 48(?), legate of Caesar in Spain in 46–45, and consul in 45, when he died in office on the last day of his term.

Gabinius, Aulus: Tribune of the plebs in 67, in which office he moved the bill creating the special command against the pirates for Pompey. Legate of Pompey in 66–63, consul in 58, governor of Syria in 57–54. He was exiled but returned under amnesty from Caesar in 49 and served as legate to Caesar in 49–48, in which position he died.

Gracchus: see Sempronius Gracchus.

Hirtius, Aulus: One of Caesar's most trusted aides, he completed Book 8 of the *Gallic War* and was likely the editor of the *Alexandrian War*. Consul in 43, in which office he died.

Juba: Son of Hiempsal II and his successor as king of Numidia, which he ruled from 60–46.

Julia (1): Daughter of Lucius Julius Caesar the consul of 90 and third cousin of Julius Caesar. Mother of Mark Antony.

Julia (2): Sister of Caesar's father and wife of Gaius Marius.

Julia (3): The elder of Caesar's two sisters, she married Lucius Pinarius and then Gaius Pedius.

Julia (4): The younger of Caesar's two sisters, she married Marcus Atius Balbus. Her daughter Atia married Gaius Octavius and was the mother of the emperor Augustus.

Julia (5): Daughter of Julius Caesar and wife of Pompey. She died in 54.

Julius Caesar, Gaius: Father of Caesar. Praetor *c.* 92 and governor of Asia *c.* 91.

Julius Caesar, Lucius (1): Praetor by 95, consul in 90, and censor in 89. Murdered by Marius's forces in 87.

Julius Caesar, Lucius (2): Son of the preceding, he was consul in 64 and served as Caesar's legate in Gaul from 52 to 49. He was the author of a history of the Julian family.

Julius Caesar, Lucius (3): Son of the preceding, he sided with Pompey in the Civil War, serving as an ambassador to Julius Caesar in 49. He continued to side with the Pompeians after Pharsalus and was executed after the battle of Thapsus.

Julius Caesar, Sextus: Caesar's paternal uncle, he was praetor by 95 and consul in 91. He died besieging Asculum in 90.

Julius Caesar Strabo Vopiscus, Gaius: Brother of Lucius Julius Caesar (1), famous for his sense of humor as an orator. Murdered by Marius's supporters in 87.

Junius Brutus, Marcus: Son of Caesar's mistress Servilia, he was quaestor in 53 and served under Pompey in 49–48, pardoned by Caesar, he was praetor in 44, in which office he became a leader of the conspiracy against Caesar in 44. Committed suicide in 42 after his defeat at the Battle of Philippi.

Labienus, Titus: Tribune of the plebs in 63; he was legate to Caesar in Gaul from 58 to 50 but deserted to Pompey in 49. He survived Pharsalus and the Thapsus campaign but died at Munda in 45.

Licinius Crassus, Marcus: Praetor in 73 (probably), he commanded Roman forces against Spartacus in 72–71 and was consul in 70, censor in 65, consul a second time in 55, and governor of Syria in 54–53. He died in battle against the Parthians at Carrhae.

Licinius Crassus, Publius: Son of the preceding. Legate of Caesar in Gaul in 57 and 56.

Lucceius, Lucius: Unsuccessful consular candidate (with Caesar) in 60. Notable historian. Sided with Pompey in the Civil War.

Lucretius Carus, Titus: Author of the *De rerum natura*, a brilliant poetic exposition of Epicurean philosophy.

Lutatius Catulus, Quintus (1): Consul in 102. As proconsul the following year, he claimed to have played a major role in winning the victory at Vercellae against the Cimbrians along with Marius. He was praised by Cicero as one of the leading orators of his generation. In 87 he sided against Marius and Cinna and committed suicide. He was the stepbrother of Lucius Julius Caesar (1) and Gaius Julius Caesar Strabo Vopiscus.

Lutatius Catulus, Quintus (2): Son of the preceding, he was consul in 78. In 87 he fled Rome to serve Sulla, whom he came to admire and whose memoirs he completed. He opposed the *Lex Gabinia* in 67 and the *Lex Manilia* in 66. He was defeated by Caesar in the election for pontifex maximus in 63.

Marius, Gaius: Served with Scipio Aemilianus in Spain in 133, tribune of the plebs in 119, praetor in 115, legate of Quintus Caecilius Metellus during the Jugurthine War in 109–108, and consul in 107, 104–100, and 86, He reorganized the Roman army during his campaigns against the Cimbrians and Teutons. He married Julia (2), the sister of Caesar's father. Exiled by Sulla in 88; he returned with Cinna to seize power in 87. He died shortly after taking office as consul in 86. Caesar presented him as a role model.

Metellus Scipio: see Caecilius Metellus Pius Scipio Nasica, Quintus.

Mithridates VI: King of Pontus from 120 to 63, he waged wars with Rome in 89–84, 83–81, and 74–63.

Mucia: Pompey's third wife, mother of his three children.

Nicomedes IV: King of Bithynia, 94–74.

Octavius, Gaius: Praetor in 63. Husband of Atia, the daughter of Julia (4) and Atius Balbus.

Octavius, Gaius (Octavian): Son of the preceding. Named as Caesar's heir, he later became the emperor Augustus.

Opimius, Lucius: Consul in 121, he passed the first *senatus consultum ultimum*, which he used to suppress (and murder) the followers of Gaius Gracchus.

Oppius, Gaius: A Roman knight who was one of Caesar's most important followers, working closely with Cornelius Balbus in Gaul and Rome. After the Ides of March he provided important assistance to Octavian. He produced a significant life of Caesar that was used by later biographers.

Petreius, Marcus: Legate in 63–62, in which role he managed the campaign against Catiline. He was also Pompey's legate in Spain in 55–49 and commanded Pompeian forces in the Lerida campaign. He also served against Caesar in the Thapsus campaign, in the wake of which he was killed.

Pompeia: Daughter of Quintus Pompeius Rufus and Cornelia, the daughter of Sulla, she married Caesar in 67. They divorced in 61 as the result of her involvement in the Bona Dea scandal.

Pompeius Rufus, Quintus: Consul in 88 as colleague of Sulla, whose daughter his son married. Murdered at the behest of Pompeius Strabo.

Pompeius Strabo, Gnaeus: Consul in 89, who played a major role in the suppression of the Italian revolt. Father of Pompey the Great. He died in 87.

Pompeius, Gnaeus (Pompey the Great): Consul in 70, 55, and 52. He raised several legions at his own expense to join Sulla's side in the civil war against the Marians (83–81) and was then given commands against Sulla's surviving rivals in Sicily and North Africa. After this he took to calling himself "the Great," suggesting he was Rome's version of Alexander. He held commands in Spain in 76–70, against the pirates in 67, and against Mithridates VI in 66–62. First Caesar's ally and then his opponent in the Civil War. Killed in Egypt in 48 after the Battle of Pharsalus.

Pompeius, Gnaeus (the Younger): Elder son of Pompey by Mucia. Died in Spain in 45.

Pompeius, Sextus: Younger of Pompey's sons by Mucia, active in the Munda campaign and subsequently a power in his own right after Caesar's assassination until he was defeated by Gaius Octavius (Octavian), the future emperor Augustus, in 36.

Pompey: see Pompeius, Gnaeus (Pompey the Great).

Porcius Cato, Marcus (the Elder): Consul in 195 and censor in 184. He was the author of the first history of Rome in Latin.

Porcius Cato, Marcus (the Younger): Caesar's most notable political adversary. Quaestor in 64, tribune of the plebs in 62, assigned to annex Cyprus in 58–57, praetor in 54. His mother Livia was the mother of Servilia by her first husband Servilius Caepio. Cato's father, Livia's second husband, was the grandson of Marcus Porcius Cato the Elder (see preceding).

Ptolemy XII: King of Egypt, 80–58 and 55–51. He was driven from his throne by an Alexandrian protest and was later restored by Aulus Gabinius.

Ptolemy XIII: King of Egypt, 51–47, as co-ruler with his sister, Cleopatra VII.

Sallust: see Sallustius Crispus, Gaius.

Sallustius Crispus, Gaius: Quaestor in 55or 54 and tribune of the plebs in 52, in which role he supported the prosecution of Milo's followers. Expelled from the Senate in 50, he was restored by Caesar and served as praetor in 46. After Caesar's assassination he wrote three major historical works, the *Conspiracy of Catiline*, the *Jugurthine War*, and the *Histories*.

Scribonius Curio, Gaius: Tribune of the plebs in 50 and legate of Caesar in 49, during which year he was killed in battle against Juba in North Africa.

Sempronius Gracchus, Gaius: Tribune of the plebs in 123–122. Younger brother of Tiberius Sempronius Gracchus.

Sempronius Gracchus, Tiberius: Tribune of the plebs in 133.

Servilia: Mother of Marcus Junius Brutus by her first husband, and Caesar's long-term mistress. She was the maternal half-sister of Marcus Porcius Cato the Younger.

Servilius Vatia Isauricus, Publius (1): Served under Sulla in the Civil War. Consul in 79. He subsequently served as governor of Cilicia, where he took the name Isauricus ("victor in Isauria," a region of Cilicia) to commemorate victories over the pirates there. Caesar served under him.

Servilius Vatia Isauricus, Publius (2): Son of the preceding. Praetor in 54 and consul in 48.

Sulla: see Cornelius Sulla, Lucius.

Sulpicius Rufus, Publius: Tribune of the plebs in 88 who sponsored a series of laws, including one changing the way new citizens would be distributed through the original thirty-five tribes and another transferring the command against Mithridates from Sulla to Marius. He was killed on Sulla's orders.

Terentius Varro, Marcus: Noted intellectual who advised both Pompey and Caesar. He was governor of Further Spain in 49.

Titurius Sabinus, Quintus: Legate of Caesar from 57 until 54, when he died in action against the Eburones. Caesar blamed him for the disaster in which he was killed. He may previously have served under Pompey.

Tullius Cicero, Marcus: The foremost literary figure of his generation. Consul in 63.

Tullius Cicero, Quintus: Younger brother of Marcus Tullius Cicero. Praetor in 62, governor of Asia in 62–58, legate of Pompey in 58–56, and legate of Caesar in 54–52.

Trebonius, Gaius: Tribune of the plebs in 55, in which office he moved the bill conferring five-year commands on Pompey and Crassus. He was legate of Caesar in 54–49, praetor in 48, governor of Further Spain in 47–46, legate of Caesar in Spain in 46–45, and consul from October 1 to December 31 of 45. He joined the conspiracy against Caesar.

Valerius Catullus, Gaius: The most brilliant poet of Caesar's generation.

Vercingetorix: Leader of the great Gallic revolt of 52.

Timeline

All dates BCE

133: Tribunate of Tiberius Gracchus.

123–122: Tribunates of Gaius Gracchus.

121: Passage of the first "ultimate decree" (*senatus consultum ultimum*); murder of Gaius Gracchus.

112: Jugurthine War begins.

107: First consulship of Gaius Marius.

106: Births of Cicero and Pompey.

105: Jugurtha captured; Cimbrians and Teutons destroy Roman armies in Gaul.

104: Second consulship of Marius.

103: First tribunate of Saturninus.

102: Fourth consulship of Marius, who defeats Teutons at Aquae Sextiae.

101: Fifth consulship of Marius, who defeats the Cimbrians at Vercellae.

100: Sixth consulship of Marius; birth of Julius Caesar on July 12; *senatus consultum ultimum* passed to suppress Saturninus.

91–88: Social War.

89–85: First Mithridatic War.

88: Tribune Sulpicius transfers command against Mithridates from Sulla to Marius; Sulla marches on Rome, massacres political rivals, and takes back command against Mithridates.

87: Marius and Cinna expel Sulla's supporters and take power in Rome; death of Pompeius Strabo, father of Pompey the Great.

86: Seventh consulship of Marius.

85: Sulla defeats Mithridates.

84: Marriage of Caesar and Cornelia.

83–81: Sulla's return to Italy.

81: Sulla captures Rome, publishes proscription edict.

80: Sullan constitutional reforms; Caesar joins staff of Minucius Thermus, awarded civic crown for valor.

78: Death of Sulla; revolt of Lepidus.

77: Pompey granted special *imperium* to defeat Lepidus and fight Sertorius in Spain.

76: Caesar prosecutes Dolabella and Antonius Hybrida.

75: Third Mithridatic War begins.

73: Spartacus's revolt begins; Caesar serves under Antonius in Greece, during which time he may have been taken hostage by pirates; Caesar's selection as a member of the college of *pontifices*.

72: Sertorian War ends; Caesar serves as military tribune under Crassus.

71: Spartacus defeated; Pompey returns to Italy.

70: First consulship of Pompey and Crassus; Caesar serves as quaestor in Further Spain.

69: Caesar delivers funeral elegies for his aunt Julia and wife Cornelia.

68: Caesar marries Pompeia.

67: *Lex Gabinia* passed, appointing Pompey to a special command to suppress piracy; Lucullus's army mutinies; Mithridates reoccupies Pontus.

66: *Lex Manilia* confers command against Mithridates on Pompey.

65: Aedileship of Caesar, who restores monuments to Marius.

63: Caesar elected *pontifex maximus* and praetor; conspiracy of Catiline; Pompey finalizes his victory over Mithridates.

62: Caesar serves as praetor; Bona Dea scandal at the end of the year; Pompey returns to Italy.

61: Caesar divorces Pompeia, begins term as governor of Further Spain.

60: Caesar elected consul for 59.

59: Caesar serves as consul and is granted Cisalpine Gaul, Transalpine Gaul, and Illyricum for five years; Julia marries Pompey; Caesar marries Calpurnia.

58: Caesar defeats Helvetians and Ariovistus; exile of Cicero.

57: Caesar defeats Belgic Tribes; Cicero returns from exile.

56: Caesar defeats Veneti; meeting at Luca between Caesar and Pompey; Cicero delivers speech *On the Consular Provinces*.

55: Pompey and Crassus consuls for the second time; Caesar defeats Usipetes and Tencteri, invades Germany and Britain; *Lex Pompeia Cassia* extends Caesar's command in Gaul for five more years.

54: Caesar invades Britain a second time; disaster of Sabinus and Cotta; Crassus governor in Syria; deaths of Aurelia and Julia.

53: Caesar avenges disaster of Sabinus and Cotta, invades Germany; Crassus killed at Carrhae.

52: Murder of Clodius; Pompey made sole consul; revolt of Vercingetorix; plebiscite supported by Pompey grants Caesar the right to stand for the consulship in absentia (*ratio absentis*); Pompey supports passage of a bill imposing a five-year interval between holding office and a provincial governorship; Pompey marries Cornelia.

49: Caesar crosses the Rubicon; Pompey withdraws to Greece; Caesar defeats Afranius and Petreius in Spain; defeat of Curio in North Africa; Caesar made dictator for the first time in December.

48: Caesar crosses the Adriatic and is defeated at Dürres; Caesar defeats Pompey at Pharsalus; Pompey murdered in Egypt; Caesar arrives at Alexandria and initiates relationship with Cleopatra.

47: Caesar installs Cleopatra as queen of Egypt; birth of their son Caesarion; defeat of Pharnaces at Zela; Caesar returns to Italy and as dictator deals with military mutinies and financial crises before leaving for Africa.

46: Caesar as dictator and consul defeats Pompeian forces at Thapsus; suicide of Cato; Caesar celebrates four triumphs in the autumn and reforms of the calendar, establishing the 365-day year; Cicero delivers *On Behalf of Marcellus* and *On Behalf of Ligarius*.

45: Caesar as dictator and consul defeats Pompeian forces at Munda, administers Italy through prefects until his return in the autumn, chooses Gaius Octavius to be his principal heir, and writes *Anti-Cato*.

44: Caesar becomes dictator for life and is assassinated on March 15.

Glossary of Terms

aediles Originally plebeian magistrates charged with overseeing plebeian cults on the Aventine hill. The office was opened to patricians in 367 BCE, when the curule aedileship was created for them. Thereafter, curule aediles and plebeian aediles were elected in alternate years (with curule aedilships falling in even-numbered years), though in some years (e.g., in 65 BCE) both plebeian and curule aediles were elected. The duties of the aediles included the holding of certain games, overseeing the marketplace, and the maintenance of public order.

comitia centuriata The Roman voting assembly based upon the division of the Roman people into five classes and 193 *centuriae* (centuries). The *comitia centuriata* could only be summoned by a magistrate with *imperium* and could elect magistrates with *imperium*, declare war and peace, and enact laws.

comitia populi tributa An assembly, created on the model of the *concilium/comitia plebis*, in which the voting units were the thirty-five tribes. Unlike the *concilium/comitia plebis*, patricians were admitted. The assembly could pass laws and elected curule aediles, quaestors, and special commissioners.

concilium/comitia plebis tributa Originally formed as an assembly of plebeians only and presided over by the tribunes. It elected tribunes of the plebs and plebeian aediles and could pass motions—plebiscites—that were binding upon all members of the Roman community. The voting units were the thirty-five tribes. Throughout the history of the Republic, this was the assembly through which laws proposed by tribunes were passed.

censors Two censors were elected every five years for eighteen-month terms. Their chief function was to draw up lists of Roman citizens, which also involved oversight of the morals of the community. They were also responsible for leasing revenue-producing public property.

cohort A military unit forming one tenth of a legion under the Marian army reforms. Each cohort had six centurions and was the basic tactical unit of the legion. Auxiliary infantry units were also raised as cohorts even though they were not gathered into legions.

consul The highest magistrate of the Roman Republic. Romans understood the term to be derived from the verb *consulo*, to take counsel, since the crucial aspect of the consulship was that there had to be two at any given time (a consul who died in office had to be replaced by a suffect). The *imperium* of a consul was superior to that of every other magistrate unless a dictator was in office.

denarius (plural **denarii**) The basic silver coin in the coinage system of the late Republic. Worth four sestertii.

dictator Originally an office only created by a senior magistrate, the holder had *imperium* superior to all other magistrates. Originally the dictator's power was defined by a specific task, upon the completion of which the office would lapse, or by a specific time limit. Sulla eliminated the notional time limit for himself.

Epicureanism Doctrine derived from the thought of the Greek philosopher Epicurus (341–270 BCE). Its central tenet was that the purpose of philosophy was to secure a happy life. Epicurus taught, based on earlier theories, that all matter was made up of atoms and that change was the result of the rearrangement of these atoms. The gods were themselves the product of atomic combination and took no thought for humans.

equestrian order Originally referring to the cavalry in the early army, by the mid-Republican period (if not before) the term "equestrian" was used to define the order that ranked just below the Senate.

flamen dialis The priest of Jupiter. He was always a patrician and was chosen by the *pontifices*. The *flamen dialis* was bound by such an elaborate system of rules and taboos that it was virtually impossible for him to have a political career.

imperium Legal power of a dictator, consul, or praetor, graded according to the office or last office held, unless special arrangement was made through a law passed by the Roman people.

master of horse (*magister equitum*) In the Republican period, this term for a cavalry commander referred to the magistrate who was second-in-command to a dictator. All dictators appointed one.

nobiles Members of the Roman aristocracy who came from families that had, at some point in their history, produced a consul.

paterfamilias The head of a Roman household. Roman law granted the *paterfamilias* power of life and death (*patria potestas*) over every member of his family and his servants within his home.

patrician A member of a ruling elite of Rome. The aristocratic families who made up the patrician order claimed descent from the city's original senators.

pilum (plural **pila**) A heavy javelin that was the standard missile weapon of the Roman legionary.

plebeian Any Roman citizen who was not a patrician.

pomerium The sacred boundary of the city of Rome.

pontifex maximus The chief of the board of *pontifices*. The position was elective.

pontifices A college of Roman priests which oversaw matters connected with the state cult—sacrifices, festivals, and other rituals—and advised magistrates on matters of religious law.

praetor Roman magistrate second in rank to the consul. Sulla increased the number of praetors from six to eight and assigned them the administration of standing courts at Rome. Caesar expanded their number to sixteen.

proscription Under Sulla the word came to mean the publication of a list of citizens who were sentenced to death as enemies of the state. Those proscribed by Sulla had no right of *provocatio*.

provocatio Literally, "an act of summoning." The term came to mean the right of any Roman citizen to appeal to the Roman people against the exercise of a magistrate's power of physical coercion.

publicanus (plural *publicani*) A contractor for public works, especially tax collection.

quaestor The lowest-ranking Roman magistrate. Quaestors had responsibilities for state finances. After Sulla's law governing the stages of the senatorial career, election to the quaestorship qualified a person to be a senator.

regnum Literally the office or power of a king, in the political vocabulary of the late Republic this term stood in opposition to *libertas* as signifying autocratic or despotic rule.

senatus consultum The "advice of the senate" or a decree of the Senate. A *senatus consultum* did not have the authority of law, which could be conferred only if an assembly of the people voted in favor of a *senatus consultum*.

senatus consultum ultimum The "ultimate decree of the Senate" supposedly conferred on magistrates the power to take whatever action they deemed necessary to protect the state from harm, including the killing of Roman citizens without trial. The *senatus consultum ultimum* was first passed in 121 BCE.

sestertius (plural **sestertii**) The basic Roman bronze coin.

Stoicism System of thought devised by Zeno of Citium (335–263 BCE), according to which the physical world is made up of material objects whose interactions are governed by the laws of fate. Stoic ethics held that virtue, which served to place things in their proper order, was sufficient for happiness, that nothing other than virtue was good, and that emotions were bad when contrary to virtue.

tribune Initially an official connected with the tribes (the word is derived from *tribus*). The number of tribunes was stabilized at ten in 455 BCE. Tribunes were plebeians and elected to office by the *concilium plebis*. They had the power to introduce legislation before the *comitia tributa* and the *ius intercessionis* (right of intercession) or veto power, which enabled them to bring public business to a halt. In theory, tribunes possessed *sacrosanctitas*, i.e., were "protected by religious sanction from harm," thus freeing a tribune while in office from the threat of violence at the hands of a holder of *imperium*.

Vestal Virgins The group of six women who were servants of Vesta, the patron goddess of the Roman hearth and home. The Vestals were charged with keeping alight the eternal flame, symbolizing the enduring strength of the state, at the Temple of Vesta in the Forum.

Notes

All abbreviations of classical works follow *Oxford Classical Dictionary*.

CHAPTER I

1. For the connection with Bovillae, see Tac. *Ann.* 2.41, 15.23.2, with S. Weinstock, *Divus Julius* (Oxford, 1971), 5–7; D. Potter, "Rome and Bovillae through the Early Decades of the Empire," in *Ancient Bovillae: History, Art and Archaeology of a Lost City on the Roman Hinterland* ed. P. Hatlie (Ann Arbor, 2025): 24–29. The effort to deny the connection in E. Badian, "From the Iulii to Caesar," in *A Companion to Julius Caesar*, ed. M. T. Griffin (Oxford, 2007), 13–14, is perverse.

2. For Caesar's birth, see M. Carroll, *Infancy and Earliest Childhood in the Roman World: "A Fragment of Time"* (Oxford, 2015), 56–59; A. Bonnell-Freidin, *Birthing Romans Childbearing and its Risks in Imperial Rome* (Princeton, 2024): 38–40 (midwives); 166–208 on the technology of hope (amulets). For speculation on the connection with Caesar's cognomen, see Plin. *HN* 7.47. See F. M. Galassi and H. Ashrafian, *Julius Caesar's Disease: A New Diagnosis* (Barnsley, 2016), 8 disproving the connection with epilepsy; and see also p. 271 below.

3. See Plut. *Mar.* 6.2 for the date of the marriage after his praetorship. On the status of the Julii at this point, see R. Syme, *Sallust* (Berkeley, 1964), 161; and E. Gruen, *The Last Generation of the Roman Republic* (Berkeley and Los Angeles, 1974), 75.

4. *CIL* 14.2387 with discussion in M.G.G. Cercere, "Inscriptions from the Area of Bovillae," in *Ancient Bovillae: History, Art and Archaeology of a Laost City on the Roman Hinterland* ed. P. Hatlie (Ann Arbor, 2025): 130–2.

5. For all the options, see SHA *Ael.* 2.3–4. For "caesarian," see Plin. *HN* 7.47; Serv. *ad Aen.* 10.316. For the elephant, see *RRC* no. 443.

6. A. Ernout and A. Meillet, *Dictionnaire étymologique de la langue latine*, 4th ed. (Paris, 2001), 84.

7. For Roman tribes in general, see L. R. Taylor, *The Voting Districts of the Roman Republic: The Thirty-Five Urban and Rural Tribes*, 2nd ed., ed. J. Linderski (Ann Arbor, 2013), 40–41, 363.

8. *FRH* 5 F11, with C. Smith, "Caesar and the History of Early Rome," in *Cesare: Precursore o visionario? Atti del convegno internazionale, Cividale del Friuli 17–19 settembre 2009*, ed. G. Urso (Pisa, 2020), 252, and, more generally, 250 253, 261 264.

9. The coin in question is *RRC* no. 320; *FRH* 5 F8 for Cato.

10. A. Erskine, *Troy between Greece and Rome: Local Tradition and Imperial Power* (Oxford, 2001), 17–23, for the mythic history of the Julii, and 147 for Aeneas in Etruria.

11. Livy 27.22.9, 29.4–6 (praetor of 208); and *CIL* 13.1 (consul of 157). He is probably also the ex-praetor in Dessau, *ILS* 19. See also Smith, "Caesar and the History of Early Rome," 251.

12. For the ancestry of the Marcii see Suet. *Iul.* 6.1.

13. R. Bagnall and B. W. Frier, *The Demography of Roman Egypt* (Cambridge, 1994), 81–90. The Egyptian evidence plainly aligns with other evidence for life expectancy in the Roman world.

14. For age at marriage, see S. Treggiari, *Roman Marriage: Iusti Coniuges from the Time of Cicero to the Time of Ulpian* (Oxford, 1991), 398–403. For Cicero and his family, see A. E. Hanson, "The Roman Family," in *Life, Death, and Entertainment in the Roman Empire*, rev. ed., ed. D. Potter and D. J Mattingly (Ann Arbor, 2010), 47–48.

15. For dowries, see Treggiari, *Roman Marriage*, 323–364.

16. See now B. D. Shaw, "The Company-State Model and the *societates publicanorum*," *Historia* 71 (2022): 78–127.

17. D. Potter, *The Origin of Empire: Rome from the Republic to Hadrian* (London, 2019), 116, on the Ligurian scam. See P. Kay, *Rome's Economic Revolution* (Oxford, 2014) on the economic expansion of the second century.

18. Cic. *Mur.* 76. For more on the aedileship, see pp. 10; 65–66 below.

CHAPTER 2

1. L. R. Taylor, *Roman Voting Assemblies* (Ann Arbor, 1966).

2. D. W. Rathbone, "The Control and Exploitation of *ager publicus* in Italy under the Roman Republic," in *Tâches publiques et enterprise privée dans le monde romain*, ed. J.-J. Aubert (Geneva, 2003), 135–178; J. Rich, "Lex Licinia, Lex Sempronia, B. G. Niebuhr and the Limitation of Landholding in the Roman Republic," in *People, Land, and Politics: Demographic Developments and the Transformation of Roman Italy, 300 BC–AD 14*, ed. L. de Light and S. Northwood (Leiden, 2008), 519–572; and S. T. Roselaar, *Public Land in the Roman Republic: A Societal and Economic History of Ager Publicus in Italy, 396–89 BC* (Oxford, 2010).

3. D. L. Stockton, *The Gracchi* (Oxford, 1979), 61–86.

4. Stockton, *Gracchi*, 114–161.

5. Cic. *Cat.* 1.4; *Phil.* 8.14; and Plut. *C. Gracch.* 14.3.

6. Sall. *Iug.* 42; and R. Syme, *Sallust* (Berkeley, 1964): 160–171, on his political views. See also D. Potter, *The Origin of Empire: Rome from the Republic to Hadrian* (London, 2019): 145, 155–157.

7. Plut. *Mar.* 3.1.

8. Plut. *Mar.* 4.2–4 (tribune), 5.3–5 (trial), 6.1 (governor of Spain); Sall. *Iug.* 8.1–2 (connection with Jugurtha, albeit without mentioning Marius directly, but a connection may be implicit in *ea tempestate in exercitu nostro fuere conplures novi atque nobiles*).

9. Sall. *Iug.* 16.5 (settlement), 20.1: *omnia Romae venalia esse*.

10. Sall. *Iug.* 26 (murders), 28.4–29 (campaign of 111), 38.9 (surrender).

11. Livy, *Per.* 63; Flor. 1.39.4; Dio Cass. 26 fr. 88; Fest. *Brev.* 9.1; Amm. Marc. 27.4.4 (defeat of Cato); Strabo 5.1.8; Livy, *Per.* 63; Vell. Pat. 2.12.2; Plut. *Mar.* 16.5; App. *Celt.* 13 (defeat of Carbo by the Cimbri); Sall. *Iug.* 40 (Scaurus); Plut. *Mar,* 4.1 (Marius as a hereditary client of the Caecilii).

12. D. Potter, "Caesar and the Helvetians," *New Perspectives on Ancient Warfare*, ed. G. Fagan and M. Trundle (Leiden, 2010), 311–312.

13. Sall. *Iug.* 64.1–4 (Metellus to Marius), 65.4–5, 73.3–7; Plut. *Mar.* 8.3–9; Dio Cass. fr. 89.3 (election of Marius); and Syme, *Sallust*, 158–160.

14. Sall *Iug.* 73.7: *Et postea populus a tribuno plebis T. Manlio Mancino rogatus, quem vellet cum Iugurtha bellum gerere, frequens Marium iussit.*

15. Sall. *Cat.* 96.

16. *FRH* 25 F66a–b; Flor. 1.38.4; Gran. Licin. p. 17B; Plut. *Mar.* 16.5, 19.2; Dio Cass. fr. 91.

17. Plut. *Mar.* 16

18. Livy, *Per* 68 (both battles); Plut. *Mar.* 17 (religious figures), 18–21 (defeat of the Teutons), 24–27; Plut. *Sull.* 4 (defeat of the Cimbrians). For the temple, see A. Carandini and P. Carafa, eds., *The Atlas of Ancient Rome: Biography and Portraits of the City,* trans. A. C. Halaveis (Princeton, 2017), 503–504.

19. Gran. Licin. p. 13F; *Auct. ad Her.* 1.14; Val. Max. 4.7.3 (trials of Caepio and Mallius); Cic. *De or.* 2.25, 28, 47; *Off.* 2.14; Val. Max. 8.5.2; Tac. *Ann.* 1.72 (*maiestas* law); Cic. *Verr.* 2.1.9; *Brut.* 62; *Rab. Post.* 4; *Balb.* 23; Asc. *Scaur.* 21C (extortion law); Livy, *Per.* 69; Val. Max. 9.7.1, 7. 3; Flor. 2.4; App. *B Civ* 1.28; [Aur.Vict,] *De vir. ill.* 73 (election of Saturninus).

20. Livy, *Per.* 69; App. *B Civ* 1.29 (land law); Cic. *Balb.* 21; [Aur.Vict,] *De vir. ill.* 73 (land law); *Auct. ad Her.* 1.12 (grain law). For examples of oath clauses, see M. H. Crawford, *Roman Laws and Statues,* BICS suppl.64 (London, 1996) no. 7, 14–22.

21. Cic. *Rab Post.* 7 *Brut.* 62; Livy, *Per.* 69; Vell. Pat. 22.12; Val. Max. 3.2.18, 8.6.2; Flor. 2.4; Plut. *Mar.* 30; App. *B Civ* 1.33, with P. Hinard's n. 233 in P. Goukowsky, ed., *Appien: Histoire romaine,* vol. 13 (Paris, 2008); Oros. 5.17; [Aur. Vict.] *De vir. ill.* 73. For the date, see J. L. Beness and T. W. Hillard, "The Death of Lucius Equitius on 10 December 100 B.C.," *CQ* 40 (1990): 269–272 (pointing out that Equitius died after the murder of Saturninus and his companions).

CHAPTER 3

1. M. Carroll, *Infancy and Earliest Childhood in the Roman World: "A Fragment of Time"* (Oxford, 2015), 63.

2. A. E. Hanson, "The Roman Family," in *Life Death, and Entertainment in the Roman Empire,* rev. ed., ed. D. Potter and D. J. Mattingly (Ann Arbor, 2010): 39–40; and Carroll, *Infancy and Earliest Childhood,* 64–65 (weaning), 72–75 (swaddling); A. Bonnell-Freidin, *Birthing Romans: Childbearing and its Risks in Imperial Rome* (Princeton, 2024): 35–37 (wetnurses).

3. Tac. *Dial.*28 (Aurelia's reputation as a mother).

4. Quint. *Inst.* 1.1.25–26.

5. Quint., *Inst.* 1.1.30–32.

6. Quint., *Inst.* 1.1.12–14.

7. August. *Conf.* 1.13.22

8. Hanson, "Roman Family," 37, fig. 2, on toys; S. Bonner, *Education in Ancient Rome: From the Elder Cato to the Younger Pliny* (Abingdon, 2012), 37.

9. For slavery as a non-productive aspect of the elite economy, and for ostentatious specialization, see S. Treggiari, "Jobs in the Household of Livia," *Papers of the British School at Rome* 43 (1975), 48–77; K. Bradley, *Slavery and Society at Rome* (Cambridge, 1995), 59–63; and G. E. M. de Ste. Croix, *The Class Struggle in the Ancient Greek World* (London, 1981), 133–173.

10. H. Mouritson, *The Freedman in the Roman World* (Cambridge, 2011), 120–205 (esp. 132–133 on age at manumission).

11. K. Hopkins, "Novel Evidence for Roman Slavery," in Potter and Mattingly, *Life, Death and Entertainment,* 110–134; and Mouritson, *Freedman in the Roman World,* 27, on sexual abuse. See also A. Richlin, *Slave Theater in the Roman Republic: Plautus and Popular Comedy* (Cambridge, 2017).

12. Cicero, *Comment. pet.* 5 (Cicero and his slaves); Mouritson, *Freedman in the Roman World*, 44–46; S. Treggiari, *Roman Freedmen During the Late Republic* (Oxford, 1969), 218–219 (on Cicero and Tiro); and E. J. Champlin, *Final Judgements: Duty and Emotion in Roman Wills, 200 B.C–A.D. 250* (Berkeley and Los Angeles, 1991), 137 (legacies to concubines).

13. For the young man with compressed disc, see: https://kslnewsradio.com/1937431/bodies-of-man-and-his-slave-unearthed-from-ashes-at-pompeii/. The claim of a mill reported at Pompeii being the site of slave punishments is overstated—it is part of a large kitchen in a large, wealthy household, for the erroneous report see: https://www.nytimes.com/2023/12/08/world/europe/pompeii-ruins-slaves.html. (I am indebted to members of the archaeological staff at Pompeii for a tour of the site in July 2024). See also Sen. *Ep.* 47 (slaves standing around at dinner parties).

14. H. Thompson, "Iron Age and Roman Slave-Shackles," *Archaeological Journal* 150 (1983): 57–168; Gai. *Inst.* 1.53 (protections for slaves in the imperial period); *AE* 1971 no. 88 (text from Pozzouli); Diod Sic. 34.4 (ill treatment of slaves and Sicilian revolt), with P. Morton, *Slavery and Rebellion in Second-Century BC Sicily: from* Bellum Servile *to* Sicilia Capta (Edinburgh, 2024), 129–152.

CHAPTER 4

1. The critical analysis of the biographical tradition remains H. Strasburger, *Caesars Eintritt in die Geschichte* (Munich, 1938), reprinted in H. Strasburger, *Studien zu alten Geschichte* (Hildesheim, 1982). See also G. B. Townend, "C. Oppius on Julius Caesar," *AJPhil;* 108 (1987): 325–342 and, for Suetonius, G. W. Bowersock, "Suetonius and Trajan." In *Hommages à Marcel Renard*, vol. 1, ed. J. Bibauw, Collection Latomus 101. (Brussels, 1969): 119–25; for Plutarch see C.B.R. Pelling, *Plutarch*, Caesar (Oxford, 2011): 13–58 *Plutarch*, Caesar. Oxford, 2011.

2. For the characterization of Strabo see Cic. *Brut.* 177. Passages quoted in the text are: Cic. *De or.* 2.270 (*Genus est perelegans et cum gravitate salsum cumque oratoriis dictionibus tum urbanis sermonibus accommodatum*); 2.273 (*"quidni" inquit "meminerim? Numquam enim recepissem, nisi tu perdidisses"*).

3. Suet. *Iul.* 55, on Caesar's use of Strabo's work; Caes. *B Gall.* 1.44.9, with p. 139 below; *BCiv.* 1.19 (*Cum vultus Domiti cum oratione non consentiret, atque omnia trepidantius timidiusque ageret, quam superioribus diebus consuesset*), with p. 209 below; Suet. *Iul.* 34 (*professus ante inter suos, ire se ad exercitum sine duce et inde reversurum ad ducem sine exercitu*), with pp. 215–216 below. See also See A. Garcea, *Caesar's* De Analogia: *Edition, Translation and Commentary* (Oxford, 2012), 19–20.

4. Suet. *Gram. et rhet.* 6.

5. See Garcea, *Caesar's* De Analogia, 20–21.

6. Suet. *Gram. et rhet.* 7.2.

7. D. Potter, *The Origin of Empire: Rome from the Republic to Hadrian 264 BC–AD 138* (London, 2021), 146–154, with bibliography on p. 406; the question of the allied contribution to Rome's armies is complex; see P.A. Brunt, *Italian Manpower 225 BC–AD 14* (Oxford, 1971), 432–433; R.E. Smith, *Service in the Post-Marian Roman Army* (Manchester, 1958): 3; 16–26; Contradictory information is provided by Vell. Pat. 2.15.1: allies contributed twice the number as Romans, wrong for the second century, though roughly correct for the period of the Hannibalic war (see Brunt, *Italian Manpower*, 678), Pol. 6.26: allied infantry were equivalent in strength to citizen units, which would not be contradicted if

garrison armies consisted of one citizen and one allied legion as appears from Plut. *Caes.* 12.1; App. *Ill.* 10; see also F. Bigloni, *The War Economy of the Roman Republic (406-100 BCE) Mnemosyne Supplement* 487 (Leiden, 2025): 102-155.

8. Malcovati, *ORF* p. 191 (speech of Gaius Gracchus about the conduct of magistrates in Italy); and Asc. *Corn.* 67C (expulsion of Italians).

9. App. *B Civ.* 1.35. See also Vell. Pat. 2.13; Livy, *Per.* 71; Diod. Sic. 37.10 (increase in the size of the Senate); App. *B Civ.* 1.35; Vell. Pat. 2.14; Flor. 2.35; Livy, *Per.* 71 (franchise); App. *B Civ.* 1.35-36; Livy, *Per.* 71 (agrarian law). Cic. *Dom.* 41, 50; *Leg.* 2.14, 31; Diod. Sic. 36.10; Asc. *Mil.* 68C; Flor. 2.5. See, in general, E. Gabba, "Rome and Italy: The Social War," in *The Cambridge Ancient History*, 2nd ed., vol. 9, ed. J. A. Crook, A. Lintoot, and E. Rawson (Cambridge, 1994), 111-113.

10. For the outbreak of the war, see App. *B Civ.* 1.38; Flor. 2.6; Livy, *Per.* 72; Obseq. 114-115, with P. A. Brunt, *The Fall of the Roman Republic* (Oxford, 1998), 98-102. For the campaigns of 90, see App. *B Civ.* 1.40-47; Livy, *Per.* 73-74; Oros. 5.18. For the *lex Julia de civitate*, see App. *B Civ.* 1.49; Gell. 4.4.3; Cic. *Balb.* 21; Vell. Pat. 2.16, with Brunt, *Fall,* 105-108.

11. App. *BC* 1.40; 46 for Sulla's return to action; for Marius's comment see Plut. *Mar.* 33.2.

12. For Strabo's campaigns, see Cic. *Balb.* 50; App. *B Civ.* 1.17; Oros. 5.18.10, 17; Livy, *Per.* 70. The inscription in question is *ILS* 8888, with N. Criniti, *L'Epigrafe di Asculum di Gn. Pompeo Strabone* (Milan, 1970).

13. App. *Mith.* 18-19, with A. N. Sherwin-White, *Roman Foreign Policy in the East, 168 B.C. to A.D. 1* (London, 1984), 121-127.

14. Plin. *NH* 33.48; App. *Mith.* 21, with B. C. McGing, *The Foreign Policy of Mithridates VI of Pontus* (Brill, 1986), 105.

15. For Mithridates and Alexander's cloak, see App. *Mith.* 117. For another Alexander fantasy, see App. *Mith.* 20, with the note in P. Goukowsky, *Appien: Histoire romaine*, vol. 7 (Paris, 2003), 147-148 and McGing, *Foreign Policy of Mithridates*, 101. For Athens, see *BNJ* 87 F36. For the massacre, see *BNJ* 434.22.9 (Memnon, a contemporary); Cic. *Man.* 7, 11; *Flac.* 57; App. *Mith.* 22, with Goukowsky *Appien: Histoire romaine*, 7:n212.

16. Plut. *Sull.* 6.8-9. For the events of 88, see also R. Seager, "Sulla," in *The Cambridge Ancient History* 2nd ed., vol. 9, ed. J. A. Crook, A. Lintoot, and E. Rawson (Cambridge, 1994), 165-173.

17. Livy, *Per.* 77; App. *B Civ.* 1.55; Plut. *Sull.* 8 (distribution of new citizens); Livy, *Per.* 77; *Auct. ad Her.* 2.45 (recall of exiles); Livy, *Per* 77; Vell. Pat. 2.18; App. *B Civ.* 1.56; Plut. *Mar.* 34; *Sull.* 8; Val. Max. 9.7; Eutr. 5.4; Flor. 2.9; [Aur. Vict.] *De vir. ill.* 67 (transfer of command to Marius); Plut. *Sull.* 8 (debt prohibition), with R. J. Evans, "The Sulpician Law on Debt: Implications for the Political Elite and Broader Ramifications," *Acta Classica* 50 (2007): 81-94.

18. Plut. *Mar.* 35.2-3 in M. Chassignet, *L'annaliste romaine*, vol. 3 (Paris, 2004): 178 F12; Plut. *Sull.* 8.3.

19. Livy, *Per.* 77; Plut. *Sull.* 9; *Mar.* 35; App. *B Civ.* 57 59.

20. Cic. *Sest.* 22; *Pis.* 19; *Planc.* 10; Vell. Pat. 2.19; Diod. Sic. 37.29; Plut. *Mar.* 35-40; *Sert.* 4; Flor. 2.9.8; Oros. 5.19 (Marius's flight; Florus and Orosius reflect Livy's version, while Cicero shows that the story was in regular circulation in his generation); *Auct. ad Her.* 1.15, 4.22; Cic. *Brut.* 64; Val. Max. 6.5.7 (death of Sulpicius).

21. App. *B Civ.* 1. 59.

22. Sall. *Hist* 2.21; Livy, *Per.* 77; Val. Max. 9.7; App. *B Civ.* 1.63 (murder of Pompeius Rufus).

23. App. *B Civ.* 1.65–66; Plut. *Mar.* 4; App. *B Civ.* 1.65, 67; Plut. *Mar.* 42.2–3; *Pomp.* 3; *Sert.* 5.1.

24. Cic. *De or.*3.8; Livy, *Per.* 80.

25. Suet., *Iul.* 1.1: *dismissa Cossutia*; the verb indicates divorce. Plut. *Caes.* 5.7 makes it clear that Pompeia was Caesar's third wife. To be *flamen dialis*, Caesar would have to be married to another patrician, which Cornelia was. Technically a *flamen dialis* could not be divorced, but the situation at the time was sufficiently irregular that an exemption was presumably sought. It may also be relevant that Caesar never actually took up the position. For the view that Cossutia was only betrothed to Caesar see, e.g., C. Meier, *Caesar: A Biography*, trans. D. McLintock (New York, 1982), 85. A. Goldsworthy, *Caesar: Life of a Colossus* (New Haven, 2006), 49, is agnostic but leans toward betrothal only on the grounds of age. L. Pedius's relationship to Caesar is implied by Suet. *Ius.* 83.2, but he did enjoy a significant career in Caesar's service (see Caes. *B Gall.* 11.2 22.3; *BCiv.* 3.32) and as consul in 43 moved the bill authorizing the proscriptions: see *BNP*, s.v. "Pedius." The marriage to Pinarius is known only through the existence of L.Pinarius Scarpus: see Suet. *Iul.* 83.2; App. *B Civ.* 3.22, with *BNP*, s.v. "L.Pinarius Scarpus." Scarpus's career indicates that he was significantly younger than L. Pedius.

26. For Caesar and the Salii, see G. Rüpke, *Fasti Sacredotium: A Prosopography of Pagan, Jewish, and Christian Religious Officials in the City of Rome 300 BC TO AD 499*, trans. D. M. B. Richardson (Oxford, 2008), 734. *Flamen dialis*: see Tac. *Ann.* 3.58, which I do think is decisive; the issue is admittedly not straightforward and Suetonius (*Iul.* 1.1) says he was *destinatus*, but that does indicate he didn't complete the process, contra Vell. Pat. 2.43.1, who explicitly states that he held the office and lost it under Sulla (*flamen dialis creatus victoria Sullae . . . amisisset id sacerdotium*). Plut. *Caes.* 1.3 seems to confirm Suetonius's version (Caesar is a candidate for a priesthood which Sulla prevents him from taking up); see also Strasburger, *Caesars Eintritt*, 80. Rüpke, *Fasti Sacerdotium*, 734n1 takes the view that he briefly held the position, but see L. R. Taylor, "Caesar's Early Career," *C Phil.* 36 (1941): 115, on Aurelia.

27. Fiscal arrangements: see App. *Mith.* 63; Plut. *Sull.* 24.3 (treaty with Mithridates); 25.2 (fine imposed on Asia), with F. Santangelo, *Sulla, the Elites and the Empire: A Study of Roman Policies in Italy and the Greek East* (Leiden, 2007), 107–133; M.H. Crawford, *Roman Republican Coinage* (Cambridge, 1975), n. 359; 366–71; 374, and now, taking in the Greece mints along with the Sullan mints see L.F. Carbone, "Financing Sulla's Wars," in D.G. Domíguez, J.G. González, and F. Santangelo eds., *Connected Histories of Roman Civil Wars (88-30 BCE)* (Berlin, 2024): 75–120; the number she allows for Sulla's army in p. 75 n. 6 is substantially larger (93,000 men) than the army with which Sulla returned to Italy numbered 40,000 men (App. *BC* 1. 363 with P. Goukowsky and F. Hinard, *Appien, histoire romaine XIII Guerres civiles I* (Paris, 2008) n. 465 on the numbers) suggesting that Sulla arrived with a substantial surplus, which was deployed to increase his army to 23 legions or c. 120,000 men after arriving in Italy; see App. *BC* 1. 489; 470 for these numbers, and Potter, *Origin of Empire*, 186–188, on the significance of the resources for the civil war.

28. Plut. Pompey, 6–7 for Pompey with R. Seager, *Pompey the Great: A Political Biography* (2nd ed.) (Oxford, 2002): 26–8. For Sulla and the Italians, see Santangelo, *Sulla*, 67–77.

29. Santangelo, *Sulla*, 78–87; and F. Hinard, *Les proscriptions de la Rome républicaine* (Paris, 1985), 67–100, on the terms of the *lex Cornelia*.

30. Plut. *Caes.* 1.4; Suet. *Iul.* 1.3 (placing the incident at different points after Sulla's return). For discussion of the meaning of this passage and its significance for Suetonius, see D. Wardle, "Sulla and the 'Prophecy' of Caesar's Destruction of the *Optimates* (Suet. *Iul.* 1.3)," *Akroterion* 66 (2021): 79–96. For the fictional aspects of the accounts of Caesar's relationship with Sulla, see Taylor, "Caesar's Early Career," 116.

31. On this point, see Strasburger, *Caesars Eintritt*, 69–70.

CHAPTER 5

1. H. Strasburger, *Caesars Eintritt in die Geschichte* (Munich, 1938): 82 (= *Kleine Schriften* 1:82).

2. App. *Mith.* 65–66; *BNJ* 434.26. with A. N. Sherwin-White, *Roman Foreign Policy in the East, 168 BC to AD 1* (London, 1984), 149–152.

3. Suet. *Iul.* 49.3, mentioning that he argued a case on her behalf; F. Russo, "Caesar's *Pro Bithynis* and Heraclea Pontica," *Antichthon* 49 (2015): 94–109; and J. Osgood, "Caesar and Nicomedes," *CQ* 58 (2008): 690–691; fragments in A Garcea, *Tout César: discours, rtaites, corespondance et commentaires* (Paris, 2020): Les discours fr. 44–5 (pp. 63–4).

4. Suet. *Iul.* 49.2; and p. 44 below.

5. Suet. *Iul.* 2; for the *corona civica*, see Plin. *NH* 6.16.5.

6. For the retirement, see Plut. *Sull.* 34.3–4; App. *B Civ.* 1.103. Caesar's comment is reported in Suet. *Iul.* 77, on which see also p. 278 below. For the location of Sulla's retirement, see App. *B Civ.* 1.104; for his behavior, see Plut. *Sull.* 36 (also for the symptoms of his final illness, on which compare https://www.mayoclinic.org/diseases-conditions/inflammatory-bowel-disease/symptoms-causes/syc-20353315, whence my suspicion he suffered from colon cancer).

7. Suet. *Iul.* 3; for Lepidus, see J. A. Rosenblitt, *Rome after Sulla* (London, 2019), 45–79.

8. For the career move, see Cic. *Cael.* 73; *De or.* 1.121; Quint. *Inst.* 12.6.1; 7.3; Tac. *Dial.* 34.7. For the trial, see Cic. *Brut.* 317; Val. Max. 8.9.3, with other sources in M. C. Alexander, *Trials in the Late Roman Republic: 149 to 50 BC* (Toronto, 1990), 71 n. 140, placing the trial in 77. I favor the date given in the text because Dolabella needed to return to Rome to celebrate a triumph in 77. The error in Tacitus *Dial.* 34.7, saying Caesar was twenty-one at the time of the trial, does not support either view. For the success of the speech, see Vell. Pat. 2.43.3, saying that the audience favored Caesar's position. For Dolabella's line, see Suet. *Iul.* 49.1, with Strasburger, *Caesars Eintritt*, 36; and Osgood, "Caesar and Nicomedes," 688; fragments in Garcea, *Tout César*, Les discours frs. 17–23 (pp. 45–9).

9. Alexander, *Trials*, 71–72 n. 141. See especially Asc. *Mil.* 87C (on the judgement of the censors); Plut. *Caes.* 4.1 and Garcea, *Tout César*, Les discours frs 24–5 (pp. 50–51).

10. Val. Max. 6.9.15.

11. Vell. Pat. 2.42; Plut. *Caes.* 2.6–7 (Juncus); Vell. Pat. 2.42; Val. Max 6.9.15; Plut. *Caes.* 2.7 (crucifixion); Suet. *Iul.* 74.1 (throat slitting); and *FRH* 70 F31 (decapitation). [Aur. Vict.] *De vir. ill.* 42.3. Suet. *Iul.* 4.2 simply mentions execution. For the place of the story in the biographical tradition, see J. Osgood, "Caesar and the Pirates, or: How to Make (and Break) an Ancient Life," *GRBS* 57 (2010): 323–327, showing that the earliest version of the story, stressing Juncus's incompetence, was likely first spread by Caesar, probably in the early 60s, but see below n. 12. It is possible that Juncus was attacked for his general inability to deal with pirates rather than Caesar's kidnapping in particular.

12. For the financial situation of Asia in this period, see Plut. *Luc.* 20. See also App. *Mith.* 83 on Lucullus's tax reduction. On the issue of Caesar's legal capacity, see L.-M. Günther,

"Caesar und die Seeräuber—Eine Quellenanalyse," *Chiron* 29 (1999): 330–331. See also A. Goldsworthy, *Caesar: Life of a Colossus* (New Haven, 2006), 74–76; and M. Wyke, *Caesar: A Life in Western Culture* (London, 2007), 74, noting that the story fits well with Caesar's image in later life. The point of the story as Günther understands it is excellently exploited in M. Edwards, *A Coin for the Ferryman* (Las Vegas, 2022): 271–281; this novel's plot involves Caesar's kidnapping by time travelers from California.

13. Polyaenus, *Strat.* 8.23.1. Strasburger, *Caesars Eintritt,* 9–10 (=*Kleine Schriften,* 1:191–192) notes correctly that the story defies analysis in the context of other versions; for the possibility that it is the closest to reality, see Günther, "Caesar und die Seeräuber," 335.

14. Suet. *Iul.* 4.2.

15. *Syll*³ 748; for the family relationship, see Plut. *Ant.* 2.1.

CHAPTER 6

1. Vell. Pat. 2.43.1, with L. R. Taylor, "Caesar's Early Career," *C Phil* 36 (1941): 117–120.

2. Suet. *Iul.* 5.1; Plut. *Caes.* 5.1, with Taylor, "Caesar's Early Career," 120–121, noting the probability that he served in the war against Spartacus.

3. Oros. 5.24.1. For collaboration between members of municipal elites and Spartacus, see Cic. *Verr.* 5.158–170 (the case of Gavius falsely accused of being a spy for Spartacus in Sicily; for his probable home in Bruttium, see Z. Rubinsohn, "Was the *Bellum Spartacium* a Servile Insurrection?," *Rivista di Filogia e di Istruzione Classica* 99 (1971): 291n2.

4. O. Rudenko, "The Making of a Soviet Hero: The Case of Spartacus," *The Soviet and Post-Soviet Review* 47 (2020): 338.

5. On the status of gladiators, see G. Ville, *La gladiature en occident des origins à la mort de Domitien* (Rome, 1981), 227–344.

6. For the evil *lanista,* see Plut. *Crass.* 8.1. On the army, see especially the battles described in Plut. *Crass.* 9.3, 7; note also Appian's stress on the acquisition of legionary equipment by Spartacus's men and his statement that free men fought with Spartacus at *B Civ.* 1.117.

7. Plut. *Crass.* 9.7; App. *B Civ.* 1.116, stressing the hasty recruitment of the Roman forces.

8. App. *B Civ.* 1.117; Plut. *Crass.* 9.7; 5; Oros. 5.24.4 (Gellius's success); Plut. *Crass.* 9.7; App. *B Civ.* 1.117–118; Oros 5.24.4–5 (Spartacus's victories); Plut. *Crass.* 11.4, with Rubinsohn, "*Bellum Spartiacum,*" 297, on the impact of regional supporters on Spartacus's movements; Plut. *Crass.* 1.2 (Vestal scandal). For the nature of Crassus's command, see F. J. Vervaet, "Erratum to Crassus' Command in the War against Spartacus (73–71 BCE): His Official Position, Forces and Political Spoils," *Klio* 97 (2015): 405–442.

9. Plut. *Crass.* 10.1; App. *B Civ.* 1.118 (decimation). For the tactical developments, see D. Potter, "Caesar and the Helvetians," in *New Perspectives on Ancient Warfare,* ed. G. Fagan and M. Trundle (Leiden, 2010), 325–328; Plut. *Crass.* 10.2–3; Cic. *Verr.* 2.5.4 (plan to escape to Sicily); Cic. *Verr.* 2.5.64 (Verres and pirates); Plut. *Crass.* 11.4–7; App. *B Civ.* 1.120 (final with https://www.archaeological.org/wall-built-to-contain-spartacus-discovered/ on the discovery of the site at Dossone della Melia in south-central Calabria in 2024).

10. App. *B Civ.* 1.120, on the mass execution; Plut. *Crass.* 11.7; *Pomp.* 21.2 (Pompey ends the war).

11. Suet. *Iul.* 74.1, on the pirates. Plutarch knows a story that Caesar said Crassus would be happy when he learned he had been captured by the pirates (*Crass.*7.5); while I agree with Straburger (*Caesars Eintritt,* 64) that the whole story is fiction, it may reflect the fact that the two were known to have known each other prior to 70. For the possibility

that Caesar's association with Crassus began at this point, see Taylor, "Caesar's Early Career," 121.

12. Cic. *Verr.* 45; for the prosecution of Verres, see E. Rawson, *Cicero: A Portrait* (Bristol, 1975), 40–41.

13. For factional politics of the *Pro Roscio Amerino*, see D. Potter, *The Origin of Empire: Rome from the Republic to Hadrian* (London, 2019), 200–201. For the change in the juries, see Cic. *Div. Caec.* 8; *Verr.* 2.2 (bill under discussion), 45 (Pompey announces that he supports reform of the courts). For the bill, see Asc. *Pis.* 17.1–7 (Clark); *Corn.* 67 11–13 (Clark), with discussion in B. A. Marshall, *A Historical Commentary on Asconius* (Columbia, 1985), 115, 237–238; Plut. *Pomp.* 22.3. Restoration of tribunician rights: see Vel. Pat. 2.30.4; Livy, *Per.* 97; Suet. *Iul.* 5.1; Plut. *Pomp.* 22.3, with R. Seager, *Pompey the Great: A Political Biography,* 2nd edition (Oxford, 2002), 37; and E. Gruen, *The Last Generation of the Roman Republic* (Berkeley and Los Angeles, 1974), 27–28. Censors of 70: see Cic. *Clu.* 119; Livy, *Epit.* 98 (general statement). For Lentulus, see Plut., *Cic.* 17.1; Dio Cass. 37.30.4. For Antonius, see Sall. *Hist.* 4.49 (Ramsay); Asc. *In toga candida* 84.20–25C. with Marshall, *Commentary,* 285.

14. In general terms I follow the view expressed in F. Millar, *The Crowd in Rome in the Late Republic* (Ann Arbor, 1998), stressing the importance of the voters and drawing heavily on the work of Cl. Nicolet, *The World of the Citizen in Republican Rome,* trans. P. S. Falla (Berkeley, 1988). As Millar rightly points out, the importance of legislative politics does not mean that the majority of citizens voted. The distinction between electoral politics and legislative politics is rightly stressed by L. R. Taylor, *Roman Voting Assemblies from the Hannibalic War to the Dictatorship of Caesar* (Ann Arbor, 1966), 68, 83; and P. A. Brunt, *The Fall of the Roman Republic and Related Essays* (Oxford, 1988), 24–25. Crucial new work on the structures of urban life, which is reflected in this paragraph, is offered by L. Mignone, *The Republican Aventine and Rome's Social Order* (Ann Arbor, 2016); and J. Hartnett, *The Roman Street: Urban Life and Society in Pompeii, Herculaneum and Rome* (Cambridge, 2017), whose p. 297 is quoted on streets in dialogue. For Cicero on neighborliness, see Cic. *Planc.* 43, 72. On venues for learning the views of the people, see Cic. *Sest.* 96–106. For samples of electoral graffiti, see A. E. Cooley and M. G. L. Cooley, *Pompeii and Herculaneum,* 2nd ed. (Cambridge, 2018), 163–180.

15. C. Rosillo-López, *Public Opinion and Politics in the Late Roman Republic* (Cambridge, 2017), 75–97.

16. On "political parties," see Potter, *Origin of Empire,* 219–224; H. Mouritsen, *The Roman Elite and the End of the Republic: The Boni, the Nobles and Cicero* (Cambridge, 2024), 110–112; and the works cited in n. 14 above.

17. Suet. *Iul.* 45.

18. Suet. *Iul.* 5.1; Garcea, *Tout César,* Les discours frs 26–27 (pp. 51–52), with Strasburger, *Caesars Eintritt,* 93; Taylor, "Caesar's Early Career," 122; and F. Hinard, *Les proscriptions de la Rome républicaine* (Paris, 1985), 168n85.

19. Suet. *Iul.* 6; Garcea, *Tout César,* Les discours frs 30 31 (pp. 54 55).

20. Plut. *Caes.* 5.2, with C. Pelling, *Plutarch,* Caesar (Oxford, 2011), 150–151.

21. Suet. *Iul.* 6: *Amitae meae Iuliae maternum genus ab regibus ortum, paternum cum diis inmortalibus coniunctum est. Nam ab Anco Marcio sunt Marcii Reges, quo nomine fuit mater; a Venere Iulii, cuius gentis familia est nostra. Est ergo in genere et sanctitas regum, qui plurimum inter homines pollent, et caerimonia deorum, quorum ipsi in potestate sunt reges.* See also p. 56 and Garcea, *Tout César,* Les discours frs 28–29 (pp. 53–54).

22. Suet. *Iul.* 46. For the significance of mixed economic neighborhoods see Mignone, *The Republican Aventine*; for Pompey's houses, see I. Shatzman, *Senatorial Wealth and Roman Politics* (Brussels, 1975), 389.

23. For the economic impact of Spanish mines, see P. Kay, *Rome's Economic Revolution* (Oxford, 2014), 44–49.

24. Suet. *Iul.* 7.2; Dio Cass. 37.52.2 (mentioning only the statue of Alexander and moving the event to his praetorship); Plut. *Caes.* 32.9 (transferring it to the crossing of the Rubicon). For the view taken here, see D. Wardle, "Suetonius, Caesar and a Dream of World-Domination," *Athenaeum* 108 (2020): 72–88.

25. For the sexual mores of the period, see S. Treggiari, *Servilia and Her Family* (Oxford, 2019), 99–102; the Catullan passages cited here are 87.3 *nulla fides ullo fuit umquam foedere tanta*; 72.5: *nunc te cognovi: quare etsi impensius uror.*

26. D. Potter, *The Victor's Crown* (London, 2011), 191, 196 for Caesar's gladiators.

27. Treggiari, *Servilia*, 102–117.

28. Suet. *Iul.* 50; and Treggiari, *Servilia*, 104–106 (allowing that the affairs might have occurred). The view taken here aligns with J. P. V. D. Balsdon, *Julius Caesar and Rome* (London, 1967), 63–64.

29. For the house and the friend see Catull. 68b.68–9. For Sempronia, see Sall. *Cat.* 25. On the family relationship, see F. Münzer, *Roman Aristocratic Parties and Families*, trans. Th. Ridley (Baltimore, 1999), 250–251. For Postumia, see Catull. 27.

30. Plut. *Brut.*, 1.5, 2.1.

31. Cic. *Lig.* 30: *Causas, Caesar, egi multas, equidem tecum, dum te in foro tenuit ratio honorum tuorum*, with H. C. Gotoff, *Cicero's Caesarian Speeches: A Stylistic Commentary* (Chapel Hill, 1993): 165 (note on *causas dicere*). See also Cic. *Fam.* 1.9.12 on his *vetus amicitia* with Caesar.

32. Cic. *Comment. pet.* 1: *Ii rogandi omnes sunt diligenter et ad eos adlegandum est persuadendumque est iis nos semper cum optimatibus de re publica sensisse, minime popularis fuisse; si quid locuti populariter videamur, id nos eo consilio fecisse ut nobis Cn. Pompeium adiungeremus.*

33. Cic. *Brut.* 252, 261–262.

34. Plut. *Luc.* 7–8; App. *Mith.* 72; Cic. *Flac.* 85; Vel. Pat. 2.33.1 for Asia and Cilicia in 74. Bithynia was added no later than 72: see Livy, *Per.* 95; for details, see A. N. Sherwin-White, *Roman Foreign Policy in the East, 168 B.C. to A.D. 1* (London, 1984), 159–185; and B. McGing, *The Foreign Policy of Mithridates VI Eupator, King of Pontus* (Leiden, 1986), 144–162.

35. *FRH* no. 22.

36. Plut. *Luc.* 20.3.

37. Plut. *Pomp.* 24.6 (kidnapping); 25–26.1; App. *Mith.* 94; Dio Cass. 36.23–36, with D. Potter, "Dio and Pompey: Explaining the Failure of the Republic," in *The Intellectual Climate of Cassius Dio*, ed. A. Kemezis, C. Bailey, and B. Poletti (Leiden, 2022), 41–43, on Gabinius's bill. See Cic. *Verr.* 2.2.8 (on Antonius's *imperium infinitum*); Vell. Pat. 2.31.3 (on this as a precedent for Gabinius). See also K. M. Girardet, "*Imperia* und *Provinciae* des Pompeius 82 bis 48 v. Chr.," *Chiron* 31 (2001): 171 n. 73.

38. Plut. *Pomp.* 25.4

39. Asc. *Corn.* 72 C; Dio Cass. 36.30.1–4, on the passage of the bill. For the "legates of Pompey," see J. M. Reynolds, "Cyrenaica, Pompey and Cn. Cornelius Lentulus Marcellinus," *JRS* 52 (1962): 97–103. See now also *ICyr.* P.100: https://ircyr2020.inslib.kcl.ac.uk/en/inscriptions/P.100.html.

40. For the settlement of pirates away from Cilicia, see Strabo 8.7.5; 14.3.3; Plut. *Pomp.* 28.3–4; App. *Mith.* 96; Serv. *ad G.* 4.127; and J. Reynolds, "Cyrenaica, Pompey and Cn. Cornelius Lentulus Marcellinus," 102.

41. Reynolds, "Cyrenaica," 99n7.

42. Sall. *Hist.* 5.11 (Ramsay); Dio Cass. 36.14.3; App. *Mith.* 90.

43. Dio Cass. 36.14.4.

44. See R. Kallet-Marx, *Hegemony to Empire: The Development of the Roman* Imperium *in the East from 148 to 62 B.C.* (Berkeley, 1995), 314–315

45. Dio Cass. 36.43.2.

46. Cic. *Leg. Man.* 27, 42–46, 50 (why Pompey?), 51–53, 59–66; note esp. *Leg. Man.* 52 on Hortensius's opposition to a single commander. See also Vell. Pat. 2.33.1; Plut. *Pomp.* 30; *Luc.* 35.7; App. *Mith.* 97; Dio Cass. 36.42–44; Girardet, "*Imperia* und *Provinciae* des Pompeius 82 bis 48 v. Chr.," 176–187 (Manilius's proposal); Dio Cass. 36.31.3 (Catulus's speech backdated to the previous year); Cic. *Leg. Man.* 60 (breaking with tradition in time of war).

47. Plut. *Crass.* 2.4 on Crassus's conduct.

48. Potter, *Victor's Crown*, 183–185.

49. Cic. *Att.* 4.8.2 (Cicero and Atticus); Suet. *Iul.* 10 (on the ban); Plut. *Caes.* 5.9 (on the number); Caes. *B Civ.* 1.14.4–5 (gladiators in 49).

50. Cic. *Mur.* 76.

51. Plut. *Caes.* 10.

52. Suet. *Iul.* 11; Plut. *Caes.* 6.1–5, with R. Morstein-Marx, *Julius Caesar and the Roman People* (Cambridge, 2021), 47 (restoration of Marius's trophies); Plut. *Caes.* 6.6–7 (Catulus's comment).

53. For the scandal in the consular election see Cic. *Sull.* 11; 49–50; 81; Sall. *Cat.* 18; Asc. *Corn.* 75C; Asc. *In toga candida* 88C; Suet. *Caes.* 9; Dio 36.44.3–5; for the censors see Plut. *Crass.*13.1–2; Dio 37.9.3.

54. Cic. *Cael.* 10–12; *Att.* 1.2.1 (on Catiline's charm).

55. For Cicero's speech *In toga candida* see Asc. 82–94C; on Asconius's statement that Caesar and Crassus backed Catiline, see R. G. Lewis, *Asconius: Commentaries on Speeches by Cicero* (Oxford, 2006), 291, arguing this was a later invention of Cicero's that Asconius picked up see Marshall, *Commentary*, 285 is less agnostic. See, in general, Rawson, *Cicero*, 56–59.

56. Suet. *Iul.* 11; Dio Cass. 37.10.2. Suetonius's statement should not be interpreted as showing that he was a *iudex quaestionis*. The crucial point is that Cicero describes him as a prosecutor (*Lig.* 12 with *schol. Grov.* 271 Stangl). Dio likewise implies a role as a prosecutor. Otherwise all that can be said is that the speech for Decius was not regarded as Caesar's best work: see Tac. *Dial.* 21. In this view, I follow Straburger, *Caesars Eintritt*, 117–119 (= *Kleine Schriften* 1:299–301); see also Gruen, *Last Generation*, 176 n. 124. Dio Cass. 37.10.3 simply says that Catiline was acquitted, not that Caesar had anything to do with the acquittal. For Cato, see Plut. *Cat. Min.* 17.4.

57. Cic. *Leg. agr.* 2.31 (powers of the *decemviri*), with discussion in G. Manuwald, *Cicero, Agrarian Speeches: Introduction, Text, Translation and Commentary* (Oxford, 2018), 258 (on the relevant *lex Sempronia* used as a model); *Leg. agr.* 1.12, 2.35–62 (finances). As for Labienus's bill, the view taken here follows Strasburger, *Caesars Eintritt*, 102n30 (= *Kleine Schriften* 1:284); L. R. Taylor, "The Election of the Pontifex Maximus in the Late Republic," *C Phil.* 37 (1942): 421–424; Rawson, *Cicero*, 69; and C. Rosillo-López, "Can a Dictator Reform an Electoral System?," in *Sulla: Politics and Reception*, ed.

A. Eckert and A. Thein (Berlin, 2019), 58–61. I now take this view because of Cic. *Leg. agr* 2.18: *ut comitiis pontifici maximi*, since it was not possible that Labienus's bill could have been passed by the time Rullus's bill was introduced. See Manuwald, *Cicero, Agrarian Speeches*, 229, on how the two bills turned the electoral procedure into a *popularis* issue. For the view that Labienus's bill was connected to the election of the pontifex maximus, see Dio Cass. 37.37.2, who places it after the Catilinarian conspiracy, which is plainly wrong in light of Sall. *Cat.* 49.2. For the view that Sulla had left the position elective while simply repealing the *lex Domitia* of 102, which made all pontifical positions elective see Meyer, E. Caesars Monarchie und das Principat des Pompejus: Innere Geschichte Roms von 66 Bis 44 V. Chr. (Stuttgart, 1919), 15. For the view that Labienus's law included the pontifex maximus, see M. Gelzer, *Caesar: Politician and Statesman*, trans. P. Needham (Oxford, 1969), 46–47 (more implicit than explicit); A. Goldsworthy, *Caesar: Life of a Colossus* (New Haven, 2006), 124–125; and J. Rüpke, *Fasti Sacerdotum: A Prosopography of Pagan, Jewish and Christian Religious Officials in the City of Rome, 300 BC to AD 499*, trans. D. M. B. Richardson (Oxford, 2008), 735n4.

58. Sall. *Cat.* 49.2; Vell. Pat. 2.43.3; Plut. *Caes.* 7.1–4; Suet. *Iul.* 13; Dio Cass. 37.37.1–3. Gelzer, *Caesar*, 47 implicitly connects Caesar's success to his expenditure on the aedilician games.

CHAPTER 7

1. H. Strasberger, *Caesar im Urteil seine Zeitgenossen*, 2nd ed. (Darmstadt, 1968), 72–73 (= *Studien*, vol. 1 [Berlin, 1982], 412–413).

2. Plut. *Caes.* 11.3–4.

3. Suet. *Iul.* 53.

4. Cic. *Cat.* 4.7; see also Suet. *Iul.* 59, noting that he would not be dissuaded from doing something by bad omens.

5. K. Volk, "Caesar the Epicurean? A Matter of Life and Death," in *Epicurus in Rome: Philosophical Perspectives in the Ciceronian Age*, ed. S. Yona and G. Davis (Cambridge, 2022), 72–86.

6. See, e.g., Cic. *Leg. agr.* 1.23–24, 2.6–7, 9–10, 15, 102–103 on why he is a true *popularis*. See also Plut. *Cic.* 12.6; Cic. *Sull.* 65 (veto threat).

7. On *perduellio*, see J. E. Gaughan, *Murder Was Not a Crime: Homicide and Power in the Roman Republic* (Austin, 2010): 106–108; for the oddity of the process in 63 see Cic. *Rab. per.* 15, 17. I place the trial after the pontifical election, which I see as taking place early in the year given that the electoral procedure was discussed in January. For a different view, seeing the trial as leading up to the election, see M. Gelzer, *Caesar: Politician and Statesman*, trans. P. Needham (Oxford, 1969), 46; Goldsworthy, *Caesar: Life of a Colossus* (New Haven, 2006), 125, places it near the end of the year.

8. Suet. *Iul.* 12; Dio Cass. 37.27.2 (circumstances of the trial); Cic. *Rab. per.* 20–21 (mob); Cic. *Rab. per.* 31 (slave rewarded); Cic. *Rab. per.* 21 (the Iulii), 27: *C. Marium, quem vere patrem patriae, parentem, inquam, vestrae libertatis atque huiusce rei publicae possumus dicere.* The reconstruction in the text follows roughly from the discussion in T. R. Holmes, *The Roman Republic*, vol. 1 (Oxford 1923): 452–455. The fact that there were two trials is secured by Cic. *Pis.* 4, which must refer to the first trial. I take Cic. *Rab. per.* 6, 9 as referring to Labienus not as a judge but as the author of the process in which the speech takes place; reference to a speech against Cicero by Labienus (*Rab. per.* 10) seems to me to be a feature of the process. See also Gelzer, *Caesar*, 45–46; and E. Rawson, *Cicero: A Portrait* (Bristol, 1975), 66–68, 87–88.

9. Cic. *Att.* 2.1.3 (speech included in his consular corpus); Dio Cass. 37.27.3 (Metellus Celer).

10. Cic. *Att.* 1.13.2; Dio Cass. 36.37.2 (Piso's victory); Plut. *Pomp.* 27.1; Dio Cass. 36.37.2–3 (the charge); Cic. *Flac.* 98: *Consul ego nuper defendi C. Pisonem; qui, quia consul fortis constansque fuerat, incolumis est rei publicae conservatus*; Sall. *Cat.* 49.2.

11. R. Seager, *Pompey the Great: A Political Biography* 2nd edition (Oxford, 2002), 59–62.

12. Suet. *Aug.* 4.1.

13. Sall. *Cat.* 35.3; the consular elections must postdate the triumph of Murena so they can hardly have been earlier than July; for Murena's departure from his province, see Cic. *Mur.* 89; see also Rawson, *Cicero*, 69, placing the consular elections in July.

14. Plut. *Ant.* 2.1.

15. Sall. *Cat.* 59.3.

16. Cic. *Cat.* 1.7 (date of Manlius's rising), 1.9; Sall. *Cat.* 27.2 (fires); Cic. *Cat.* 1.10 (warned); Sall. *Cat.* 28.2 (Fulvia's role); 31.7 (Cicero as a transplant), 36.1; Dio Cass. 37.33 (Catiline and consular insignia).

17. Cic. *Mur.* 72: *Odit populus Romanus privatam luxuriam, publicam magnificentiam diligit*; and *Mur.* 22: *rei militaris virtus praestat ceteris omnibus.*

18. Plut. *Caes.*; Suet. *Iul.* 13.

19. Cic. *Mur.* 22 (military glory preferred to knowledge of the laws), 61, 74 (Cato's stoicism), and 77 (give up gladiators). For the debate, see Plut. *Brut.* 5.3–4; *Cato Min.* 24.1–2. Plutarch implies that this incident occurred during the debate over the punishment of the conspirators; see the discussion in Treggiari, *Servilia and Her Family* (Oxford 2019), 110–111. The absence of the incident from Sallust is perhaps the result of his desire to highlight the characters of Cato and Caesar through the debate, but what Plutarch implies at *Brut.* 5.3 is that this is an earlier debate, since the Senate had become aware of the conspiracy.

20. Plut. *Caes.* 8.2.

21. Cic. *Cat.* 4.7; Sall. *Cat.* 51.

22. Cic. *Cat.* 4.9: *Si eritis secuti sententiam C. Caesaris, quoniam hanc is in re publica viam, quae popularis habetur, secutus est . . . sicut ipsius dignitas et maiorum eius amplitudo postulabat.*

23. Plut. *Cato Min.* 26.1; *Caes.* 8.6.1–2 (grain bill), 26.3 (Metellus's bill). See also Rawson, *Cicero*, 89.

24. Cic. *Fam.* 5.1, 2 (letter from Metellus and Cicero's response); Suet. *Iul.* 15 (replacing Catulus); Dio Cass. 37.44.1–2; Cic. *Att.* 2.24.3 (replacing him with Pompey).

25. Suet. *Iul.* 16 (for Caesar); Plut. *Cato Min.* 27–29; Dio Cass. 37.43 (Metellus); see also Gelzer, *Caesar*, 56–58.

26. Sall. *Cat.* 59.4 (Petreius); 61.4–5 (Catiline and his army), 61.7 (Antonius's losses).

27. Suet. *Iul.* 17.

CHAPTER 8

1. Suet. *Iul.* 71.1.

2. Dio Cass. 37.49.1; Cic. *Att.* 1.12.1 shows that he was in Italy before the end of 62. See Cic. *Att.* 1.13.4 (Pompey's style); Plut. *Pomp.* 43.2 (speech to the soldiers), 44.1 (power); App. *B Civ.* 2.31 (Pompey at the peak of his power), with D. Potter, "Dio and Pompey: Explaining the Failure of the Republic," *The Intellectual Climate of Cassius Dio: Greek*

and *Roman Pasts*, ed. A. Kemezis, C. Bailey, and B. Poletti (Leiden, 2022), 44–48. See Plut. *Pomp.* 44.1; and p. 84 above for Nepos; Plut. *Pomp.* 44.3 on the consular election, the reference here is specifically to Afranius's candidature.

3. Cic. *Att.* 1.12.3, saying the divorce was generally approved; Plut. *Pomp.* 42.7. See also R. Seager, *Pompey the Great: A Political Biography*, 2nd edition (Oxford 2002), 76.

4. Plut. *Caes.* 9.4–7 (description of the rites).

5. Plut. *Caes.* 10.1–5; *Cic.*, 28.2–4; Suet. *Iul.* 6.2.

6. Cic. *Att.* 1.13.3; Suet. *Iul.* 6.2 74.2; Plut. *Caes.* 10.9, *Cic.* 29.2; Dio Cass. 37.45.2.

7. Cic. *Att.* 1.13.3 on Clodius's position. On the issue of Caesar's authority as pontifex maximus, see A. Lintott, *Cicero as Evidence: A Historian's Companion* (Oxford, 2008), 155. Plut. *Cic.* 29.9 states that Caesar appeared as a witness; Dio Cass. 38.12.1 puts it more correctly when he says Caesar refused to accuse Clodius of adultery. On Caesar's thinking, see W. J. Tatum, *The Patrician Tribune: Publius Clodius Pulcher* (Chapel Hill, 1999), 67–71.

8. Plut. *Caes.* 11.2 (debts); Suet. *Iul.* 71 (Masintha).

9. Plut. *Cic.* 29.1. On the statement here that Cicero acted to appease Terentia, who was angry about his relationship with Clodia, see S. Treggiari, *Terentia, Tullia and Publilia: The Women of Cicero's Family* (London, 2007), 49–50, suggesting, quite reasonably, that this was an invention of late date.

10. Plut. *Caes.* 12.1; Suet. *Iul.* 54 (Caesar's greed); Dio Cass. 37.52–53 (including details on the naval action). For financing provincial armies, see p. 39 n. 27 below; for the tax reduction see Caes. *B. Hisp.* 42.2; see also A. Goldsworthy, *Caesar: Life of a Colossus* (New Haven, 2006), 148–151, who sees the campaign presaging Caesar's style of operation in Gaul. See also Plut. *Caes.* 12.4; Suet. *Iul.*18.1; Dio Cass. 54.1; App. *B Civ.* 2.27 (triumph).

11. Plut. *Caes.* 12.2–3 (debt law); Cic. *Balb.* 63 (Balbus as *praefectus fabrum*). For Lucullus's handling of debt, see p. 62 above.

12. Cic. *Att.* 1.20.5; and Seager, *Pompey the Great*, 81–82.

13. Cic. *Att.* 1.19.4.

14. Cic. *Att.* 1.18.7, 19.6 (*publicani*), 2.1.8 (Cato).

15. Cic. *Att.* 1.19.2; see also p. 133 below.

16. For the triumph, see Plut. *Caes.* 13.1; *Cat. Min.* 31.3; Suet. *Iul.* 18.1; Dio Cass. 38.54.2; App. *B Civ.* 2.28. The view that the requirement to make profession in person dates to 63 depends on Cicero's statement, in January of that year, that this was not the case (*Leg. agr.* 2.24) and on the fact that Cicero was responsible for the last attested law on *ambitus* prior to 60: see Th. Mommsen, *Römische Staatsrecht*, vol. 1³ (Berlin, 1871), 503n3. For Cicero's law, see Dio Cass. 37.29.1; Cic. *Planc.* 83: *mea lege*. For Caesar's presence in Italy in early June, see Cic. *Att.* 2.1.9; note also 2.1.7: *si etiam Caesarem cuius nunc venti valde sunt secundi reddo meliorem, num tantum obsum rei publicae?* This presumably anticipates the outcome of the consular election given that, as Shackleton Bailey, *CLA*, points out, 2.1.9 (*Favonius meam tribum tulit honestius quam suam, Luccei perdidit*) must refer to elections in 61. This is presumably also a prediction of his chances in the forthcoming consular election. On the election, see Suet. *Iul.* 19.1, with S. G. Crissanthos, *The Year of Julius and Caesar* (Baltimore, 2019), 33.

17. Cic. *Att.* 2.1.7 (see note 14 above); Suet. *Iul.* 19.2 for the provincial allocation.

18. Cic. *Att.* 2.3.3–4: *Nam fuit apud me Cornelius, hunc dico Balbum, Caesaris familiarem. is adfirmabat illum omnibus in rebus meo et Pompei consilio usurum daturumque*

operam ut cum Pompeio Crassum coniungeret. [4] *Hic sunt haec, coniunctio mihi summa cum Pompeio, si placet, etiam cum Caesare, reditus in gratiam cum inimicis, pax cum multitudine, senectutis otium.* The significance of this passage is rightly stressed in E. Meyer, *Caesars Monarchie und das Principat des Pompejus: innere Geschichte Roms von 66 bis 44 v. Chr.* (Stuttgart, 1919), 59–62; see also Chrissanthos, *Year of Julius and Caesar*, 36, 48. The passage plainly contradicts the later narrative tradition, for which see Plut. *Caes.* 14.1; *Pomp.* 47.2; *Crass.* 13.3–4; Dio Cass. 37.54.3–58; Livy, *Per.* 103, dating the alliance to the summer of 60 before the consular election; Suet. *Iul.* 19.2, dating it toward the end of 60, after the consular election. Vell. Pat. 2.44.1 is not precise but dates the alliance after the election; see also Hor. *Carm.* 2.1.1.

19. For the opening of the consular year see also C. Meier, *Caesar: A Biography*, trans. D. McLintock (New York, 1982), 204–206; and Chrissanthos, *Year of Julius and Caesar*, 50–53.

20. Suet. *Iul.* 20.1 (*acta senatus*), 21 (Crassus to speak first until the marriage of Julia and Pompey).

21. App. *B Civ.* 2.10; Dio Cass. 38.1.1 (speech to Bibulus). I follow M. Gelzer, *Caesar: Politician and Statesman*, trans. P. Needham (Oxford, 1969), 71, in putting the speech on January 1. Appian alone says he addressed Bibulus, Dio reports essentially the same content as a speech to the *optimates*.

22. Terms of the land bill. see App. *B Civ.* 2.10 (conflating the two land bills of 59); Dio Cass. 38.1.2–6; Cic. *Fam.* 13.4.2 (land tenure not challenged); Dio Cass. 38.1.5; Cic. *Dom.* 23 (money from Pompey). For the board of twenty, see Dio Cass. 38.1.6; Cic. *Att.* 2.6.2, 7.3. For the board of five, see Cic. *Att.* 2.7.4; *Prov. cons.* 41; *ILS* 46; see also Gelzer, *Caesar*, 72.

23. Dio Cass. 38.3.

24. See Morstein-Marx, *Julius Caesar and the Roman People* (Cambridge, 2021), 127–128, on these precedents.

25. Dio Cass. 38.7.2; for earlier cases, see p. 19 n. 20 above.

26. Dio Cass. 38.4.4–5.5; Plut. *Pomp.* 47.3–5; *Caes.* 14.4–6.

27. For the date, see Morstein-Marx, *Julius Caesar and the Roman People*, 136n73, following L. R. Taylor, "Dating Major Legislation and Elections in Caesar's First Consulship," *Historia* 17 (1968):174–177, contra Crissanthos, *Consulship of Julius and Caesar*, 63–64, who follows Meyer, *Caesars Monarchie*, 71, in putting the vote on the agrian law in April, specifically on April 4, but, as Taylor (p. 174) shows, the commissioners created under the law were being appointed in mid-April (Cic. *Att.* 2.6.2).

28. Dio Cass. 38.6.1–4; Plut. *Pomp.* 48.1–2 (conflating this law with the later law on the Campanian land); for the date, see Taylor, "Dating Major Legislation," 180.

29. Suet. *Iul.* 20.1; Dio Cass. 38.6.4–5. Both Suetonius and Dio say that Bibulus retired to his house for the rest of the year, but both appear to be confusing his withdrawal with this occasion, when it should be connected with the passage of the Campanian land bill; the suggestion that he refused to attend meetings of the Senate in February is mine and is supported by Caes. *B Gall.* 1.43.4 (see next note).

30. Caes. *B Gall.* 1.31.9 (Diviciacus), 1.35.1, 40.2–3, and esp. 43.4 on Caesar's role: *Ubi eo ventum est, Caesar initio orationis sua senatusque in eum beneficia commemoravit, quod rex appellatus esset a senatu, quod amicus, quod munera amplissime missa*, See also App. *B Civ.* 2.9.

31. Plut. *Caes.* 14.16, *Cic.* 30.1; App. *B Civ.* 2.14; Dio Cass. 38.12.1–2.

32. Cic. *Att.* 2.9.2. On the chronology, see Chrissanthos, *Year of Julius and Caesar*, 60, 66–67, contra Taylor, "Dating Major Legislation," 182–188. Plut. *Caes.* 14.10 and Suet. *Iul.* 22.1 imply that the law was passed after the marriage between Pompey and Julia; Dio Cass. 38.7.5 places it before the wedding.

33. The author is to be distinguished from Marcus Terentius Varro, a loyal supporter of Pompey who served on the land commission: see Plin. *NH* 7.176.

34. Marriages: Plut. *Caes.* 14.7, *Pomp.* 47.6; App. *B Civ.* 2.14. The date, before mid-May, is secured by Cic. *Att.* 2.17.1.

35. V. Moesch, *La Villa dei Papiri* (Naples, 2009), for the finds, on the papyri themselves, see R. Janko, "New Fragments of Epicurus, Metrodorus, Demetrius Laco, the *Carmen de Bello Actiaco* and other Texts in Oxonian Disegni of 1788–1792," *Cronache Ercolanesi* 38 (2008): 35–42, on *PHerc.* 238a.

36. Cic. *Att.* 2.9.2 (dominion of the Senate); Cic. *Att.* 2.16.2 (mission to Egypt); and Suet. *Iul.* 54 (non-payment). See also M. Siani-Davis, "Ptolemy XII Auletes and the Romans," *Historia* 46 (1997): 316.

37. Suet. *Iul.* 20; Dio Cass. 38.7.3. I think this is the point at which Bibulus locked himself up in his house for the remaining eight months of his term (Plut. *Pomp.* 48.4), and I attribute that to the excrement.

38. Plut. *Caes.* 14.13; for the date see Cic. *Att.* 2.24.4.

39. Suet. *Iul.* 49 (queen of Bithynia); see also Cic. *Att.* 2.19.5.

40. Suet. *Iul.* 20 (consulship of Julius and Caesar), 22; Dio Cass. 38.8.5 (addition of Transalpine Gaul), with Morstein-Marx, *Julius Caesar and the Roman People*, 168–181. In the context of this discussion it should be noted that, when he granted Ariovistus the title of "friend and ally" of the Roman people, Caesar seems to have explicitly been eliminating friction that could cause war in Transalpine Gaul, which is also connected with the extreme length of his justification for war with Ariovistus, on which see p. 136 below. See also Suet. *Iul.* 22 (Semiramis).

41. Cic. *Att.* 2.19.3 (theater); Cic. *Att.* 2.14.1, 16.2, 17.1–2, 23.2 (Sampsigeramus); Cic. *Att.* 2.18.2 (Pompey on the agrarian bill); *Att.* 2.16.1.

42. Cic. *Att.* 2.19.2 (Bibulus in heaven); Cic. *Att.* 2.2–4; Cic. *Vat.* 24–26; Suet. *Iul.* 20; Dio 38.9, with Lintott, *Cicero as Evidence*, 173–174 (Vettius).

43. Cic. *Att.* 2.19.1 (Clodius's threats, July); Cic. *Att.* 2.20.2, 2.21.6, 2.24.5 (Pompey says Clodius won't be able to do anything to him, July and November). See also Cic. *Att.* 2.12.2 (ambivalence of the relationship between Clodius and Caesar), 2.18.3, 19.4 (Caesar offers Cicero a position, July).

44. Suet. *Iul.* 23; A Garcea, *Tout César: discours, rtaites, corespondance et commentaires* (Paris, 2020): Les discours fr. 38–40 (pp. 61–62) and Morstein-Marx, *Julius Caesar and the Roman People*, 182–183.

45. For the *collegia*, see Cic. *Pis.* 8, with Asc. *Pis.* 6–7C and H. Flower, *The Dancing Lares and the Serpent in the Garden: Religion at the Roman Street Corner* (Princeton, 2017), 243. For the form of the name—Clodius rather than Cloelius—see Asc. *Pis.* 8; *Mil.* 30; 33, 37. The fact that Asconius knew him as Clodius rather than Cloelius would suggest that Clodius is actually the correct form of his name; for the case that the name was Cloelius see D. R. Shackleton Bailey, "Sextus Clodius-Sextius Cloelius," *CQ* 10 (1960): 41–42. I am grateful to Professor Shackleton Bailey for his discussion of this issue with me (and his agreement to disagree). For Sextus Clodius's background, see B. Hartman, *The Scribes of Rome: A Cultural and Social History of the* Scribae (Cambridge, 2020), 90, 116. On the legislative program, see Tatum, *The Patrician Tribune*, 114–138.

46. For the legislation concerning Cyprus, see L. Cavelli, *Il tesoro di Cipro: Clodio, Catone e la conquista romana dell'isola* (Venice, 2020), 25–98. For Cicero on his prospective safety, see Cic. *Fam.* 1.2.16, with Lintott, *Cicero as Evidence*, 172.

47. Tatum, *Patrician Tribune*, 150–156 (Cicero's exile).

CHAPTER 9

1. Caes. *B Gall.* 1.1.1.

2. Caes. *B Gall* 1.1; for the genocide of 53 BCE, see esp. N. Roymans and N. Fernádez-Goetz, "Caesar in Gaul: New Perspectives on the Archaeology of Mass Violence," in *Proceedings of the Twenty-Fourth Annual Theoretical Roman Archaeology Conference*, ed. T. Brindle, M. Allen, E. Dunham, and A. Smith (Oxford, 2015), 77–79, with Cic. *Off.* 1.34 on the limit of vengeance, and discussion in A. M. Riggsby, *Caesar in Gaul and Rome: War in Words* (Austin, 2006): 159, 188–189.

3. What follows as Posidonius is derived from Diodorus Siculus Book 5, which, following E. Schwartz, *Griechische Gesichtschreiber* (Leipzig, 1957), 58, I take to be derived from Posidonius (see also the parallels between Diodorus and fragments of Posidonius identified as such, in notes 5 and 6 below).

4. Diod Sic. 5.33.1 (physical appearance and boasting), 28.3 (moustaches), 26.3 (slave for an amphora of wine), and 30.1 (clothing). For textiles, see I. Ralston, "The Gauls on the Eve of the Roman Conquest," in *Julius Caesar's Battle for Gaul: New Archaeological Perspectives*, ed. A. P. Fitzpatrick and C. Haselgrove (Oxford, 2019), 29–30.

5. Diod. Sic. 5.33.2 (armor), 30.3 (nudity), 29.1 (war chariots), 32.7 (same-sex relationships), 29.4–5 (collecting heads), with *BNJ* 87 F55 (Posidonius quoted from Strabo).

6. Diod. Sic. 5.31.3 (human sacrifice), with *BNJ* 87 F55.3 (parallel account quoted by Strabo); and Ralston, "Gauls on the Eve of the Roman Conquest," 36–38. For affirmation of aristocratic power, see M. Poux and M. Demierre, *Le sanctuaire de Corent (Puy-de-Dôme, Auvergene)* (Paris, 2015).

7. Caes. *B Gall.* 6.16.2–5.

8. Caes. *B Gall.* 6.17.1–3, with B. Cunliffe, *The Celtic World* (New York, 1979), 70–75, for an outline of issues.

9. Caes. *B Gall.* 3.22, with A. Goldsworthy, *The Roman Army at War, 100 BC–AD 200* (Oxford, 1996), 54.

10. Caes. *B Gall.* 1.18.5 (mounted retainers of Dumnorix); see also 7.31.5 for the cavalry retainers of Teutomatus; 7.38.1 (slaughter of the Aeduan cavalry equated with the slaughter of the aristocracy), and *B Gall.* 3.59.1 (Allobrogian aristocrats and their cavalry retainers), 7.19 (clan groupings), 5.56 (annual muster), 5.30.7, 6.3.4, [Caes.] *B Gall.* 8.8.3 (raids before the muster), with Goldsworthy, *Roman Army*, 56. I use the words "state or community" rather than "tribe" to describe Gallic groups because, as Y. Le Bohec, *Peuples et fédérations en Gaule (58–51 avant J.-C): Lecture socio-juridique du Bellum Gallicum; De l'archéologie à l'histoire* (Paris, 2009) points out, the word "tribe" is an inappropriate translation for the Latin *civitas* (Caesar's term); see also S. B. Dunham, "Caesar's Perception of Iron Age Gallic Social Structures," in *The Celtic World: Critical Concepts in Historical Studies*, vol. 3, *Celtic History*, ed. R. Karl and D. Stifter (London, 2007), 161–172.

11. Caes. *B Gall.* 6.13.1–3, 20 (aristocrats), but for more detail see e.g. *B Gall.* 5.54.2 (expulsion of a leader appointed by Caesar *publico concilio*). Caesar then deals with the tribal senate at 5.54.3; note also the implication that bad decisions are made by a popular assembly at [Caes] *B Gall.* 8.22.2; see also 5.4.1, where Caesar reconciles the *principes* of

the Treviri to his candidate. See also B. Debatty, "Les organs du politique chez les Sénons," in *Les Sénones. Archéologie et histoire d'un people gaulois*, ed. L. Baray (Gand, 2018), 333–334. On the archaeology see S. Fichtl, "Des campagnes gauloises largement hiérarchisées," in Baray, *Sénones*, 109–117; and Dunham, "Caesar's Perception," 165–169.

12. Caes. *B Gall.* 6.12 (Aeduan organization); *B Gall.* 1.15.1, 18.9, 4.6.5, 7.1, 12.1–3 (Gallic auxiliary cavalry); and *B Gall.* 4.2, 12, 7.67.5 (superiority of German tactics).

13. Diod. Sic. 5.27 (gold); for roads and surplus, see Ralston, "Gauls on the Eve of Roman Conquest," 26–30; for coinage, see C. Haselgrove, "The Development of Iron Age Coinage in Belgic Gaul," *Numismatic Chronicle* 159 (1999): 134–149; N. Roymans and S. Scheers, "Eight Gold Hoards from the Low-Countries: A Synthesis," in *Gold Hoards from the Low Countries and the Caesarian Conquest of Northern Gaul Amsterdam Archaeological Studies*, ed. N. Roymans, G. Creemers, and S. Scheers 18 (2012): 1–46; P. Nouvel, "Historiographie du monnayage sénon," in Baray *Sénones*, 167–169 (summary); Y. Le Bohec, "César et l'économie pendant la guerre des Gaules," in *Krieg— Gesellschaft—Institutionen: Beitrage zur einer vergleichenden Kriegsgeschichte*, ed. B. Meßner, O. Schmitt, and M. Somme (Berlin, 2005), 326–330; and S. Nieto-Pelletier, A. Lefort, and D. B. Foucray, "Les monnaies celtiques et les rouelles: Du sanctuaire celtique et gallo-romain du site des 'Grèves' á la Villeneuve-au-Châtelot (10)," in Baray *Sénones*, 172–193. For Caesar on Pompey, see p. 221 below.

CHAPTER 10

1. D. Potter, "Caesar and the *Bellum Gallicum*," in *People and Institutions in the Roman Empire: Essays in Memory of Garrett G. Fagan*, ed. A. F. Gatzke, L. L. Brice, and M. Trundle (Leiden, 2020), 33–43 anticipates the case made in this chapter about the composition of the *Bellum Gallicum*; the argument is supported by the pattern of cross references between books outlined on pp. 39–41. See Cic. *Fam.* 15.1–2 for the reports; Caes. *B Gall.* 5.52.5 (*idque adeo haud scio mirandumne . . .*); Caes. *B Gall.* 2.35.4, 4.38.5, 7.90.7 (celebrations); Caes. *B Gall.* 2.28.2 (slaughter of the Nervii), 2.33.7 (53,000 Atuatuci sold into slavery), *B Gall.* 5.49.1 (around 60,000 detached from the siege of Cicero's camp, tribes involved were the Eburones, Nervii, and Atuatuci: see *B Gall.* 5.39.3). See also Plin. *NH* 7.91–92; Plut. *Caes.* 15.5 for the carnage claimed by Caesar; Plin. *NH* 97–98; Plut. *Pomp.* 45.3 for Pompey. See, in general, D. S. Potter, "Measuring the Power of the Roman Empire," in *East and West in the Roman Empire of the Fourth Century: An End to Unity?*, ed. R. Dijkstra; S. Van Poppel, and D. Slootjes (Leiden, 2015), 26–48.

2. Public performance: see T. P. Wiseman, "The Publication of *De Bello Gallico*," in *Julius Caesar as Artful Reporter: The War Commentaries as Political Instruments*, ed. K. Welch and A. Powell (London, 1998), 4–6; for the range of communication from Gaul see R. Morstein-Marx, *Julius Caesar and the Roman People* (Cambridge, 2021): 208–15. For Ariovistus, see Caes. *B Gall.* 1.44.12, with p. 139 below. Melian Dialogue: Caes. *B Gall.* 1.36.1 (*ius est belli, ut qui vicissent, iis quos vicissent, quemadmodum vellent, imperarent*), with Thuc. 5.105. See also J. F. Gaertner and B. C. Hausburg, *Caesar and the* Bellum Alexandrinum*: An Analysis of Style, Narrative Technique, and the Reception of Greek Historiography* (Göttingen, 2013), 137–139, on other Thucydidean elements. See also Caes. *B Gall.* 5.27 (Ambiorix), 20–30.1 (Sabinus in council), 33.1 (Sabinus's behavior during the ambush). For Sabinus, see Caes. *B Gall.* 3.17.7, with "Julius Caesar and the Presentation of Massacre." *In Julius Caesar as Artful Reporter: The War*

Commentaries as Political Instruments, edited by K. Welch and A. Powell, London, *1998*, 111–137. Vesontio: Caes. *B Gall.* 1.40.1: *quod aut quam in partem aut quo consilio ducerentur sibi quaerendum aut cogitandum putarent.*

3. Dumnorix's assassination: Caes. *B Gall.* 5.6.1; note also 5.3.1, referring to 1.37.3. Crassus: Potter, "Caesar and the *Bellum Gallicum*," 41. Pompey: Caes. *B Gall.* 6.1.2, 7, 7.1.1, 6.1.

4. For the literary quality of this ethnography see E. Allen-Hornblower, "Beasts and Barbarians in Caesar's *Bellum Gallicum* 6.21–8," *CQ* 64 (2014): 682–693. T. Creer, "Ethnography in Caesar's Gallic War and its Implications for Composition," *CQ* 69 (2019): 246–263 argues that the ethnography continues the portrait of the Gauls in Books 1–5 and thus Books 1–6 are a unit. The ethnography anticipates the conduct Caesar describes in Book 7 as irresponsible Gallic aristocrats betray Rome in their own self-interest. For the British ethnography, see Caes. *B Gall.* 5.12–14.

5. Caes. *B Gall.* 6.13.2–3; [Caes.] *B Gall.* 8.22.

6. Caes. *B Gall.* 6.24.2, with Allen-Hornblower, "Beasts and Barbarians," 685.

7. [Caes.] *B Gall.* 8 praef. 7; Cic. *Brut.* 261. On *populus Romanus*, see Potter, "Caesar and the *Bellum Gallicum*," 41.

8. Caes. *B Gall.* 2.20.1 (doing everything at once), 25.2 (calling on centurions by name). For Baculus, see Caes. *B Gall.* 2.25.1; 3.5.; 6.38.1. For the status of centurions, see D. Potter, "Caesar and the Helvetians," in *New Perspectives on Ancient Warfare*, ed. G, Fagan and M. Trundle (Leiden, 2010), 313. For hierarchy and *virtus*, see A. M. Riggsby, *Caesar in Gaul and Rome: War in Words* (Austin, 2006), 92–93.

9. Caes. *B Gall.* 7.19.4–5 (Avaricum); Caes. *B Civ.* 1.7, 85 (speeches on the reasons for the civil war); Caes. *B Gall.* 1.25.1 (sending away horse); [Caes]. *B Alex.* 10.5 (no slackness unnoticed); [Caes.] *B Alex.* 16.3–4 (Alexandrian harbor); [Caes.] *B Afr.* 71 (*lanista*).

10. Helvetians: Caes. *B Gall.* 1.12.6, with M. Rambaud, *La deformation historique chez César* (Paris, 1966), 251–254. Nervii: Caes. *B Gall.* 5.52.6. Ambiorix: Caes. *B Gall.* 6.30.5. For the active role of Fortune, see Caes. *B Gall.* 1.53.7, 5.44.14, 6.30.2, 6.30.3, 6.35.2, 7.20.4. For fortune as "fate," see *B Gall.* 2.31.6, 5.55.2, 7.62.7, 7.89.2; as "luck," *B Gall.* 2.16.3, 2.22.2, 5.34.2; as "opportunity," *B Gall.* 6.37.7; as "result," *B Gall.* 2.31, 4.26.5; as "well-being," *BG* 5.3.7, 6.7.6; as "situation," *B Gall.* 1.37.4, 7.1.5, 7.8.4, 7.40.7, 7.54.4, 7.77.1; as "chances," *B Gall.* 3.12.3. Caes. *B Gall.* 3.6.6 (*quod saepius fortunam temptare Galba nolebat*; Galba didn't want to tempt Fortune again) isn't attributing decisive action to a divinity. See also Rambaud, *La deformation*, 256–264. On the deliberate contrast with Sulla, see U. Gotter, "Writing Down Uncivil Wars, or: How Roman Generals Justified Themselves in the Wake of Civic Bloodshed," in *A Culture of Civil War: Bellum Civile and Political Communication in Late Republican Rome*, ed. H. Börm, U. Gotter, and W. Havener (Stuttgart, 2023), 192.

11. Caes. *B Gall.* 1.81 (Rhône fortifications), 1.10.3 (legions in 58), 2.2.1 (legions in 57), 1.23.1 (grain at Bibracte), 3.9.1 (construction of a fleet). For the Rhine bridge, see n. 24 below. See also Caes. *B Gall.* 2.12.5 (Suessiones), 2.31.1 (Atuatuci), 3.14.5 (dismasting Gallic ships), 7.69, 73 (siege works at Alesia). See also Riggsby, *Caesar in Gaul and Rome*, 73–83.

12. Caes. *B Gall.* 4.17.1–2: *sed navibus transire neque satis tutum esse arbitrabatur neque suae neque populi Romani dignitatis esse statuebat. Itaque, etsi summa difficultas faciendi pontis proponebatur propter latitudinem, rapiditatem altitudinemque fluminis, tamen id sibi contendendum aut aliter non traducendum exercitum existimabat.*

13. Caes. *B Gall.* 4.25.3 (eagle-bearer), 7.88.1 (Caesar at Alesia).

14. Caes. *B Gall.* 1.7.4 (earlier Helvetian victory), with Riggsby, *Caesar in Gaul and Rome*, 175–176; Caes. *B Gall.* 1.45.2 (Fabius Maximus), 2.3.1–2 (*deditio* of the Remi), 4.20.1

(Britons assisting Gauls), 4.16.1 (decision to cross the Rhine); 2.33.6–7 (enslavement of the Veneti);3.16.4 (execution of the council of the Veneti who had briken their agreement); 6.34–5 (ravaging the land of the Eburones); 7.11.9 (destruction of Cenabum).

15. Caes. *B Gall.* 1.7, 10 (Helvetian campaign), 2.2–3.1 (Belgic campaign), 5.48.2 (rescue of Quintus Cicero), 7.8–9 (campaign of 52).

16. Caes. *B Gall.* 1.16.1, 28.3, 37 (logistics in 58), 2.2.2, 4 (logistics in 57), 3.7.3 (logistics in 56), 4.7.1, 29–32 (logistical issues in 55), 5.8.1, 20.3–4, 24.1, 6, 47.2 (logistical issues in 54), 6.10.2, 29.4, 33.4, 43.3, 4.3 (logistics in 53), 7.3.1, 10.1, 16.3, 17.2–3, 32.1, 34.1, 36.1, 73.1, 74.2, 75.1, 90.7 (logistical issues, omitting Gallic discussion thereof, in 52). On Samarobriva as a central headquarters, see Caes. *B Gall.* 5.24.1, 47.2; Cic. *Fam* 7.11.2. On Cenabum as headquarters, Caes. *B Gall.* 7.3.1. See also Y. Le Bohec, "César et l'économie pendant la guerre des Gaules," in *Krieg—Gesellschaft—Institutionen: Beitrage zur einer vergleichenden Kriegsgeschichte*, ed. B. Meßner, O. Schmitt, and M. Somme (Berlin, 2005), 319–322.

17. Caes. *B Gall.* 4.5: *His de rebus Caesar certior factus et infirmitatem Gallorum veritus, quod sunt in consiliis capiendis mobiles et novis plerumque rebus student, nihil his committendum existimavit. Est enim hoc Gallicae consuetudinis, uti et viatores etiam invitos consistere cogant et quid quisque eorum de quaque re audierit aut cognoverit quaerant et mercatores in oppidis vulgus circumsistat quibus ex regionibus veniant quas ibi res cognoverint pronuntiare cogat. His rebus atque auditionibus permoti de summis saepe rebus consilia ineunt, quorum eos in vestigio paenitere necesse est, cum incertis rumoribus serviant et pleri ad voluntatem eorum ficta respondeant.* For prisoners and deserters, see, e.g., *B Gall.* 1.50.3–4, 2.16.1–2, 5.9.1, 18.4, 48.2, 52.4, 7.18.1.

18. Caes. *B Gall.* 1.39.1 (Vesontio), 1.16.5, 18–20, 31, 41.4: *eorum satisfactione accepta et itinere exquisito per Diviciacum, quod ex Gallis ei maximam fidem habebat,* 2.5.2, 14.1, 15.1, 12.5, 7.39.1 (Diviciacus), 1.47.4 (Mettius), 4.21.7 (praise of Commius), 1.50.3–4, 2.116.1–2, 5.9.1, 18.4, 48.2, 7.18.1 (prisoners and deserters). For merchants as sources, see *B Gall.* 4.20–21, 6.24, with Le Bohec, "César et l'economie," 323.

19. Caes. *B Gall.* 2.17.2 (Nervii), 1.21–22 (Considius), 7.47.2, 52.2 (Gergovia), 6.36.1 (Quintus Cicero); *B Civ.* 3.51.4: *aliae enim sunt legati partes atque imperatoris: alter omnia agere ad praescriptum, alter libere ad summam rerum consulere debet.*

20. [Caes.] *Bell. Afr.* 54, with S. G. Chrissanthos, "Caesar and the Mutiny of 47 BC," *JRS* 91 (2001): 62.

21. Caes. *B Gall.* 1.18, 5.6.2 (Dumnorix). See also *B Gall.* 5.1.7, on the Pirustae blaming a raid on individuals without state backing.

22. Caes. *B Gall.* 5.25.2–4 (Tasget), 5.6.2 (Dumnorix), 4.21.7 (Commius); Cic. *Fam.* 7.5.2 (joke).

23. Caes. *B Gall.* 4.19.2: *more suo concilio habito nuntios in omnes partes dimisisse,* 5.2.4: *quod hi neque ad concilia veniebant,* 5.4.3 (Cingetorix), 6.3.4: *Concilio Galliae primo vere, ut instituerat,* 6.3.6: *Hac re pro suggestu pronuntiata.* See also Caes. *B Civ.* 3.59 on the benefits of service.

24. Cic. *Cat* 4.9, with p. 83 n. 22 above.

25. On Pompey's enterprise, see Caes. *BCiv.* 1.85.

CHAPTER II

1. Caes. *B Gall.* 1.47.4 (Valerius Procillus), 1.19.3 (Valerius Troucillus), 5.36.1 (Quintus Pompeius). See Just. *Epit.* 43.5.12 on the father of the historian. Note also Quintus

Iunius, a man from Spain who was accustomed to hunt with Ambiorix (*B Gall.* 5.27.1). See Caes. *B Civ.* 3.59.1–2 for the Allobrogians.

2. Cic. *Prov. cons.* 32 on Pomptinus. The date of his departure is conjectural. For the likely date of his successor's demise, see p. 102 above.

3. Caes. *B Gall.* 1.2–5.

4. See Caes. *B Gall.* 1.32.1–3, with p. 136 below, for the Sequani who claimed to be oppressed by Ariovistus.

5. Caes. *B Gall.* 1.10.1 on the destination.

6. Caes. *B Gall.* 1.10.3.

7. For the size of Caesar's army see J. Harmand, *L'armée et le soldat a Rome de 107 à 50 avant notre ère* (Paris, 1967), 29, showing that a newly raised legion numbered about 4,000 men. For the dietary requirements, see J. P. Roth, *The Logistics of the Roman Army at War, 264 BC–AD 235* (Leiden, 1995), 42. The claim that the document was in Greek (Caes. *B Gall.* 1.29.1–3) adds a note of verisimilitude to the story: see A. Mullen, *Southern Gaul and the Mediterranean: Multilingualism and Multiple Identities in the Iron Age and Roman Periods* (Cambridge, 2013), 113, noting that the document itself may be a fabrication.

8. For basic training in the US army, see: https://www.goarmy.com/army-life/basic-training.html. For training in the Roman army, see Harmand, *L'armée et le soldat*, 314–320.

9. Caes. *B Gall.* 1.10.5. For the date, see K. A. Raaflaub and J. T Ramsay, "The Chronology of Caesar's Campaigns," in *The Landmark Julius Caesar*, ed. and trans. K. A. Raaflaub (New York, 2017), 137.

10. Caes. *B Gall.* 1.9.3–4.

11. Caes. *B Gall.* 1.35.4. For events in 61, see Cic *Att.* 1.19.2: *Nam Haedui fratres nostri pugnam nuper malam pugnarunt, et Helvetii sine dubio sunt in armis excursionesque in provinciam faciunt Senatus decrevit, ut consules duas Gallias sortirentur, delectus haberetur, vacationes ne valerent, legati cum auctoritate mitterentur, qui adirent Galliae civitates darentque operam, ne eae se cum Helvetiis coniungerent.* In light of the contents of the senatorial decree, the *et* in the first clause is conjunctive.

12. On the Tigurini, see Caes. *B Gall.* 1.12.4–7, with D. Potter, "Caesar and the Helvetians," in *New Perspectives on Ancient Warfare*, ed. G. Fagan and M. Trundle (Leiden, 2010), 306. On Divico, see Caes. *B Gall.* 1.13.2.

13. Caes. *B Gall.* 1.15 (cavalry encounter), 1.16–18 (grain). For the Dumnorix theme, see D. Potter, "Caesar and the *Bellum Gallicum*," in *People and Institutions in the Roman Empire: Essays in Memory of Garrett G. Fagan*, ed. A. F. Gatzke, L. L. Brice, and M. Trundle (Leiden, 2020), 33–43; and p. 117 above.

14. Caes. *B Gall.* 1.21–22, with p. 124 above. See also K. Welch, "Caesar and his Officers in the Gallic War Commentaries," in *Julius Caesar as Artful Reporter: The War Commentaries as Political Instruments*, ed. K. Welch and A. Powell (London, 1998), 101.

15. For the location, see T. R. Holmes, *C. Julii Caesaris commentarii rerum in Gallia gestarum VII A. Hirtius commentarius VIII* (Oxford, 1914), 26, on *B Gall.* 1.24.1.

16. Caes. *B Gall.* 1.24 (dispositions), 1.25.1 (horse).

17. Plut. *Mar.* 25.1–2. See also Potter, "Caesar and the Helvetians," 313–314; A. Goldsworthy, *The Roman Army at War*, 197–206; and Caes. *B Gall.* 1.25.2–3 (Caesar on *pila*), 1.25.6–7 (Helvetian surrender).

18. Plut. *Mar.* 19.2–7, with Potter, "Caesar and the Helvetians," 325.

19. Caes. *B Gall.* 1.31–2.

20. Caes. *B Gall.* 1.34; for the legal issue lurking behind this narrative see R. Morstein-Marx, *Julius Caesar and the Roman People* (Cambridge, 2021): 200–203.

21. Caes. *B Gall.* 1.35–6.

22. Caes. *B Gall.* 1.37.3.

23. For a more rapid march, see the discussion in Raaflaub and Ramsay, "Chronology," 138. I differ from them in thinking that, in light of *B Gall.* 1.16.3, Caesar would have relied on river transportation for his supplies.

24. Caes. *B Gall.* 1.391.1 (frightening Germans), 1.39.2–5 (troops writing wills).

25. Caes. *B Gall.* 1.40.2–4 (Germans in Spartacus's army), 1.40.8 (Ariovistus's tactics against the Aedui), 1.41.1–2 (Tenth legion). See also A. Goldsworthy, *Caesar: Life of a Colossus* (New Haven, 2006), 224–228.

26. Caes. *B Gall.* 1.44.9: *non se tam barbarum neque tam imperitum esse rerum ut non sciret neque bello Allobrogum proximo Haeduos Romanis auxilium tulisse neque ipsos in iis contentionibus quas Haedui secum et cum Sequanis habuissent auxilio populi Romani usos esse*; Caes. *B Gall.* 1.44.12: *Quod si eum interfecerit, multis sese nobilibus principibusque populi Romani gratum esse facturum (id se ab ipsis per eorum nuntios compertum habere)*, on the implied communication see R. Morstein-Marx, *Julius Caesar and the Roman People* (Cambridge, 2021): 213.

27. Caes. *B Gall.* 1.45–46.2.

28. Caes. *B Gall.* 1.47.4–6.

29. For the location, see C. B. R. Pelling, "Caesar's Battle-Descriptions and the Defeat of Ariovistus," *Latomus* 40 (1981): 751–766.

30. Caes. *B Gall.* 1.54.2–3.

31. For the poem, see E. Courtney, *The Fragmentary Latin Poets* (Oxford, 1993), 238 (Varro Atacinus frs. 1–2). For Caesar and Catullus's father, see Suet. *Iul.* 73, with Goldsworthy, *Caesar*, 236–237.

32. Caes. *B Gall.* 2.1.2 (Belgae), 2.5.2 (Diviciacus), 2.3.1–2 (*deditio in fidem*).

33. Caes. *B Gall.* 2.3.2–3 (the offer of hostages was part of the approach from the Remi).

34. For the location of this battle, see Pelling, "Caesar's Battle Descriptions," 742–747. I accept the Berry-au-Bac location, which, as Pelling notes, is controversial because of the proximity to the Aisne, which is crucial to the narrative.

35. Caes. *B Gall.* 2.7.1 (new units), 2.8–9 (tactics).

36. Caes. *B Gall.* 1.40.8.

37. Caes. *B Gall.* 2.10.4: *ipsos res frumentaria deficere coepit, concilio convocato constituerunt optimum esse domum suam quemque reverti, et quorum in fines primum Romani exercitum introduxissent, ad eos defendendos undique convenirent, ut potius in suis quam in alienis finibus decertarent et domesticis copiis rei frumentariae uterentur.* See also Ph. Richardot, *Les erreurs stratégiques des Gaulois face à César* (Paris, 2006), 48.

38. Caes. *B Gall.* 2.12.5–13.1: *et petentibus Remis ut conservarentur impetrant. Caesar, obsidibus acceptis primis civitatis atque ipsius Galbae regis duobus filiis armisque omnibus ex oppido traditis, in deditionem Suessiones accipit.* Caes. *B Gall.* 2.15.1: *Caesar honoris Diviciaci atque Haeduorum causa sese eos in fidem recepturum et conservaturum dixit.* See also Goldsworthy, *Caesar*, 243.

39. Caes. *B Gall.* 2.17.1–2, 19.2 (line of march). For the location see P. Turquin, "La bataille de la Selle (du Sabis) en l'an 57 avant J.-C.," *Études Classiques* 23 (1955): 113–156.

40. Caes. *B Gall.* 2.22.1 (cannot form a single line), 2.23 (deployment), 2.26.1 (Caesar's intervention), 2.26.3–4 (Labienus).

41. Caes. *B Gall.* 2.28.2. See p. 116 above on this issue.

42. For discussion of the site, see N. Roymans, "Caesar's Conquest and the Archaeology of Mass Violence in the Germanic Frontier Zone" in *Julius Caesar's Battle for Gaul: New Archaeological Perspectives*, ed. A. P. Fitzpatrick and C. Haselgrove (Oxford, 2019), 115. For the surrender, see Caes. *B Gall.* 2.31–33, with L. Grillo, *The Art of Caesar's* Bellum Civile: *Literature, Ideology and Community* (Cambridge, 2012), 95–99, on the point Caesar is making.

43. Caes. *B Gall.* 2.34, 3.7.

44. Raaflaub and Ramsay, "Chronology," 144.

CHAPTER 12

1. Caes. *B Gall.* 3.2.3–5. See also K. M. Riggsby, *Caesar in Gaul and Rome: War in Words* (Austin, 2006), 184–187.

2. Caes. *B Gall.* 2.35, 3, 3.7.1, 9.1–2 (on which see T. R. Holmes, *C. Julii Caesaris commentarii rerum in Gallia gestarum VII A. Hirtius commentarius VIII* [Oxford, 1914], 107, noting that a reference to the meeting at Luca is concealed here).

3. Caes. *B Gall.* 3.8.3: *ut in ea libertate quam a maioribus acceperint permanere quam Romanorum servitutem perferre malint.*

4. Plut. *Pomp.* 49.2 (alleged assassination); Dio Cass. 38.30 (Pompey's annoyance with Clodius in 58), 39 6 (Milo versus Clodius) with R. Seager, *Pompey the Great: A Political Biography,* 2nd ed. (London, 2002): 103–108.

5. Cic. *Red. pop.* 21; *Sest.* 70; *Dom.* 75 (Cicero's recall); *Att.* 4.1.6–7; *Dom.* 34; *Red. pop.* 34; Plut. *Pomp.* 49.4–5, 50; App. *B Civ.* 2.18.20; Dio Cass. 39.9.3 (grain law). See also Seager, *Pompey The. Great*, 108–9; and K. M. Girardet, "*Imperia* und *provinciae* des Pompeius 82 bis 48 v. Chr.," *Chiron* 31 (2002): 188–190 for Pompey's management of the situation. For Cicero's role in the vote of the thanksgiving for Caesar, see Cic. *Prov. cons.* 25–26; see also Plut. *Caes.* 21.1 and discussion in R. Morstein-Marx, *Caesar and the Roman People* (Cambridge, 2021): 219–21.

6. For differing accounts of his departure, see Plut. *Pomp.* 49.6–7; Dio Cass. 39. 12.2–13.3; Livy, *Per.* 104, with P. M. Fraser, *Ptolemaic Alexandria* (Oxford, 1972), 125; and M. Siani-Davis, "Ptolemy XII Auletes and the Romans," *Historia* 46 (1997): 318–319, 322–323. If the affair reported at Plut. *Ant.* 25.4 happened, it is likely at this point; for the possibility that Pompey had visited Ptolemy in Egypt during the Mithridatic War, see Siani-Davis, "Ptolemy XII Auletes and the Romans," 314–315.

7. Cic. *Rab. Post.* 6 (loans for bribes); *Fam.* 1.1 (Ptolemy wants Pompey); Plut. *Pomp.* 49.6 (the proposal of Caninius). The version of the oracle in the text is reconstructed from Cic. *Rab. Post.* 4 and *Q Fr.* 2.3; *Fam.* 1.7. Dio purports to quote the actual oracle at 39.15.2, but his text omits the line quoted by Cicero in the *Pro Rabirio Postumo*; see also Siani-Davis, "Ptolemy XII Auletes and the Romans," 326–327.

8. See R. G. Austin, *M. Tullii Ciceronis pro M. Caelio oratio*, 3rd ed. (Oxford, 1959), viii, 152–154 (Caelius); Catull. 66.13–16, 79–82 (Berenice), 29, 113 (Pompey), 49 (Cicero), 29, 57, 93 (Caesar).

9. Cic. *Q Fr.* 2.3.1–2; *Fam.* 1.5b1, with Seager, *Pompey the Great*, 114–15; E. Gruen, *The Last Generation of the Roman Republic* (Berkeley and Los Angeles, 1974), 442; and W. J. Tatum, *The Patrician Tribune: P. Clodius Pulcher* (Chapel Hill, 1999), 211–213.

10. On the Campanian land, see Cic. *Q Fr.* 2.7.2; *Fam.* 1.9.8. On the Caesarian proposals, see Cic. *Q Fr.* 5.3: *Hunc igitur Catonem Lentulus a legibus removit et eos, qui de Caesare monstra promulgarunt, quibus intercederet nemo.* These are presumably the measures

Cicero supported later: see *Fam.* 1.7.10; *Balb.* 69; *Prov.cons.* 28; Suet. *Iul.* 23: *Mox et ipse a Lucio Antistio tr. pl. postulatus appellato demum collegio optinuit, cum rei publicae causa abesset reus ne fieret.* On the identity of Antistius, see Shackleton Bailey's note on Cic. *Q Fr.* 2.1.3 and E. Rawson, *Cicero: A Portrait* (Bristol, 1975), 127–128.

11. Cic. *Fam.* 1.9.9 on the order of the events connected with Luca (including Crassus's prior meeting with Caesar at Ravenna with Seager, *Pompey the Great,* 118 correctly stressing the point that Crassus was not at Luca). For exaggeration, see Plut. *Caes.* 21.5–7; *Pomp.* 51.3; Cic. *Att.* 4.5.1, with discussion in L. Grillo, *Cicero's* De provinciis consularibus oratio (Oxford, 2015), 15–16. For Cicero and the bill in favor of Caesar, see Cic. *Prov. cons.* 29. For the provincial commands see Plut. *Pomp.*52; *Crass.* 14.6 specify that the agreement about the provincial commands was reached at Luca; Dio 39. 33 preserves a version in which the extension of Caesar's command was not part of the agreement.

12. Cic. *Prov. cons.* 17–18, 25–26.

13. Cic. *Prov. cons.* 19.

14. Caes. *B Gall.* 3.8–9.3. On the context, see C. Ando, "Aliens, Ambassadors and the Integrity of Empire," *Law and History Review* 26 (2008): 496–497.

15. Caes. *B Gall.* 3.14.1 (behavior of the Veneti), 3.15 (decisive battle), 3.16.4 (fate of the leadership of the Veneti).

16. Caes. *B Gall.* 3.18.5–7 (people who believe what they want), 19.3 (inexperience and exhaustion), 3.19.6 (Gauls starting wars).

17. Caes. *B Gall.* 3.23.5: *Duces vero ii deliguntur qui una cum Q. Sertorio omnes annos fuerant summamque scientiam rei militaris habere existimabantur.*

18. Caes. *B Gall.* 3.28.1: *quod omni Gallia pacata Morini Menapiique supererant, qui in armis essent neque ad eum umquam legatos de pace misissent.*

19. Cic. *Att.* 4.8a.2, with Seager, *Pompey the Great,* 126–129.

20. D. Potter, *The Origin of Empire* (London, 2018), 249–250, on Gabinius.

21. Morstein-Marx, *Julius Caesar and the Roman People,* 267, for a succinct statement of the issue. See also P. J. Cuff, "The Terminal Date of Caesar's Command," *Historia* 7 (1958): 445–471 on the point that the terminal date was not clearly defined.

22. Suet. *Iul.* 73, referring to poems 29 and 57. For the social origins of Caesar's associates see R. Syme, *The Roman Revolution* (Oxford, 1939), 71–75.

23. Tac. *Ann.* 12.60; For the description of Caesar's kindness and energy as general, see Suet. *Iul.* 55 (indifference to cuisine, from Oppius), 72 (kindness to Oppius when ill), 57 (energy). F. Vonder Mühl (*RE,* s.v. "Hirtius") and F. Münzer (*RE,* s.v. "Oppius") date the formation of the "cabinet" to the aftermath of the defeat of Sabinus and Cotta in 54, but it seems to me that it must be earlier, as Catullus 29 (on Mamurra's wealth) dates to 56 or 55, which suggests that the core group had come together before 54. Vonder Mühl's suggestion that Hirtius replaced Pompeius Trogus as Caesar's secretary is intriguing, but Caesar's cabinet seems not to have had a strict hierarchy so no one person needed to replace another.

24. Caes. *B Gall.* 4.1.1–2. For the location, see n. 28 below.

25. A. Garcea, *Caesar's* De Analogia: *Edition, Translation and Commentary* (Oxford, 2012), 24, pointing out that the work should be dated after the summer of 56.

26. The passage quoted is Caes. *B Gall.* 4.6.5: *eorumque animis permulsis et confirmatis equitatuque imperator bellum cum Germanis gerere constituit.* For the negotiations, see *B Gall.* 4.7–8.

27. Caes. *B Gall.* 4.9.3 (return of cavalry), 4.12–13 (noble Aquitanian). For Cato, see Plut. *Caes.* 22.4; *Cato Min.* 51.1–2; Suet. *Iul.* 24.3 (not mentioning Cato by name); App. *Celt.* 18, with K. Morrell, "Caesar, Cato and the Germani," *Antichthon* 49 (2015): 73–93; and J. Osgood, "The Pen and the Sword: Writing and Conquest in Caesar's Gaul," *Cl. Ant.* 28 (2009): 339.

28. For discussion of the site, see N. Roymans, "Caesar's Conquest and the Archaeology of Mass Violence in the Germanic Frontier Zone," in *Julius Caesar's Battle for Gaul: New Archaeological Perspectives*, ed. A. P. Fitzpatrick and C. Haselgrove (Oxford, 2019), 115–125.

29. Caes. *B Gall.* 4.16.1.

30. Caes. *B Gall.* 4.16.4: *populi Romani imperium Rhenum finire; si se invito Germanos in Galliam transire non aequum existimaret, cur sui quicquam esse imperii aut potestatis trans Rhenum postularet?*

31. Caes. *B Gall.* 4.18.1, 19.4 (bridge building and length of campaign), 4.19.4: *satis et ad laudem et ad utilitatem profectum arbitratus se in Galliam recepit pontemque rescidit.*

32. For the date, see K. A. Raaflaub and J. T Ramsay, "The Chronology of Caesar's Campaigns," in *The Landmark Julius Caesar*, ed. and trans. K. A. Raaflaub (New York, 2017), 152. See also Caes. *B Gall.* 4.20.1 (Britons and Gauls); 4.20.3–4, 21 (Commius's mission).

33. Strabo 4.5.2 for the ancient location (Ition); for the identification of the modern site, see A. P. Fitzpatrick, "Caesar's Landing Sites In Britain and Gaul in 55 and 54 BC: Critical Places, Natural Places," in Fitzpatrick and Haselgrove, *Julius Caesar's Battle for Gaul*, 137. For Sabinus and Cotta, see Caes. *B Gall.* 4.22.5.

34. The case for Pegwell Bay is made by Fitzpatrick, "Caesar's Landing Sites," 149–155. See also Caes. *B Gall.* 4.23.5 (Volusenus), 4.25.3: *ego certe meum rei publicae atque imperatori officium praestitero.*

35. Caes. *B Gall.* 4.27.2–4.

36. Caes. *B Gall.* 4 30–5, with Osgood, "The Pen and the Sword," 342–343, on the literary enhancement of the British operation.

37. Cic. *Att.* 4.16.7, 18.5 (quoted n. 47 below); R. Hingley, *Conquering the Ocean* (Oxford, 2022), 29 (anticipated returns); Caes. *B Gall.* 5.14, with Hingley, *Conquering the Ocean*, 33–34 (actual returns).

38. Cic. *Att.* 4.16.8; Plin. *NH* 36.103; Suet. *Iul.* 26.1, specifying that the forum was built with plunder from Gaul. See also R. Raja and J. Rüpke, "Creating Memories in and of Urban Rome: The Forum Iulium," in *Caesar's Past and Posterity's Caesar*, ed. T. A Hass and R. Raja (Turnhout, 2021), 53–66.

39. Cic. *Fam.* 7.5.2 (Trebatius to be a king in Gaul); Caes. *B Gall.* 5.3.4 (Treviri don't show up).

40. Caes. *B Gall.* 5.3.5–6.

41. Caes. *B Gall.* 5.4.3.

42. Potter, "Caesar in the *Bellum Gallicum*," in *People and Institutions in the Roman Empire: Essays in Memory of Garrett G. Fagan*, ed. A. F. Gatzke, L.L. Brice, and M. Trundle (Leiden, 2020), 38–39.

43. Caes. *B Gall.* 5.6.

44. Caes. *B Gall.* 5.7.

45. Caes. *B Gall.* 5.8.5–6 (landing), 9. 3–4 (for the location, see Holmes, *C. Julii Caesaris commentarii*, 180–181n, on 5.9.3–4, accepted by Hingley, *Conquering the Ocean*, 31), 5.11.8 (election of Cassivellaunus), with Holmes, *C. Julii Caesaris commentarii*, 184, on the location. For the battle, see Caes. *B Gall.* 5.18–19.

46. Caes. *B Gall.* 5.20 (Trinovates), with Hingley, *Conquering the Ocean*, 35–36.

47. Caes. *B Gall.* 5.22.4–5. See also Cic. *Att.* 4.18.5: *confecta Britannia, obsidibus acceptis, nulla praeda, imperata tamen pecunia exercitum ex Britannia reportabant.*

48. Cic. *Q Fr.* 3.1.10: *De Britannicis rebus cognovi ex tuis litteris nihil esse nec quod metuamus nec quod gaudeamus.*

49. Cic. *Q Fr.* 3.1.17, for the date when Caesar received the news. For his reaction, see Plut. *Pomp.* 53.4; Dio Cass. 39.64; Cic. *Q Fr.* 3.1.17.

50. W. Allen, "The British Epics of Quintus and Marcus Cicero," *TAPA* 86 (1955): 143–159.

51. Catull. 29.4. Catull. 20 implies at least one British campaign had been completed, and the poem may postdate the lunch reported at Suet. *Iul.* 73. See also Cic. *Q Fr.* 2.9.3: *Lucretii poemata, ut scribis, ita sunt: multis luminibus ingenii, multae etiam artis* (he had the poem in February). The quotation is Lucr. 1.1–2. For Caesar's use of the poem, see C. B. Krebs, "Caesar, Lucretius and the Dates of *De rerum natura* and the *Commentaries*," *CQ* 63 (2013): 772–779.

52. Lucr. 1.50–53 (advice to Memmius); for the bribe, see Cic. *Att.* 4.17.2. For the sum, see Shackleton Bailey's note on the text of Cic. *Att.* 4.17.2. Appian *B Civ.* 2.19 gives the sum as being nearly twenty million sesterces, which is outside the range of a typical senatorial fortune. See also Cic. *Att.* 4.17.3 (Caesar's reaction).

53. Plut. *Crass.* 16.3–5.

CHAPTER 13

1. Caes. *B Gall.* 5.25.

2. Caes. *B Gall.* 5.55.

3. Caes. *B Gall.* 5.28.1; for the identification of Aduatuca with Tongeren, see Y. Le Bohec, *César, chef de guerre: Stratégie et tactique de la République romaine* (Monaco, 2001), 231.

4. Caes. *B Gall.* 5.26–7 (initial attack and embassy); for the portrayal of Ambiorix, see also J. Barlow, "Noble Gauls and Their Other in Caesar's Propaganda," in *Julius Caesar as Artful Reporter: The War Commentaries as Political Instruments*, ed. K. Welch and A. Powell (London, 1998), 149–150; and Caes. *B Gall.* 5.27 (Ambiorix's advice).

5. Caes. *B Gall.* 5.28.3–6; see also A. M. Riggsby, *Caesar in Gaul and Rome* (Austin, 2006), 193.

6. Caes. *B Gall.* 5.30; see also Powell, A. "Julius Caesar and the Presentation of Massacre," in *Julius Caesar as Artful Reporter: The War Commentaries as Political Instruments*, ed. K. Welch and A. Powell (London, 1998), 111–137.

7. Caes. *B Gall.* 5.33.1–4.

8. Caes. *B Gall.* 5.37.

9. Plut. *Crass.* 31.

10. Caes. *B Gall.* 5.38.

11. Caes. *B Gall.* 5.36.7 (prisoners), 40.1 (writes immediately to Caesar), 41 (refuses to negotiate), 44 (Pullo and Vorenus).

12. Caes. *B Gall.* 5.46–48 (Caesar to the rescue).

13. Caes. *B Gall.* 5.49.1 (number of Gauls), 49.7 (number of Romans), 50–51 (rout of the Gauls).

14. Caes. *B Gall.* 5.52.5.

15. Caes. *B Gall.* 5.53.5 (conspiracies), 5.54.1 (Caesar and Gallic leaders).

16. Caes. *B Gall.* 6.54.2 (Senones), 56.5 (expulsion of Cingetorix), 58.1–6 (death of Indutiomarus).

17. Caes. *B Gall.* 5.54.5: *Idque adeo haud scio mirandumne sit, cum compluribus aliis de causis, tum maxime quod ei, qui virtute belli omnibus gentibus praeferebantur, tantum se eius opinionis deperdidisse ut a populo Romano imperia perferrent gravissime dolebant.* For the use of the first person here, see p. 115 above.

18. Caes. *B Gall.* 6.1.2–4 (Pompey's assistance); *B Civ.* 1.85.9 (the law on provincial administration a sign of Pompey's ill will); for the terms of the law, see K. Morrell, *Pompey, Cato, and the Governance of the Roman Empire* (Oxford, 2017): 214–33.

19. Caes. *B Gall.* 6.1.2–4.

20. Caes. *B Gall.* 3.1–3 (Nervii), 4.2–3 (Senones and Aedui), 4.5 (Remi and Carnutes).

21. For the archaeological evidence, see N. Roymans, "Caesar's Conquest and the Archaeology of Mass Violence in the Germanic Frontier Zone," in *Julius Caesar's Battle for Gaul: New Archaeological Evidence*, ed. A. P. Fitzpatrick and C. Hazelgrove (Oxford, 2019), 125–131. See also Caes. *B Gall.* 6.6 (surrender of the Menapii), 43.5–6 (Ambiorix's escape), 6.31.5 (Catuvolcus).

22. Caes. *B Gall.* 6.8.4: *praestate eandem nobis ducibus virtutem, quam saepe numero imperatori praestitistis, atque illum adesse et haec coram cernere existimate.*

23. Caes. *B Gall.* 6.9.2 (decision to cross the Rhine), 6.9.5–8 (Ubii), 29.1 (decision to withdraw).

24. Caes. *B Gall.* 6.30.2, 5 (Ambiorix's escape), 35.1, 42.1 (Tongeren).

25. Caes. *B Gall.* 6.42.3.

26. Asc. *Mil.* 30–33C; App. *B Civ.* 2.21; Dio Cass. 40.48.2. On the specific circumstances see D.H. Barry, "Clodius, Milo and the battle of Bovillae," in *Ancient Bovillae: History, Art and Archaeology of a Lost City in the Roman Hinterland* ed. P. Hatlie (Ann Arbor, 2025): 85–99. See, in general, E. Gruen, *The Last Generation of the Roman Republic* (Berkeley and Los Angeles, 1974), 150–154. See also G. Sumi, "Power and Ritual: The Crowd at Clodius' Funeral," *Historia* 46 (1977): 80–92.

27. Dio Cass. 40.45 (consular elections of 53); Asc. *Mil.* 30C (consular elections for 52).

28. Asc. *Mil.* 34C (*senatus consultum*). For these events, see J. T. Ramsay, "How and Why Was Pompey Made Sole Consul in 52 BC," *Historia* 65 (2016): 298–324. For Caesar's actions, see Caes. *B. Gall.* 7.1.2, with T. R. Holmes, *C. Julii Caesaris commentarii rerum in Gallia gestarum VII A. Hirtius commentarius VIII* (Oxford, 1914), 271; and C. B. Krebs, *Caesar Bellum Gallicum Book VII* (Cambridge, 2023), 117–118: Caesar may have been replacing losses from the previous year since the total strength of the army is given as ten legions at *B Gall.* 6.44.2 and 7.34.2.

29. Asc. *Mil.* 36C (for the election); Caes. *B Civ.* 1.32.3; Cic. *Att.* 7.1.4 (Cicero's role), 3.4, 6.2; *Fam.* 6.6.5, 8.3.3, 16.12.3; *Phil.* 2.34; Suet. *Iul.* 26.1, 28; Plut. *Pomp.* 56; App. *B Civ.* 2.25; Dio Cass. 40.51.2. For the chronology, see Ramsay, "How and Why Was Pompey Made Sole Consul," 321.

30. Caes. *B Gall.* 6. 44.2 (execution of Acco), 7.1.4 (complaints about Acco's murder). For the Carnutes initiating the conspiracy, see Krebs, *Caesar Bellum Gallicum Book VII*, 119–120.

31. Caes. *B Gall.* 7.3.1; for the form of the name Gutuatrus see [Caes.] *B Gall.* 8.38.3, with Holmes, *C. Julii Caesaris commentarii*, 387 and Krebs, *Caesar Bellum Gallicum Book VII*, 123–4. The plural *ducibus* indicates it is a name not a religious title, but, along with Y. Le Bohec, "Le clergé celtique et la guerre des Gaules historiographie et politique," *Latomus* 64 (2005): 871–881, I think it entirely plausible that druids supported the revolt, but the distinction between religious grounds for this support and political ones (since the druids were members of the aristocracy) perhaps cannot really be made.

32. Caes. *B Gall.* 7.4–5.

33. Caes. *B Gall.* 7. 8–9.

34. Caes. *B Gall.* 7.9.5, 11. The number of legions is again controversial. K. M. Girardet, *Januar 49 v. Chr.: Caesars Militärputsch; Vorgeschichte, Rechtslage, politische Aspekte* (Bonn, 2017), 61, adds an eleventh despite the clear implication of the Latin that the whole army was with Caesar at the end of the summer of 53. The dispositions described here are confirmed at Caes. *B Gall.* 7.9.3 (two legions with the Lingones), 10.4 (the bulk of the army at Agedincum/Sens). At 34.2 Caesar specifically states that the army consisted of ten legions; see also the note on 10.34.2 in C. R. Krebs, *Caesar* Bellum Gallicum *Book VII*, 209–210.

35. Caes. *B Gall.* 7.12–13.

36. Caes. *B Gall.* 7.14.

37. Caes. *B Gall.* 7. 17.2 (incompetence of the Boioi and Aedui), 17.3 (endurance of hardship), with J. E. Lendon, "The Rhetoric of Combat: Greek Military Theory and Roman Culture in Julius Caesar's Battle Descriptions," *Cl. Ant.* 18 (1999), 295–304. See also Caes. *B Gall.* 19.5 (interest in the safety of the men).

38. Caes. *B Gall.* 7.32.1–2, with K. A. Raaflaub and J. T Ramsay, "The Chronology of Caesar's Campaigns," in *The Landmark Julius Caesar*, ed. and trans. K. A. Raaflaub (New York, 2017), 169, for the chronology, 7.32.3–5 (meeting with the Aedui).

39. Caes. *B Gall.* 7.34.2 (Labienus's mission), 36.1 (Caesar on Gergovia). For the site, see https://musee-gergovie.fr/en/the-gergovie-plateau/archaeological-digs/.

40. Caes. *B Gall.* 7. 39–42 (the Aeduan issues).

41. Caes. *B Gall.* 7.43.5.

42. Caes. *B Gall.* 7.45–51, with M. Reddé, "Recent Archaeological Research on Roman Military Engineering Works of the Gallic War," in *Julius Caesar's Battle for Gaul: New Archaeological Perspectives*, ed. A. P. Fitzpatrick and C. Haselgrove (Oxford, 2019), 94–98.

43. Caes. *B Gall.* 7.52 (Caesar on what went wrong), 54–55 (Aeduan revolt). On the politics, see Ph. Richardot, *Les erreurs stratégiques des Gaulois face à César* (Paris, 2006), 70–71.

44. Caes. *B Gall.* 7.62.10; for the inconsistency in the narrative, see Krebs, *Caesar* Bellum Gallicum *Book VII*, 271.

45. Caes. *B Gall.* 7.65–66.1.

46. Suet. *Iul.* 28.2–3 (Pompey's electoral law and Caesar) with R. Morstein-Marx, Julius Caesar and the Roman People (Cambridge, 2021) 265–266 esp. 265 n. 20 discussing the issue of whether the new law had undone the law of the ten Tribunes; Dio Cass. 56.1 (provincial commands, electoral law), 56.2 (extension of the Spanish command).

47. For the chronology, see Raaflaub and Ramsay, "Chronology," 173; and Krebs, *Caesar* Bellum Gallicum *Book VII*, 271–272. See also Caes. *B Gall.* 7.66–68. For the debate over the location of Alesia, and the solution adopted here, see Le Bohec, *César chef de guerre*, 270–276.

48. Caes. *B Gall.* 7.73.1, with M. Reddé, "Recent Archaeological Research," 98–106.

49. Caes. *B Gall.* 7.74.2, with J. F. Donahue, "Sieges, Deception and Bioterrorism: Logistics and Strategy of Food and Drink during the Republic," in *Brill's Companion to Diet and Logistics in Greek and Roman Warfare*, ed. J. F. Donahue and L. L. Brice (Leiden, 2023), 296–301.

50. Caes. *B Gall.* 7.76.2; compare *B Gall.* 5.54.5 and p. 175 above; for the numbers see the discussion in *Caesar* Bellum Gallicum *Book VII*, 303–304 pointing out that Caesar himself is inconsistent in the numbers he gives.

51. Caes. *B Gall.* 7.77–8.

52. Caes. *B Gall.* 7.80–83.

53. Caes. *B Gall.* 7.88.1–3 with discussion in Krebs, *Caesar* Bellum Gallicum *Book VII*, 336–337.

54. Caes. *B Gall.* 7.90; on Pompey's conduct see n. 46 above.

55. [Caes.] *B Gall.* 8.4–5, with 8.38.3, where the manuscript reads *Gutrualtum*, but it is clear from context that this is the same person mentioned in *B Gall.* 7.3.1. See note xxx above.

56. [Caes.] *B Gall.* 8.21.4–22.

57. [Caes.] *B Gall.* 8.31.1–4, with 38.3 (n. 31 above).

58. [Caes.] *B Gall.* 8.44.

59. Suet. *Iul.* 35 on the tribute. For the comparison with the forum, see A. Goldsworthy, *Caesar: Life of a Colossus* (New Haven, 2006), 355; see also p. 164 above on the cost. The date is derived from [Caes.] *B Gall.* 8.49.3: *nulla onera iniungendo defessam tot adversis proeliis Galliam condicione parendi meliore facile in pace continuit*, referring to the summer of 50, suggesting that the tribute was fixed in 51.

60. [Caes.] *B Gall.* 8.49.1. For the number of legions, the critical discussion remains H. M. Ottmer, *Die Rubikon-Legende: Untersuchungen zu Caesar und Pompeius' Strategie vor und nach Ausbruch des Bürgerkriegs* (Boppard am Rhein, 1979), 36; see also Girardet, *Januar 49 v. Chr.*, 144–147.

CHAPTER 14

1. For the Senate meeting, see Caes. *B Civ.* 1.1–2. For the chronology, see K. A. Raaflaub and J. T Ramsay, "The Chronology of Caesar's Campaigns," in *The Landmark Julius Caesar*, ed. and trans. K. A. Raaflaub (New York, 2017), 180. I will give the traditional Roman months, occasionally indicating the dates according to the Julian calendar when necessary for clarity. For the quotation from Lucan, see Luc. 1.125–126. *nec quemquam iam ferre potest Caesarue priorem / Pompeiusue parem*, with A. Goldsworthy, *Caesar: Life of a Colossus* (New Haven, 2006): 372.

2. Caes. *B Civ.* 7.4.1 (Celtillus) with C. B. Krebs, *Caesar* Bellum Gallicum *Book VII* (Cambridge, 2023): 126–127. For Cicero on Pompey, see Cic. *Dom.* 65: *Cn. Pompeium, quem omnium iudicio longe principem esse civitatis videbat*; see also *Rep.* 3.26. For Caesar on losing the top position, see Suet. *Iul.* 29; for Caesar working for years to obtain the top position, see Cic. *Phil.* 2.116.

3. [Caes.] *B Gall.* 8.49.2: *Nihil enim minus volebat quam sub decessu suo necessitatem sibi aliquam imponi belli gerendi, ne, cum exercitum deducturus esset, bellum aliquod relinqueretur quod omnis Gallia libenter sine praesenti periculo susciperet.*

4. [Caes.] *B Gall.* 8.50; for the date of the election, see Cic. *Fam.* 8.12.4, 14.1. For the text, see R. Morstein-Marx, *Julius Caesar and the Roman People* (Cambridge, 2021), 278 n. 72.

5. Cic. *Att.* 11.2; Suet. *Iul.* 28; Plut. *Caes.* 29.1; App. *B Civ.* 2.26. See also discussion in L. Canfora, *Julius Caesar: The Life and Times of the People's Dictator*, trans. M. Hill and K. Windel (Berkeley and Los Angeles, 2007), 129–131.

6. Cic. *Fam* 8.1.2; Suet. *Iul.* 28 (behavior of Marcellus), 8.2.2, 5.3 (business brought to a halt); Cic. *Att.* 8.5.3 (Pompey's statement). The month in question would be June by our reckoning. For the problem with the wording of the law, see pp. 157–158 above; note also Cic. *Att.* 7.7.6, explicitly stating that Caesar was retaining his command after its legal expiration. Caesar's own view is stated clearly at Caes. *B Civ.* 1.9.2: *ereptoque semenstri imperio in urbem retraheretur, cuius absentis rationem haberi proximis*

comitiis populus iussisset, with J. M. Carter, *Julius Caesar: The Civil War, Books I and II* (Warminster, 1990), ad loc.

7. Cic. *Fam.* 8.8.5–8 (Caesar's veterans), 8.8.9 (Pompey's statement).

8. [Caes.] *B Gall.* 8.52.2–3.

9. Cic. *Att.* 4.17.7; *Fam.*8.4.4; Plut. *Caes.* 29.3; Val. Max. 9.1.6; Vell. Pat. 2.48.4 (size of the bribe; Valerius puts it at 60,000,000 sesterces, Velleius at 10,000,000); Plut. *Caes.* 29.3; Cic. *Fam.* 8.6.5 (on Curio's shift, but attributing it to frustration with the consuls). See also Cic. *Att.* 6.3.4 (expressing disappointment in Paullus and Curio in June).

10. Cic. *Fam.* 8.4.4.

11. Suet. *Caes.* 30.3–4; Plut. *Caes.* 46.1. Both these passages repeat Asinius Pollio, on whom see *FRH* 56 F31b, with Drummond's discussion ad loc. For Caelius on Caesar's fear, see Cic. *Fam.* 8.14. I accept here the view of Morstein-Marx, *Julius Caesar and the Roman People*, 622–624, that Caesar's fear was rhetorical rather than genuine.

12. Cic. *Fam.* 8.14.2 (loves and bickerings), 8.14.3.

13. Plut. *Pomp.* 53 (consequences of Julia's death), with R. Syme, *The Roman Revolution* (Oxford, 1939), 40.

14. Suet. *Iul.* 50.

15. Plut. *Pomp.* 57.1–3; see also Dio Cass. 41.6.5.

16. Plut. *Pomp.* 57.5 (foot stamping). For Caesar's offer see Suet. *Iul.* 29, with K. M. Girardet, *Januar 49 v. Chr.: Caesars Militärputsch; Vorgeschichte, Rechtslage, politische Aspekte* (Bonn, 2017), 127–132. The date is derived from Cic. *Fam.* 8.14.2 and referred to by Caesar at *B Civ.* 1.9.3, 32.4; for an alternative view, that this passage refers to Caesar's letter in January of 49, see Morstein-Marx, *Julius Caesar and the Roman People*, 288 n. 127, but that letter was not read out and the correspondence between the proposal and Curio's motion seems too close. For Curio's motion, see [Caes.] *B Gall.* 8.52.3–5; the proposal was clearly Caesar's: see Cic. *Fam.* 8.14.2. For Marcellus with the sword, see App. *B Civ.* 2.31. Plut. *Pomp.* 59.1 has Marcellus lead members of the Senate to Pompey's house to ask him to undertake the defense of the state.

17. Cic. *Att.* 7.5.4.

18. Suet. *Iul.* 29 (Caesar's proposals about the provinces). See esp. Cic. *Fam.* 16.11.2, summing up Caesar's position; see also *Att.* 7.9.2, raising two possibilities for peace: that Caesar retains his army and becomes consul or gives up his army, hands over his province, and becomes consul. The two choices are plainly those offered by the two sides.

19. Cic. *Att.* 7.7.6. The statement of Atticus in October that Caesar had four legions at Placentia, reported at *Att.* 6.9.5, looks like it might be hearsay; for the actual number, see Girardet, *Januar 49 v. Chr.*, 136–144; for the false tradition, passed on in later historiography, that Caesar had only one legion, see R. W. Westall, *Caesar's Civil War: Historical Reality and Fabrication* (Leiden, 2017), 2–3.

20. [Caes.] *B Gall.* 8.52.3 (rumors that Labienus's loyalty was being tampered with in the summer of 50); for Labienus's original connection to Pompey, see R. Syme, "The Allegiance of Labienus," *JRS* 38 (1938):113–125 (= R. Syme, *Roman Papers* 1 [Oxford, 1979]: 62–75).

21. See Dio Cass. 41.4.3–4 on the relationship between Caesar and Labienus at this point; see also Syme, *Roman Revolution*, 42.

22. Cic. *Att.* 7.4.2.

23. Cic. *Att.* 7.4.3 (Cicero's hope that Caesar will not put everything at risk), 7.5.4 (result will be a tyrant); 7.6.2; cf Cic. *Att.* 7.7.6–7 (increase in Caesar's power), 7.8.5 (Antony's speech), 7.8.4 (Pompey has no interest in peace).

24. App. *B Civ.* 2.32; Dio Cass. 41.1.3–4 (letter); Caes. *B Civ.* 1.1–2 (on the meeting), with Morstein-Marx, *Julius Caesar and the Roman People*, 303–307. It is likely that Caesar gave some details of the letter; the text of the *Bellum Civile* as it stands opens with an ablative absolute, which cannot be the original opening: see Carter, *Julius Caesar: The Civil War, Books I and II*, ad loc. for a clear discussion of the issue. See also Cic. *Fam.* 16.11.2, referring to the contents of the letter as threatening. See also Caes. *B Civ.* 1.2.1 (Scipio's speech sent from Pompey's mouth), 1.2.6 (demand that Caesar dismiss his army). For the qualities of Caesar's description, see W. Batstone and C. Damon, *Caesar's Civil War* (Oxford, 2006), 43–55, with 109–113 on the characterization of Metellus Scipio.

25. Caes. *B Civ.* 1.2.7, 5.5; Cic. *Fam.*16.11.2; Plut. *Ant.* 5.5; Dio Cass. 41.2.2; and Morstein-Marx, *Julius Caesar and the Roman People*, 307–308.

26. Caes. *B Civ.* 1.7–8, with Batestone and Damon, *Caesar's Civil War*, 56–59; L. Grillo, *The Art of Caesar's Bellum Civile: Literature, Ideology and Community* (Cambridge, 2012), 137; and R. W. Westall, *Caesar's Civil War: Reality and Fabrication* (Leiden, 2017), 49. See also R. MacMullen, "Personal Power in the Roman Empire," *AJPhil.* 107 (1986): 516–518 (Caesar's *dignitas*).

27. Plut. *Caes.* 32.4–8; App. *B Civ.* 2.35 see Pollio fr. 32a–b in *The Fragments of the Roman Historians*, ed. T. Cornell (Oxford, 2013) with Drummond's note.

28. Luc. 1.185–205.

29. Suet. *Iul.* 31–32; for the different versions, see L. Fezzi, *Crossing the Rubicon*, trans. R. Dixon (New Haven, 2019), 149–165.

30. Cic *Att.* 7.22.1 (*celeritas*).

31. Cic. *Att.* 7.10, 11.3 (decision to abandon Rome irrational), 7.21.2 (consuls sent to get the money from the treasury). For Pompey's command authority as a proconsul, see K. M. Girardet, "*Imperia* und *Provinciae* des Pompeius 82 bis 48 v. Chr.," *Chiron* 31 (2001): 202–206.

32. Cic. *Att.* 7.11.1 (mentioning Labienus's desertion on January 19), 7.13a2 (for his encounter with Lucius Caesar at Minturnae on January 23). See also H. Cornwell, "Negotiation as a Tool for Legitimacy in the Roman Civil War of 49–48 BCE: A New Policy for Achieving Victory," in *New Perspectives on the Roman Civil Wars of 49–30 BCE*, ed. R. Westall and H. Cornwell (London, 2024), 23–24.

33. Caes. *B Civ.* 1.14.4–5.

34. Cic. *Att.* 7.14. (Caesar's proposal), 7.14.2; Caes. *B Civ.* 1.14.4–5 (Pompey's reply), 1.9.10–11.3 (Pompey's terms via Lucius Caesar); Cic. *Att.* 7.19 (Curio ridicules Lucius Caesar's mission); Caes. *B Civ.* 1.32.8 (Pompey has no further interest in negotiating).

35. Cic. *Att.* 7.21.1 (Cicero to Atticus on February 8), 8.11b.3 (Cicero does not know what Pompey intends). See also Cic. *Att.* 7.23.3 (recruits not showing up), 8.3.1: *si Pompeius Italia excedat, quod eum facturum esse suspicor*. Certainty is evident on February 21 (Cic. *Att.* 8.7.2: Pompey is planning to leave Italy). For Pompey's question, see Cic. *Att.* 9.10.2: *Sulla potuit, ego non potero?* (March 18); see also *Att.* 7.11.2.

36. Cic. *Att.* 8.12d (Pompey's letter). The description of Domitius is borrowed from Syme, *Roman Revolution*, 61.

37. Caes. *B Civ.* 1.19.1–4 (Domitius's decline), 1.19.3, 20–22 (surrender); see also Fezzi, *Crossing the Rubicon*, 201–209; and, on the scene of the surrender, U. Gotter, "Writing Down Uncivil Wars, or: How Roman Generals Justified Themselves in the Wake of Civic Bloodshed," in *A Culture of Civil War? Bellum civile and Political Communication*

in Late Republican Rome, ed. H. Börm, U. Gotter, and W. Havener (Stuttgart, 2023), 191–192. For the topography of the site, see V. La Salvia and M. Moderato, "Ghost Walls and Vanishing Towns: The Case of Caesar's Siege of Corfinium between Historical Sources and Archaeological-Topographical Data," in Westall and Cornwell, *New Perspectives*, 127–140.

38. Cic. *Att* 9.7c.1, with H. Cornwell, "Negotiation as a Tool for Legitimacy in the Roman Civil War of 49–48 BCE: A New Policy for Achieving Victory," in Westall and Cornwell, *New Perspectives*, 15–16.

39. Cic. *Att.* 9.15a (quoted in the text), 9.10.6 ("to Sulla"); see also Canfora, *Julius Caesar*, 152–156.

40. Caes. *B Civ.* 1.30.2–3; 31.2; App. *B Civ.* 2.40; Dio Cass. 41.1.

41. R. Macfarlane, "*Ab inimicis incitatus*: On Dating the Composition of Caesar's *Bellum Civile*," *Syllecta Classica* 7 (1996): 107–132, on Caesar's language. See also Cic. *Att.* 9.10.2, 11.6.6. For Pompey, see Caes. *B Civ.* 1.33.2. For the shift in terminology in subsequent chapters, see p. 226 below. On the issue of composition, see the summary of scholarship in Grillo, *Art of Caesar's* Bellum Civile, 178–179. My own view is that Caesar issued summaries of operations, as he had in Gaul, a conclusion which is supported by Macfarlane's study of linguistic variation in Book 1, and the consistent picture of Pompey's army as barbarians. I suspect that the treatment of Cleopatra in Book 3 does indicate that Caesar completed the commentaries as we have them in 46, which would agree with J. F. Gaertner and B. C. Hausburg, *Caesar and the* Bellum Alexandrinum: *An Analysis of Style, Narrative Technique, and the Reception of Greek Historiography* (Göttingen, 2013), 39–40, who argue that the early chapters of the *Alexandrian War* were drafted by Caesar. The level of inconsistency may well show that the draft was not given to the public as it is plainly less finished than the *Gallic War*: see in particular C. Damon, *Studies in the Text of Caesar's* Bellum Civile (Oxford, 2015), esp. 10 n. 28.

42. Fundamental discussions are Syme, *The Roman Revolution*, 61–69; and Morstein Marx, *Julius Caesar and the Roman People*, 352–378.

43. For Servilius Isauricus and Aemilius Lepidus, see S. Treggiari, *Servilia and Her Family* (Oxford, 2019), 132–133. For Crassus, Fabius, and Sulpicius Rufus, see Morstein-Marx, *Julius Caesar and the Roman People*, 375–378. For Publius Sulla, see J. T. Ramsay, "Who's Who in Caesar," in Raaflaub, *Landmark Julius Caesar*, 661, with D. R. Shackleton Bailey, *Letters to Atticus* (Cambridge, 1965–1970) on Cic. *Att.* 4.3.3 for the identification.

44. For Piso, see Morstein-Marx, *Julius Caesar and the Roman People*, 365. For Lucius Caesar the younger, see Suet. *Iul.* 75.3; Dio Cass. 43.12.3, with Morstein-Marx, *Julius Caesar and the Roman People*, 484. For Cassius and Brutus, see Morstein-Marx, *Julius Caesar and the Roman Peple*, 482. For Cicero's decision, see P. A. Brunt, "Caesar's *Officium* in the Civil War," *JRS* 76 (1986): 12–32.

45. Caes. *B Civ.* 1.32.2–9; Dio Cass. 41.15.2–4.

46. Cic. *Att.* 10.4.8; Plut. *Pomp.* 62; Caes. 35.3–4; App. *B Civ.* 2.41; Dio Cass. 41.17.2, with R. Evans, *Questioning Reputations: Essays on Nine Roman Republican Politicians* (Pretoria, 2003), 74–76.

47. Cic. *Att.* 10.4.9 ("everything comes from me"), 10.4.8 (does not hold a public meeting), 10.4.11 (not angry with Cicero).

48. Dio Cass. 41.16.1; see *RRC* no. 442.

CHAPTER 15

1. For the dispositions and number of the legions, see H. M. Ottmer, *Die Rubikon-Legende: Untersuchungen zu Caesar and Pompeius' Strategie vor und nach Ausbruch des Bürgerkreiges* (Boppard am Rhein, 1979), 85 n. 326.

2. Caes. *B Civ.* 1.35.1–36.4.

3. Caes. *B Civ.* 1.40–41, with T. R. E. Holmes, *The Roman Republic and the Founder of Empire*, vol. 3 (London, 1923), 390–391, on the battlefield; and W. Batstone and C. Damon, *Caesar's* Civil War (Oxford, 2006), 126.

4. Caes. *B Civ.* 1.44.2; see also A. Goldsworthy, *Caesar, Life of a Colossus* (New Haven, 2006), 400.

5. Caes. *B Civ.* 1. 54–55.

6. Caes. *B Civ.* 1.53; for Cicero's thinking, see P. A. Brunt, "Cicero's *Officium* in the Civil War," *JRS* 76 (1986): 12–32.

7. Caes. *B Civ.* 1.61.

8. Caes. *B Civ.* 1.64.1–3.

9. Caes. *B Civ.* 1.64.7 (cavalry action), 67 (mini mutiny), with A. Peer, *Julius Caesar's* Bellum Civile *and the Composition of a New Reality* (Abingdon, 2015), 68–69.

10. Caes. *B Civ.* 1.72.2; see also L. Grillo, *The Art of Caesar's* Bellum Civile: *Literature, Ideology and Community* (Cambridge, 2012), 18–19, on the theme of speed.

11. Caes. *B Civ.* 1.74–76 with Peer, *Caesar's* Bellum Civile, 74–75.

12. Caes. *B Civ.* 1.84.3–5.

13. Caes. *B Civ.* 1. 85.5 (sentiments quoted in the text), 1.87.4–5 (dismissal of the Pompeian army); see also Westall, *Caesar's* Civil War, 104–107.

14. Caes. *B Civ.* 2.17.1–2 (communication with Caesar), 2.17.3 (Varro responds to news from Lerida), 2.18 (Varro's preparations), esp. 2.18.4, (on money).

15. Caes. *B Civ.* 2.21.2–4; *RRC* no. 443, with B. Woytek, *Arma et Nummi: Forschungen zur römischen Finanzgeschichte und Münzprägung der Jahre 49 bis 42 v. Chr.* (Vienna, 2003), 127–131; and C. Rowan, *From Caesar to Augustus (c. 49 BC–AD 14): Using Coins as Sources* (Cambridge, 2019), 24.

16. Caes. *B Civ.* 2.12.4 (ambassadors' speech), 2.14–16 (Massiliote treachery), 2.22 (surrender), with Grillo, *Art of Caesar's* Bellum Civile, 92–95.

17. Caes. *B Civ.* 2. 23.6 (passage quoted); and K. A. Raaflaub and J. T Ramsay, "The Chronology of Caesar's Campaigns," in *The Landmark Julius Caesar*, ed. and trans. K. A. Raaflaub (New York, 2017), 187, for the date.

18. For the date, see H. C. Avery, "A Lost Episode in Caesar's Civil War," *Hermes* 121 (1993): 457. For the location, see Caes. *B Civ.* 3.10.5 with Damon, *Caesar's* Bellum Civile, 221–223, with Avery, "Lost Episode," 457n18. On the betrayal by Pulo, see note 19 below. For the conditions, see Dio Cass. 41.40; Florus 2.13.30–33.

19. For the dating of this event relative to the defeat of Antonius, note Caes. *B Civ.* 2.23.1: *Eisdem temporibus.* The reference cannot be to the end of the siege of Marseilles narrated in the previous chapter, making it likely that some section of Book 2 has dropped out. The cross-reference at Caes. *B Civ.* 3.67.5, *Tito Pulione, cuius opera proditum exercitum G. Antonii demonstravimus,* shows that there must have been a narrative of these events in Caesar's writings at some point. Klotz marks a lacuna at this point in his text; see also Avery, "Lost Episode," 459–460.

20. R. Westall, *Caesar's* Civil War: *Historical Reality and Fabrication* (Leiden, 2017), 191–192.

21. Caes. *B Civ.* 2.25.3–4; Curio's proposal was not a novelty, since this had also been proposed in 63: see Cic. *Leg. agr.* 2.58. See p. 86 for the beard pulling.

22. Caes. *B Civ.* 2.38.1–2 (false intelligence), 2.42 (Juba's victory), with Grillo, *Art of Caesar's* Bellum Civile, 35, on how Curio's mistakes absolve Caesar of responsibility.

23. Dio Cass. 41.26.1; App. *B Civ.* 2.47.

24. Dio Cass. 41. 29–24; for the propaganda, stressing the Gallic War at this point, see Rowan, *From Caesar to Augustus*, 28–30.

25. Dio Cass. 41.34.5; App. *B Civ.* 2.47, with S. G. Chrissanthos, "Caesar and the Mutiny of 47 BC," *JRS* 91 (2001), 68.

26. Caes. *B Civ.* 2.21.5; see also Plut. *Caes.* 37.1, who misunderstands the process by saying Caesar was made dictator by the Senate; see also Matthias Gelzer, *Caesar: Politician and Statesman*, trans. P. Needham (Oxford, 1969), 219; and M. B. Wilson, *Dictator: The Evolution of the Roman Dictatorship* (Ann Arbor, 2021), 309–317.

27. Caes. *B Civ.* 3.1.2–3; Suet. *Iul.* 42.3; Plut. *Caes.* 37.1; App. *B Civ.* 2.13; Dio Cass. 41.37–38; for the issue, see also Cic. *Att.* 7.18.4, 9.9.4, 10.11.2, with Gelzer, *Caesar*, 221; and Goldsworthy, *Caesar*, 409–410.

28. Plut. *Caes.* 37.2; Cic. *Fam.* 13.8.2, with F. Hinard, *Les proscriptions de la Rome républicaine* (Paris, 1985), 217–222 (sons of the proscribed); Caes. *B Civ.* 3.1.5 (Caesar on the restorations). See also R. Syme, *The Roman Revolution* (Oxford, 1939), 61–62. On Messalla, see also *MRR* 2, 285 no. 9; for Antonius, see Cic. *Phil.* 2.98; Strabo 2.13.

29. For the problem of the publication date, see chapter 14 n. 41. On the same principle that Wiseman propounds for the *Bellum Gallicum*, what follows allows that individual sections reflect communications to the public in the course of 49–48.

30. See R. T. Macfarlane, "*Ab inimicis incitatus*: On Dating the Composition of Caesar's *Bellum Civile*," *Syllecta Classica* 7 (1996): 107–132; and p. 211 above. The critique in Gaertner and Hausburg, *Caesar and the* Bellum Alexandrinum, 185–188, misses the point in adducing *B Civ.* 3.16.3, 83.4 in that Caesar is referring in those places to personal animosities, not to the totality of the opposition, which is the case in Book 1.

31. M. Rambaud, *L'art de la déformation historique dans les Commentaires de César* (Paris, 1966), 257–259, drawing attention to the contrast with Pompey; and p. 120 above on the *Gallic War*.

32. *Commentum Cornuti in Persium* 6.55, on Bovillae; for the event, see Dio Cass. 41.39.2–3 with D. Potter, "Rome and Bovillae through the Early Decades of the Empire," in *Ancient Bovillae: History, Art and Archaeology of a Lost City on the Roman Hinterland* ed. P. Hatlie (Ann Arbor, 2025): 24–6.

33. T. R. Holmes, *The Roman Republic* (Oxford 1923), 3:434–435.

34. Goldsworthy, *Caesar*, 410, on this point.

35. Luc. 5.44–49 on the appointment and date before the end of 49, with Caes. *B Civ.* 3.16.4, referring to the "opinion of the council" that Pompey be given control of the war. See also Dio Cass. 41.43 on the Senate in exile, with no mention of Pompey's appointment. Despite Vell. Pat. 2.49.2, Pompey did not have official control of the operation prior to this: see esp. Cic. *Att.* 8.12.b2 and p. 207 above; see also Holmes, *The Roman Republic*, 3:432–432; and K. M. Girardet, "*Imperia* und *Provinciae* des Pompeius 82 bis 48 v. Chr.," *Chiron* 31 (2001): 202–203.

36. Dio Cass. 41.44 1 on Pompey at Thessalonica; for the army at Veroia, see Plut. *Pomp.* 64.1; for the theme of barbarism in Pompey's army, see Grillo, *Art of Caesar's* Bellum Civile, 110–117; and Westall, *Caesar's* Civil War, 204–206.

37. Caes. *B Civ.* 3.6.3, with Raaflaub and Ramsay, "Chronology," 187 and Westall, *Caesar's Civil War*, 199–200.

38. Caes. *B Civ.* 3.8.3, with discussion in Peer, *Julius Caesar's* Bellum Civile, 144, for Bibulus; Caes. *B Civ.* 3.15.8 on public knowledge of Vibullus's mission, with Grillo, *Art of Caesar's* Bellum Civile, 28–32. Note also Dio's view (41.47.2) that this was not a serious offer but rather a delaying tactic.

39. Caes. *B Civ.* 3.13.1; and Holmes, *Roman Republic*, 3, 120–121.

40. Caes. *B Civ.* 3.10, with Peer, *Julius Caesar's* Bellum Civile, 117–120, rightly drawing attention to the connection with the story at Suet. *Iul.* 30.4.

41. Caes. *B Civ.* 3.18.3–5.

42. Caes. *B Civ.* 3.18.4. I do not see the need to assume a lacuna after *sum*, though I find Kuebler's *ex qua profectus <tamquam fugituvus> reductus* very attractive. For the characterization of Pompey here, see Peer, *Julius Caesar's* Bellum Civile, 130.

43. Caes. *B Civ.* 3.17 (Libo), 3.19.8 (Labienus).

44. Caes *B Civ.* 3.18.1 (death of Bibulus), 3.25.2 (multiplicity of commanders for the fleet), 3.26, 29 (Antony's voyage), 3.30 (Antony and Caesar join forces).

45. Caes. *B Civ.* 3.44 (extension of siege lines), 47.2–3 (resupply of Pompey's forces).

46. Caes. *B Civ.* 3.47.3–48.2, 58.3–5; see also App. *B Civ.* 2.61 and Westall, *Caesar's* Civil War, 32 n. 126 for other versions of the story.

47. Caes. *B Civ.* 3.55.1–2.

48. Caes. *B Civ.* 3.61.2 (first men to desert), 63.4–5; and Goldsworthy, *Caesar*, 419 (information).

49. Caes. *B Civ.* 3.68.1 (Fortune), 70.1 (Pompey could have won the war, a comment picked up in the later tradition: see App. *B Civ.* 2. 62),70.2 (decision to withdraw). See also Batstone and Damon, *Caesar's* Civil War, 123–127.

50. Caes. *B Civ.* 3.73.

51. Caes. *B Civ.* 3.34.3–4.

52. Caes. *B Civ.* 3.80.1.

53. Caes. *B Civ.* 3.81.3 with D.G. Domínguez, "Pain and Gain. Violence against Provincial Cities in the Age of Civil War," in *Connected Histories of the Roman Civil Wars (88-30 BCE)*, ed. D.G. García Domínguez, J. García González, and F. Santangelo (Berlin/Boston, 2024): 127–31.

54. Caes. *B Civ.* 3.72 (confidence in the troops), 81–82 (postwar plans and Pompey's wishing to stay in command), with Batstone and Damon, *Caesar's* Civil War, 113–118.

55. Cic. *Att.* 11.6.2.

56. J. D. Morgan, "Palaepharsalus—The Battle and the Town," *AJArch.* 87 (1983): 23–54.

57. Caes. *B Civ.* 3.86.2–4 (Pompey's plan), with Grillo, *Art of Caesar's* Bellum Civile, 114, on the contrasting styles; Plut. *Caes.* 45.2–3 (Caesar's instructions).

58. Caes. *B Civ.* 3.91.3–4.

59. Caes. *B Civ.* 3.92.5.

60. Caes. *B Civ.* 3.96.3–4.

61. Caes. *B Civ.* 3.99.1–4, but see App. *B Civ.* 2.82, Plut. *Caes.* 46.3; *Pompey*, 72.4 (Pollio frs 4 a–c in *The Fragments of the Roman Historians* ed. T. Cornell (Oxford, 2013) with Drummond's note. Pollio put the losses for the Pompeian side at 6,000. See also Goldsworthy, *Caesar*, 430.

CHAPTER 16

1. Dio Cass.42.2.4–6 (against the truth of the tradition), but see 41.55.3, stating that Orodes did not send aid to Pompey despite being offered Syria in exchange. From here to the end of the book the dates will be given according to modern reckoning.

2. Caes. *B Civ.* 3.102–103.

3. *BGU* 8.1828, with J. Bingen, *Hellenistic Egypt: Monarchy, Society, Economy, Culture,* edited with an introduction by R. Bagnall (Berkeley and Los Angeles, 2007), 68; and D. W. Roller, *Cleopatra: A Biography* (Oxford, 2010), 53.

4. *BGU* 8.1730, with Bingen, *Hellenistic Egypt,* 69; Caes. *B Civ* 3.110.6 (killing of Bibulus's sons). For Ptolemy XIII's entourage, see Caes. *B Civ.* 3.108.1 (Pothinus); Plut. *Pomp.* 77.2 (adding Theodotus and Achillas); see also App. *B Civ.* 2.90 and P. M. Fraser, *Ptolemaic Alexandria* (Oxford, 1972), 126; and Roller, *Cleopatra,* 55–59.

5. Plut. *Ant.* 25.4 on the "Senate's" decree with C. Pelling, *Plutarch: Life of Antony* (Cambridge, 1988), ad loc.; For Egyptian contributions to Pompey's army, see Caes. *B Civ.* 3.3.1, 111.3; App. *B Civ.* 2.71 (ships; Appian puts the number at sixty), 4.1 (Gabinians).

6. Caes. *B Civ.* 3.103.2; Strabo 17.1.11 (flight to Syria); Plut. *Pomp.* 77; App. *B Civ.* 2.84; Dio Cass. 43.1, with Fraser, *Ptolemaic Alexandria,* 126; T. R. Holmes, *The Roman Republic and the Founder of the Empire,* vol. 3 (Oxford, 1923), 126; and Roller, *Cleopatra,* 58–59.

7. Caes. *B Civ.* 3.103.4 (conversations with Gabinians); Plut. *Pomp.* 78.3; App. *B Civ.* 2.84 (Pompey killed to please Caesar). Luc. 8. 483–505 makes Pothinus the person giving the advice.

8. Caes. *B Civ.* 3.104.2–3; Plut. *Pomp.* 78–79 (assassination); Vell. Pat. 2.53.3; Plin. *NH* 37.13; Dio Cass. 42.5.5. For Plutarch's dates, see Plut. *Pomp.* 79.5; *Cam.,* 19.11; *Mor.* 717c; see also R. Seager, *Pompey the Great: A Political Biography* 2nd edition (Oxford, 2002), 168.

9. Seager, *Pompey,* 168.

10. Caes. *B Civ.* 3.102.1.

11. Cic. *Att.* 10.5.3, 7.1; *Fam.* 7.3.3; *Deiot.* 29; Plut. *Cat. Min.* 55.2; *Cic.* 39.1, with Holmes, *Roman Republic* 3:220–221.

12. Caes. *B Civ.* 3.106.12. For the Sixth Legion, see also Caes. *B Civ.* 3.102.1; [Caes.] *B Alex.* 33.3; for the other legion, see *B Civ.* 3.106.1. For the miracles, see Caes. *B Civ.* 3.105. For discussion of the money see R.W. Westall, *Caesar's* Civil War: *Historical Reality and Fabication* (Leiden, 2017): 263–70.

13. J. F. Gaertner and B. C. Hausburg, *Caesar and the* Bellum Alexandrinum: *An Analysis of Style, Narrative Technique, and the Reception of Greek Historiography* (Göttingen, 2013), 153–163, arguing, convincingly, that the author is Hirtius, but that chapters 1–21 are based on a draft left behind by Caesar and plainly intended to be published with what are now the concluding chapters of the *Bellum Civile*: note especially [Caes.] *B Alex.* 4.1, where "as was shown above" (*ut supra demonstratum*) is a reference to *B Civ.* 3.112.10–11.

14. Caes. *B Civ.* 3.106.4 (objection to the *fasces*); Plut. *Caes.* 48.2; *Pomp.* 77–80 on Pompey's head, with D. Potter, "Dio and Pompey: Explaining the Failure of the Republic," in *The Intellectual Climate of Cassius Dio,* ed. A. Kemezis, C. Bailey and B. Poletti (Leiden, 2022), 34.

15. Caes. *B Civ.* 3.108 (offer to mediate), 3.109.4–6 (takes custody of Ptolemy), 3.111.6 (dockyard), 3.112.1 (lighthouse), 3.112.5–6 (summons assistance), 3.112.12 (Pothinus). On the question of whether the fire destroyed the library, see Dio Cass. 42.38.2; Plut. *Caes.* 49.6; Gell. *NA* 7.17.3; Livy in Sen. *Tranq.* 9.4–5; Luc. 10.486–505; Oros. 6.15.31–32. For a thorough discussion, concluding that the library itself was not destroyed, see L. Tiberi, "La biblioteca di Alessandria e l'incendio che non la distrusse, I: Riflessioni moderne fino a Giusto Lupsio," *Bibliothecae.it* 9 (2020): 4–100.

16. Dio Cass. 42.34.5–35.1; Plut. *Caes.* 49.8 (demand for repayment), with R. W. Westall, *Caesar's* Civil War: *Historical Reality and Fabrication* (Leiden, 2017), 297–298. The passage quoted is Plut. *Caes.* 49.1–3. See also Roller, *Cleopatra*, 61, favoring Plutarch's version.

17. The date derives from Demotic Stele (Louvre 335): see H. Heinen, "Cäsar und Kaesarion," *Historia* 18 (1969): 181–203, who does an admirable job of summarizing (and eliminating) the various alternative hypotheses; see also Roller, *Cleopatra*, 64; and A. Goldsworthy, *Antony and Cleopatra* (New Haven, 2010), 192–193.

18. Suet. *Iul.* 52.

19. See Goldsworthy, *Antony and Cleopatra*, 174, for the parallel with Servilia.

20. Caes. *B Civ.* 3.108.4–5 (not mentioning Cyprus); Dio Cass. 42.35.2 (Ptolemy's behavior), 42.35.5 (terms of the agreement including Cyprus).

21. See also Goldsworthy, *Antony and Cleopatra*, 176, on the possible Cato factor in Caesar's decision-making.

22. Caes. *B Civ.* 3.110–111 (outbreak of the war presented as a mutiny on Achillas's part); Dio Cass. 42.36–7 (outbreak of the war because Caesar favors Cleopatra); Caes. *B Civ.* 3.112.10; Dio Cass. 42.39.1 (escape of Arsinoe).

23. [Caes.] *B Alex.* 4.1–2; the cross reference at 4.1 to *B Civ.* 3.112.10–11 supports the view of Gaertner and Hausburg (n. 13 above) that the opening section of the work is based on notes prepared by Caesar.

24. [Caes.] *B Alex.* 9.3–11.

25. [Caes.] *B Alex.* 20.5–6; Plut. *Caes.* 49.7–8; Suet. *Iul.* 64 (in this version he saves his cloak by dragging it in his teeth); Dio Cass. 42.40.3–5; App. *B Civ.* 2.90.

26. [Caes.] *B Alex.* 23–24. Dio Cass. 42.42.1–2 states that Ptolemy was now in command.

27. [Caes.] *B Alex.* 26; Joseph. *BJ* 14.127–137; Dio Cass. 41.41.1.

28. [Caes.] *B Alex.* 26–31 (battle), 32 (surrender); Dio Cass. 42.42.2–6; Oros 6.16.1–2.

29. [Caes.] *B Alex.* 33.2–4 (short stay); Suet. *Iul.* 52.1; App. *B Civ.* 2.90 (long trip); Dio Cass. 42.45.1 (short stay). For the chronology, see K. A. Raaflaub and J. T. Ramsay, "The Chronology of Caesar's Campaigns," Web Essay BB for *The Landmark Julius Caesar*, ed. K. A. Raaflaub (New York, 2017), 193 (https://thelandmarkcaesar.com/LandmarkCaesarWebEssays_5Jan2018.pdf). See Cic. *Att.* 11.25.2, showing that the statement Caesar was in Egypt for nine months at App. *B Civ.* 2.90 extends his actual stay by two months. For the garrison, see [Caes.] *B Alex.* 33.3–4.

30. [Caes.] *B Alex.* 39.1. Calvinus also supported Octavian very strongly, which accords with the author's perspective, which is critical of Antony. For the date, see Raaflaub and Ramsay, "Chronology," 192.

31. [Caes.] *B Alex.* 61.1. Dio Cass. 42.45.1 attributes his departure to news of Pharnaces, but the editor of the *Bellum Alexandrinum* says he only learned what had happened when he reached Antioch.

32. [Caes.] *B Alex.* 12.65.1.

33. [Caes.] *B Alex.* 69; App. *B Civ.* 2.92 (adding the detail that Pharnaces offered Caesar his daughter in marriage); [Caes.] *B Alex.* 69–70 (Caesar's reply).

34. [Caes.] *B Alex.* 72.2.

35. [Caes.] *B Alex.* 75–76 (battle); App. *Mith.* 120 (death).

36. Dio Cass. 42.48.2 (trophy); [Caes.] *B Alex.* 77.1 (on the speed of the victory). For the chronology accepted here, see Suet. *Iul.* 35.2 (five days); see also Raaflaub and Ramsay, "Chronology," 194; Suet. *Iul.* 37.2 ; Plut. *Caes.* 50; App. *B Civ.* 2.91 (*veni, vidi, vici*).

CHAPTER 17

1. Caes, *B Civ.* 3.20.1–3; Dio Cass. 42.22.3–4 (Caelius's first proposal); Caes. *B Civ.* 3. 21.21–3; Dio Cass. 42.23.2–3 (Caelius's subsequent actions and the *senatus consultum ultimum*).

2. Caes. *B Civ.* 3, 21. 4; ILS 8393 with J. Osgood, *Turia: A Roman Woman's Civil War* (Oxford, 2014), 38.

3. Dio Cass. 43.25; Vell. Pat. 2.26.2–3.

4. Plut. *Ant.* 9.4–5; see also Cic. *Phil.* 2.24–25 and W. J. Tatum, *A Noble Ruin: Mark Antony, Civil War and the Collapse of the Republic* (Oxford, 2024), 86, 92 (Pompey's house).

5. Plut. *Ant.* 9.1–2; Dio Cass. 42.29–32, with T. R. Holmes, *The Roman Republic and the Founder of the Empire*, vol. 3 (Oxford, 1923), 227–228; and Tatum, *A Noble Ruin*, 87–91.

6. [Caes.], *B Alex.* 65.1 (referring to the *indiligentia* of the officers); Cic. *Att.* 11.20.2, 11.22.2; [Caes.] *B Afr.* 54; Plut. *Caes.* 51.2; App. *B Civ.* 2.92; Dio Cass. 42.52, with S. G. Chrissanthos, "Caesar and the Mutiny of 47 BC," *JRS* 91 (2001): 63–75, esp. 69, on the officers involved. For Antony, see Tatum, *A Noble Ruin*, 88.

7. Plut. *Caes.* 48.1; App. *B Civ.* 5.19; Dio Cass. 42.6 for 48 BCE. The statement in Plutarch and Appian that he reduced payments by a third could be a reduction from the money collected by Pompey: see C. Pelling, *Plutarch*, Caesar (Oxford, 2011), 379, but Dio's description does make it appear that this was a permanent reduction from the sums collected by the *publicani*. See also P. A. Brunt, *Roman Imperial Themes* (Oxford, 1990), 380, 388–389, For extractions after Zela, see Dio Cass. 43.49; Strabo 14.1.42, with B. Woytek, Arma et Nummi: *Forschungen zur römischen Finanzgeschicte und Münzprägung der Jahre 49 bis 42 v. Chr.* (Vienna, 2003), 162–171.

8. Dio Cass. 42.51.1–2.

9. Dio Cass. 42.50.2–5 (Caesar raises money). For Pompeian property, see Plut. *Ant.* 10.2. The one person who does not seem to have been required to pay full price was Servilia. See also C. Meier, *Caesar: A Biography*, trans. D. McLintock (New York, 1982), 418–419.

10. Dio Cass. 42.52.2 (Sallust's adventure); Dio Cass. 42.52.2; Plut. *Caes.* 51 (the praetorian victims), with Chrissanthos, "Caesar and the Mutiny," 72–73.

11. Suet. *Iul.* 70 (the short version); Plut. *Caes.* 51.2; App. *B Civ.* 2.93; Dio Cass. 42.53.3–54.2, 42.55.2 (settlement with the rest of the army). App. *B Civ.* 2.94 has Caesar explicitly contrast his policy with Sulla's. For the legions which did not go to Africa, see Chrissanthos, "Caesar and the Mutiny," 74.

12. For the characteristics of the author, see A. Bouvet, *Pseudo-César: Guerre d'Afrique* (Paris, 2002), xxi–xxx, xxxviii–xliii; see also R. Cluett, "In Caesar's Wake: The Ideology of the Continuators," in *Caesar against Liberty: Perspectives on his Autocracy*, ed. F. Cairns and E. Fantham, Papers of the Langford Latin Seminar 11 (Cambridge, 2003), 118–131.

13. For the cause of the antipathy see Plut. *Cat. Min.* 7.1–2; for Metellus's book, see Plut. *Cat. Min.* 57.2; see Plut. *Cat. Min.* 58.5–6 for Cato's lack of confidence in Metellus.

14. [Caes.] *B Afr.* 2.5 (ships go astray), 3.1 (landing at Sousse), 11.2 (missing ships arrive at Sousse).

15. [Caes.] *B Afr.* 34.4–5, 52.1.

16. [Caes.] *B Afr.* 3.77.3.

17. Suet. *Iul.* 59 (Cornelian); Dio Cass. 42.58.3 ("I've got you, Africa!"). See Plut. *Cat. Min.* 57.3 for the belief that Scipio would be successful in Africa.

18. [Caes.] *B Afr.* 1.4; the number of elephants is given here and at 19.5: there are sixty when the royal army is said to be complete at *B Afr.* 48.4 and sixty-four at *B Afr.* 86.1. The number of legions under Scipio's command is put at ten at 1.4, along with four legions belonging to Juba. See also [Caes.] *B Afr.* 16.4 (new recruits overwhelmed by fear), 19.2 (Labienus employs tactics to confuse new soldiers), 31.9–10 (Caesar didn't want to take heavy losses winning with an inexperienced army so he waited for his veterans). See also [Caes.] *B Afr.* 35.1 (Scipio puzzled because he expected Caesar to take the initiative), 18.4 (battle with Labienus), 71.1 (Caesar as *lanista*), 72.4 (elephants).

19. [Caes.] *B Afr.* 86.1; Plut. *Caes.* 53.4 (casualties).

20. For the veterans' complaints, see App. *B Civ.* 2.47; note the earlier complaint at Caes. *B Civ.* 1.72–3, 3.90 (now perhaps significant). See also Chrissanthos, "Caesar and the Mutiny," 70. For Faustus Sulla and Afranius see [Caes,] *B Afr.* 95.1–3, but see also Dio Cass. 43.12.2, saying the order came from Caesar. For Scipio and his companions, see *B Afr.* 95.1–2; Plut. *Cat. Min.* 60.3. App. *B Civ.* 100 says he died fighting.

21. Plut. *Cat. Min.* 68–70.

22. Plut. *Cat. Min.* 72. For Lucius Caesar, see Cic. *Fam.* 9.7.1; Suet. *Iul.* 75.3; Dio Cass. 43.12.3. [Caes.] *B Afr.* 89.4–5 states that Caesar spared him in accordance with his "usual policy."

23. [Caes.] *Bell. Afr.* 94; App. *BC* 2.100.

24. Suet. *Iul.* 52.1 (Eunoe); see also D. J. Mattingly, *Between Sahara and Sea: Africa in the Roman Empire* (Ann Arbor, 2023), 156, 229–230; and A. Goldsworthy, *Caesar: Life of a Colossus* (New Haven, 2006), 467. For Sulci, see [Caes]. *B Afr.* 98.

25. See Dio 43.14.3; *AE* 2005 no. 1487; *SEG* 55.1452; S. Mitchell, "The Treaty between Rome and Lycia of 46 BC (MS 2070)," in *Papyri Graecae Schøyen*, ed. M. Pintaudi, *Papyrologica Florentina* 35 (Florence, 2005), 163–243; and G. Kantor, "Roman Treaty with Lycia (SEG LV 1452) and the Date of Caesar's Third Dictatorship," *ZPE* 190 (2014): 135–136.

26. Cic. *Phil* 13.32 on Hirtius's law; Dio Cass. 43.15ff.; Plin. *NH* 7.94 on the correspondence. See further E. Meyer, *Caesars Monarchie und das Principat des Pompejus: Innere Geschichte Roms von 66 bis 44 v. Chr.* (Stuttgart, 1919), 382, 400.

27. Dictatorship: see Dio Cass. 43.14.4. *Cura morum*: see Dio Cass. 43.14.4; Cic. *Fam.* 9.15.5, 26.3; *Att.* 12.35, 13.6.1, 7.1; Suet. *Iul.* 43.

28. M. Beard, *The Roman Triumph* (Cambridge, MA, 2007), 219–238.

29. Suet. *Iul.* 37.2 (broken wheel and elephants), 51 (bald adulterer), 49.4 (soldier's song on Nicomedes); Dio Cass. 43.21.1–2 (broken axle and ascent to the temple on his knees), with Beard, *Roman Triumph*, 249; Dio Cass. 43.20.4 (Caesar's oath about Nicomedes and response).

30. Suet. *Iul.* 52.1; Dio Cass. 43.7.3; App. *B Civ.* 2.102. I am assuming that the official reason for her visit was the triumph; in Dio her presence is associated with the celebration of Venus Genetrix; see also D. W. Roller, *Cleopatra: A Biography* (Oxford, 2010), 71.

31. Dio Cass. 43.20.4 (response to Caesar's oath).

32. On the dedication of the temple of Venus, see Dio Cass. 43.21.1; App. *B Civ.* 2.102, adding the detail that Caesar dedicated a statue of Venus with the features of Cleopatra, which is confusion on his part since the statue was placed there by Augustus after Actium: see Dio Cass. 51.22.3, with P. Goukowsky, *Appien: Histoire romaine*, vol. 14

(Paris, 2021), ccxxiii, 189 n. 473. For the Laberius anecdote, see Cic. *Fam.* 12.18.2; Macrob. *Sat.* 2.2.3, 2.10 (restoration). See also Meyer, *Caesars Monarchie*, 387; Holmes, *Roman Republic* 3:541; W. D. Lebek, "Moneymaking on the Roman Stage," in *Roman Theater and Society*, ed. W. J. Slater (Ann Arbor, 1996), 45–47; and D. Potter, *The Victor's Crown: A History of Ancient Sport from Homer to Byzantium* (London, 2011), 212–213.

33. Dio Cass. 43.22.3–23 (on the games), 43.24.1 (on the bloodshed).

34. Suet. *Iul.* 38.1, giving the figure of six thousand denarii, but see Dio Cass. 43.21.3; App. *B Civ.* 2.102, giving five thousand. For the version given in the text, rejecting Suetonius, see Woytek, Arma et Nummi, 183–184. For the gifts to the people on the grain rolls, see Dio Cass. 43.21.3 (specifying that it was this group only); Suet. *Iul.* 38.1 is less precise. On the numbers involved see Woytek, Arma et Nummi, 188.

35. Dio Cass. 43.25.1 (reform of juries), 43.25.3 (limitation on governors' terms), 43.47.2 (increase in the number of praetors and quaestors, wrongly placed after the return from Spain, since details of the prefects who were appointed at the beginning of the year follow), 43.47.3 (increase of the Senate to nine hundred). See also Suet. *Iul.* 41.1, 80.2 (non-Roman origin of some new senators); Cic. *Phil.* 11.12, 13.27; and R. Syme, *The Roman Revolution* (Oxford, 1939), 78–96. On the division between elected and appointed magistrates, see Suet. *Iul.* 41.2–3.

36. For free tenant farmers, see Suet. *Iul.* 42.1; for Corinth and Carthage, see Plut. *Caes.* 57.8; Dio 43.50.3–4. The alternative date of 44 for Carthage in App. *Pun.* 136 is certainly wrong and contradicted by his story in this context that Caesar proposed the refoundation after having a dream when he was encamped at Carthage. Diod. Sic. 37.27.1 ("about a hundred years") is simply imprecise. See also B. D. Shaw, "The Elder Pliny's African Geography," *Historia* 30 (1981): 438–440. For the program in general, see P. A. Brunt, *Italian Manpower, 225 BC–AD 14* (Oxford, 1971), 255–259, 319–324, 589 (Narbo, Arles and Baeterrae), 593–594 (Carthage, Clupeo, Curubis, Carpis, Neapolis, Hippo Diarrhytus), 597–598 (Salonae, Narona, and Epidaurum, founded as *municipia* by Caesar), 598 (Corinth), 600 (Lampsacus, Sinope).

37. Sall. *Cat.* 54.2, with E. Wistrand, *Caesar and Contemporary Roman Society* (Göteborg, 1978), 55–56.

38. Suet. *Iul.* 40; Dio Cass. 43.26; Goldsworthy, *Caesar*, 479; and D. Feeney, *Caesar's Calendar: Ancient Rome and the Beginning of History* (Berkeley and Los Angeles, 2007), 197–199.

39. Cic. *Marcell.* 7 (Fortune yields to Caesar), 8, 12, 15, 17, 19 (Caesar's mercy), 18 (Pompeian behavior), 2–23 (threats to Caesar's life), 23 (moral fiber), 25 (Caesar has done enough for glory or nature).

40. Cic. *Fam.* 6.6.10–11.

41. Quint. *Inst.* 11.178, on the charge.

42. Cic. *Lig.* 15, 29, 32, 37, for the points made in the text.

43. For the negotiation, see Cic. *Fam.* 6.14. For Caesar's reaction, see Plut. *Caes.* 39.6–7. For the publication of the speech, see p. 279 below.

44. On the Spanish campaign as background to the trial of Ligarius, see Cic. *Fam.* 6.14; for the management of policy, see Cicero's complaints at *Fam.* 9.19 (*reges*), with 9.17, 7.20.

45. The subsequent debate over Caesarion's paternity shows that, even if Cleopatra was calling him Caesarion at this point, Caesar never acknowledged the paternity: see Suet. *Iul.* 52.1–2. For the contemporary biography, see Nic. Dam. *Aug.* 16–20, with M. Toher, *Nicolaus of Damascus: The Life of Augustus and The Autobiography* (Cambridge, 2016), 192–203, esp. 195–196. For the significance of Caesar's decision, see R. Billows, *Julius Caesar: The Colossus of Rome* (London, 2009), 257.

46. The discussion here derives from F. M. Galassi and H. Asrafian, *Julius Caesar's Disease: A New Diagnosis* (London, 2016), 128–129, 149. For the date of Caesar's departure from Rome, November 5, see Raaflaub and Ramsay, "Chronology," 200.

47. [Caes.] *B Alex.* 48–64.

48. Dio Cass. 43. 29–30; see also Cic. *Fam.* 15.21 for Trebonius' return to Spain in December of 46.

49. For the number of Pompey's troops in January, see Cic. *Fam.* 6.18.2, repeating information from Caesar himself. The thirteen legions at Munda may reflect a later expansion of the army: see [Caes.] *B Hisp.* 7.4, which does give thirteen legions at the beginning of the campaign and at Munda (30.1, 31.11). See the discussion in N. Diouron, *Pseudo-César: Guerre d'Espagne* (Paris, 1999), xxxiii–iv, on the Pompeian army, and lxii–lxiv, for the Caesarians. For Afranius's veterans and African survivors, see Dio Cass. 40.30.4.

50. Dio Cass. 43.33.1 on the consular election *contra* Plut. *Caes.* 56.1; Eutr. 6.24.1. For Dio's priority, see M. Gelzer, *Caesar: Politician and Statesman*, trans. P. Needham (Oxford, 1969), 294 n. 5 and Pelling, *Plutarch*, Caesar, 416. For Balbus managing a reform of municipal government, see Cic. *Fam.* 6.18, with M. H. Crawford, *Roman Statutes*, vol. 1 (London, 1996), 361. On the assignment of the prefects, see Suet. *Iul.* 76; Dio 43.28, 48. The confusion about the number of prefects, six or eight, is presumably because two, separate from the others, were assigned the task of managing the *aerarium*: for this solution and the decision to use prefects in place of elected officials, see Meyer, *Caesars Monarchie,* 428–430. The letter to the prefect quoted is Cic. *Fam.* 13.7 (in the autumn of 45). On Balbus as a *rex*, see Cic. *Fam.* 9.19 (August, 46) and, on the *regia condicio* he sets on a dowry, Cic. *Att.* 12.12.1 (March, 45).

51. Suet. *Iul.* 56; Dio Cass. 43.32.1 (Caesar's men surprised), 43.32.6 (illness).

52. For Cassius, see Cic. *Fam.* 15.19.4. On the author's perspective, see N. Diouron, *Pseudo-César: Guerre d'Espagne*, lx–lix.

53. The passage quoted is [Caes.] *B Hisp.* 30–31. For Pompey and Caesar on the battlefield, see Dio Cass. 43.36.4, giving Caesar's statement as quoted here. For a more elaborate version, see App. *B Civ.* 2. 104; Plut. *Caes.* 56.4; the statement seems to be misinterpreted in Suet. *Iul.* 36.2. The author of the *Bellum Hispaniense* does not mention Caesar's personal role in the fighting.

54. Dio Cass. 43.38.2–3; Flor. 2.81.2–3, on Bogud's maneuver and Labienus's reaction; [Caes.] *B Hisp.* 31.4–5 has pressure from the Tenth Legion cause the move, and then the cavalry getting around the flank of the Pompeian army causing the collapse. See also Holmes, *Roman Republic* 3:549–551. For Labienus's body, see [Caes.] *B Hisp.* 31.9. For the wall of dead bodies, see [Caes.] *B Hisp.* 32.2.

55. [Caes.] *B Hisp.* 38–39 (death of Pompey), 41 (speech at Seville).

56. For Caesar and Spain in this period, see Dio Cass. 43.39, with A. T. Fear, *Rome and Baetica: Urbanization in Southern Spain, c. 50 BC–AD 150* (Oxford, 1996), 77–80, 117–119; and Brunt, *Italian Manpower*, 592. For Octavius, see Nic. Dam. *Aug.* 26, with Toher, *Nicolaus of Damascus,* 211.

57. Suet. *Iul.* 83.1; Nic. Dam. *Aug.* 30, with Toher, *Nicolaus of Damascus,* 103–104; and Holmes, *Roman Republic* 3:317–318.

CHAPTER 18

1. Cic. *Phil.* 2.34, on the meeting at Narbo.

2. See R. Cluett, "In Caesar's Wake: The Ideology of the Continuators," in *Caesar against Liberty: Perspectives on His Autocracy*, ed. F. Cairns and E. Fantham, Papers of the

Langford Latin Seminar 11 (Cambridge, 2003), 128, on the point emerging from the Caesarian continuators that all things descend from Caesar. See also H. Strasburger, *Caesar im Urteil seine Zeitgenossen*, 2nd ed (Darmstadt, 1968), 62–63 (= H. Strasburger, *Studien zur Alten Geschichte*, ed W. Schmitthenner and R. Zoepffel [Berlin, 1982], 402–403).

3. Sall. *Cat.* 54.2–6.

4. R. Laffont, *Tout César: discours, traités correspondance et commentaire* (Paris, 2020): 92-7, L'Anti-Caton. (Cicero as Pericles and Theramenes), fr. 1 (Cicero's cultural achievement), fr. 4 (Cato's drinking), fr. 7 (sex life), fr. 6 (disagreeable).

5. Caesar's response is first read through a work issued by Hirtius on May 11 (Cic. *Att.* 12.41.4). The letter of advice is mentioned in Cic. *Att.* 12. 51 on May 20; then in *Att.* 12.52 a day later; the role of Oppius and Balbus, the *amici* of *Att.* 13.1.3, appears therefore on May 24; at *Att.* 13.27.1, Cicero fears the letter will be seen as a "peace offering" in the wake of the *Cato*. See, further, Meyer, *Caesars Monarchie und das Principat des Pompejus: Innere Geschichte Roms von 66 bis 44 v. Chr.* (Stuttgart, 1919), 438.

6. For the Greek models, see Cic. *Att.* 12.40, 13.28.2–3 (May 26), with Meyer, *Caesars Monarchie*, 439–440; and Strasburger, *Caesar im Urteil seine Zeitgenossen*, 59 (= Strasburger, *Studien zur Alten Geschichte*, 399).

7. The Parthian war as an aspect of the letter is mentioned at Cic. *Att.* 13.27.1, and *Att.* 13.31.3 (28 May) mentions a letter of Caesar stating that he will not go to Parthia before "settling matters here," as Cicero says he had recommended; see also Cic. *Att* 12.5.1, on the difficulty Cicero experiences with the subject matter. For Caesar's comment on Sulla, see Suet. *Iul.* 77.

8. Cic. *Att.* 13.19.2 (response to the *pro Ligario* on June 24).

9. Caes. *B Gall.* 7.4, with p. 196 above.

10. Cic. *Q Fr.* 1.7; *Att.* 6.2.9.

11. Dio Cass. 43.45.1 (consulship for ten years and elections); Cic. *Deiot.* 33; Dio Cass. 43.45.4 (statue with the kings of Rome), 43.45.2; Cic. *Att.* 12.45.2, 48.1 (with Shackleton Bailey's note ad loc. in *CLA*); Cic. *Att.* 13.28.3 (for the events of the Parilia), 13.44 (on the procession at the *ludi Victoriae*, July 28?, 45), with Shackleton Bailey, *CLA*, ad loc. For the statues, see S. Weinstock, *Divus Julius* (Oxford, 1971), 185–186. For the inscription, see Weinstock, *Divus Julius*, 186–188.

12. Dio Cass. 43.42.1 (Spanish triumph in bad taste); Suet. *Iul.* 78 (Pontius).

13. G. Sumi, *Ceremony and Power: Performing Politics in Rome between Republic and Empire* (Ann Arbor, 2005), 64–65.

14. Dio Cass. 43.42.2, with Sumi, *Ceremony and Power*, 65, on the date (triumphs for Fabius and Pedius); on the large staff and lack of opportunities for newcomers, see Cic. *Fam.* 6.19.

15. Dio Cass. 43.43.1, 44.4.2 (triumphal attire), 44.2 (imperator), 43.43.2 (king of Alba) with D. Potter, "Rome and Bovillae During the Early Decades of the Empire," in P. Hatlie ed. *Ancient Bovillae: History, Art and Archaeology of a Lost City in the Roman Hinterland* (Ann Arbor, 2025): 25; Dio 44.4.3 (returning from the *feriae Latiniae* on horseback), 43.44.1 (liberator), 43.44.2 (imperator). On Caesar's rejection of privileges Dio Cass. 43.46.1 as overtly monarchical.

16. Dio Cass. 44.5.2 (Senate House).

17. Cic. *Att.* 13.52; see also *Deiot.* 21. On emetic theory, see Celsus, *Med.* 1.3.19–23.

18. Cic. *Deiot.* 9–12 (people who followed Pompey), 14 (fights with Caesar at Zela), 17 (plot to kill Caesar), 33 (criticism of Caesar); *Fam.* 9.12 (for the date). See, in general,

H. C. Gotoff, *Cicero's Caesarian Speeches: A Stylistic Commentary* (Chapel Hill, 1993), xvii–xl.

19. Cic. *Att.* 14.1.2, quoting Matius, who had said he knew he was hated if he had been keeping Cicero waiting. See also Cic. *Fam.* 6.13.3, 14.2, with Strasburger, *Caesar im Urteil seine Zeitgenossen*, 57 (= Strasburger, *Studien zur Alten Geschichte*, 397).

20. Suet. *Iul.* 78.1; Plut. *Caes.* 60; Dio Cass. 44.8.1–4; App. *B Civ.* 2.107, with T. R. Holmes, *The Roman Republic and the Founder of Empire*, vol. 3 (Oxford, 1923), 333–334; A. Goldsworthy, *Caesar: Life of a Colossus* (New Haven, 2006), 502; and J. M. Madsen, "Between Dynast and Legitimate Monarch: Imperial Reflections of Julius Caesar," in *Caesar's Past and Posterity's Caesar*, ed. T. A. Hass and R. Raja (Tunhout, 2021), 124–125 for the implication of Dio's handling of the business. There is a significant alternative version in Nic. Dam. *Aug.* 78–79, which places this incident after the Lupercalia and gives Antony a significant role, leading the senatorial embassy. My suspicion is that this version was devised to cast blame on Antony for the assassination, but see otherwise W. J. Tatum, *A Noble Roman: Mark Antony, Civil War and the Collapse of the Roman Republic* (Oxford, 2024), 110.

21. Cic. *Fam.* 7.30. 1–2 (quoted), 7.30.1 (on the consulship of Caninius, later repeated in SHA *Tyr. Trig.* 8.2); Macrob. *Sat.* 2.2.6, 7.3.10. See also Suet. *Iul.* 80.2, reporting negative comments about the short consulship of Fabius, which suggests that Cicero's view was widespread. See also Plut. *Caes.* 58.3. For another Ciceronian joke about Caninius, see Macrob. *Sat.* 2.2.6, 7.3.10. See also Suet. *Iul.* 76.2; for Caesar's letter, see Suet. *Iul.* 77.

22. Dio Cass. 44.9.2–10.4; Suet. *Iul.* 79, with Holmes, *Roman Republic* 3:334; and Sumi, *Ceremony and Power*, 69.

23. For *parens patriae*, see Cic. *Phil.* 13.33; Dio Cass. 44.4.4; *RRC* 480/19–20. For the portrait coins from the mint at Rome, see *RRC* 480/2a–c, 3, 4, 5a–b, with Caesar as dictator for the fourth time, giving a date in January; *RRC* 480/6–16, with *dictator(i) (in) perpetuo*, the title assumed sometime between January 26 and February 15; *RRC* 480/17–18, with the legend *Caesar imperator*. See also *RRC* 481, an *aureus* with a bust of Venus. For the renaming of Quintilis as Julius, see Suet. *Iul.* 76.1; App. *B Civ.* 2.106; Dio Cass. 44.5.2; Censorinus, *DN* 22.16; Macrob. *Sat.* 1.12.34. For Caesar as sole censor, see Dio Cass. 44.5.3; Vell. Pat. 2.68.4; and Holmes, *Roman Republic*, 3:332n2. For the oath to uphold Caesar's decisions, see App. *B Civ.* 2.106. For the oath to protect his life, see Suet. *Iul.* 84.2, 86.1; Dio Cass. 44.7.4; App. *B Civ.* 2.124, 145. For Caesar's deification, see Cic. *Phil.* 2.110, 13.41; Dio Cass. 44.6.4. For honors as a feature of the conspiracy, see Cic. *Fam.* 11.28; Nic. Dam. *Aug.* 59, 67, 70, 80; Plut. *Caes.* 57.2–4; Dio Cass. 44.7.3–4.

24. Number of legions: see P. A. Brunt, *Italian Manpower, 225 BC–14 AD* (Oxford, 1971), 480. Plan of campaign: see Suet. *Iul.* 44; and Goldsworthy, *Caesar*, 491, rightly noting that other versions of the plan were fantasies.

25. Nic. Dam. *Aug.* 75 as translated in M. Toher, *Nicolaus of Damascus: The Life of Augustus and The Autobiography* (Cambridge, 2016). On the point of the business, I am in agreement with Goldsworthy, *Caesar*, 499–500.

26. Plut. *Brut.* 10–12. See also Cic. *Off.* 2.23 (Caesar's tyranny), 42 (leadership), 78 (legislation), 3.19, 90 (murdering a tyrant). See also G. Woolf, *Et Tu, Brute? A Short History of Political Murder* (London, 2007), 45–7).

27. For graffiti concerning Brutus, see Suet. *Iul.* 80. For other comments urging Brutus to live up to his name, see Plut. *Brut.* 9.5–6; *Caes.* 62.7; App. *B Civ.* 2.112. For the accusation that Antony and Dolabella were plotting, see Plut. *Brut.* 8.2; *Caes.* 62.10. Suspicion

of Dolabella is implied at Cic. *Att.* 13.52. For Caesar's assumption of indispensability and dismissal of his bodyguard, see Suet. *Iul.* 86.

28. For the Sibylline oracle, see Suet. *Iul.* 79; App. *B Civ* 2.110. For the date at which the conspiracy took shape, see App. *B Civ.* 2.111; it is implied in Plut. *Caes.* 62, which places it after the Lupercalia, and is stated explicitly by Nic. Dam. *Aug.* 75.

29. Suet. *Iul.* 87 (dinner with Lepidus).

30. Plut. *Caes.* 63; Suet. *Iul.* 81 (portents); Plut. *Caes.* 64.1; Suet. *Iul.* 81 (role of Decimus Brutus).

31. See Dio Cass. 44.19.1 for Trebonius and Antony. Plut. *Caes.* 66.4 has Decimus Brutus in the role but Trebonius at *Brutus* 17.1; see also App. *B Civ.* 2.117; Cic. *Fam.* 10.28.

32. Suet. *Iul.* 82; Plut. *Caes.* 66.5–13; *Brut.* 4–7, with Woolf, *Et Tu, Brute*, 10–14.

CHAPTER 19

1. G. Sumi, *Ceremony and Power: Performing Politics in Rome between Republic and Empire* (Ann Arbor, 2005), 97–112.

2. For the period after Caesar's death see Sumi, *Ceremony and Power*, 125–58; R.Syme, *The Roman Revolution* (Oxford, 1939): 112–22; for the meeting at Antium see Cic. *Att.* 15.11).

3. Cic. *Fam.* 11.28 (Matius to Caesar on the *ludi Victoriae Caesaris*), with Sumi, *Ceremony and Power*, 150–153.

4. For Lucan, see the convenient summary in C. Walde, "Caesar, Lucan's *Bellum Civile*, and Their Reception," in *Julius Caesar in Western Culture*, ed. M. Wyke (Oxford, 2006), 45–61. For Suetonius, see G. W. Bowersock, "Suetonius and Trajan," in *Hommages à Marcel Renard*, vol. 1., ed. J. Bibauw, Collection Latomus 101 (Brussels, 1969), 119–125 (showing that Trajan's attitude toward Caesar likely influenced his decision). For the first Julio-Claudian Caesar, see B. England, "Caesar's Place in the Course of Tiberian Historiography," in *Caesar's Past and Posterity's Caesar*, ed. T. A. Hass and R. Raja (Turnhout, 2021), 81–93. For the later tradition, see J. M. Madsen, "Between Dynast and Legitimate Monarch: Imperial Reflections of Julius Caesar," in Hass and Raja, *Caesar's Past and Posterity's Caesar*, 111–126.

5. Tac. *Ann.* 12.60.4.

6. Suet. *Claud.* 10.4; Joseph. *AJ* 19.1.14 does say the people were happy to recover their democracy and that the guard imposed Claudius.

7. Dante, *Inferno*, canto 34.

8. 2.1.175, 182–183; 2.2.10–11, 34–35. See further M. Dimitrova, *Julius Caesar's Self-Created Image and Its Dramatic Afterlife* (London, 2018), 115–153.

9. R. Melrose, "Obama/Trump/Caesar," *Medium* (web site), June 14, 2017 (https://medium.com/@robmelrose/obama-trump-caesar-f81bf985ac67); and M. Paulson and S. Deb, "How Outrage Grew over a Shakespearian Depiction of Trump," *New York Times*, June 12, 2017.

10. J. Osborne, "St. Peter's Needle and the Ashes of Julius Caesar: Invoking Rome's Imperial History at the Papal Court, ca. 1100–1300," in Wyke, *Julius Caesar*, 95–110 (medieval Rome).

11. T. Biskup, "Ancient Contemporary History and Enlightened Philosophy of History: Caesar and Voltaire as Models for Frederick the Great' Historiography," in Hass and Raja, *Caesar's Past and Posterity's Caesar*, 183–198. For Napoleon, see Cl. Nicolet. "Caesar and the Two Napoleons," in *A Companion to Julius Caesar*, ed. M. T. Griffin

(Oxford, 2009), 410–414; and N. Bonaparte, *Napoleon's Commentaries on the Wars of Julius Caesar*, trans. R. A. Maguire (Barnsley, 2018).

12. Nicolet, "Caesar and the Two Napoleons," 414–417; and L. Canfora, "Caesar for Communists and Fascists," in Griffin, *Companion to Julius Caesar*, 432.

13. Canfora, "Caesar for Communists and Fascists," 432–434.

14. Canfora, "Caesar for Communists and Fascists," 436–437 (Mussolini); M. Wyke, "Caesar, Cinema and National Identity," in Wyke, *Julius Caesar*, 170–189 (Italian film); G. Pucci, "Caesar the Foe: Roman Conquest and National Resistance in French Popular Culture," in Wyke, *Julius Caesar*, 190–201; M. Wyke, *Caesar in the USA* (Berkeley and Los Angeles, 2012), 167–202 (Caesar the villain); and M. Wyke, "Lessons in History: Bernard Shaw's Discomforting Caesar," in Hass and Raja, *Caesar's Past and Posterity's Caesar*, 199–212.

Bibliography

Alexander, M. C. *Trials in the Late Roman Republic: 149 to 50 BC*. Toronto, 1990.

Allen, W. "The British Epics of Quintus and Marcus Cicero." *TAPA* 86 (1955): 143–159.

Allen-Hornblower, E. "Beasts and Barbarians in Caesar's *Bellum Gallicum* 6.21–8." *CQ* 64 (2014): 682–693.

Ando, C. "Aliens, Ambassadors and the Integrity of Empire." *Law and History Review* 26 (2008): 491–515.

Austin, R. G. *M. Tullii Ciceronis Pro M. Caelio oratio*. 3rd ed. Oxford, 1959.

Avery, H. C. "A Lost Episode in Caesar's Civil War." *Hermes* 121 (1993): 452–469.

Badian, E. "From the Iulii to Caesar." In *A Companion to Julius Caesar*, edited by M. T. Griffin. Oxford, 2007.

Bagnall, R., and B. W. Frier. *The Demography of Roman Egypt*. Cambridge, 1994.

Balsdon, J. P. V. D. *Julius Caesar and Rome*. London, 1967.

Batstone, W. W., and C. Damon. *Caesar's Civil War*. Oxford, 2006.

Barlow, J. "Noble Gauls and Their Other in Caesar's Propaganda." In *Julius Caesar as Artful Reporter: The War Commentaries as Political Instruments*, edited by K. Welch and A. Powell. London, 1988.

Barry, D. H. "Clodius, Milo and the Battle of Bovillae," in *Ancient Bovillae: History, Art and Archaeology of a Lost City in the Roman Hinterland*, edited by P. Hatlie. AnnArbor, 2025.

Beard, M. *The Roman Triumph*. Cambridge, MA, 2007.

Beness, J. L., and T. W. Hillard. "The Death of Lucius Equitius on 10 December 100 B.C." *CQ* 40 (1990): 269–272.

Bigloni, F. *The War Economy of the Roman Republic (406–100 BCE) Mnemosyne Supplement* 487. Leiden, 2025.

Billows, R. *Julius Caesar: The Colossus of Rome*. London, 2009.

Biskup, T. "Ancient Contemporary History and Enlightened Philosophy of History: Caesar and Voltaire as Models for Frederick the Great's Historiography." In *Caesar's Past and Posterity's Caesar*, edited by T. A. Hass and R. Raja, 183–198. Turnhout, 2021.

Bonaparte, N. *Napoleon's Commentaries on the Wars of Julius Caesar*. Translated by R. A. Maguire. Barnsley, 2018.

Bonner, S. *Education in Ancient Rome: From the Elder Cato to the Younger Pliny*. 5th ed. Abingdon, 2012.

Bouvet, A. *Pseudo-César: Guerre d'Afrique*. Paris, 2002.

Bowersock, G. W. "Suetonius and Trajan." In *Hommages à Marcel Renard*, vol. 1, ed. J. Bibauw, 119–125. Collection Latomus 101. Brussels, 1969.

Bradley, K. *Slavery and Society at Rome*. Cambridge, UK. 1995.

Brunt, P. A. *Italian Manpower, 225 BC–AD 14*. Oxford, 1971.

Brunt, P. A. "Cicero's *Officium* in the Civil War." *JRS* 76 (1986): 12–32.

Brunt, P. A. *The Fall of the Roman Republic and Related Essays*. Oxford, 1988.

Brunt, P. A. *Roman Imperial Themes*. Oxford, 1990.

Canfora, L. *Julius Caesar: The Life and Times of the People's Dictator*. Translated by M. Hill and K. Windel. Berkeley and Los Angeles, 2007.

Canfora, L. "Caesar for Communists and Fascists." In *A Companion to Julius Caesar*, edited by M. T. Griffin, 431–440. Oxford, 2009.

Carandini, A., and P. Carafa, eds. *The Atlas of Ancient Rome: Biography and Portraits of the City*. Translated by A. C. Halaveis. Princeton, 2017.

Carbone, L.F. "Financing Sulla's Wars." In *Connected Histories of Roman Civil Wars (88-30 BCE)*, edited by D.G. Domíguez, J.G. González, and F. Santangelo eds, 75–120. Berlin, 2024.

Carroll, M., *Infancy and Earliest Childhood in the Roman World: "A Fragment of Time."* Oxford, 2015.

Carter, J. M. *Julius Caesar:* The Civil War *Books I and II*. Warminster, 1990.

Cavelli, L. *Il Tesoro di Cipro: Clodio, Catone e la Conquista romana dell'isola*. Venice, 2020.

Cercere, M.G.G. "Inscriptions from the Area of Bovillae," in *Ancient Bovillae: History, Art and Archaeology of a Lost City on the Roman Hinterland*, edited by P. Hatlie, 130–49. Ann Arbor, 2025.

Champlin, E. J. *Final Judgements: Duty and Emotion in Roman Wills, 200 B.C–A.D. 250*. Berkeley and Los Angeles, 1991.

Cluett, R. "In Caesar's Wake: the Ideology of the Continuators." In *Caesar against Liberty?· Perspectives on his Autocracy*, edited by F. Cairns and E. Fantham, 118–131. Papers of the Langford Latin Seminar 11. Cambridge, 2003.

Cooley, A. E., and M. G. L. Cooley. *Pompeii and Herculaneum*. 2nd ed. Cambridge, 2018.

Cornwell, H. "Negotiation as a Tool for Legitimacy in the Roman Civil War of 49–48 BCE: A New Policy for Achieving Victory." In *New Perspectives on the Roman Civil Wars of 49-30 BCE*, edited by R. Westall and H. Cornwell, 13–31. London, 2024.

Courtney, E. *The Fragmentary Latin Poets*. Oxford, 1993.

Crawford, M. H. *Roman Laws and Statues*. Bulletin of the Institute of Classical Studies Supplement 64. London, 1996.

Creer, T. "Ethnography in Caesar's Gallic War and Its Implications for Composition." *CQ* 69 (2019): 246–263.

Crissanthos, S. G. "Caesar and the Mutiny of 47 BC." *JRS* 91 (2001): 63–75.

Crissanthos, S. G. *The Year of Julius and Caesar*. Baltimore, 2019.

Cuff, P. J. "The Terminal Date of Caesar's Command." *Historia* 7 (1958): 445–471.

Cunliffe, B. *The Celtic World*. New York, 1979.

Damon, C. *Studies in the Text of Caesar's* Bellum Civile. Oxford, 2015.

Debatty, B. "Les organs du politique chez les Sénons." In *Les Sénons: Archéologie et histoire d'un peuple gaulois*, edited by L. Baray, 333–334. Gand, 2018.

Dimitrova, M. *Julius Caesar's Self-Created Image and Its Dramatic Afterlife*. London, 2018.

Diouron, N. *Pseudo-César: Guerre d'Espagne*. Paris, 1999.

D.G. Domínguez, "Pain and Gain. Violence against Provincial Cities in the Age of Civil War," in *Connected Histories of the Roman Civil Wars (88-30 BCE)* edited by D.G. Garcia Domínguez, J. García González, and F. Santangelo, 121–42. Berlin/Boston, 2024.

Donahue, J. F. "Sieges, Deception and Bioterrorism: Logistics and Strategy of Food and Drink during the Republic." In *Brill's Companion to Diet and Logistics in Greek and Roman Warfare*, edited by J. F. Donahue and L. L. Brice, 287–310. Leiden, 2023.

Dunham, S. B. "Caesar's Perception of Iron Age Gallic Social Structures." In *The Celtic World*, vol. 3, *Celtic History*, edited by R. Karl and D. Stifter, 161–172. Critical Concepts in Historical Studies. London, 2007.

Edwards, M. *A Coin for the Ferryman.* Las Vegas, 2022.

Ernout, A., and A. Meillet. *Dictionnaire étymologique de la langue latine.* 4th ed. Paris, 2001.

Erskine, A. *Troy between Greece and Rome: Local Tradition and Imperial Power.* Oxford, 2001.

Evans, R. *Questioning Reputations: Essays on Nine Roman Republican Politicians.* Pretoria, 2003.

Evans, R. "The Sulpician Law on Debt: Implications for the Political Elite and Broader Ramifications." *Acta Classica* 50 (2007): 81–94.

Fear, A. T. *Rome and Baetica: Urbanization in Southern Spain, c. 50 BC–AD 150.* Oxford, 1996.

Feeney, D. *Caesar's Calendar: Ancient Time and the Beginning of History.* Berkeley and Los Angeles, 2007.

Fezzi, L. *Crossing the Rubicon.* Translated by R. Dixon. New Haven, 2019.

Fichtl, S. "Des campagnes gauloises largement hiérarchisées." In *Les Sénons. Archéologie et histoire d'un peuple gaulois,* edited by L. Baray, 109–117. Gand, 2018.

Fitzpatrick, A. P. "Caesar's Landing Sites in Britain and Gaul in 55 and 54 BC: Critical Places, Natural Places." In *Julius Caesar's Battle for Gaul: New Archaeological Perspectives,* edited by A. P. Fitzpatrick and C. Haselgrove, 135–158. Oxford, 2019.

Flower, H. *The Dancing Lares and the Serpent in the Garden: Religion at the Roman Street Corner.* Princeton, 2017.

Fraser, P. M. *Ptolemaic Alexandria.* Oxford, 1972.

Gaertner, J. F., and B. C. Hausburg. *Caesar and the* Bellum Alexandrinum: *An Analysis of Style, Narrative Technique, and the Reception of Greek Historiography.* Göttingen, 2013.

Galassi, F. M., and H. Asrafian. *Julius Caesar's Disease: A New Diagnosis.* London, 2016.

Garcea, A. *Caesar's* De Analogia: *Edition, Translation, and Commentary.* Oxford, 2012.

Garcea, A. *Tout César: discours, rtaites, corespondance et commentaires.* Paris, 2020.

Gaughan, J. E. *Murder Was Not a Crime: Homicide and Power in the Roman Republic.* Austin, 2010.

Gelzer, M. *Caesar: Politician and Statesman.* Translated by P. Needham. Oxford, 1969.

Girardet, K. M. "*Imperia* und *Provinciae* des Pompeius, 82 bis 48 v. Chr." *Chiron* 31 (2001): 153–209.

Girardet, K. M. *Januar 49 v. Chr.: Caesars Militärputsch; Vorgeschichte, Rechtslage, politische Aspekte.* Bonn, 2017.

Goldsworthy, A. *The Roman Army at War, 100 BC–AD 200.* Oxford, 1996.

Goldsworthy, A. *Caesar: Life of a Colossus.* New Haven, 2006.

Goldsworthy, A. *Antony and Cleopatra.* New Haven, 2010.

Gotoff, H. C. *Cicero's Caesarian Speeches: A Stylistic Commentary.* Chapel Hill, 1993.

Gotter, U. "Writing Down Uncivil Wars: Or: How Roman Generals Justified Themselves in the Wake of Civic Bloodshed." In *A Culture of Civil War?* Bellum civile *and Political Communication in Late Republican Rome,* edited by H. Börm, U. Gotter, and W. Havener, 177–196. Stuttgart, 2023.

Goukowsky, P., ed. *Appien: Histoire romaine.* 13 vols. Paris, 2008.

Grillo, L. *The Art of Caesar's* Bellum Civile: *Literature, Ideology and Community.* Cambridge, 2012.

Grillo, L. *Cicero's* De provinciis consularibus oratio. Oxford, 2015.

Gruen, E. *The Last Generation of the Roman Republic.* Berkeley and Los Angeles, 1974.

Günther, L.-M. "Caesar und die Seeräuber—Eine Quellenanalyse." *Chiron* 29 (1999): 321–338.

Hanson, A. E. "The Roman Family." In *Life, Death, and Entertainment in the Roman Empire,* new and expanded edition, ed. D. Potter and D. J. Mattingly, 19–66. Ann Arbor, 2010.

Harmand, J. *L'armée et le soldat à Rome de 107 à 50 avant notre ère*. Paris, 1967.

Hartman, B. *The Scribes of Rome: A Cultural and Social History of the* Scribae. Cambridge, 2020.

Hartnett, J. *The Roman Street: Urban Life and Society in Pompeii, Herculaneum and Rome* Cambridge, 2017.

Haselgrove, C. "The Development of Iron Age Coinage in Belgic Gaul." *Num. Chron.* 159 (1999): 134–149.

Heinen, H. "Cäsar und Kaesarion." *Historia* 18 (1969): 181–203.

Hinard, F. *Les proscriptions de la Rome républicaine*. Paris, 1985.

Hingley, R. *Conquering the Ocean*. Oxford, 2022.

Holmes, T. R., ed. *C. Julii Caesaris Commentarii rerum in Gallia gestarum VII; A. Hirti Commentarius VIII*. Oxford, 1914.

Holmes, T. R. *The Roman Republic and the Founder of Empire*. 3 vols. Oxford, 1923.

Hopkins, K. "Novel Evidence for Roman Slavery." In *Life, Death, and Entertainment in the Roman Empire*, new and expanded edition, edited by D. Potter and D. J. Mattingly, 110–134. Ann Arbor, 2010.

Janko, R., "New Fragments of Epicurus, Metrodorus, Demetrius Laco, the *Carmen de Bello Actiaco* and Other Texts in Oxonian Disegni of 1788–1792." *Cronache Ercolanesi* 38 (2008): 5–95.

Kallet-Marx, R., *Hegemony to Empire: The Development of the Roman* Imperium *in the East from 148 to 62 B.C.* Berkeley, 1995.

Kantor, G. "Roman Treaty with Lycia (SEG LV 1452) and the Date of Caesar's Third Dictatorship." *ZPE* 190 (2014): 135–136.

Kay, P. *Rome's Economic Revolution*. Oxford, 2014.

Krebs, C. B. "Caesar, Lucretius and the Dates of *De rerum natura* and the *Commentaries*." *CQ* 63 (2013): 772–779.

Krebs, C. B. *Caesar* Bellum Gallicum *Book 7*. Cambridge, 2023.

La Salvia, V., and M. Moderato. "Ghost Walls and Vanishing Towns: The Case of Caesar's Siege of Corfinium between Historical Sources and Archaeological-Topographical Data." In *New Perspectives on the Roman Civil Wars of 49–30 BCE*, edited by R. Westall and H. Cornwell, 127–140. London, 2024.

Lebek, W. D. "Moneymaking on the Roman Stage." In *Roman Theater and Society*, edited by W. J. Slater, 29–48. Ann Arbor, 1996.

Le Bohec, Y. *César, chef de guerre: Stratégie et tactique de la République romaine*. Monaco, 2001.

Le Bohec, Y. "César et l'économie pendant la guerre des Gaules." In *Krieg—Gesellschaft— Institutionen: Beitrage zur einer vergleichenden Kriegsgeschichte*, edited by B. Meßner, O. Schmitt, and M. Somme, 317–333. Berlin, 2005.

Le Bohec, Y. "Le clergé celtique et la guerre des Gaules historiographie et politique." *Latomus* 64 (2005): 871–881.

Le Bohec, Y. *Peuples et fédérations en Gaule (58–51 avant J.-C.): Lecture socio-juridique du Bellum Gallicum; De l'archéologie à l'histoire*. Paris, 2009. Lendon, J. E., "The Rhetoric of Combat: Greek Military Theory and Roman Culture in Julius Caesar's Battle Descriptions," *CA* 18 (1999): 273–329.

Lintott, A. *Cicero as Evidence: A Historian's Companion*. Oxford, 2008.

Macfarlane, R. "*Ab inimicis incitatus*: On Dating the Composition of Caesar's *Bellum Civile*." *Syllecta Classica* 7 (1996): 107–132.

MacMullen, R. "Personal Power in the Roman Empire." *AJPhil.* 107 (1986): 512–524.

Madsen, J. M. "Between Dynast and Legitimate Monarch: Imperial Reflections of Julius Caesar." In *Caesar's Past and Posterity's Caesar*, edited by T. A. Hass and R. Raja, 111–126. Turnhout, 2021.

Manuwald, G. *Cicero, Agrarian Speeches: Introduction, Text, Translation, and Commentary*. Oxford, 2018.

Marshall, B. A. *A Historical Commentary on Asconius*. Columbia, 1985.

Mattingly, D. J. *Between Sahara and Sea: Africa in the Roman Empire*. Ann Arbor, 2023.

McGing, B. *The Foreign Policy of Mithridates VI Eupator, King of Pontus*. Leiden, 1986.

Meier, C. *Caesar: A Biography*. Translated by D. McLintock. New York, 1982.

Melrose, R. "Obama/Trump/Caesar." *Medium* (web site), June 14, 2017. https://medium. com/@robmelrose/obama-trump-caesar-f81bf985ac67.

Meyer, E. *Caesars Monarchie und das Principat des Pompejus: Innere Geschichte Roms von 66 bis 44 v. Chr*. Stuttgart, 1919.

Mignone, L. *The Republican Aventine and Rome's Social Order*. Ann Arbor, 2016.

Millar, F. *The Crowd in Rome in the Late Republic*. Ann Arbor 1998.

Mitchell, S. "The Treaty Between Rome and Lycia of 46 BC (MS 2070)." In *Papyri Graecae Schøyen*, edited by M. Pintaudi, 163–243. Papyrologica Florentina 35. Florence, 2005.

Moesch, V. *La Villa dei Papiri*. Naples, 2009.

Mommsen, Th. *Römische Staatsrecht* I³ Berlin, 1871.

Moorstein-Marx, R. *Julius Caesar and the Roman People*. Cambridge, 2021.

Morgan, J. D. "PalaePharsalus—The Battle and Town." *AJArch*. 87 (1981): 23–54.

Morrell, K. "Caesar, Cato and the Germani." *Antichthon* 49 (2015): 73–93.

Morrell, K. *Pompey, Cato, and the Governance of the Roman Empire*. Oxford, 2017.

Morton, P. *Slavery and Rebellion in Second-Century BC Sicily: From Bellum Servile to Sicilia Capta*. Edinburgh, 2024.

Mouritson, H. *The Freedman in the Roman World*. Cambridge, 2011.

Mouritson, H. *The Roman Elite and the End of the Republic: The Boni, the Nobles and Cicero* Cambridge, 2024.

Mullen, A. *Southern Gaul and the Mediterranean: Multilingualism and Multiple Identities in the Iron Age and Roman Periods*. Cambridge, 2013.

Münzer, F. "Oppius." *RE* 18.1: 729–736

Münzer, F. *Roman Aristocratic Parties and Families*. Translated by Th. Ridely. Baltimore, 1999.

Nicolet, Cl. *The World of the Citizen in Republican Rome*. Translated by P. S. Falla. Berkeley, 1988.

Nicolet, Cl. "Caesar and the Two Napoleons." In *A Companion to Julius Caesar*, edited by M. T. Griffin, 410–417. Oxford, 2009.

Nieto-Pelletier, S., A. Lefort, and D. B. Foucray. "Les monnaies celtiques et les rouelles: Du sanctuaire celtique et gallo-romain du site des "Grèves" à la Villeneuve-au-Châtelot (10)." In *Les Sénons: Archéologie et histoire d'un peuple gaulois*, edited by L. Baray, 172–193. Gand, 2018.

Nouvel, P. "Historiographie du monnayage sénon." In *Les Sénons: Archéologie et histoire d'un people gaulois*, edited by L. Baray, 167–169. Gand, 2018.

Osborne, J. "St. Peter's Needle and the Ashes of Julius Caesar: Invoking Rome's Imperial History at the Papal Court, ca. 1100–1300." In *Julius Caesar in Western Culture*, edited by M. Wyke, 95–110. Oxford, 2006.

Osgood, J. "Caesar and Nicomedes." *CQ* 58 (2008): 687–691.

Osgood, J. "The Pen and the Sword: Writing and Conquest in Caesar's Gaul." *Cl. Ant.* 28 (2009): 328–358.

Osgood, J. "Caesar and the Pirates: Or How to Make (and Break) an Ancient Life." *GRBS* 57 (2010): 319–336.

Osgood, J. *Turia: A Roman Woman's Civil War.* Oxford, 2014.

Ottmer, H. M. *Die Rubikon-Legende: Untersuchungen zu Caesar and Pompeius' Strategie vor und nach Ausbruch des Bürgerkreiges.* Boppard am Rhein, 1979.

Paulson, M., and S. Deb. "How Outrage Grew over a Shakespearian Depiction of Trump." *New York Times,* June 12, 2017.

Pelling, C. B. R. "Caesar's Battle-Descriptions and the Defeat of Ariovistus." *Latomus* 40.4 (1981): 751–766.

Pelling, C. B. R. *Plutarch, Caesar.* Oxford, 2011.

Peer, A. *Julius Caesar's* Bellum Civile *and the Composition of a New Reality.* Abingdon, 2015.

Potter, D. "Caesar and the Helvetians." In *New Perspectives on Ancient Warfare*, edited by G. Fagan and M. Trundle. Leiden, 2010.

Potter, D. *The Victor's Crown: A History of Ancient Sport from Homer to Byzantium.* London, 2011.

Potter, D. "Measuring the Power of the Roman Empire." In *East and West in the Roman Empire of the Fourth Century: An End to Unity?*, edited by R. Dijkstra, S. Van Poppel, and D. Slootjes, 26–48. Leiden, 2015.

Potter, D. *The Origin of Empire.* London, 2019.

Potter, D. "Caesar in the *Bellum Gallicum*." In *People and Institutions in the Roman Empire: Essays in Memory of Garrett G. Fagan,* edited by A. F. Gatzke, L. L. Brice, and M. Trundle, 33–43. Leiden, 2020.

Potter, D. "Dio and Pompey: Explaining the Failure of the Republic." In *The Intellectual Climate of Cassius Dio,* edited by A. Kemezis, C. Bailey, and B. Poletti, 35–58. Leiden, 2022.

Potter, D. "Rome and Bovillae through the Early Decades of the Empire," in *Ancient Bovillae: History, Art and Archaeology of a Laost City on the Roman Hinterland,* edited by P. Hatlie, 13–34. Ann Arbor, 2025.

Poux, M., and M. Demierre. *Le sanctuaire de Corent (Puy-de-Dôme, Auvergene).* Paris, 2015.

Powell, A. "Julius Caesar and the Presentation of Massacre." In *Julius Caesar as Artful Reporter: The War Commentaries as Political Instruments,* edited by K. Welch and A. Powell, 111–137. London, 1998.

Pucci, G. "Caesar the Foe: Roman Conquest and National Resistance in French Popular Culture." In *Julius Caesar in Western Culture,* edited by M. Wyke, 190–201. Oxford, 2006.

Raaflaub, K. A., and J. T. Ramsay. "The Chronology of Caesar's Campaigns." Web Essay BB in *The Landmark Julius Caesar,* edited and translated by K. A. Raaflaub. New York, 2017. https://thelandmarkcaesar.com/LandmarkCaesarWebEssays_5Jan2018.pdf.

Raja, R., and J. Rüpke. "Creating Memories in and of Urban Rome: The Forum Iulium." In *Caesar's Past and Posterity's Caesar,* edited by T. A, Hass and R. Raja, 53–66. Turnhout, 2021.

Ralston, I. "The Gauls on the Eve of the Roman Conquest." In *Julius Caesar's Battle for Gaul: New Archaeological Perspectives,* edited by A. P. Fitzpatrick and C. Haselgrove, 19–47. Oxford, 2019.

Rambaud, M. *L'art de la deformation historique dans les Commentaires de César.* Paris, 1966.

Ramsey, J. T. "How and Why Was Pompey Made Sole Consul in 52 BC?" *Historia* 65 (2016): 298–324.

Rathbone, D. W. "The Control and Exploitation of *ager publicus* in Italy under the Roman Republic." In *Tâches publiques et enterprise privée dans le monde romain*, edited by J.-J. Aubert, 135–178. Geneva, 2003.

Rawson, E. *Cicero: A Portrait*. Bristol, 1975.

Reynolds, J. "Cyrenaica, Pompey and Cn. Cornelius Lentulus Marcellinus." *JRS* 52 (1962): 97–103.

Rich, J. "Lex Licinia, Lex Sempronia, B. G. Niebuhr and the Limitation of Landholding in the Roman Republic." In *People, Land and Politics: Demographic Developments and the Transformation of Roman Italy, 300 BC–AD 14*, edited by L. de Light and S. Northwood, 519–572. Leiden, 2008.

Richardot, Ph. *Les erreurs stratégiques des Gaulois face à César*. Paris, 2006.

Richlin, A. *Slave Theater in the Roman Republic: Plautus and Popular Comedy*. Cambridge, 2017.

Riggsby, A. M. *Caesar in Gaul and Rome: War in Words*. Austin, 2006.

Roller, D. *Cleopatra: A Biography*. Oxford, 2010.

Roselaar, S. T. *Public Land in the Roman Republic: A Societal and Economic History of Ager Publicus in Italy, 396–89 BC*. Oxford, 2010.

Rosenblitt, J. A. *Rome after Sulla*. London, 2019.

Rosillo-López, C. *Public Opinion and Politics in the Late Roman Republic*. Cambridge, 2017.

Rosillo-López, C. "Can a Dictator Reform an Electoral System?" In *Sulla: Politics and Reception*, edited by A. Eckert ad A. Thein, 55–70. Berlin, 2019.

Roth, J. P. *The Logistics of the Roman Army at War, 264 BC–AD 235*. Leiden, 1995.

Rowan, C. *From Caesar to Augustus (c. 49 BC–AD 14): Using Coins as Sources*. Cambridge, 2019.

Roymans, N. "Caesar's Conquest and the Archaeology of Mass Violence in the Germanic Frontier Zone." In *Julius Caesar's Battle for Gaul: New Archaeological Perspectives*, edited by A. P. Fitzpatrick and C. Haselgrove, 115–125. Oxford, 2019.

Roymans, N., and N. Fernádez-Goetz. "Caesar in Gaul: New Perspectives on the Archaeology of Mass Violence." In *Proceedings of the Twenty-Fourth Annual Theoretical Roman Archaeology Conference*, edited by T. Brindle, M. Allen, E. Dunham, and A. Smith, 70–80. Oxford, 2015.

Roymans, N., and S. Scheers. "Eight Gold Hoards from the Low-Countries: A Synthesis." In *Gold Hoards from the Low Countries and the Caesarian Conquest of Northern Gaul*, edited by N. Roymans, G. Creemers, and S. Scheers, 1–46. Amsterdam Archaeological Studies 18. Amsterdam, 2012.

Rudenko, O. "The Making of a Soviet Hero: The Case of Spartacus." *Soviet and Post-Soviet Review* 47 (2020): 333–356.

Rüpke, J. *Fasti Sacerdotum: A Prosopography of Pagan, Jewish and Christian Religious Officials in the City of Rome 300 BC to AD 499*. Translated by D. M. B. Richardson. Oxford, 2008.

Russo, F. "Caesar's *Pro Bithynis* and Heraclea Pontica." *Antichthon* 49 (2015): 94–109.

Ste. Croix, G. E. M. de. *The Class Struggle in the Ancient Greek World*. London, 1981.

Santangelo, F. *Sulla, the Elites and the Empire: A Study of Roman Policies in Italy and the Greek East*. Leiden, 2007.

Schwartz, E. *Griechische Gesichtschreiber*. Leipzig, 1957.

Seager, R. *Pompey the Great. A Political Biography* (2nd ed.). Oxford, 2002.

Shackleton Bailey, D. R. "Sextus Clodius-Sextius Cloelius," *CQ* 10 (1960): 41–42.

Shatzman, I. *Senatorial Wealth and Roman Politics*. Brussels, 1975.

Shaw, B. D. "The Elder Pliny's African Geography." *Historia* 30 (1981): 424–471.

Shaw, B. D. "The Company-State Model and the *societates publicanorum*." *Historia* 71 (2022): 78–127.

Sherwin-White, A. N. *Roman Foreign Policy in the East, 168 B.C. to A.D. 1*. London, 1984.

Siani-Davis, M. "Ptolemy XII Auletes and the Romans." *Historia* 46 (1997): 306–340.

Smith, C. "Caesar and the History of Early Rome." In *Cesare: Precursore o Visionario? Atti del convegno internazionale Cividale del Friuli, 17–19 settembre 2009*, edited by G. Urso. Pisa 2020.

Stockton, D. L. *The Gracchi*. Oxford, 1979.

Strasburger, H. *Caesars Eintritt in die Geschichte*. Munich, 1938. Republished as H. Strasburger, *Studien zur Alten Geschichte*, edited by W. Schmitthenner and R. Zoepffel (Berlin, 1982), 181–323.

Strasburger, H. *Caesar im Urteil seine Zeitgenossen*. 2nd ed. Darmstadt, 1968. Republished as H. Strasburger, *Studien zur Alten Geschichte*, edited by W. Schmitthenner and R. Zoepffel (Berlin, 1982), 345–405.

Sumi, G. "Power and Ritual: The Crowd at Clodius' Funeral." *Historia* 46 (1977): 80–92.

Sumi, G. *Ceremony and Power: Performing Politics in Rome between Republic and Empire.* Ann Arbor, 2005.

Syme, R. "The Allegiance of Labienus." *JRS* 38 (1938): 113–125. Republished as R. Syme, *Roman Papers*, vol. 1 (Oxford, 1979), 62–75.

Syme, R. *The Roman Revolution*. Oxford, 1939.

Syme, R. *Sallust*. Berkeley, 1964.

Tatum, W. J. *The Patrician Tribune: Publius Clodius Pulcher*. Chapel Hill, 1999.

Tatum, W. J. *A Noble Ruin: Mark Antony, Civil War and the Collapse of the Republic*. Oxford, 2024.

Taylor, L. R. "Caesar's Early Career." *CPhil.* 36 (1941): 113–132.

Taylor, L. R. "The Election of the Pontifex Maximus in the Late Republic." *CPhil.* 37 (1942): 421–424.

Taylor, L. R. *Roman Voting Assemblies*. Ann Arbor, 1966.

Taylor, L. R. "Dating Major Legislation and Elections in Caesar's First Consulship." *Historia* 17 (1968): 173–193.

Taylor, L. R. *The Voting Districts of the Roman Republic: The Thirty-Five Urban and Rural Tribes*. 2nd ed. Edited by J. Linderski. Ann Arbor, 2013.

Thompson, H. "Iron Age and Roman Slave-Shackles." *Arch. Journ.* 150 (1983): 57–168.

Tiberi, L. "La biblioteca di Alessandria e l'incendio che non la distrusse, I: Riflessioni moderne fino a Giusto Lupsio." *Bibliothecae.it* 9 (2020): 4–100.

Treggiari, S. *Roman Freedmen during the Late Republic*. Oxford, 1969.

Treggiari, S. "Jobs in the Household of Livia." *PBSR* 43 (1975): 48–77.

Treggiari, S. *Roman Marriage: Iusti Coniuges from the Time of Cicero to the Time of Ulpian*. Oxford, 1991.

Treggiari, S. *Terentia, Tullia and Publilia: The Women of Cicero's Family*. London, 2007.

Treggiari, S. *Servilia and Her Family*. Oxford, 2019.

Turquin, P. "La Bataille de la Selle (du Sabis) en l'an 57 avant J.-C." *Études Classiques* 23, no. 2 (1955): 113–156.

Volk, K. "Caesar the Epicurean? A Matter of Life and Death." In *Epicurus in Rome: Philosophical Perspectives in the Ciceronian Age*, edited by S. Yona and G. Davis, 72–86. Cambridge, 2022.

Vonder Mühll, F. "Hirtius." *RE* 8.2: 1956–1962.

Walde, C. "Caesar, Lucan's *Bellum Civile*, and their Reception." In *Julius Caesar in Western Culture*, edited by M. Wyke, 45–61. Oxford, 2006.

Wardle, D. "Suetonius, Caesar and a Dream of World-Domination." *Athenaeum* 108 (2020): 72–88.

Welch, K. "Caesar and his Officers in the Gallic War Commentaries." In *Julius Caesar as Artful Reporter: The War Commentaries as Political Instruments*, edited by K. Welch and A. Powell, 85–110. London, 1998.

Westall, R. W. *Caesar's Civil War: Historical Reality and Fabrication.* Leiden, 2017.

Weinstock, S. *Divus Julius.* Oxford, 1971.

Wiseman, T. P. "The Publication of *De Bello Gallico*." In *Julius Caesar as Artful Reporter: The War Commentaries as Political Instruments*, edited by K. Welch and A. Powell, 1–9. London, 1998.

Wistrand, E. *Caesar and Contemporary Roman Society.* Göteborg, 1978.

Woolf, G. Et Tu, Brute? *A Short History of Political Murder.* London, 2007.

Woytek, B. Arma et Nummi: *Forschungen zur römischen Finanzgeschichte und Münzprägung der Jahre 49 bis 42 v. Chr.* Vienna, 2003.

Wyke, M. "Caesar, Cinema and National Identity," in *Julius Caesar in Western Culture*, edited by M. Wyke, 170–189. Oxford, 2006.

Wyke, M. *Caesar: A Life in Western Culture.* London, 2007.

Wyke, M. *Caesar in the USA.* Berkeley and Los Angeles, 2012.

Wyke, M. "Lessons in History: Bernard Shaw's Discomforting Caesar." In *Caesar's Past and Posterity's Caesar*, edited by T. A. Hass and R. Raja, 199–212. Turnhout, 2021.

Index

For the benefit of digital users, indexed terms that span two pages (e.g., 52–53) may, on occasion, appear on only one of those pages.